Fashion and Costume
in American Popular Culture

**Recent Titles in
American Popular Culture**

Animation: A Reference Guide
Thomas W. Hoffer

Variety Entertainment and Outdoor Amusements: A Reference Guide
Don B. Wilmeth

Women in Popular Culture: A Reference Guide
Katherine Fishburn

Sports: A Reference Guide
Robert J. Higgs

Play and Playthings: A Reference Guide
Bernard Mergen

American Popular Music: A Reference Guide
Mark W. Booth

American Popular Illustration: A Reference Guide
James J. Best

Recreational Vehicles and Travel: A Resource Guide
Bernard Mergen

Magic: A Reference Guide
Earle J. Coleman

Newspapers: A Reference Guide
Richard A. Schwarzlose

Radio: A Reference Guide
Thomas Allen Greenfield

Popular American Housing: A Reference Guide
Ruth Brent and Benyamin Schwarz, editors

FASHION AND COSTUME IN AMERICAN POPULAR CULTURE

A Reference Guide

VALERIE BURNHAM OLIVER

American Popular Culture
M. Thomas Inge, Series Editor

Greenwood Press
Westport, Connecticut • London

Library of Congress Cataloging-in-Publication Data

Oliver, Valerie Burnham.
   Fashion and costume in American popular culture : a
reference guide / Valerie Burnham Oliver.
     p.   cm. — (American popular culture, ISSN 0193–6859)
   Includes index.
   ISBN 0–313–29412–7 (alk. paper)
   1. Costume—United States—Bibliography. I. Title. II. Series.
Z5694.U5045 1996
016.391'00973—dc20   96–161

British Library Cataloguing in Publication Data is available.

Library of Congress Catalog Card Number: 96–161
ISBN: 0–313–29412–7
ISSN: 0193–6859

First published in 1996

Greenwood Press, 88 Post Road West, Westport, CT 06881
An imprint of Greenwood Publishing Group, Inc.

Printed in the United States of America

∞™

The paper used in this book complies with the
Permanent Paper Standard issued by the National
Information Standards Organization (Z39.48–1984).

10 9 8 7 6 5 4 3 2

To Charles,
who has been there always.
Thank you.

2000

Contents

Preface   xi

1. **Guides to the Literature**   1
   Fashion and Costume   1
   Business, Entertainment, American History, Textiles, and Material and Popular Culture   4
   Selected Bibliography   8

2. **Encyclopedias**   11
   General Encyclopedias   11
   Costume and Fashion Encyclopedias   13
   Specialized Encyclopedias   15
   Selected Bibliography   16

3. **Histories of Fashion and Costume in the United States**   19
   Pre-1600s   19
   1600s   20

1700s   23

1800s   26

1900s   32

Selected Bibliography   36

Popular Perspective—Dolls   45

4. **Specific Clothing and Accessories**   49

Clothing   50

Accessories   74

Clothing and Accessories in Performance   85

Collecting Clothing and Accessories   93

5. **Psychological, Sociological, and Cultural Aspects**   97

Monographs   97

Theses   108

6. **Dictionaries**   123

Costume, Fashion, Clothing, and Dress   124

Textiles and Embroidery Dictionaries   125

Biographical Dictionaries and Related Sources   126

7. **Specialized Bibliographies**   129

General   129

Clothing for the Elderly and Disabled   132

Clothing and Accessories   132

Popular Culture and Performance   134

Types of Publications   137

8. **Indexing and Abstracting Services**   139

Monographs and Periodicals   139

Theses and Dissertations   145

Fashion and Costume   147

Selected Bibliography   151

9. **Media**   159

Specific Clothing and Accessory Publications   160

Fashion and Costume History   165

Advertising and Clothing 166

10. **Research Centers** 171
Directories 171
Research Centers 173

11. **Costume Museums and Collections** 183
Costume Collection Surveys 185
Museum Histories 187
Selected Bibliography 189
The Museums and Collections 190

12. **Professional Organizations and Related Conference Proceedings** 199
Selected Organizations 200

13. **Periodicals** 203
American Periodicals' History 203
Women's Periodicals 205
Fashion Periodicals 207
Fashion-Related Periodicals 214
Theses on Fashion Periodicals 218
The Periodicals 221

Appendix: Clothing and Accessory Terms Used in the *OCLC/WorldCat* Database July 6, 1995 (Sorted for Books, Serials, and Media in English) 231

Notes 241

Author Index 247

Subject Index 261

Preface

This work concentrates on reviewing monographic literature, with some exceptions, reflecting domestic fashion and costume subjects. The inclusion of selected master's and Ph.D. theses allows for reflection on educational and student interests in the subjects. Certain topics are not included, such as the business aspects of the fashion industry, fashion illustration and photography, fashion merchandising generally, military uniforms, and Native American costume and clothing. Additionally, the use of fashion, clothing, and accessory terminology in works of literature is not included.

Essentially the literature is allowed to speak for itself. Even the publishers' names offer interesting insights as to the wide variety of groups involved in these subjects. The sources identified here were located mainly using standard bibliographic tools, all mentioned in the text. Some sources were included from materials in my own collection. I created the database represented in the Appendix to determine which types of clothing and accessories were getting the most attention by writers. It is not an exact measure but a good approximation.

The Internet as a major source of information has not been included because of time and space constraints. It is an evolving information source and does reflect many of the same interests as the print or audiovisuals studied. For instance, it contains sales catalogs for clothing and costumes and promotional pages for fashion designers; information about museums—their collections and exhibition schedules; library catalogs worldwide; electronic discussion groups on all kinds of subjects; electronic conferences and journals; and many other sources. Internet searching tools such as Lycos and WebCrawler as well as Netscape and Mosaic are available, as well as print guides. Libraries offer the public much help in accessing the Internet, and a growing number of services are being developed to organize the Internet by subject, such as the NetFirst service, offered as one of the databases on the FirstSearch service, released in January 1996 by OCLC in Dublin, Ohio.

I thank Robert Vrecenak, head of the Interlibrary Loan Department, Homer Babbidge Library, University of Connecticut, and his staff: Lana Babij, Judy DeLottie, Lucy Marsalisi, and Lynn Sweet. Without their efforts on my behalf, I could not have entertained undertaking this project at all. I would also thank the staff of my own Research and Information Services Department, Homer Babbidge Library, University of Connecticut, for their patience as I worked on this book.

1

Guides to the Literature

FASHION AND COSTUME

Four books outline or provide guides to fashion and costume literature and study. In 1973 Janet Arnold wrote *A Handbook of Costume* in which she acknowledged that "over the last ten years more people than ever before seem to have acquired an interest in costume" (p. 7). Her work, which concentrates on the British perspective and source materials, examines primary sources; dating costume from construction techniques; costume conservation storage and display; costume collections in England, Scotland, and Wales; and costume for children, students, and the stage. It also provides a bibliography.

Eleanor Lambert's *World of Fashion: People, Places, Resources* (1976) looks at the world fashion industry through fashion designers and firms, "fashion influentials" (nondesigners who had an impact on the industry), trade associations and organizations, honors and awards, fashion education, costume and fashion archives, and fashion publications. The book is arranged geographically by country, but the section on the United States takes up almost 200 of the 361-page volume. Biographies of people and descriptions of organizations, awards, and education programs are supplemented by a listing of fourteen costume and fashion archives or museum collections in the United States. The publications listed for each geographic area are limited to periodicals devoted to the fashion industry. A separate chapter on the Hall of Fame as well as an appendix listing Coty Award Winners, 1943–1975, and a bibliography conclude the work. Lambert's work now serves as a historical look at the people and organizations influencing the industry during the 1970s. She appreciated the importance of the worldview many years prior to the 1990s' emphasis on looking at business and economics globally.

In 1979 Jackson Kesler produced *Theatrical Costume: A Guide to Information Sources,* part of Gale Research Company's Performing Arts Information Guide series. The actual guide might be considered the selected bibliographies, dictionaries, encyclopedias, glossaries, and sourcebooks and guidebooks in the first eleven pages, together with several later sections on illustrated social history materials, textile history and conservation, and fashion designers and the fashion world. The major portion of the volume is an annotated bibliography of publications, mainly from 1957 to 1979. The works are arranged by subject and are indexed by subject, author, and title for ease of access to specific sources. Western and Eastern theatrical costume, as well as costume for the dance and cinema, are included, followed by historical costume arranged geographically, special types of clothing (e.g., occupational, sports), and more general aspects such as costume design and construction, ornamentation, and textile dyeing. The emphasis is on materials easily obtainable at libraries, although three Ph.D. dissertations are noted as being of "particular interest to students of theatrical costuming in the American professional stage."[1] Kesler's *Guide* holds much value today because of the careful annotations, cross-references, and indexing. Combining its use with online library catalogs and other bibliographic databases, the theatrical designer should be able to keep current in any search for specific design sources and materials for design inspiration.

The Costume Society of America, Region I, supported the printing of Valerie B. Oliver's *Costume/Clothing/Fashion, Information Access, Sources and Techniques* (1993). Although probably somewhat limited in its distribution as a society publication, it does provide the first look at the literature from many vantage points and serves as a complement to this book. It brings into focus a complex field of study as it describes, outlines, and annotates types of sources, with examples, sample search techniques, and ways to keep current with the literature. Print and electronic sources are included, with a discussion of manual and electronic literature searching methods. The book contains selected guides, encyclopedias, dictionaries, directories, bibliographies, and indexing and abstracting services. Detailed lists of costume, clothing, and fashion terms are included for the indexes and some bibliographies to show their focus on these topics. Information on how to locate library collections of interest and sources for the study of

American periodicals, especially for women, fashion, and related fields, is included, as well as the location of visual sources in print materials, microfiche/microfilm, photographs, portraits, slides, and films. Separate sections explain how to locate primary sources and introduce computer networks. The volume concludes with author, keyword subject/selected title indexes, and list of abbreviations/acronyms. This guide looks at the subject from the social science, humanities, business, and technical perspectives with the student in mind. It also can provide the nonspecialist costume/clothing/fashion enthusiast with a wealth of ideas for learning more about these subjects.

Other discussions of the literature can be found in chapters or sections of books. In 1939 Hilaire Hiler, a costume book collector, discussed various facets of costume study in his *Bibliography of Costume*. His essay, "Costumes and Ideologies," discusses the fields of philosophy, psychology, the social sciences, politics, and law and their relation to costume and clothing. Clothing theories, the influence of religion, military and nonmilitary uniforms, biology, fashion, architecture, fine arts, and the theater and cinema are also discussed. Within all these discussions he includes advice and publications for further information. "Compilation of the Bibliography" completes this early guide to the literature by discussing general works, periodicals, encyclopedias, newspapers, and library and museum collections available for research in the late 1930s. The listing of periodical publications within the *Bibliography* itself is a unique resource, providing quick access to lists of fashion periodicals published chronologically by country. Doreen Yarwood's 1978 *Encyclopedia of World Costume* includes a six-page sources of information on costume. Some standard reference sources—encyclopedias and dictionaries—are included, although the major emphasis is on histories by subject (e.g., the Americas, furs and hides, cosmetics and perfumery, nursing and maternity wear).

Vicki L. Berger provides both a historical overview and a beginning guide to the literature in her chapter, "Fashion," for the 1989 *Handbook of American Popular Culture*. The focus is the United States, beginning with ready-to-wear clothing in the early nineteenth century and continuing to the late 1980s. The information outlined includes suggested subject headings used in library catalogs, encyclopedias, biographical dictionaries, selected indexing/abstracting services, bibliographies, and dictionaries. Museum collections and directories are included. Of interest is Berger's discussion of fashion history and theory books, which is not limited to just those for U.S. fashion and costume. She arranges them into several groups for discussion, including historical surveys, classic historic costume books in reprint, social-psychological materials, fashion design and illustration, and fashion marketing. The review concludes with a discussion of trade publications, several nineteenth-century periodicals and books featuring reprinted materials from them, mail order catalogs, scholarly journals in the field, and anthologies and reprints. Berger's bibliography of some 228 articles and books is followed by a list of 62 periodicals containing fashion and costume articles.

BUSINESS, ENTERTAINMENT, AMERICAN HISTORY, TEXTILES, AND MATERIAL AND POPULAR CULTURE

For those studying various aspects of clothing, consultation of literature guides for the areas can be enlightening. Both historical and contemporary sources are important. For the field of business, Harvard University personnel have contributed several classic texts, such as Henrietta M. Larson's 1948 *Guide to Business History: Materials for the Study of American Business History and Suggestions for Their Use.* Larson exhibited her strong knowledge and understanding of the sources in the materials listed but even more in the advice contained throughout. Her emphasis is on business history generally and the history of specific types of businesses; social, cultural, and economic background materials, as well as biographical and autobiographical works on administrators, are included. A few manufacturers of clothing and shoes and of textiles are included, as well as a list of administrators in the advertising, retailing, and recreation industries. The importance of the textile, clothing, and related industries is emphasized by their inclusion in the sections on the "history of industries," which covers retail distribution, advertising, fur trade, and manufacturing (clothing, leather, shoe, textile, cotton, silk/rayon, and wool/worsted products and industries). Cyclical changes in fashion are noted in the index, with reference to Young's *Recurring Cycles of Fashion, 1760–1937.*[2] Robert W. Lovett's *American Economic and Business History Information Sources* (1971) is intended to supplement Larson's work; it includes publications mainly from 1948 to 1970 in those areas "receiving most attention by scholars."[3] It does contain information on the leather, shoe, and textile industries but nothing in the index or contents page specifically on the history of the fashion or clothing industries.

Lorna M. Daniells's third edition of her award-winning[4] *Business Information Sources* (1993) is a comprehensive, up-to-date analysis of reference materials and other sources for learning about business today. Sources for locating facts, business trends, and company, industry, management, and marketing information are covered. She includes a separate annotated list of textile and apparel statistics sources and department and specialty store information.

Gale Research Company also provides a current look at business information sources but in a very different way. Its *Encyclopedia of Business Information Sources,* published annually, lists up to seventeen types of materials for each business subject included (e.g., directories, online databases, encyclopedias/dictionaries, handbooks, statistics sources, trade associations and journals, periodicals/newsletters, price sources). The volume, arranged alphabetically by topic, provides a quick way of obtaining a brief list of current sources of information. Many fashion and clothing topics are included in addition to related subjects, among them, antiques as an investment, auctions, barber and beauty shops, children's apparel industry, the clocks and watch industry, the clothing industry, the cosmetics industry, consumer surveys, direct marketing, display of merchandise, fairs, the fashion industry, the fitness industry, the fur industry, gems and gemstones, the glove industry, the hosiery industry, the knit goods industry, labels and labeling, the luggage industry, the mature consumer market, the men's clothing industry, the perfume industry, the shoe industry, show business, the silk industry, the toy industry, the underwear industry, uniforms, the women's clothing industry, and the youth market.

For those interested in the costuming aspects of various forms of entertainment there are several specific guides available. Blanch M. Baker's 1952 *Theatre and Allied Arts* features costume as an "allied art" and outlines books on costume for North America, children, ceremony and religious purposes, uniforms, theater, accessories, and includes some Miscellaneous works. Makeup, dance, marionettes and puppets, and other types of stage entertainments are also covered, such as the circus and variety shows. This H. W. Wilson publication contains excellent annotations, including costume pattern information and other specific details with author and subject index (not limited to the U.S. theater). Claudia Jean Lowe compiled *Guide to Reference and Bibliography for Theatre Research* (1971), which includes a separate listing of thirteen sources specifically useful for stage scenery and costume. Robert A. Armour's *Film: A Reference Guide* (1980), although not isolating a separate chapter for costume, contains useful information especially on the impact of film on society. It includes sections for film histories, production and production personnel, special film types (e.g., musicals), film and visual arts, reference works and periodicals, American film chronology, and research collections. Don B. Wilmeth's 1982 *Variety Entertainment and Outdoor Amusements: A Reference Guide* does not isolate costume or clothing as a focus. It provides historical background and sources for studying U.S. musical reviews, variety shows, vaudeville, circuses, and Wild West shows, among other types of performances. Armour and Wilmeth provide excellent, even if indirect, insights to literatures that are full of clothing illustrations and other primary sources where the costumes have contributed to the impact of performances.

Knowledge of American history will aid in understanding how political, social, economic, and technical developments have influenced clothing, costume, and fashion. The *American Historical Association's Guide to Historical Literature* (1961) contains an index listing "Clothing and Dress." Although Francis P. Prucha's 1987 *Handbook for Research in American History* does not include any mention of costume, clothing, fashion, garment, apparel, or uniform(s) in the index, it does offer several sections of importance in doing clothing research: "Guides to Newspapers," "Military History," "Blacks," "American Indians," "Regional Material," and "Travel Accounts." The work includes analysis of the literature as well as bibliographies and a combined author, title, and subject index.

Because clothing is the final result of a sculpturing of fabric or fabrics with or without other embellishments, the study of the textiles can provide the necessary background for understanding a particular fashion. My own *Textile Reference Sources* appeared in 1973 as part of the University of Connecticut Library's Reference Bibliography series and included sources from the business, social sciences, technical, and arts perspectives. Also in 1973 Helen G. Sommar produced *A Brief Guide to Sources of Fiber and Textile Information,* focusing more on the technical literature. In 1974 the Textile Institute, building on earlier work by the Aslib (Association of Libraries) Textile Group, published Carolyn A. Farnfield's *Guide to Sources of Information on the Textile Industry* with a British industry focus but of importance for learning about the literature. Business sources are emphasized including standards, patents, and statistics, as well as information on textile organizations, periodicals, directories and dictionaries, and selected books about various aspects of textiles. A more current source is *The Textile Industry, an Information Sourcebook* (1989) by J. Thomas Vogel and Barbara W. Lowry, a well-annotated guide that provides a worldview with emphasis on business materials published since 1980, including electronic information sources. The authors write, "The apparel industry deserves a volume of its own," although they do include materials on the interaction of "fabric producer and apparel manufacturer."[5] In 1974 a United Nations document, *Information Sources on the Clothing Industry,* was published; it has not been updated. On a more design and artistic level the 1991 *New Textiles: Trends and Traditions* by Chloe Colchester provides analysis, including a section on textiles in fashion, with over 300 excellent photographs (over half in color). It also provides some guidance for locating further information. Biographies of over eighty textile and fiber artists, galleries and museums worldwide, selected exhibitions, selected books, periodicals, articles, and a glossary conclude the volume.

Within guides to the literature for material and popular culture, costume, clothing, and fashion subjects are sometimes covered. Thomas J. Schlereth's *Material Culture Studies in America* (1982), an anthology of selected material culture studies, contains an important overview of the history of material culture study in the United States. "Material Culture Studies in America, 1876–1976" comprises the first seventy-five pages of the volume. It contains tables to illustrate the author's classification of material culture into several periods: 1876–1948, characterized by collecting and classifying; 1948–1965, characterized by describing or developing histories of objects; and since 1965, as a period of more detailed analysis of materials, such as placing them in a social context or using computers to store and analyze data.[6] A bibliographical essay includes discussion of survey and specialized bibliographies, anthologies, periodicals and newsletters, dissertations and exhibit catalogs, and a bibliography. Although clothing as material culture is not the major focus in any of the selected studies, it is included indirectly in several. Of major value is the historical perspective, people, institutions, research methods, and the classic and other publications listed.

A more specialized material culture guide by Nancy J. Parezo, Ruth Perry, and Rebecca Allen, *Southwest Native American Arts and Material Culture: A Guide to Research* (1991) contains several sections that together form a guide to the literature: "A Beginner's Guide to Southwest Native American Material Culture," "Sources for Researching Southwest Native American Arts and Material Culture," "Journals and Series Containing Numerous Articles," a glossary of cultures, and definitions of key terms. This work specifically includes the subjects of clothing and ceremonial costume, as well as headwear, footwear, jewelry, masks, and textiles. The major portion of the two-volume work is a bibliography of some 8,400 works published between 1844 and 1988, arranged alphabetically by author. Easiest access to the clothing and costume materials is accomplished if studying a specific group of people. Indexes provide access by cultural group, then by subject, then by group.

Larry N. Landrum's *American Popular Culture: a Guide to Information Resources* (1982) recognizes fashion and dress as a section within "Material Culture" in the Contents, but other clothing sources are noted in other sections (nine publications within "Aspects of Everyday Life" and three in both "General Works" and "Anthologies," for example). One work identified as covering clothing under "Material Culture" but not in the specific section on "Fashion and Dress" is Train's 1941 *Story of Everyday Things,* which provides "descriptions of things . . . bringing them alive into an evolutionary pattern,"[7] placing the work neatly into Schlereth's period of classifying for material culture works from 1876 to 1948. A more specialized work on popular culture is represented by *Folklife Sourcebook: A Directory of Folklife Resources in the United States* (1994) by Peter T. Bartis and Hillary Glatt. This book does not indicate clothing or costume as a focus but describes sources full of visual materials and possibly text on the subjects as it covers archive collections, societies, periodicals and newsletters, specialized publishers, and mail order dealers, among other materials and resources. An index by state serves to isolate regional resources.

SELECTED BIBLIOGRAPHY

Costume and Fashion

Arnold, Janet. *A Handbook of Costume*. London: Macmillan, 1973. 336p.

Berger, Vicki L. "Fashion." In *Handbook of American Popular Culture*, v.1, 417–443. Edited by M. Thomas Inge. 2d ed., rev. and enl. Westport, CT: Greenwood Press, 1989. 2v.

Hiler, Hilaire. "Costumes and Ideologies." In *Bibliography of Costume*, xi–xxxix. Compiled by Hilaire and Meyer Hiler. New York: H. W. Wilson Company, 1939.

Kesler, Jackson. *Theatrical Costume: A Guide to Information Sources*. Performing Arts Information Guide Series, v. 6. Detroit: Gale Research Company, 1979. 308p.

Lambert, Eleanor. *World of Fashion: People, Places, Resources*. New York: R. R. Bowker, 1976. 361p.

Oliver, Valerie B. *Costume/Clothing/Fashion: Information Access, Sources and Techniques*. n.p.: Costume Society of America, Region I, 1993. 101p.

Yarwood, Doreen. "Sources of Information on Costume" and "Bibliography." In *Encyclopedia of World Costume*, 453–459. New York: Charles Scribner's Sons, 1978.

Business, Entertainment, American History, Textiles, Material, and Popular Culture

American Historical Association's Guide to Historical Literature. New York: Macmillan, 1961. 962p.

Armour, Robert A. *Film: A Reference Guide*. Westport, CT: Greenwood Press, 1980. 251p.

Baker, Blanch M. *Theatre and Allied Arts: A Guide to Books Dealing with the History, Criticism, and Technic of the Drama, and Theatre and Related Arts and Crafts*. New York: H. W. Wilson Company, 1952. 536p.

Bartis, Peter T., and Hillary Glatt. *Folklife Sourcebook: A Directory of Folklife Resources in the United States*. Washington, D.C.: Library of Congress, 1994. 165p.

Colchester, Chloe. *New Textiles: Trends and Traditions*, with over 250 illustrations, 153 in color. New York: Rizzoli International Publications, 1991. 192p.

Daniells, Lorna M. *Business Information Sources*. 3d ed. Berkeley: University of California Press, 1993. 725p.

Farnfield, Carolyn A. *Guide to Sources of Information on the Textile Industry*. 2d ed. rev. and enl. Manchester: Textile Institute, 1974. 130p.

Landrum, Larry N. *American Popular Culture: A Guide to Information Sources*. Detroit: Gale Research Company, 1982, 435p.

Larson, Henrietta M. *Guide to Business History: Materials for the Study of American Business History and Suggestions for Their Use*. Cambridge, MA: Harvard University Press, 1948. 1,181p.

Lovett, Robert W. *American Economic and Business History Information Sources*. Detroit: Gale Research Company, 1971. 323p.

Lowe, Claudia J. *Guide to Reference and Bibliography for Theatre Research.* Columbus: Ohio State University Libraries, 1971. 137p.

Parezo, Nancy J., Ruth M. Perry, and Rebecca Allen. *Southwest Native American Arts and Material Culture: A Guide to Research.* New York: Garland, 1991. 2 vols. 1506p.

Prucha, Francis P. *Handbook for Research in American History: A Guide to Bibliographies and Other Reference Works.* Lincoln: University of Nebraska Press, 1987. 289p.

Ralston, Valerie H. *Textile Reference Sources: A Selective Bibliography.* Storrs, CT: University of Connecticut Library, 1973. 47p.

Schlereth, Thomas J. *Material Culture Studies in America.* Compiled and edited with introductions and bibliography by Thomas J. Schlereth. Nashville, TN: American Association for State and Local History, 1982. 419p.

Sommar, Helen G. *Brief Guide to Sources of Fiber and Textile Information.* Washington, D.C.: Information Resources Press, 1973. 138p.

United Nations Industrial Development Organization. *Information Sources on the Clothing Industry.* New York: United Nations, 1974. 116p. UNIDO/LIB/ser.D/12.

Vogel, J. Thomas, and Barbara W. Lowry. *Textile Industry: An Information Sourcebook.* Phoenix, AZ: Oryx Press, 1989. 246p.

Wilmeth, Don B. *Variety Entertainment and Outdoor Amusements: A Reference Guide.* Westport, CT: Greenwood Press, 1982. 242p.

2

Encyclopedias

GENERAL ENCYCLOPEDIAS

The five multivolume general encyclopedias reviewed all include costume, clothing, and fashion subjects, provide information about contributors' professional affiliations, include illustrative materials, and identify sources for further study. There are, however, some subtle differences in the presentation of data to their respective audiences, in their choice of terminology for lead articles, and in their special features.

Encyclopaedia Britannica, first published in 1768 in Scotland, provides a scholarly approach and the most extensive bibliographies for further study. The fifteenth edition, first produced in 1974, is entitled *The New Encyclopaedia Britannica* in its 1993 printing. It is now produced in Chicago with editorial advice from the University of Chicago. "Dress and Adornment" is the major article, with some fifty pages of text, color photographs, and other illustrations. It covers ancient Egypt to Europe and America in the nineteenth and twentieth centuries, as well as Eastern dress, the purpose of dress, and a separate review of jewelry. "Dress" was written by Diana J. A. de Marly, author and lecturer, and "Jewelry" was contributed by Guido Gregorietti, a former museum curator and author. The clothing worn by leaders of society is featured rather than religious, military, academic, or professional garb. Although characterized by its use of *Micropaedia* (ready reference with short articles), *Macropaedia* (lengthy articles), and *Propaedia* offering various methods of access to information, it can still be used to best advantage by starting with index volumes. The *Propaedia* or *Outline of Knowledge* offers an organized method for self-study and serves as an index to both *Macro-* and *Micropaedias,* showing what subjects are covered.

The *Encyclopedia Americana,* produced in the United States since 1829, uses (in the 1991 edition) "costume" in the index to provide access to academic, religious, and theatrical aspects of the subject and "dress" to provide a more detailed look at special types of clothing and accessories. The main article on dress covers garments, cosmetics, and jewelry and was written by Millia Davenport, author of *The Book of Costume.* Clothing, the clothing industry, and fashion articles were written by academicians: Elizabeth E. Bacon, Michigan State University, Sweetman R. Smith, Fashion Institute of Technology (FIT), and Maurice Valency, Columbia University, respectively. Produced for a wide audience, one special feature is the indexing of glossaries.

The *World Book Encyclopedia,* produced since 1917 for elementary, middle school, and high school students and families, uses "costume" in the 1991 edition index to highlight the performance aspects of the subject. The major article, "Clothing," by Richard Martin, FIT, includes four pages of clear color drawings representing traditional costumes. The article sections are, "Why We Wear Clothes," "Clothing around the World," "Clothing through the Ages," "Clothing Industry," and "Career Opportunities." The article on "Fashion" by Valerie Steele, also of FIT, covers "Origins of Fashion," "Why People Follow Fashion," "Why Fashion Changes," and the "Fashion Industry." The articles conclude with study aids indicating related material in the *World Book,* bibliographies, and a clear outline of the material presented. These features, plus excellent cross references and a focus on the younger student, characterize the *World Book.*

Colliers Encyclopedia, published since 1950, offers a more scholarly approach. The 1992 edition's "Fashion and Clothing" article provides a review from ancient times to the twentieth century and contains "The History of Western Dress, a Color Portfolio," twelve plates of drawings by Douglas Gorsline. Contributors to this article are Bernice G. Chambers, Pennsylvania State University; Elizabeth A. Madeira, former fashion editor of *Women's Home Companion;* Rachel Kemper, FIT; Jack Freeman, former associate editor of *Apparel Arts Magazine;* Oscar E. Schoeffler, fashion adviser to Esquire Inc.; and Alfred V. Sloan Jr., FIT. Military uniforms receive special attention, with drawings of selected U.S. uniforms; U.S. Army, Air Force, Navy, and Marine insignia; insignia from other branches such as the Dental Corps; and forty color figures depicting military uniforms of the world. Bibliographies are in the index volume, where arrangement is by a general outline of knowledge rather than by article. For example, in the bibliography section "The Arts," theater and drama sources are listed under "costume," "makeup," "masks," and "marionettes." In the "Home and Family" section, other sources are listed under "clothing." Bibliographic sources are indicated in the index but must be looked up separately.

The *Academic American Encyclopedia,* first produced in 1980, provides similar coverage for a wide audience but includes notation for illustrations and bibliography in the index, a very helpful device. The major article in the 1991 edition is "Costume," by E. M. Plunkett, an art historian. Illustrations are used, including drawings for entire costumes (outerwear, underwear, and accessories), which appear in paper-doll-like fashion. "Fashion Design," also written by Plunkett, contains a bibliography of thirteen references, ten published in the 1970s. The "Clothing Industry" article, although brief, features development in the United States from the 1800s. Written by Linda Olsheim, FIT, it contains these sections: "Development of the American Clothing Industry" ("Women's Clothing," "Growth of Garment Unions," "Seventh Avenue"), "Production of a Line," "U.S. Industry Today," and "The Industry in Europe." Theatrical aspects of the subject have been contributed by Douglas A. Russell, Stanford University.

All of these encyclopedias are published annually or are kept up-to-date with yearbooks. None deals solely with fashion and costume in the United States but instead provides general background and history for various aspects of the subjects. Many provide separate index access to specific subjects—for example, dolls or fashion dolls, fans, hats, jewelry, masks, and shoes. More specialized encyclopedias on costume or fashion subjects are also available.

COSTUME AND FASHION ENCYCLOPEDIAS

Millia Davenport's *Book of Costume* (1948), combines historical summaries with descriptions of paintings or other primary art sources grouped to illustrate a particular historical period or various styles of the same type of garment. Coverage is from the ancient Orient to nineteenth century English, French, German, and American costume (to the end of the American Civil War). Complete documentation appears in the appendix. Davenport's belief that documented pictures are crucial to the study of costume is evident in her presentation. The index, unlike that of a general encyclopedia, is full of specific costume and fashion terminology, representing costume subjects reflected in the photographs of the primary art works as well as names of artists and location of biographies. François Boucher's *20,000 Years of Fashion* (1967) also presents a historic discussion, emphasizing France, the rest of the Continent, and England from prehistoric time to the period 1920–1947. Political, social, and economic factors as well as textile availability enhance the costume descriptions. No specific focus on North America or the United States is provided. Documented photographs of art works are liberally included throughout. Some special sections are: "First Historical Engraving of Costume" (sixteenth century), "Fashion Trades and Publications" (seventeenth century), and "Creators and Fashion Publications" (eighteenth century). A general bibliography, glossary, and index conclude the volume.

Esquire's Encyclopedia of 20th Century Men's Fashion (1973), by O. E. Schoeffler and W. Gale, looks at men's clothing from 1900 to the 1970s. Each type of garment is treated chronologically; toiletries, hair styles, and accessories (including luggage and leather goods) are considered in the same way. Personal anecdotes, illustrations, technical and manufacturing background, impact of color, other influences, a glossary, and an index enhance the work. Five years later, Doreen Yarwood's *Encyclopedia of World Costume* was published. Arranged in dictionary format and containing black and white line drawings, it represents a departure from both the Davenport and Boucher works. As in Schoeffler and Gale's book, illustrations and discussion of specific garments or accessories are presented together so that the differences over time and in style from different parts of the world can be compared easily. For example, sleeves are described and illustrated by thirty-nine figures and overcoats with thirty-one figures. English-speaking countries are featured, with religious and military attire omitted. A bibliography and an index are provided.

The Fashion Encyclopedia: An Essential Guide to Everything You Need to Know about Clothes (1982), by Catherine Houck, provides a more popular approach to a contemporary aspect of fashion. Written in dictionary format, it is more of a consumer guide to fashion terms, trade names linked to company, designers, and "elusive tidbits of information about clothes." Georgina O'Hara's *Encyclopedia of Fashion* (1986) also appeals to a general audience, with illustrations and photographs, some in color, adding to its attractiveness. O'Hara focuses on the five major fashion centers: Paris, London, New York, Rome, and Milan. Also in dictionary format it includes clothing terms, trade names, and artists, designers, and other influential people and covers a period from about 1840 to the 1980s. The introduction by Carrie Donovan, fashion editor of the *New York Times Magazine*, provides interesting commentary. Illustrations are documented, and an excellent bibliography is included. Both volumes abound with clothing terms that have become part of American popular culture (e.g., bikini, button-down shirt, crewneck, duffel coat, dungaree, leotard, mackintosh, Mary Jane shoes, v-neck, wedgies, zoot suit).

SPECIALIZED ENCYCLOPEDIAS

Some encyclopedias that focus on special topics contain specific sections on clothing, costume, dress or fashion. Those interested in learning about fabrics and textiles should consult the *Encyclopedia of Textiles* (1992), a dictionary with bibliography and index by Judith Jerde; *Encyclopedia of Textiles* (1980), by the editors of *American Fabrics and Fashions Magazine* (including a separate "Dictionary of Textile Terms"), and *English and American Textiles from 1790 to the Present* (1989), by Mary Schoeser and Celia Rufey. *The Encyclopedia of Chemical Technology* (1978 to 1984) and the *Encyclopedia of Polymer Science and Engineering* (1985–1990) provide more technical and scientific background on natural and synthetic fibers—their development, properties, applications, and manufacture.

The *Encyclopedia of World Art* (1958–1989) contains a separate section on costume discussing costume as art, fashion and fashion publications, and special types of costume: royal, civil, military, ecclesiastical, and European folk. Embroidery, lace, and textiles are included as separate index entries. Further background on religious clothing can be found in *Encyclopaedia Judaica* (1971–1972), *Encyclopedia of Religion* (1987), and the *New Catholic Encyclopedia* (1987).

The eight-volume *Dictionary of American History* (1978) contains an article on dress from colonial times to the 1970s by Jo Anne C. Olian, a curator and art historian. Army uniforms are covered separately. The three-volume *Encyclopedia of American Social History* (1993) contains an article on clothing and personal adornment by Nancy Rexford, a costume consultant. She covers Native Americans and the seventeenth through twentieth centuries, including a bibliography. More specialized types of sources can also be consulted, such as the Smithsonian's *Handbook of North American Indians* (1978–), with a section on clothing for each group of people. Volume 4, *History of Indian-White Relations* (1988), includes essays on Indian hobbyists and the Indian in literature, movies, and American popular culture. The *Encyclopedia of Southern Culture* (1989) includes "Clothing" by Bill McCarthy and "Fashion" by Jeanette C. Lauer and Robert H. Lauer. The *Encyclopedia of Black America* (1981) does not include fashion or dress but does include the subject of dance. *The Blackwell Companion to Jewish Culture: From the Eighteenth Century to the Present* (1989), includes costume.

The reason to use these encyclopedias is to gain some preliminary insights into the subject and to learn about the classic works and other sources for study. Although the more scholarly sources provide greater depth and detail, all the encyclopedias provide good background material. The examples cited here are only representative. Sources devoted to the history of costume or fashion in a given time period and place also serve as encyclopedias for the subject, as do monographs on specific types of clothes or accessories.

SELECTED BIBLIOGRAPHY

General

Academic American Encyclopedia. Danbury, CT: Grolier, 1991. 21v. 1980–. Annual.
Colliers Encyclopedia. New York: Macmillan, 1992. 24 v. 1950–. Annual.
Encyclopaedia Britannica. 15th ed. New York, Encyclopaedia Britannica, 1993. *Micropaedia* v. 1–12; *Macropaedia* v. 13–29; *Propaedia* v. 30; Index v. 31–32. 1768– ; 1936–. Annual.
Encyclopedia Americana. International ed. Danbury, CT: Grolier, 1990. 34v. 1829–; 1936–. Annual.
World Book Encyclopedia. Chicago: World Book, 1992. 22v. 1917–; 1933–. Annual.

Costume and Fashion

Boucher, François. *20,000 Years of Fashion: The History of Costume and Personal Adornment.* New York: Harry N. Abrams, 1967. 441p.
Davenport, Millia. *The Book of Costume.* New York: Crown Publishers, 1948, 1976. 958p. 2v. in 1.
Houck, Catherine. *The Fashion Encyclopedia: An Essential Guide to Everything You Need to Know about Clothes.* New York: St. Martin's Press, 1982. 236p.
O'Hara, Georgina. *The Encyclopedia of Fashion.* Introduction by Carrie Donovan. New York: Harry N. Abrams, 1986. 272p.
Schoeffler, Oscar E., and William Gale. *Esquire's Encyclopedia of 20th Century Men's Fashions.* New York: McGraw-Hill, 1973. 709p.
Yarwood, Doreen. *The Encyclopedia of World Costume.* New York: Charles Scribner's Sons., 1978. 471p.

Specialized

The Blackwell Companion to Jewish Culture: From the Eighteenth Century to the Present. Edited by Glenda Abramson et al. New York: Blackwell Reference, 1989. 853p.
Dictionary of American History. Rev. ed. New York: Charles Scribner's Sons, 1978. 8v.
Encyclopaedia Judaica. Jerusalem, Israel: Keter Publishing House, 1971–1972. 16v.
Encyclopedia of American Social History. Edited by Mary K. Cayton, Elliot J. Gorn, and Peter W. Williams. New York: Scribner, 1993. 2,653p. 3v.
Encyclopedia of Black America. Edited by W. Augustus Low and Virgil A. Clift. New York: McGraw-Hill, 1981. 921p.
Encyclopedia of Chemical Technology. 3d ed. New York: John Wiley, 1978–1984. 24v. plus supplement and index.

Encyclopedia of Polymer Science and Engineering. 2d ed. New York: John Wiley & Sons, 1985–1990. 17v. plus supplements.

Encyclopedia of Religion. Edited by Mircea Eliade. New York: Macmillan, 1987. 16 v.

Encyclopedia of Southern Culture. Edited by Charles R. Wilson et al. Chapel Hill: University of North Carolina Press, 1989. 1,634p.

Encyclopedia of Textiles. Judith Jerde. New York: Facts on File, 1992. 260p.

Encyclopedia of Textiles: An Illustrated and Authoritative Source Book on Textiles, Presenting a Complete and Practical Coverage of the Entire Field—Its History and Origins, Its Art and Design, Its Natural and Manmade Fibers, Its Manufacturing and Finishing Processes, Color and Dyes, Textile Printing, Specialty End Uses. Editors of American Fabrics and Fashions Magazine. 3d ed. Englewood Cliffs, NJ: Prentice-Hall, 1980.

Encyclopedia of World Art. New York: McGraw-Hill, 1959–1968. 15v.

Handbook of North American Indians. Gen. ed., William C. Sturtevant. Washington, D.C.: Smithsonian Institution, 1978–. 20v planned. V. 4–11, 15 published to date. SI 1.20/2: v. no.

New Catholic Encyclopedia. New York: McGraw-Hill, 1967. 15v. plus supplements.

Schoeser, Mary, and Celia Rufey. *English and American Textiles: From 1790 to the Present.* New York: Thames and Hudson, 1989. 256p.

3

Histories of Fashion and Costume in the United States

PRE-1600s

Several books provide an overview of costume and fashion history including pre-1600s information. Douglas W. Gorsline's *A History of Fashion: A Visual Survey of Costume from Ancient Times* (1955) includes mention of the United States for the period 1840–1925. The chronological arrangement provides for both background discussion and black and white drawings from documented primary sources. Gorsline indicates that "existing costume books . . . tend to overlook the character of the people who wore a given dress."[1] His drawings attempt to portray the variety of individuals who wore the different styles of clothing—for example, lumberjacks and cowboys. American costume is represented by a separate bibliography. Ruth T. Wilcox's *Five Centuries of American Costume* (1963) provides a highly visual survey with her own black and white drawings of men, women, and children. The American Indian, early settlers, military uniforms, colonists, civil dress, and a section on children's clothing are included. Twentieth-century material proceeds to 1960, with the table of contents serving as the index. *Mirror, Mirror: A Social History of Fashion* (1977), by Michael and Ariane Batterberry, provides an overview of fashion history from ancient times to the twentieth century, with the United States coming into focus with World War I. Mention of individuals and their contributions add to the volume's usefulness as a social history. Fashions are visually represented in many colored and black and white photographs; there is less emphasis on children. The same time period is covered by Maggie P. Murry in *Changing Styles in Fashion: Who, What, Why* (1989). The major focus of this history is to explain fashion cycles and how clothing evolves and reflects culture. Coverage is from ancient times to the twentieth century. Murry concludes with thoughts on the "slowly merging cohesiveness in the clothing of mankind" as a "reflection of an emerging similarity in us all."[2] *Common Threads: A Parade of American Clothing* (1992), by Lee Hall, also reflects this theme, as her title indicates. This too is a highly visual account, with many black and white photographs covering the period 1492 to the twentieth century. This is the only source in this group that discusses masters and slaves, in a section on the southern hierarchy and clothing. All of these titles, highly visual, have bibliographies and are written for the general public. Diana De Marly covers the period 1492 through 1800 in her *Dress in North America,* volume 1: *The New World* (1990). Special features include a chronology of major clothing events, such as the start of the homespun business in Boston in 1767; a glossary of textile terms; and two appendixes, "English Cloth and Clothing Exports to the American Colonies and Canada" and the "Commencement of American Cloth Production."

One Ph.D. dissertation, by Lydia Wares, concentrates on the "Dress of the African American Woman in Slavery and Freedom: 1500–1935."

1600s

Alice M. Earle's 1903 classic work, *Two Centuries of Costume in America,* covering 1620–1820, was preceded by many earlier works on colonial life.[3] Her book contains documented illustrations of paintings, portraits, and drawings from publications, as well as quotations from many primary sources. Arrangement is by costume subject, with information presented chronologically within two volumes or parts. Separate sections include "Venerable Hood," "Batts and Broags, Boots and Shoes," "Commodes, Mobs and Pinners," and "Bridal Dress." Men, women, and children receive attention, as do fashion dolls and fashion plates, "Masculine Vanities—Muffs and Ear-Rings," Quaker dress, the riding habit, mourning dress, and uniforms.

In 1904 Elisabeth McClellan, working in Philadelphia, produced *Historic Dress in America, 1607–1870,* illustrated with black and white drawings by Sophie B. Steel and Cecil W. Trout. The arrangement is in two volumes or parts: volume 1, *The Seventeenth Century,* focuses on English and Dutch colonies, and volume 2, *The Eighteenth Century,* focuses on women's, children's, and men's clothing each from 1700 to 1800. The drawings are meant to reveal hair styles and accessories, and all sources of illustrations are identified. However, the documentation is not precise in linking an illustration to a specific source, as indicated by statements such as "from a print."[4] "Authorities Consulted" serves as the bibliography, showing the depth of study and research. The text focuses on the clothing itself and is interspersed with many quotations. The result is somewhat disjointed. Special features include a glossary, lists of European rulers and U.S. presidents, an introduction on Spanish settlements in Florida and California, 1565–1764, and French settlements in the South, 1680–1764. The clothing items with the most entries in the index are, in volume 1, wigs and periwigs, thirteen; hoods, eight; shoes, eight. In volume 2, they are bonnets, sixty; coiffure, thirty-four; sleeves, thirty-one; waistcoats and vests, twenty-three; and hats, thirty-three. Uniforms are featured for the period 1775–1800, with readers referred to an 1889 U.S. government publication covering the topic, "fully illustrated," from 1800 to 1870, although no actual source is provided.[5]

Twenty-four years later, in 1929, Edward Warwick, dean of the Philadelphia Museum College of Art, and Henry C. Pitz, a period illustrator,[6] published their *Early American Costume* covering the period from about 1607 to the frontier years of Daniel Boone, or about 1790. The work includes black and white photographs, many credited to the collection of Elisabeth McClellan, and drawings by Pitz designed to show the "shape, character, and method of wearing" of the clothes.[7] Chapters emphasize clothing for men and women in Virginia, New England, New York, and Pennsylvania, and also reflect changes in colonial life between 1675 and 1775, the Revolution and New Republic, and life on the frontier. Special sections are "Sources and Authorities" and "Bibliographical Notes," which serve as an excellent guide to the literature. The index reveals several items of clothing receiving more attention than others: the bodice, body garments (the term *underwear* is not used), boots, and breeches. In fact, knickerbockers or knee breeches are mentioned as the type most worn by Puritan/Pilgrim men. This work was reissued in 1965 with modifications to text and illustrations by Alexander Wycoff, an editor and scholar, and Pitz to reflect a more accurate depiction of clothing worn in America. A new chapter is "Children in North America: 1585–1790." The introduction elaborates on American artists, works on early painters are included in the bibliography, and the authors caution on the use of illustrative source materials in making decisions about what people wore. The original foreword from the 1929 volume is not included. Plates and drawings covering the period 1440 to 1790–1800 are grouped chronologically, with their page locations.

The Story of Everyday Things (1941), by Arthur Train, Jr., provides an overview of American material culture from the 1600s to the early 1900s, with clothes receiving attention, along with houses, furniture, food, agriculture, transportation, industry, and community life. Train looks at this time period and suggests that the material background reveals seventeenth-century "simplicity," eighteenth-century "comfort," nineteenth-century "bad taste," and the twentieth-century as the "dawn of a new aestheticism" where machine-made things became "simple" and "functional."[8] Each chronological section discusses the items, with a few black and white drawings included. The clothing covered provides Train's idea of popular clothing items for each century. One particularly interesting chapter, "Our Days: An Age of Transition," mentions the "first American competition in designs for women's wear" in 1916 and the opening the next year of the Metropolitan Museum's "new textile gallery." Also from this section he mentions a t-shirt trend of the early twentieth century, where cartoon characters were used for decoration. The clothes discussion concludes:

When men got out and stuck each other through with rapiers, they were not afraid to wear frills on their wrists. But the man who spends the better part of his waking life in a swivel chair avoids any hint of interest in beauty for fear of seeming effeminate. He dresses as much like a sparrow or a mole as he can, and stubbornly resists any efforts to improve his sartorial lot. Athwart his serge or broadcloth bosom falls the shadow of his Puritan forefathers.[9]

A bibliography with a separate section for clothes (twelve items) precedes the index. There are no footnotes. Also from the 1940s is Paul McPharlin's *Life and Fashion in America 1650–1900* (1946), providing a brief review of life and fashion in America directed to the young reader. It includes extremely colorful drawings featuring men, women, and children, including slaves. This volume is more of a collectors' item today than a source for historical data.

In 1980 Estelle Worrell wrote and illustrated *Children's Costume in America, 1607–1910*. Arrangement is chronological, with brief sociocultural background information followed by groups of drawings of children in various styles of clothing for that period. Each costume is fully described. Worrell indicates that between 1770 and 1800, children's clothing began to have its own character rather than simply copying adult attire. Many popular trends she brings into focus include the close association (1840–1870) of girl's clothing to toys, especially dolls; the popularity of boy's baseball suits designed after the first American baseball team was founded in Cincinnati in 1869; similar development of sailor suits and pea coats from U.S. Navy uniforms and official regulation wear in the early 1880s; overalls or apron overalls originally advertised for work that evolved into modern children's playwear between 1890 and 1900; the middy for girls, which became "almost an American school girl uniform" (1900–1910); and the teddy bear, often depicted with a sleeping child wearing night clothes, which appeared between 1900 and 1919. Worrell concludes, "There have been few new concepts in children's clothing design since [1900] only variations on and improvements in those already conceived." This high-quality production is a pleasure to read, as are the black and white and some colored drawings to view, although there are no footnotes, bibliography, or index. Acknowledgments are provided for various institutions and people who assisted the author in her research.

Clues to American Dress, completed by magazine writer E. F. Hartley in 1994, is part of a series of small-size *Clues to . . .* booklets by Starhill Press. It covers the period from 1600 to 1990 and includes a glossary, an index, and a selection of quotations on fashion by famous people.

Several theses cover these early years. In 1957 Emma Briscoe at Colorado State University researched Spanish colonial embroidery in New Mexico. Sumptuary laws affecting appearance in the seventeenth century were studied by Joana Phillips in 1961. Analyzing childhood using costume as one of several artifacts was researched by Karin Calveri in her 1984 Ph.D. dissertation, and the social and economic mobility of servants and gentlemen in Massachusetts bay as visible in costume was studied by Donna Bartsch in 1988.

1700s

Histories beginning coverage with the eighteenth century range from those where the United States is only mentioned and does not receive major focus to those that concentrate solely on this country. Iris Brooke in 1930, Agnes B. Young in 1937, and Jane Dorner in 1974 provide sources that serve mainly as background. Brooke's *Encyclopedia of Children's Costume since 1775* provides a British focus. She states that the earliest record of a distinctly child costume was in 1770 or 1775.[10] The author's drawings accompany text and descriptions by decade. Young's *Recurring Cycles of Fashion, 1760–1937* analyzes women's dress with helpful illustrations. Dorner's *Fashion: The Changing Shape of Fashion through the Years, 1700–1970*s, is a highly visual treatment emphasizing, for example, "sexual display," "decorative dandyism," "physical freedom," "social equality," and "self expression."[11] "American Influences" provides a cursory discussion from the 1620s to the 1970s. Regional studies include Catherine Fennelly's *The Garb of Country New Englanders, 1760–1840* (1966) and Ellen J. Gehret's *Rural Pennsylvania Clothing* (1976).

The celebration of the U.S. bicentennial in 1975 provided the opportunity to publish materials on historic American costume. The few items examined were cheaply produced but represent a beginning look at a larger body of ephemeral materials. Alan Armstrong and Ken Small's *American Costume of 1776* (1975) was intended to show how to reproduce basic clothes for working-class and fashionable men, women, and children.

It was printed on newsprint and has deteriorated over the years. *Women's Wear Daily* celebrated with Tobi Nyberg's *The Changing American Woman, WWD, 200 Years of American Fashion,* Covering 1776–1976. Text plus advertisements reflecting decades are arranged from the 1970s back to 1900, then conclude with 1850–1900 and 1776–1850. This book too was produced on poor-quality paper; it is in tabloid format. Advertisements, many designed for the occasion, provide much popular interest—for example: Wamsutta's display of fabrics from 1846 to 1976, De Weese swimwear designs from the 1930s through the 1970s, and changing styles of the shirtdress from 1905 to 1976 reflected in an advertisement by David Crystal of New York City.

In 1977 Peter F. Copeland completed *Working Dress in Colonial and Revolutionary America* covering 1710–1810, the period before mass-produced clothes were available. Arranged by type of occupation (e.g., transportation workers, household servants, criminals), it concludes with a glossary, a bibliography, and an index. Drawings are documented if taken from other sources. Copeland found very little change over the years, especially in clothing for the farmer, waggoner, and sailor.[12] Linda Baumgarten, curator of textiles at Colonial Williamsburg Foundation, wrote *Eighteenth Century Clothing at Williamsburg* (1986). The colored and black and white photographs of documented paintings and clothing of Virginia for men, women, and children complement the excellent text. The volume is the first in a series to introduce subjects to "intelligent lay people."[13] Both formal dress and informal "undress" plus accessories are covered, with clear explanations of clothing terms used during the eighteenth century.

The 1990s has brought to the light one aspect of costume and fashion that previously received little attention: African-American dress. Barbara Starke, Lillian Holloman, and Barbara Nordquist have produced an edited volume of essays, *African American Dress and Adornment: A Cultural Perspective* (1990). Covering the 1700s to the 1980s, it is the first attempt at documenting clothing and adornment of African Americans in the commercial press (see Wares's 1981 Ph.D. dissertation, which focused on the African-American woman from 1500 to 1935). Clothing, accessories, hair treatment, jewelry, and cosmetics are included, with chapters written by different scholars and arranged in three subject groupings: "African Historical Perspectives" (three essays), "African American Slave Clothing" (three essays), and "20th Century African American Dress and Adornment" (ten essays). Special features are lists of African-American designers with biographical information, a selected bibliography on African-American dress, and bibliographies for each chapter. In 1990, as Vermont prepared to celebrate its bicentennial the following year, Meredith Wright wrote *Put on Thy Beautiful Garments: Rural New England Clothing 1783–1800.* Illustrated by Nancy Rexford, the volume includes historical background as well as patterns to assist in the reproduction of the garments. The bibliography and a list of costume pieces in museum collections are special features. Also in 1991, Nancy Rexford, herself a costume consultant, completed *Shoes,* the first volume of her own series, *Women's Clothing in America 1795–1930.* Her research is being sponsored by the National Endowment for the Humanities.

Letters originally appearing in the *Muzzleloader,* a periodical for "black powder shooters and living history interpreters" between 1984 and 1992, form the basis of *Tidings from the 18th Century* (1993) by Beth Gilgun. A seamstress and writer, Gilgun has addressed the reader from the point of view of a person living in the eighteenth century. Photographs in black and white of contemporary models in period clothing plus pattern designs and sources of supplies add value for those seeking to replicate this type of clothing for men, women, and children. The afterword is a practical and helpful discussion of how to go about obtaining information on period clothing. All chapters conclude with references.

Although not specifically focused on the United States, Farid Chenoune's excellent and well-researched *A History of Men's Fashion* (1993) provides an enlightening panorama from 1760 to 1990 of world influences and interrelationships that make up the history of men's fashion. The work was sponsored by the Federation Française des Industries du Vetement Masculin and has been translated from the French by Deke Dusinberre. Richard Martin, curator of the Costume Institute, Metropolitan Museum of Art, in his preface mentions the "great historical codifications—*ancien regime elegance.* Empire austerity. Victorian embellishment. rational repression. the modern in dress and the emergence of the body" reflecting changes in men's as well as women's wear and exhibiting "themes of consonance as much as . . . styles of difference."[14] The phenomenon of men's fashions' being adopted by women and the important influence of gay men's clothing styles on men's fashion generally is covered. The volume looks at four periods: "Dress Coat and Frock Coat, 1760–1850"; "Overcoat and Mourning Coat, 1850–1914," on European ready-to-wear; "Lounge Suit and Business Suit, 1914–1940," the "new American elegance"; and "Pin Stripes and Black Leather, 1940–1990," covering topics such as antifashion, unstructured tailoring, "Tribes and Fashion Victims," and "Fashion Winners. Fashion Losers." Notes, a bibliography, an index, and photographic credits conclude the volume. The index is by proper name followed by an "Index of the Male Wardrobe" by clothing type. Most entries refer to coats, jackets, pants, and suits.

Exhibition catalogs include *Of Men Only: A Review of Men's and Boy's Fashions, 1750–1975,* published in 1975 for the Brooklyn Museum exhibition. "Pattern of Male Fashion" by Elizabeth A. Coleman, costume curator, provides the overview; most of the catalog consists of colored photographs of clothing and accessories in the exhibition. The Smithsonian's exhibit *Men and Women: A History of Costume, Gender, and Power* covers the period from 1780 to the 1980s. The printed catalog, written by Barbara C. Smith and Kathy Peiss in 1989, analyzes gender themes and includes the "black is beautiful" movement of the 1960s as an attempt to provide an alternative to the "white" idea of beauty. The exhibit sought to encourage thinking about how fashion and appearance came to be of more concern to women than men and how strength and muscular bodies came to be associated with men. The popular culture aspects of this exhibit are evidenced in the use of early magazines, the theater, movies, and television. The authors admit that their work and that of other costume researchers focuses on middle- and upper-class white Americans at the expense of "working-class immigrants and Black Americans." Although these groups do appear in the exhibit and catalog, the authors write that "scholars do not yet know enough about their behaviors and ideals."

Several theses touch on the eighteenth century. Nancy Oberseider in 1966 looked at women's clothing in Westmoreland County, Virginia, 1700–1775; Eunice Glosson wrote in 1985 on the influence of fashionable dress on American stage costume; and Terri Riggs studied male servant's dress in North Carolina from 1770 to 1794 in 1989.

1800s

Monographs focusing on the nineteenth century include an esoteric source written in 1885 by Mary E. Tillotson, *History of the First Thirty-five Years of the Science Costume Movement in the United States of America.* It chronicles incidents of repression experienced by dress reformers in the movement to establish a healthy "scientific system of garmenture."[15] In 1974 Stella M. Newton wrote *Health, Art and Reason: Dress Reform of the 19th Century,* covering 1850 to the 1980s, with her focus on the movement in England. Illustrations, a bibliography, and an index are provided.

Kathryn Weibel's 1977 *Mirror, Mirror: Images of Women Reflected in Popular Culture* provides a look at various images from 1827 to 1977 as reflected in fashion. These images come from fiction, television, movies, women's magazines, magazine advertisements, and fashionable women themselves. Written during the women's movement of the 1970s, it reflects that interest but pays no specific attention to the minority woman's image (or lack of it) as reflected in the same media forms. Some of her points include that until the turn of the century, fashion was designed for the "idle" woman; that fashion became less complicated as women entered the workforce; and that "suburban housewife" clothing became a fashion of its own in the 1950s. Weibel provides an overview of trends from about 1810 to the 1970s in "Images of the Fashionable Woman." Notes, clear black and white drawings, and an index are provided.

Estelle A. Worrell, a lecturer on Americana and a designer of dolls, doll houses, puppets, and miniature period clothing, wrote and illustrated

American Costume, 1840–1920 (1979). The arrangement is chronological, with text followed by her drawings and their descriptions. Although she states that she tells the "story even when it's shameful because I show what slaves and Indians wore as well as child laborers, minority groups," there are no illustrations of slaves in the volume. The last chapter, "Design and Construction," includes drawings of patterns for men's and women's basic clothing as well as trimmings. The volume is not footnoted but does include acknowledgments and an index.

A very different visual approach is provided in William H. Shaw's *American Men's Wear, 1861–1982* (1982). Shaw's illustrations are black and white photographs from his own collection and from clothing industry archives. The chapters center around major historical periods, with each chapter containing historical events, notes on innovation in clothing styles, and specific types of clothing (e.g., coat, vest, trousers), with characteristics, fabrics discussion, and photographs to illustrate the period. Emphasis is on ordinary men and boys from all walks of life; military, sports, and religious clothing is not included. The photographs are documented with date, location, and other descriptive information. There is an index of people in the photographs, as well as a bibliography.

In 1985 and 1986 two works were published focusing on western clothing: Betty J. Mills's *Calico Chronicle: Texas Women and Their Fashions, 1830–1910* and E. L. Reedstrom's *Historic Dress of the Old West.* Mills focuses on women's frontier clothing using the collections at the Museum of Texas Tech University. Calico as an important fabric of the time is used to symbolize, as it did then, a "badge of respectability, . . . [a way] to make a decent appearance."[16] Mills used many primary sources in her study and benefited from donations of frontier clothing for the Ranching Heritage Center at Texas Tech University, established in 1967. Special features include the foldout "Capsule Fashion Commentary 1830–1910," which links seven time periods to fabric choices, colors, design, trim, general observations, and silhouette emphasis, and seven line drawings by L. C. Ross. A glossary, a bibliography, and an index are provided. A popular culture connection is that the research completed for the book was first used in 1983–1984 to produce the Amanda series of paper dolls produced by Texas Tech University.

Reedstrom's *Historic Dress of the Old West* includes thirty-two colored plates plus many black and white drawings by the author that include the weapons, saddles, and other gear in common use. Clothing for men and women is featured, with arrangement by occupation (e.g., soldiers, hunters, outlaws, cattlemen, hurty-gurty girls, and cowboy) and including historical background, with plates and their descriptions. A western illustrator, Reedstrom's research technique included personal interviews, including those with western outfitters and historians, visits to various institutions and exhibits including gun shows, and use of photographs from libraries and archives from around the country. A bibliography and an index are included.

Caroline R. Milbank, in *New York Fashion: The Evolution of American Style* (1989), emphasizes the history of U.S. design and style. The first chapter, on the nineteenth century, is followed by one for each decade of the twentieth century, to the 1980s. Only women's styles are covered, with black and white and some colored photographs making up a major portion of the presentation. Beginning with the 1950s, brief biographical information is included on selected designers, noting when they worked, for what companies, and special features of their designs. In some cases costs of garments are discussed. Simplicity is mentioned as a major American style element, symbolizing both "self-sufficiency" and "the freedoms inherent in a democracy." This style was reflected at the end of the nineteenth century by the popular "Gibson Girl's shirtwaist and skirt, a fashion that was easily manufactured and appropriate to all classes." This oversized, glossy volume appealing to the general audience has a bibliography, an index, and documentation for all photographs.

Exhibition catalogs are more plentiful for this period. *Costumes and Portraits of Newarkers* by Elizabeth A. Coleman and Robert R. Kerr was published by the Newark Museum, Newark, New Jersey, for an exhibition in 1966. *Flashes of Fashion: 1830–1972* by Betty Mills, curator of historic fashion and textiles, Texas Tech University Museum, was produced by the West Texas Museum Association in 1973 as a follow-up to a fashion show. The show, exhibit, and catalog were produced to promote the costume collection at the museum. The catalog consists of colored photographs of local models wearing costumes from the collection with descriptions of the garments, including provenance. Photographs are arranged by type of costume—for example, "unusual" and "traditional" wedding dresses, "color on black," "jewels on black," "the pink look," and "Duchess Gowns from Fiesta de San Jacinto." This last category represents the recognition in the collection of the local San Antonio celebration of Texas's independence from Mexico. During the celebration a queen is crowned, and elaborate dresses are designed for the occasion. A bibliography including periodicals is provided. Also in 1972, from the Brooklyn Museum came Elizabeth A. Coleman's *Changing Fashions, 1800–1970,* accompanying the first exhibition in the "newly designed Costume Galleries." The catalog consists of thirty-four photographs of costumed mannequins with brief descriptions of the costumes. Clothing worn by American women is featured.

A major research effort is exemplified in the classic *Suiting Everyone: The Democratization of Clothing in America* (1974), by Claudia B. Kidwell, associate curator, Division of Costume and Furnishings, and Margaret C. Christman. The publication, supported by Sears, Roebuck and Company, Chicago, and complementing the Smithsonian exhibit of the same name, hoped to inspire scholars to explore this area of study. Clothes for men and women made from woven cloth are featured. It became necessary during preparations for the Smithsonian exhibit to appeal to the American public for donations of daytime and sportswear clothing for the period 1920–1970. The public responded with examples from both "our industries' greatest designers" and "clothing worn by the majority of Americans."[17] Black and white and some color photographs illustrate the manufacturing aspects, which are the major focus of the volume, but also show examples of American clothing itself depicted in advertisements, company catalogs, posters, lithographs, brochures, and other primary sources. A bibliography is included. Other catalogs produced in the 1970s include *What She Wore: Fashion in America, 1870–1900* for the 1977 exhibition at the Helen Ward Memorial Costume Room, Allen Memorial Art Museum, Oberlin, Ohio; *Eight Chicago Women and Their Fashions, 1869–1929* (1978), by Elizabeth Jachimowicz for the Chicago Historical Society; and *Women's Clothing and Accessories, 1800–1930* (1979), a booklet produced for the Dartmouth College Museum and Galleries exhibition in 1979, with an introduction by Margaret E. Spicer.

A Stitch in Time: Clothing the Middle Class Family, 1850–1910 (1980), published by the Margaret Woodbury Strong Museum, Rochester, New York, was accompanied by transparencies and slides. Also in the 1980s the Crocker Art Museum, Sacramento, California, produced *A Century of Women's Costume, 1814–1914* from its own collections; the catalog was designed by Ardwe Strich with photographs by Hilary F. Marks. Another museum collection was featured in *An Elegant Art; Fashion and Fantasy in the Eighteenth Century* (1983); collections of the Los Angeles County Museum of Art are the focus. Museum director Earl A. Powell III mentions costume as a fairly recently recognized art form and costume history as a relatively new area for academic research; the exhibit and catalog required nearly four years of research and planning. Also in 1983 Riverside, California, celebrated its centennial with *A Century of Costume, 1883–1983* by Brenda B. Focht in cooperation with B. Vincent Moses. Many wedding gowns are featured. The Los Angeles County Museum of Art's Edward Maeder with Dale C. Gluckman organized in 1984 *Dressed for the Country, 1860–1900;* an essay by Evelyn Ackerman is provided in the catalog. Sports clothes from the United States and Europe are featured. At the Museum of Art, Rhode Island School of Design, *American Style: Masterpieces of Fashion, 1880–1968* accompanied the 1986 exhibit. The introduction is by Susan A. Hay, curator of costumes and textiles, with text by Phyllis Feldkamp. Biographies of fifteen designers conclude the catalog. Otto C. Thieme, curator of costumes and textiles, Cincinnati Art Museum, produced *Simply Stunning: 200 Years of Fashion from the Cincinnati Art Museum* in 1988.

Beate Ziegert's *American Clothing: Identity in Mass Culture, 1840 to 1990* was published as part of the special 1991 spring issue of the *Human Ecology*

Forum, devoted to the Cornell University costume exhibit of the same name and the costume collection at Cornell. Clothing as popular culture is emphasized. In 1992 the Mint Museum of Art, Charlotte, North Carolina, produced *The Gilded Cage: Victorian Bustle Fashion 1867 through 1889* to accompany its exhibit. *With Grace and Favor: Victorian and Edwardian Fashion in America* by Otto C. Thieme, Elizabeth A. Colemen, Michelle Oberly, and Patricia Cunningham represented a major traveling exhibition first shown at the Cincinnati Art Museum in 1993. Thieme mentions in his acknowledgments that the "catalogue is the first major publication devoted to our understanding of the dynamics of women's fashion in the United States between 1837 and 1910."[18] It includes color photographs of clothing in the exhibit, as well as a glossary and a bibliography.

In 1994 Richard Martin and Harold Koda collaborated to produce *Orientalism: Visions of the East in Western Dress* for the exhibition "Exoticism in Art" at the Metropolitan Museum of Art. Also in 1994 Barbara A. Schreier wrote *Becoming American Women: Clothing and the Jewish Immigrant Experience, 1880–1920* for the exhibition first shown at the Chicago Historical Society and then at the Ellis Island Immigration Museum and the National Museum of American Jewish History in Philadelphia.

Theses noted for this period include an early 1923 work for the Faculty of Household Arts Education at Columbia University by Anna Wilson, "History of American Dress as Affected by Political, Social, and Economic Conditions." In 1945 at Cornell, Elizabeth Brown wrote "American Woman's Dress as Seen in a Fashion Publication, 1870–1899, the Bustle Era." In 1955 Lois Foreman, at Cornell, and Betty Henshaw, at the University of Colorado, researched urban men's clothing and the dress reform movement of the 1850s, respectively. Marilyn Clifford wrote "The Evolution of American Children's Clothing from 1890 to 1930" (1957), while during the next two years, Mississippi plantation clothing practices and dress reform received attention from Lucy Sibley and Jane Purdy, respectively.

The 1960s reveals a thesis by Lorraine Simpson (1960) on women's Civil War clothing, Dorothy Smith's (1961) work on the industrial revolution's effects on nineteenth-century costume, and a doctoral dissertation by Roberta Baker (1962) on high fashion as an expression of social and artistic trends, 1870–1900. In 1963 Georgia Parker focused on the clothing of William Henry Harrison and his associates, while two other theses concentrated on women's clothing in specific regions: Suman Shenoi on Minnesota (1967) and Barbara Fargo on Kansas (1969).

In 1970 the Sears catalogs were used by Janet Jelen to analyze changes in style and customs. Sally Helvenston (1975) related children's costume, 1841–1885, to the child's role in society, and Barbara Ekeland wrote "The Evolution of Women's Fashions in the United States and the Development of the Ready-to-Wear Garment Industry . . . 1890–1900" (1976). The other theses noted during this decade focus on regions of the United States: Carmen Abbott (1971) studied Knoxville, Tennessee, women's dress, 1895–1910, and relationships to socioeconomic and political factors; Kristine Halleran (1974) compared northern and southern women's dress, 1830–1850; Debra Bennett (1976) researched Mormon dress in Nebraska, 1840–1860; Joyce Larson (1978) studied pioneer women's clothing in the Dakotas, 1861–1889; and Margaret Ordonez completed "A Frontier Reflected in Costume, Tallahassee, Leon County, Florida: 1824–1861" (1978).

The 1980s reveal the most numerous theses covering the nineteenth century. Play in American culture using costume, 1890–1930, was studied by Michael Dominque (1980). The male image as reflected in popular humor about dress during the period 1880–1910 was researched by Jo Paoletti (1980). Other theses featuring popular culture and clothing include Hae Kim's 1989 look at how *Harper's Bazaar* revealed Eastern influences on dress during the period 1890–1927. Several master's theses concentrate on methods of dating and categorizing clothing. Joyce Shore (1982) tested an "Instrument Developed to Categorize Adult Female Clothing . . . 1870 to 1898"; Pamela Rabalais (1986) evaluated a "Dating Procedure Applied to Fashion Illustrations in *Godey's Lady's Book* from 1870 to 1897"; and Julie Renner (1988) researched the "Dating Process of a Nineteenth-Century Dress and Bodice." Regional studies include non-Indian clothing of the Sonoran Desert area, Arizona, 1880–1930, by Brenda Brandt (1985); Kansas women's clothing, 1845–1985, by Sally Helvenston (1985); and rural North Carolina men's clothing, 1860–1870, by Rebecca Cornwell (1985). Health issues were studied in 1986 by Ernabeth Rey for the period 1860–1910, in 1988 by Nancy Taylor for the period 1851–1897, and in 1989 by Christina Serra for the period 1890–1920s, with a focus on "Health Advice Concerning Children's Clothing." Other works cover the "fashionable silhouette" and the crinoline, 1850–1870, by Janis Burch (1987); "Navajo Women's Dress . . . 1860–1910," by Cynthia Grounds (1988); and the "Dress of the James J. Hill Family, 1863–1916" (Minnesota) by Carol Colburn (1989).

Theses noted completed during the first half of the 1990s reflect some new interests, such as: "Clothing Adaptations of Civil War Amputees" by Laurann Figg, "The Influence of Fashion on the Dress of African-American Women in Georgia, 1870–1915" by Patricia Hunt, and "pre-Raphaelite influences" on Victorian women's dress by Pamela Radcliffe, all completed in 1990. Morman clothing, 1840–1850, was researched by Carma de Jung Anderson in 1992. In 1993 "The Role of Dress in Eastern Dakota and White Interaction, 1834–1862" was researched by David Trayte where dress was seen as a "symbol in contending cultures."

1900s

Monographs featuring the twentieth century include the 1940 David L. Cohn publication, *The Good Old Days: A History of American Morals and Manners as Seen through the Sears, Roebuck Catalogs 1905 to the Present.* The foreword by Sinclair Lewis was written on December 22, 1939. Cohn uses the Sears merchandise to show how American products expressed U.S. independence from Europe. Clothing and accessories featured include watches and watch cases, beauty products, hair products, hats, silk stockings, corsets, underwear, bathing suits, and men's sports equipment, underwear, and night shirts. In the section "Clothes Make the Man," the "Staunton suit" is mentioned as winning friends and influencing people, a product so designed by Sears with Dale Carnegie's ideas in mind that one could experience the benefits of wearing the suit while paying only two dollars a month.[19] Part 4 concentrates on the history and influence of the Sears catalogs on Americans. An index and some illustrations by the author are included.

Some British authors provide helpful background on twentieth-century European fashion generally. Jane Dorner has written for the general audience on this period: *Fashion in the Twenties and Thirties* (1973) and *Fashion in the Forties and Fifties* (1975). Both are highly visual, using many photographs in black and white and some in color, as well as cartoons. Arrangement is by topic. Each chapter contains a few pages of text followed by the illustrations. Forewords by Prudence Glynn and James Laver, respectively, add further analysis to the presentations. The focus is on everyday clothing. Elizabeth Ewing's first edition of *History of Twentieth Century Fashion* was also produced in England in 1974. It provides background as well and generated enough interest for second and third editions in 1986 and 1992. The 1992 edition, revised and updated by Alice Mackrell, is arranged chronologically, with an index and bibliography, and including 307 illustrations. British journalist Ernestine Carter wrote *The Changing World of Fashion, 1900 to the Present* (1977). The volume is dedicated to Doris Langley Moore and states that due to her "perseverence and generosity Britain owes its unique Museum of Costume at Bath." Carter discusses the "best of the best (and the most typical)" styles for women, according to Diana Vreeland's introduction. Vreeland adds that Carter's opinions and theories on how "certain silhouettes evolved" are enlightening and include comparisons between the American and European fashion centers. The chapter "Where America Leads" presents Carter's thoughts on American fashion. Illustrations in color and black and white are documented; notes, a bibliography, and an index are provided. The 1960s are featured again from the British viewpoint in Barbara Bernard's 1978 overview. Mostly photographs, the volume provides background on the Quant phenomenon and the mods as well as Chelsea shops and styles.

In 1981 the Men's Fashion Association produced *Generation of Change: A History of Male Fashion Trends, 1956–1980*. Written to commemorate the twenty-first anniversary of the founding of the association in 1955, Norman Kerr, the executive director, wrote in the foreword that the association was established to heighten men's interest in clothes by promoting "a unified industry campaign." The promotional materials produced by this alliance included articles for consumer magazines and broadcast media, fashion reports in January and June, and press kits and supplements for hundreds of newspapers in the fall and spring. Other campaign efforts featured "back-to-school," "active sportswear," "Father's Day" and other holiday materials; slide kits for retail stores; videotapes for some one hundred television stations every six months; and even promoting awards such as the Cutty Sark Men's Fashion Design Awards and the Lulu Awards for fashion journalism. In addition to recounting the history of the association's work and fashion changes for men, it includes many advertisements for men's wear to commemorate the occasion.

Sears's *Everyday Fashions* are again featured in 1981, this time with reprints of catalog pages from the 1920s. Stella Blum, costume curator at the Metropolitan Museum of Art, New York, provides the introduction and a comment on each year for 1919 through 1930–1931, which helps the reader see the trends and influences. A visual reminder of what products were for sale to the public, the presentation of clothing on people allows the viewer to see hair styles and accessories, such as shoes and hats, as well. Blum points out that the catalogs offered a reflection of Paris fashion about a year later than introduced in Paris. The advertisement text itself with prices adds to our knowledge of the attitudes and economics of the decade, just as the models themselves portray the white population, to the exclusion of any minority presence. A similar publication, *Everyday Fashions of the Thirties*, also edited by Blum, appeared in 1986.

Ellen Melinkoff's *What We Wore: An Offbeat Social History of Women's Clothing, 1950 to 1980* (1984) reflects her interest in people, clothing, and journalism. A freelance writer in Los Angeles, she presents signed excerpts from women's letters reflecting on their own clothing experiences during the 1950s, 1960s, and 1970s. Entertaining reading (remembering " 'falling' off those darned high platform shoes"), the letters reveal common issues and attitudes.[20] A special feature is the last chapter, "Fashion Magazines in General and *Mademoiselle*'s College Issue in Particular."

The photographer's view is artfully and colorfully presented in Richard Martin and Harold Koda's *Jocks and Nerds: Men's Style in the Twentieth Century* (1989). This oversize volume groups men and their attire into twelve categories that represent "persistent style modes of the twentieth century."[21] The introductory and chapter text present analysis as only these two fashion experts could provide. The choice of photographs, most of them from the United States and Europe, does begin to present a reflection of society as it is, with people from minority groups appearing: "The Jock" contains three men of color out of twenty-eight whites; "The Worker," three of thirty-four; "Military Man," one of twenty; "Sportsman," one Asian out of fifty; and "The Dandy," three black out of forty-nine. No minorities are seen in the sections on the "Businessman," "Cowboy," "Hunter," "Joe College," "Nerd," "Man about Town," or "Rebel." The authors point out that because tradition is so important in men's clothing, even a subtle change in dress, such as the color of a man's socks, can alter "the role and the man." Many photographs are of famous entertainers and artists; clothing advertisement and "fashion editorials" are included as well. All photographs are documented. The bibliography provides an excellent look at the literature on men's clothing.

Women are featured in Jane Gaines and Charlotte Herzog's edited volume, *Fabrications: Costume and the Female Body* (1990). Movies provide the evidence to support their views on how women and their bodies are represented to the public. "Fabrications" was chosen to symbolize "fictions for the eye."[22] One essay, for example, by Herzog, is entitled " 'Powder Puff' Promotion: The Fashion-Show-in-the Film." A few of the eleven individual essays are reprinted materials. In 1992 Elane Feldman, writer and adjunct assistant professor at New York University, published an eye-catching volume, *Fashions of a Decade, the 1990s.* Obviously unable to review the whole decade, she features a few themes, such as the influences of sportswear, relaxed office wear, miniskirted suits, clothes for larger women, and "ecowear," or the reflection of various societal causes and other influences on fashion. She also talks about the future. Geared to a young audience, the book includes a glossary and mostly colored photographs with original drawings by Robert Price. The volume is part of a new series, Fashions of a Decade, edited by Valerie Cumming, Museum of London. Sears catalogs were again featured by Dover in 1992 with *Everyday Fashions of the Forties.* Continuity of the Dover series and text is provided by costume curator JoAnne Olian of the Museum of the City of New York. Popular clothing of that decade examined includes the Chesterfield coat, cardigan sweaters, denim play clothes, and Roy Rogers cowboy-type clothing for children. One value to the Sears catalogs is that they offer a look at clothing and accessories available for men, women, and children. Newer publications include *50s Popular Fashions for Men, Women, Boys and Girls* (1995) by Roseann Ettinger.

Exhibition catalogs identified that feature twentieth-century costume include the 1975 Metropolitan Museum of Art's *American Women of Style* whose exhibit included "fashions designed by and/or worn by 10 well-known American women." Diana Vreeland and Stella Blum provide the text; nineteen illustrations are included. In 1979 the Indianapolis Museum of Art complemented an exhibition of American costumes representing the period 1900 to 1927 with a catalog entitled *A Rustle of Silk: Costumes from the Caroline Burford Danner Estate*. S. P. Schoelwer describes the costumes and provides biographical information on Danner and her two dress designers, Girolamo D. Giuseffi and Geroge P. Meier. Wearable art, including costumes, hats, and shoes, is featured by *Maximum Coverage: Wearables by Contemporary American Artists* sponsored by the Kohler Arts Center in Wisconsin for a 1980 exhibit. *Mystique and Identity: Women's Fashions of the 1950s* held at the Chrysler Museum in Virginia in 1984 featured the "feminine mystique" (term first used by Betty Friedan in 1963 to describe the middle-class housewife) as seen in clothing, advertisements, and cartoons.[23] The text by Barbara A. Schreier includes a historical discussion covering the period. Some of the more popular advertisements for products, which might help create such "mystique," are Warnaco's Merry Widow Bras, Helena Rubenstein's "How-to-Be-Blond" promotion, and Revlon's "Fire & Ice" makeup. Most of the costumes were from the collection of Jean Outland Chrysler; thirty black and white photographs and twelve colored plates are included in the catalog.

In 1985 the Kohler Arts Center produced an exhibition catalog on a very different theme, *Hmong Art: Tradition and Change,* with essays by Timothy Dunnigan, Amy Catlin, and Joanne Cubbs. Changes experienced by Laotian Hmong refugees in the United States are reflected by various handmade artifacts. Hmong ceremonial clothing, color significance in their clothing, and jewelry are included in an essay written by Cubbs on their art. Their experiences with adapting to the United States are also explained. Back at the Metropolitan Museum of Art in New York, *Diana Vreeland; Immoderate Style* was produced as a boxed edition containing catalog and portfolio in 1993, with text by Richard Martin and Harold Koda.

Most theses identified dealing with the twentieth century explore influences on clothing. The impact of war as a drastic event is researched by Janet Eiger in her "Effects of World War II Shortages and Regulations on American Women's Fashions, 1942–1945" (1980) and by Melissa Fullam in "Just for the Duration: American Women's Fashions during World War Two" (1994). Less violent and more general societal influences are researched: effects on the fashion silhouette (Revere, 1960); work outside the home (Houdek, 1961); for women's fashion 1939–1948 (Hornback, 1967); women's rights movements (Boynton, 1974); sociocultural reflections on women's clothing, 1919–1929 (Tindel, 1975); costume and Anglo-American social history, 1900–1925 (DePaul, 1981); socioeconomic effects of the Texas Spindletop oil boom about 1990 on female fashions in Beaumont, Texas (Reitz, 1983); and social aspects of middle-class 1950s clothing (Tingle, 1985).

Design or artistic influences are represented by two studies on the flapper fashion design, by Barbara Allen (1960) and Paulette Kontos (1974);

analysis of "Fashion Curves in Women's Clothing Styles, 1930–1979" by Marilyn Burns (1982); and "Art Deco Influences on Women's Dress from 1915 to 1925" by Robyn Gibson-Quick (1990). Paul Poiret's influence for the period 1905–1915 was studied by Catherine Young (1979), and his influence on "Society Women's Fashions as Reported by the *San Francisco Chronicle*, 1910–1915" was studied by Willette Cantua (1985). Chanel's impact on women's fashion was covered by Florence Bailey (1970). Hollywood film costume influence in the 1930s was researched by Susan Prichard (1982).

Other design influences include those from groups within the United States to foreign influences generally. In 1957 Edith C. Donaldson studied effects of Navaho costume on southwestern fashions, and Sandra Sibson examined the French influence on women's clothing, 1917–1927, in 1965. Two theses cover the impact of Egyptian fashion: Insaf Nasr in 1966 and Sara Pape in 1983. "Indian Influence on American Costume from 1960 to 1975" was studied by Hye Kim in her 1990 Ph.D. thesis.

Ethnic group clothing itself is represented by Virginia Anderson's 1957 study of Montana Flat Head and Kutenai Indian reservation costume, Margaret Hunter's 1960 study of selected Indian clothing and its relation to culture change, Mary Jacobsen's 1972 work on Norwegian-American ethnic clothing, and Pamela Sandage's 1977 study of Mexican-American clothing. Young people's clothing is researched by Sister Marie Mayer in her 1956 inventory of teenage girls' clothing and by Ann Stroup in her 1967 study of children's dress, 1930–1941. Women's "consciousness" and "identity" are reflected through clothing studies in 1981 by Kathy Sherman for the 1920s and in 1986 by Catherine Cerny for a group of Minnesota quilters. One comparative study concludes the review. It compares selected clothing in Salt Lake City, Utah, with those in New York City, 1900–1909, and was by Karen Janes in 1972.

SELECTED BIBLIOGRAPHY

Monographs

Armstrong, Alan, and Ken Small. *American Costumes of 1776: An Illustrated and Informative Manual Describing Bicentennial Dress for Women, Men, Children, and Soldiers during the Revolutionary Period.* Illustrated by Pat Raabe. Santa Barbara, CA: Channel Press, 1975. 76p.

Batterberry, Michael, and Ariane Batterberry. *Mirror, Mirror: A Social History of Fashion.* New York: Holt, Rinehart and Winston, 1977. 400p.

Baumgarten, Linda. *Eighteenth-Century Clothing at Williamsburg.* Introduction by Mildred B. Lanier. Williamsburg, VA: Colonial Williamsburg Foundation, 1986, 79p.

Bernard, Barbara. *Fashion in the 60's.* London: Academy Editions; New York: St. Martin's Press, 1978, 87p.

Blum, Stella, ed. *Everyday Fashions of the Thirties, as Pictured in Sears Catalogs.* New York: Dover, 1986. 133p.

———. *Everyday Fashions of the Twenties, as Pictured in Sears and Other Catalogs.* New York: Dover, 1981. 152p.

Brooke, Iris. *Encyclopedia of Children's Costume since 1775.* Illustrated by the author. London: A. & C. Black, 1930. 88p.

Carter, Ernestine. *The Changing World of Fashion, 1900 to the Present.* Introduction by Diana Vreeland. New York: G. P. Putnam's Sons, 1977, 256p.

Chenoune, Farid. *A History of Men's Fashion.* Translated from the French by Deke Dusinberre. Preface by Richard Martin. Paris: Flammarion, 1993.

Cohn, David Lewis. *The Good Old Days: A History of American Morals and Manners as Seen through the Sears, Roebuck Catalogs 1905 to the Present.* Introduction by Sinclair Lewis. New York: Simon and Schuster, 1940. 597p.

Copeland, Peter F. *Working Dress in Colonial and Revolutionary America.* Westport, CT: Greenwood Press, 1977. 223p.

De Marly, Diana. *Dress in North America.* New York: Holmes & Meier, 1990. 221p.

Dorner, Jane. *Fashion in the Forties and Fifties.* New Rochelle, NY: Arlington House Publishers, 1975. 160p.

———. *Fashion in the Twenties and Thirties.* London: Ian Allan, 1973, 130p.

———. *Fashion: The Changing Shape of Fashion Through the Years.* Foreword by Elizabeth A. Colemen. London: Octopus Books, 1974.

Earle, Alice Morse. *Two Centuries of Costume in America, 1620–1820.* New York: Macmillan, 1903. 2v. in 1. 824p. (various reprint editions published).

Ettinger, Roseann. *50s Popular Fashions for Men, Women, Boys and Girls.* Atglen, PA: Schiffer, 1995.

Ewing, Elizabeth. *History of Twentieth Century Fashion.* Rev. and updated by Alice Mackrell. 3d ed. Lanham, MD: Barnes & Noble Books, 1992. 300p (1st ed. 1974, 2d ed. 1986).

Feldman, Elane. *Fashions of a Decade: The 1990s.* Original illustrations by Robert Price. New York: Facts on File, 1992. 64p.

Fennelly, Catherine. *The Garb of Country New Englanders, 1790–1840: Costumes at Old Sturbridge Village.* Meriden, CT: Gravure Co., 1966. 47p.

Gaines, Jane, and Charlotte Herzog, eds. *Fabrications: Costume and the Female Body.* New York: Routledge, 1990. 295p.

Gehret, Ellen J. *Rural Pennsylvania Clothing: Being a Study of the Wearing Apparel of the German and English Inhabitants Both Men and Women, Who Resided in Southeastern Pennsylvania in the Late Eighteenth and Early Nineteenth Century: Also Including Sewing Instructions and Patterns Which Are Profusely Illustrated.* York, PA: Liberty Cap Books, 1976.

Gilgun, Beth. *Tidings from the 18th Century.* Texarkana, Texas: Rebel Publishing Co., 1993. 277p.

Gorsline, Douglas. *A History of Fashion: A Visual Survey of Costume from Ancient Times.* London: Fitzhouse Books, 1991, 1955. 266p. (first copyright by Gorsline in 1953.)

Hall, Lee. *Common Threads: A Parade of American Clothing.* Boston: Little, Brown, 1992. 324p.

Hartley, Elizabeth F. *Clues to American Dress.* Illustrated by Jonel B. Sofian. Washington, D.C.: Starrhill Press, 1994. 72p.

McClellan, Elisabeth. *Historic Dress in America, 1607–1870.* Illustrated by Sophie B. Steel and Cecil W. Trout. New York: Tudor Publishing Company, 1937. 661p. 2v. in 1. Reprint of the author's *Historic Dress in America, 1607–1800* (published in 1904) and *Historic Dress in America, 1800–1870* (published in 1910). Also reissued in New York: B. Blom, 1969. 454p. 2v. in 1.

McPharlin, Paul. *Life and Fashion in America, 1650–1900.* Pictured and annotated by Paul McPharlin. New York: Hastings House, 1946. 40p.

Martin, Richard, and Harold Koda. *Jocks and Nerds: Men's Style in the Twentieth Century.* New York: Rizzoli International, 1989. 223p.

Melinkoff, Ellen. *What We Wore: An Off Beat Social History of Women's Clothing, 1950 to 1980.* New York: William Morrow & Co., 1984. 203p.

Men's Fashion Association. *Generation of Change: A History of Male Fashion Trends, 1956–1980, on the Occasion of the 25th Anniversary of the Founding of the Men's Fashion Association.* New York: Men's Wear Magazine for the Men's Fashion Association, 1981. 84p.

Milbank, Caroline Rennolds. *New York Fashion: The Evolution of American Style.* New York: Abrams, 1989.

Mills, Betty J. *Calico Chronicle: Texas Women and Their Fashions, 1830–1910.* Lubbock, TX: Texas Tech Press, 1985. 191p.

Murry, Maggie Pexton. *Changing Styles in Fashion: Who, What, Why.* Illustrated by Polly Tribolet. New York: Fairchild, 1989. 252p.

Newton, Stella Mary. *Health, Art and Reason: Dress Reformers of the 19th Century.* London: John Murray, 1974. 192p.

Nyberg, Tobi, ed. *The Changing American Woman: WWD, 200 Years of American Fashion.* Special issue of *Women's Wear Daily.* New York: Fairchild, 1976. 147p.

Olian, JoAnne, ed. *Everyday Fashions of the Forties, as Pictured in Sears Catalogs.* New York: Dover, 1992. 122p.

Reedstrom, Ernest Lisle. *Historic Dress of the Old West.* Illustrated by the author. New York: Cassell, 1992. 160p. Originally published: Poole: Blanford, 1986.

Rexford, Nancy. *Women's Clothing in America 1795–1930.* New York: Holmes & Meier, 1991–. v.1: *Shoes.* 1991.

Shaw, William Harlan. *American Men's Wear, 1861–1902.* Baton Rouge, LA: Oracle Press, 1982. 302p.

Starke, Barbara M., Lillian O. Holloman, and Barbara K. Nordquist. *African American Dress and Adornment: A Cultural Perspective.* Dubuque, IA: Kendall/Hunt Pub. Co., 1990. 218p.

Tillotson, Mary Ella. *History of the First Thirty-Five Years of the Science Costume Movement in the United States of America.* Vineland, NJ: Weekly-Independent Book & Job Office, 1885. 14–132p.

Train, Arthur, Jr. *The Story of Everyday Things.* Illustrated by Chichi Lasley. New York and London: Harper & Brothers, 1941. 428p.

Warwick, Edward, and Henry C. Pitz. *Early American Costume.* Illustrated by the authors. New York: Century, 1929. 319p.

Warwick, Edward, Henry C. Pitz, and Alexander Wycoff. *Early American Dress: The Colonial and Revolutionary Periods.* New York: Bonanza Books, 1965. 428p.

Weibel, Kathryn. *Mirror, Mirror: Images of Women Reflected in Popular Culture.* Garden City, NY: Anchor Books, 1977. 256p.

Wilcox, Ruth Turner. *Five Centuries of American Costume.* New York: C. Scribner's Sons, 1963. 207p.

Worrell, Estelle Ansley. *American Costume, 1840–1920.* Illustrated by the author. Harrisburg, PA: Stackpole Books, 1979. 206p.

———. *Children's Costume in America, 1607–1910.* Illustrated by the author. New York: C. Scribner's Sons, 1980. 216p.

Wright, Meredith. *Put on Thy Beautiful Garments: Rural New England Clothing, 1783–1800.* Illustrated by Nancy Rexford. East Montpelier, VT: Clothes Press, 1990. 113p.

Young, Agnes Brooks. *Recurring Cycles of Fashion, 1760–1937.* New York: Harper & Brothers Publishers, 1937. 216p.

Exhibition Catalogs

Colemen, Elizabeth Ann. *Changing Fashions, 1800–1970.* Brooklyn, NY: Brooklyn Museum, 1972. 71p.

———. *Of Men Only: A Review of Men's and Boy's Fashions, 1750–1975.* Brooklyn, NY: Brooklyn Museum, 1975. 32p.

Colemen, Elizabeth Ann, and Robert R. Kerr. *Costumes and Portraits of Newarkers.* Newark, NJ: Newark Museum, 1966. 27p. Catalog of an exhibition held at the Newark Museum.

Crocker Art Museum. *A Century of Women's Costume, 1814–1914.* Sacramento: Crocker Art Museum, 1980. [16]p. Exhibition held at the museum, January 19–March 2, 1980.

Dartmouth College, Museum Galleries. *Women's Clothing and Accessories, 1800–1930.* Introduction by Margaret E. Spicer. [1979?] [10]p. "An exhibition in the Jaffe-Friede and Straus Galleries, and Barrows printroom, windows and rotunda, Hopkins Center, 7 Dec. 1979 to 27 Jan. 1980."

Focht, Brenda Buller, in cooperation with H. Vincent Moses. *A Century of Costume, 1883–1983.* Riverside, CA: Riverside Municipal Museum, 1983. 60p.

Jachimowicz, Elizabeth. *Eight Chicago Women and Their Fashions, 1860–1929.* Color photography by Frederick D. Countiss. Chicago: Chicago Historical Society, 1978. 65p. Biographical accompaniment to an exhibition at the Chicago Historical Society.

Kidwell, Claudia Brush, and Margaret C. Christman. *Suiting Everyone: The Democratization of Clothing in America.* Washington, D.C.: Smithsonian Institution Press, 1974. 208p.

Kohler Arts Center. *Hmong Art: Tradition and Change.* Sheboygan, WI: Kohler Arts Center, 1985(?). 153p. Includes essays by Timothy Dunnigan, Amy Catlin, and Joanne Cubbs.

———. *Maximum Coverage; Wearables by Contemporary American Artists.* Sheboygan, WI: Kohler Arts Center, 1980? 66p. Includes essays by J. Schafler and T. L. Lonier.

Los Angeles County Museum of Art. *An Elegant Art: Fashion and Fantasy in the Eighteenth Century.* Essays by Edward Maeder et al. Los Angeles: Los Angeles County Museum of Art; New York: H. N. Abrams, 1983. 255p.

———. *Dressed for the Country, 1860–1900.* Exhibition organized by Edward Maeder and coordinated by Dale Carolyn Gluckman; essay by Evelyn Ackerman. Los Angeles: Los Angeles County Museum of Art, 1984. 48p. Exhibition held June 28–September 9, 1984.

Margaret Woodbury Strong Museum. *A Stitch in Time: Clothing the Middle Class Family, 1850–1910.* Rochester, NY: Strong Museum, ?1980/1989. 10, [4] leaves. (7 transparencies, 6 slides)

Martin, Richard, and Harold Koda. *Vreeland: Immoderate Style.* New York: Metropolitan Museum of Art, 1993. 31p. booklet plus 37 loose plates in case. Published for exhibition at Metropolitan Museum of Art, December 9, 1993–March 20, 1994.

———. *Orientalism: Visions of the East in Western Dress.* New York: Metropolitan Museum of Art, 1994. 95p.

Mills, Betty. *Flashes of Fashion, 1830–1972.* Costume selection and text by Betty Mills, photography by Gene Aker, designed and edited by Gale Webber. Lubbock: West Texas Museum Association, 1973. 192p.

Mint Museum of Art. *The Gilded Cage: Victorian Bustle Fashion 1867 through 1889.* Edited by Jane E. Starnes. Charlotte, NC: The Museum, 1992. 32p.

Rhode Island School of Design, Museum of Art. *American Style: Masterpieces of Fashion, 1880–1968.* Providence: The Museum, 1986. [16]p. Text, "American Style," by Phyllis Feldkamp.

Schoelwer, S. P. *A Rustle of Silk: Costumes from the Caroline Burford Danner Estate.* Indianapolis, IN: Indianapolis Museum of Art, October 30–December 30, 1979. 24p.

Schreier, Barbara A. *Becoming American Women: Clothing and the Jewish Immigrant Experience, 1880–1920.* Chicago: Chicago Historical Society, 1994. 154p.

———. *Mystique and Identity: Women's Fashions of the 1950s.* Norfolk, VA: Chrysler Museum, 1984. 106p.

Smith, Barbara Clark, and Kathy Peiss. *Men and Women: A History of Costume, Gender, and Power.* Exhibition at the National Museum of American History, Smithsonian Institution. Washington, D.C.: Smithsonian Institution Press, 1989. 80p.

Thieme, Otto Charles. *Simply Stunning: 200 Years of Fashion from the Cincinnati Art Museum.* Eden Park, Cincinnati, OH: The Museum, 1988. 125p. "Catalog of an Exhibition Held at the Cincinnati Art Museum from May 3–September 3, 1988."

Thieme, Otto Charles, Elizabeth Ann Coleman, Michelle Oberly, and Patricia Cunningham. *With Grace and Favour: Victorian and Edwardian Fashion in America.* Cincinnati, OH: Cincinnati Art Museum, 1993. 102p.

Train, Arthur K. *The Story of Everyday Things.* New York: Harper, 1941. 428p.

Vreeland, Diana, and Stella Blum. *American Women of Style.* New York: Metropolitan Museum of Art, 1975. 42p.

What She Wore: Fashion in America, 1870–1900. Oberlin, OH: Allen Memorial Art Museum, 1977. 43 leaves. Catalog of exhibition opening May 10, 1977, Helen Ward Memorial Costume Room, Allen Memorial Art Museum.

Ziegert, Beate. "American Clothing: Identity in Mass Culture, 1840–1990." *Human Ecology Forum* 19 (Spring 1991): 5–9, 31. Special issue serving as the catalog for an exhibition at Cornell University, May and June 1991.

Theses

Abbott, Carmen Marie. "The Relationship of Women's Dress to the Social, Economic, and Political Conditions, in Knoxville, Tennessee between the Years 1895 to 1910." Master's thesis, University of Tennessee, 1971.

Allen, Barbara. "The Flapper: A Study of the Evaluation of an American Fashion Stereotype from 1910 to 1929." Master's thesis, Michigan State University, 1960.

Anderson, Carma de Jung. "A Historical Overview of the Mormons and Their Clothing, 1840–1850." Ph.D. diss., Brigham Young University, 1992.

Anderson, Virginia Leal. "Native Costumes of the Flat Head and Kutenai Indian Tribes of the Flat Head Indian Reservation in Montana." Master's thesis, Kansas State College, 1957.

Bailey, Florence Hubbard. "The Influence of Gabrielle Chanel on the American Women's Fashions in Twentieth Century Fashions." Master's thesis, University of Maryland, 1970.

Baker, Roberta Hardy. "A Study of High Fashion in the United States as an Expression of Major Social and Artistic Trends from 1870–1900." Ph.D. diss., Northwestern University, 1962.

Bartsch, Donna. "Social and Economic Mobility of Servants and Gentlemen in Massachusetts Bay as Visible in Costume." Master's thesis, University of Connecticut, 1988.

Bennett, Debra Sue. "Dress of the Mormans Who Traveled through Scotts Bluff, Nebraska between 1840 and 1860." Master's thesis, Iowa State University, 1976.

Boynton, Bonnie. "The Relationship between Women's Rights Movements and Fashion and Changes." Master's thesis, Florida State University, 1974.

Brandt, Brenda. "Anglo-American Clothing of the Sonoran Desert Region of Arizona, 1880 to 1930." Ph.D. diss., Florida State University, 1985.

Briscoe, Emma H. "Origins and Adaptations of Available Designs Used in Spanish Colonial Embroidery of New Mexico." Master's thesis, Colorado State University, 1957.

Brown, Elizabeth S. "American Women's Dress as Seen in a Fashion Publication, 1820–1899, the Bustle Era." Master's thesis, Cornell University, 1945.

Burch, Janis G. "The Fashionable Silhouette of American Women Using the Crinoline during the Victorian Period of 1850 through 1870." Master's thesis, University of Wisconsin, 1987.

Burns, Marilyn M. "Fashion Diffusion Process: Quantitative Analysis of the Dimensions of Fashion Curves in Women's Clothing Styles, 1930–1979." Ph.D. diss., Oklahoma State University, 1982.

Calveri, Karin L. F. "To Be a Child: An Analysis of the Artifacts of Childhood (furniture, costume)." Ph.D. diss., University of Delaware, 1984.

Cantua, Willette Diane. "The Impact of Paul Poiret on Society Women's Fashions as Reported by the *San Francisco Chronicle,* 1910–1915." Master's thesis, San Francisco State University, 1985.

Cerny, Catherine A. "Dressing as a Means of Identity: An Academic Study of Minnesota Quilters." Ph.D. diss., University of Minnesota, 1986.

Clifford, Marilyn White. "The Evolution of American Children's Clothing from 1890 to 1930." Master's thesis, Cornell University, 1957.

Colburn, Carol Ann. "The Dress of the James J. Hill Family, 1863–1916." Ph.D. diss., University of Minnesota, 1989.

Cornwall, Rebecca Ann. "Men's Costume of Rural North Carolina, 1860–1870." Master's thesis, East Carolina University, 1985.

DePaul, Frances Terese. "Costume as an Expression of Anglo-American Social History, 1900–1925." Ph.D. diss., University of Pittsburgh, 1981.

Dominique, Michael Joseph. "Play Elements in American Culture: An Analysis of the Play Theory of Johann Huizinga Using Historic American Costume, 1890–1930." Master's thesis, Louisiana State University, 1980.

Donaldson, Edith C. "Influence of the Costume of Navaho Women on Modern Southwest Fashions." Master's thesis, Colorado State University, 1957.

Eiger, Janet Nancy. "The Effects of World War II Shortages and Regulations on American Women's Fashions, 1942–1945." Master's thesis, University of Texas at Austin, 1980.

Ekeland, Barbara Kirsch. "The Evolution of Women's Fashions in the United States and the Development of the Ready-to-Wear Garment Industry with Particular Reference to the Years 1890–1900." Master's thesis, University of Connecticut, 1976.

Fargo, Barbara Mary. "Clothing of Kansas Women, 1854–1870." Master's thesis, Kansas State University, 1969.

Figg, Laurann. "Clothing Adaptations of Civil War Amputees." Master's thesis, Iowa State University, 1990.

Foreman, Lois Joan. "A Study of the Evolution of American Men's Clothing in the Urban Areas of the United States during the Years 1810–1840." Master's thesis, Cornell University, 1955.

Fullam, Melissa Lynn. "Just for the Duration: American Women's Fashion during World War Two." Thesis for School of Social Science, Hampshire College, 1994.

Gibson-Quick, Robyn. "Art Deco Influences on Women's Dress from 1915 to 1925." Master's thesis, Ohio State University, 1990.

Glosson, Eunice Alexine. "The Influence of Fashionable Dress on Theatrical Costume as Seen in Theatrical Portrait Engravings of Actresses Who Performed on American Stages, 1760–1860." Master's thesis, University of Rhode Island, 1985.

Grounds, Cynthia Tso. "Navajo Women's Dress as Associated with Navajo History from 1860–1910." Master's thesis, Iowa State University, 1988.

Halleran, Kristine. "The American Idiom in Costume: A Comparison of American Northern and American Southern Women's Dress, 1830 to 1850." Master's thesis, Cornell University, 1974.

Helvenston, Sally. "American Children's Costume in the Period 1841–1885 and Its Relationship to the Child's Role in Society." Master's thesis, Florida State University, 1975.

———. "Feminine Response to a Frontier Environment as Reflected in Clothing of Kansas Women: 1854–1985." Ph.D. diss., Kansas State University, 1985.

Henshaw, Betty Lou. "The Bloomer Costume: The Woman's Dress Reform Movement of the 1850's." Master's thesis, University of Colorado, 1955.

Hornback, Betty C. "The Influences upon and Identifying Criteria of Women's Fashion in the United States from 1939–1948." Master's thesis, Indiana University, 1967.

Houdek, Mary Fox. "Modification of Wardrobes due to Changes of Working Status of Wives of Oklahoma State University Employees and of Home Economists." Master's thesis, Oklahoma State University, 1961.

Hunt, Patricia Kay. "The Influence of Fashion on the Dress of African American Women in Georgia, 1870–1915." Ph.D. diss., Ohio State University, 1990.

Hunter, Margaret. "Relation of Costume to Cultural Change of a Selected Group of Indians of Middle America." Master's thesis, Oregon State University, 1960.

Jacobsen, Mary Ann. "Norwegian-American Ethnicity and Ethnic Clothing, Textiles, and Household Objects." Master's thesis, Oregon State University, 1972.

Janes, Karen. "A Comparison of Selected Clothing in Salt Lake City, Utah; Logan, Utah; and New York City from 1900 to 1909." Master's thesis, Utah State University, 1972.

Jelen, Janet Lynn. "The Nation's Wishbook: Changing Americana as Seen through the Pages of the Sears, Roebuck Catalogs." Master's thesis, Stephen F. Austin State University, 1970.

Kim, Hae Jeon. "Far Eastern Influence on Western Women's Dress in *Harper's Bazaar*, 1890–1927." Ph.D. diss., University of Minnesota, 1989.

Kim, Hye Kyung. "Indian Influence on American Costume from 1960 to 1975." Ph.D. diss., University of Maryland, 1990.

Kontos, Paulette G. "Fashion and Social Change: A Look at the Flapper of the 1920's." Master's thesis, Indiana State University, 1974.

Larson, Joyce M. "Clothing of Pioneer Women of Dakota Territory, 1861–1889." Master's thesis, South Dakota State University, 1978.

Mayer, Sister Marie Lawrence. "Clothing Inventories of 41 Teen–Age Girls, 1956." Master's thesis, Cornell University, 1956.

Nasr, Insaf Hassen. "Modern Adaptations from Ancient Egyptian Fashions." Master's thesis, University of Maryland, 1966.

Oberseider, Nancy Lou. "The Wearing Apparel of the Women of Westmoreland County, Virginia, 1700–1775." Master's thesis, College of William and Mary, 1966.

Ordonez, Margaret Thompson. "A Frontier Reflected in Costume, Tallahassee, Leon County, Florida: 1824–1861." Ph.D. diss., Florida State University, 1978.

Paoletti, Jo Barraclough. "Changes in the Masculine Image in the United States, 1880–1910: A Content Analysis of Popular Humor about Dress." Ph.D. diss., University of Maryland, 1980.

Pape, Sara Medina. "The Egyptian Influence in Women's Fashions following the Discovery of Tutenkhamen in 1922." Master's thesis, University of Texas at Austin, 1983.

Parker, Georgia Holt. "Costumes Worn by William Henry Harrison and His Associates about the Year 1811." Master's thesis, Indiana State College, 1963.

Phillips, Joana W. "Sumptuary Legislation and Other Regulations Pertaining to

Personal Appearance in the Seventeenth Century." Master's thesis, Women's College, University of North Carolina, 1961.

Prichard, Susan Perez. "The Influence of Hollywood Film Costume on American Fashion in the 1930s." Master's thesis, San Francisco State University, 1982.

Purdy, Jane Beryl. "The American Dress Reform Movement of the 19th Century." Master's thesis, Cornell University, 1959.

Rabalais, Pamela Pace. "Accuracy and Precision of a Dating Procedure Applied to Fashion Illustrations in *Godey's Lady's Book* from 1870 to 1897." Master's thesis, Louisiana State University, 1986.

Radcliffe, Pamela M. "Pre-Raphaelite Influences on Women's Dress in the Victorian Era." Ph.D. diss., Florida State University, 1990.

Reitz, Jan Johnson. "The Social and Economic Impact of the Spindletop Oil Boom on Women's Fashions in Beaumont, Texas at the Turn of the Twentieth Century." Master's thesis, Lamar University, 1983.

Renner, Julie Anne. "A Mystery of Origin: The Dating Process of a Nineteenth Century Dress and Bodice." Master's thesis, University of Texas at Austin, 1988.

Revere, Helen Jones. "A Fashion Silhouette and Social Changes: A Study of Society and Its Influences on Fashion in Twentieth Century America." Master's thesis, University of Oklahoma, 1960.

Rey, Ernabeth Elnora. "Women's Fashions and Health: 1860–1910." Master's thesis, Florida State University, 1986.

Riggs, Terri Ann. "Male Servant's Dress of a North Carolina Governor's Household, 1770–1794." Master's thesis, East Carolina University, 1989.

Sandage, Pamela J. "An Analysis of Clothing Worn by Mexican-Americans of the Southwest." Master's thesis, San Jose State University, 1977.

Serra, Christina M. "Health Advice Concerning Children's Clothing of the 1890s and the 1920s." Master's thesis, Iowa State University, 1989.

Shenoi, Suman Anantha. "Women's Costume in Minnesota during the Nineteenth Century." Master's thesis, University of Minnesota, 1967.

Sherman, Kathy Lynne. "Women's Changing Consciousness in the 1920's as Reflected through her Fashions." Master's thesis, Tulane University, 1981.

Shore, Joyce Elizabeth. "Empirical Test of an Instrument Developed to Categorize Adult Female Clothing Worn in the United States from 1870 to 1989." Master's thesis, Louisiana State University and Agricultural and Mechanical College, 1982.

Sibley, Lucy A. R. "A Historical Study of Clothing Practices on Some Mississippi Plantations, 1838–1861." Master's thesis, Alabama Polytechnic Institute, 1958.

Sibson, Sandra Joan. "A Study of French Influence upon Clothing Available to Women in the United States from 1917–1927." Master's thesis, Cornell University, 1965.

Simpson, Lorraine Hennings. "A Historical Survey of Women's Clothing during the Civil War Decade, 1860–1870." Master's thesis, University of Maryland, 1960.

Smith, Dorothy Jean. "A Study of the Effects of the Industrial Revolution on Developments in Nineteenth Century Costume." Master's thesis, University of Washington, 1961.

Stroup, Ann Helen. "An Investigation of the Dress of American Children from 1930 through 1941 with Emphasis on Factors Influencing Change." Master's thesis, Cornell University, 1967.

Taylor, Nancy Jean. "The American Dress Reform Movement, 1851–1897: Nexus of Fashion, Victorian Womanhood, and Social Change." Master's thesis, University of Texas at Austin, 1988.

Tindel, Cynthia Jean. "Sociological and Cultural Reflections upon Women's Fashion from 1919 to 1929 in the United States." Master's thesis, Texas Tech University, 1975.

Tingle, Jennifer. "The Meaning of Middle-Class Clothing in 1950s America." Master's thesis, Harvard University, 1985.

Trayte, David John. "The Role of Dress in Eastern Dakota and White Interaction, 1834–1862: A Symbol in Contending Cultures." Ph.D. diss., University of Minnesota, 1993.

Wares, Lydia J. "Dress of the African American Woman in Slavery and Freedom: 1500–1935." Ph.D. diss., Purdue University, 1981.

Wilson, Anna C. "History of American Dress as Affected by Political, Social, and Economic Conditions." Thesis for Diploma of Instructor in Household Arts, Columbia University, 1923.

Young, Catherine Anne. "Paul Poiret's Fashion Innovations and Their Influence on American Clothing, 1905–1915." Master's thesis, University of Texas at Austin, 1979.

POPULAR PERSPECTIVE—DOLLS

The literature on the history of costume and fashion in the United States encompasses a group of publications on dolls, doll clothes, paper dolls, and even a few coloring books. These represent a glimpse of the many sources on the topic, generally from the dolls themselves to the varied promotional literature found in advertisements, official documentation, and related paraphernalia and collectibles.

A major series of paper dolls by Ted Tierney and published by Dover covers many periods in American history. The earliest set of dolls located was dated 1978 and represented movie stars of the 1930s. Tierney also included several presidents (Carter, Jefferson, Lincoln, Nixon, Reagan, and Truman) and their families, as well as the Martin L. King family for his paper doll series. Other paper doll publications include *Dresses Worn by the "First Ladies"* (1937); antique Dolly Dingle dolls by Grace Drayton (1979); from the Boston Children's Museum collection, *Antique Fashion Paper Dolls of the 1890s* (1984); and colonial brides by Peggy Rosamond (1980). Two paper doll story presentations are Edelstein's 1985 story of family life during the 1950s, 1960s, and 1970s, in which the doll characters are dressed for the times and surrounded by drawings of popular products and symbols, and the Texas Tech University *Seven Sisters Follow a Star* (1987) by Betty J. Mills. Advertisements in magazines and in museum shop catalogs often reveal paper dolls—for example, the "My Victorian Doll" series offered in 1994 by the Boston Museum of Fine Arts where velcro eliminates all fussing with paper tabs. Some dolls even have their own paper dolls, such as the French paper dolls offered as an accessory with the Samantha doll in the *American Girls Collection Holiday Catalogue—1994.*

Publications on three-dimensional or fashion dolls reflecting U.S. history include a 1953 work on the *Godey Lady Doll,* including patterns, by Charlotte Eldridge. Other works on doll clothes are Dorothy Coleman's collectors' volume (1975); Albina Bailey's focus on underwear (1981); Hazel Ulseth's children's fashions (1982); the Haines's description of their brides' collection (1982) and Donna Felger's *Bridal Fashions* (1986), which includes a 1889 doll gown pattern. Also in the 1980s, Pieter Bach's *Textile, Costume, and Doll Collections in the United States and Canada* was published. It is interesting to note that doll collections are frequently represented in auction catalogs, such as *The Samuel Pryor Doll Collection, Part 1,* auctioned by Sotheby Park Bernet Inc., in 1982 and *The Legendary Collection of Helen Jo Payne of Arlington, Virginia,* consisting of paperdolls, 1850–1950, auctioned by Theriault's in 1986.

One of the most popular twentieth-century fashion dolls has been Barbie. Books reflecting this interest include Billie Roy's *Barbie: Her Life and Times* (1987); Glenn Mandeville's *Contemporary Doll Stars* (1992); and M. Lord's *Forever Barbie* (1994). Susan Dickey wrote about the appeal of Barbie's clothes and compiled a bibliography in 1991. *Bloomingdale's BY MAIL* 1994 holiday catalog included several Barbie items in celebration of the doll's thirty-fifth birthday. *Barbie: What a Doll* (1994) by Laura Jacobs, along with Bloomingdale's promotion of Savvy Shopper Barbie, outfitted by Nicole Miller and carrying a Boomingdale's shopping bag, were pictured. Other Barbie costumes include Barbie and Ken dressed as Scarlet and Rhett as advertised in *The Horchow Collection, Christmas Joy 1995* catalog. Even a Ph.D. dissertation (1990) has taken note of the doll industry; the author, Miriam Formanek-Brunell, focuses on gender issues.

Numerous periodical and catalog advertisements depict dolls. "Little Maids of the Thirteen Colonies" porcelain doll collection was advertised in *Metropolitan Home* (March 1984). Representing the American cowgirl, Rodeo Rosie, accompanied by two cowboy hats, cowboy boots, chaps, and several outfits, is ready for "Western adventure" in *The 1995 Christmas Book, Neiman Marcus.* The handmade tradition of Sharon Andrews's Harvest Spirit dolls, reflecting the old Southwest, feature Native American trading blanket fabrics (*Sundance Catalog,* 1994). Fashion coloring books have also been noted by Peter Copeland (1975) and Sharon Tate (1984).

Selected Bibliography

Antique Fashion Paper Dolls of the 1890s from the Collection of the Boston Children's Museum. Introduction by Sylvia D. Sawin. New York: Dover, 1984. 161p.

Bach, Pieter, ed. *Textile, Costume, and Doll Collections in the United States and Canada.* Lopez, WA: R. L. Shep, 1981. 69p.

Bailey, Albina. *19th and 20th Century Underwear for Dolls.* 1981(?), 67p.

Coleman, Dorothy S., Elizabeth A., and Evely J. *Collector's Book of Doll's Clothes: Costumes in Miniature, 1700–1929.* New York: Crown, 1975. 794p.

Copeland, Peter F. *Everyday Dress of the American Colonial Period Coloring Book.* New York: Dover, 1975.

———. *Everyday Dress of the American Revolution Coloring Book.* New York: Dover, 1975.

Dickey, Susan J. "We Girls Can Do Anything—Right Barbie!" In *Dress and Popular Culture,* 19–30. Edited by Patricia A. Cunningham and Susan V. Lab. Bowling Green, OH: Bowling Green State University Press, 1991. Includes "A Survey of Barbie Doll Fashions" [bibliography].

Drayton, Grace G. *More Dolly Dingle Paper Dolls: Full-Color Reproductions of 30 Antique Paper Dolls.* New York: Dover, 1979. [16]p.

Dresses Worn by the "First Ladies" of the White House: (Paper Doll Cutouts). Akron, OH: Saalfield Pub., 1937. [n.p.]

Edelstein, Sally. *This Year's Girl.* Garden City, NY: Doubleday, 1985. [n.p.]

Eldridge, Charlotte B. *The Godey Lady Doll: The Story of Her Creation with Patterns for Dresses and Doll Furniture.* New York: Hastings House, 1953. 209p.

Felger, Donna H. *Bridal Fashions: Victorian Era.* Cumberland MD: Hobby House Press, 1986. 166p. Includes patterns for doll's 1889 bridal gown.

Formanek-Bronell, Miriam. "Guise and Dolls: The Rise of the Doll Industry and the Gender of Material Culture, 1830–1930." Ph.D. diss., Rutgers University, 1990.

Haines, Frank, and Elizabeth Haines. *Early American Brides, A Study of Costume and Tradition, 1595–1820.* Cumberland, MD: Hobby House Press, 1982. 151p.

Jacobs, Laura. *Barbie: What a Doll! by Barbie as Told to Laura Jacobs.* New York: Artabras, 1994. 144p.

The Legendary Collection of Helen Jo Payne of Arlington, Virginia: Les Poupees de Papier: A Catalogued Auction of Paperdolls, 1850–1950 from the Payne Portfolio, September 7, 1986. Annapolis, MD: Theriault's, 1986. [32]p.

Lord, M. G. *Forever Barbie: The Unauthorized Biography of a Real Doll.* New York: Morrow, 1994. 326p.

Mandeville, A. Glenn. *Contemporary Doll Stars: 40 Years of the Best, Featuring Fashion Dolls, Barbie, Alexander, Celebrity.* Cumberland MD: Hobby House Press, 1992. 192p.

Mills, Betty J. *Seven Sisters Follow a Star: A P.O.E. Saga as Told through Paper Dolls.* Illustrations by Lynette C. Ross. Lubbock, TX: Texas Tech University Press, 1987. [14] leaves.

Rosamond, Peggy J. *American Colonial Brides Paper Dolls: Six Historic Brides with Complete Period Costumes in Full Color.* Cumberland MD: Hobby House Press, 1980, 1989. [6] leaves.

Roy, Billie. *Barbie!: Her Life and Times, and the New Theater of Fashion.* New York: Crown, 1987. 192p.

The Samuel Pryor Doll Collection, Part 1: Auction October 16, 1982: Exhibition, October 13–15, 1982. New York: Sotheby Parke Bernet Inc., 1982. 52p.

Tate, Sharon L. *The Fashion Coloring Book.* New York: Harper and Row, 1984. 192p.

Tierney, Tom. Paper doll series published by Dover, New York. Consult publishers' catalog or *Books in Print* for complete list of available titles. Brief title and date of publication: *Abraham Lincoln and His Family*, 1989; *American Family of the Civil War Era*, 1985; *American Family of the Colonial Era*, 1983; *American Family of the Early Republic*, 1988; *American Family of the 1890s*, 1987; *American Family of the 1950s*, 1994. *American Family of the 1930s*, 1991; *American Family of the 1920s*, 1988; *American Family of the Pilgrim Period*, 1987; *American Family of the Victorian Era*, 1986; *Fashions of the Old South*, 1989; *Glamorous Movie Stars of the Thirties*, 1978; *Great Black Entertainers*, 1984; *Great Fashion Designs of the Fifties* (haute couture), 1985; *Great Fashion Designs of the Forties* (haute couture), 1987; *Great Fashion Designs of the Sixties* (haute couture), 1991; *Great Fashion Designs of the Twenties* (haute couture), 1983; *Great Fashion Designs of the Victorian Era*, 1987; *Harry S. Truman and His Family*, 1991; *Jimmy Carter and His Family*, 1983; *Richard Nixon and His Family*, 1992; *Ronald Reagan*, 1984; *Thomas Jefferson*, 1992.

Ulseth, Hazel. *Antique Children's Fashions, 1880–1900: A Handbook for Doll Costumers.* Cumberland, MD: Hobby House Press, 1982. 124p.

Ware, Jane, and Cynthia Musser. "Cutouts of Fashion." *Americana* 15, no. 3 (July–August 1987): 41–45.

4

Specific Clothing and Accessories

An analysis of publications over time can reveal which types of clothing and accessories have received the most attention by writers. Monographic works, serials and periodicals, and media or audiovisuals can be studied. Large bibliographic databases allow for this type of analysis.

For this chapter the *OCLC Online Union Catalog* (*WorldCat,* as the database is known in the FirstSearch service from OCLC) was utilized. The subject headings on clothing in *LC Subject Headings* were used, with searches run to create statistical counts for each subject heading. Each basic group of publications was then limited, first to those in English, then to books in English, to serial format in English, and to media format in English. By creating a database of this information and categorizing each item as clothing or as accessory, the items with the highest counts were readily apparent. It should be noted that *WorldCat* returns various editions of the same work as separate counts; thus, one title published in four editions could be in the database at least four times—and possibly several more times if the cataloging information provided by a particular library is different from that provided by other libraries. Nevertheless, the relative counts of publications seem to provide information on what topics have received attention and provide comparisons between types of publication format.

Fifty-eight subject headings were searched on July 6, 1995, including the general subject headings of "clothing and dress," "men's clothing," "children's clothing," "dress accessories," and "color in clothing." Of the fifty-three specific clothing terms, thirty were for clothing and twenty-three for accessories. Looking at the counts for books in English "clothing and dress," 5,723; "men's clothing," 793; and "children's clothing," 719 all appear in the top ten, as one might expect. When one begins to look at specific clothing or accessory terms the leader in counts for books in English for the database as a whole is the accessory jewelry, with 3,162. Shoes, boots, hats, eyeglasses, footwear, hosiery, sweaters, coats, and gloves make up the remaining top ten. If just clothing is considered, the top ten are sweaters, coats, underwear, fur garments, sport clothes, trousers, skirts, work clothes, leather garments, and t-shirts. The top ten accessory terms are jewelry, shoes, boots, hats, eyeglasses, footwear, hosiery, gloves, millinery, and buttons. (See the Appendix for the complete database.)

An analysis of the types of monographs located for the top ten clothing and accessory items follows. Overall, the characteristics noted seem to illustrate first our cultural interests in making and decorating clothing, exemplifying qualities of individuality, creativity, and, possibly, frugality and industriousness. The economic value of clothing represented by sales catalogs and advertisements is significant, as is the power of the clothing to attract consumers, collectors, advertisers, educators, entertainers, and the ordinary individual.

Library of Congress, Subject Headings. 17th ed. Washington, D.C.: Library of Congress, Cataloging Distribution Service, 1994. 4v.

CLOTHING

Sweaters

Monographs on the history of the sweater concern British (Guernsey and Jersey) and Irish (Arans) sweaters—their knitting techniques and patterns. The many knitting instruction and pattern booklets produced over time for knitters attest to the popularity of sweaters and also of the knitting or creative process itself. Examples of this type of book are *Snowtime Sweaters* (1948) by Gretchen Baum, for ski sweaters that can be worn by "every member of the family," and *Knitting* (1977) by the Editors of Ladies' Home Journal Needle&Craft, which has patterns for a man's chevron-striped sweater, a woman's rainbow-striped pullover, and a boy's and teddy bear's tennis sweater. Sales catalogs also offer handknit or commercially knit sweaters and represent a part of the literature.

Badger Knitted Sports Wear. Sheboygan, WI: Hand Knit Hosiery Co., 1983. 16p.

Baum, Gretchen. *Snowtime Sweaters: Instructions for Knitting Ski and Sport Sweaters, Complete with Graphs and Illustrations.* N.p.: Plays, Publishers, 1948. v.2. 27p.

Compton, Rae. *The Complete Book of Traditional Guernsey and Jersey Knitting.* London: Batsford, 1985. 144p.

Goodwear Knitting Mills. *Catalogue Fall and Winter 1927–1928.* New York: Goodwear, 1927. 30p.

Knitting. Editors of Ladies' Home Journal Needle&Craft. New York: Mason/Charter, 1997. 128p.

Nicholas, Kristin. *Knitting the New Classics: 60 Exquisite Sweaters from Elite.* New York: Sterling Pub. Co., 1995. 159p.

Schlegel, Lee-Lee. *Arans—A Saga in Wool: A Study of the History, Origins, and Development of the Aran Island Gansey and Its Ornamentation.* Detroit: Harlo, 1980. 110p.

Coats

Most of the literature on coats represents manufacturers' catalogs and sewing instruction and pattern type materials. Some early twentieth-century examples are the C. J. Bailey & Co., Boston, *Catalogue of Auto Coats, Rain Coats, Mackintosches* (1910) and Flora Klickmann's *Popular Knitting Book* (1922), which included "sports coats" and "children's coats." Butterick Fashion Marketing in 1971 produced a series *Everything about Sewing . . . from Vogue Patterns.* It included *Easy Unlined Jackets, Coats, etc.*

Contemporary interest in quilting can be seen by Judy Murrah's *Jacket Jazz Encore* (1994), which includes patchwork patterns for quilted coats and vests and the even quicker "no-sew appliqué" technique used to produce an instant folk art coat or jacket, as described by Patrick Lose (1995).

The raincoat is also featured in several early twentieth-century catalogs, at least one instruction book by the Apparel Institute, and a report entitled *Rainwear for Men and Women* (1986) by the Oregon State University Extension Service. *The Story of the Trenchcoat* (1993) published by Burberry's of London is a brief piece on this garment's origins in World War I.

Apparel Institute in cooperation with Kogos International Corp. *How to Make Raincoats and Weatherproofs.* Great Neck, NY, 1961. 64p.

Burberry's of London. *The Story of the Trenchcoat.* London, 1993. [8]p.

C. J. Bailey & Co. *Catalogue of Auto Coats, Rain Coats, Mackintosches.* Boston: The Company, 1910. 48p.

Everything about Sewing . . . from Vogue Patterns. New York: Butterick Fashion Marketing Co., 1971. V.1, *Easy Unlined Jackets, Coats, etc.* [n.p.]

Klickmann, Flora, ed. *The Popular Knitting Book, Showing the Newest Designs for Jumpers, Sports Coats and Underwear, Children's Coats, Jerseys and Caps, in Plain and Fancy Patterns.* New York: Frederick A. Stokes Co., 1922. 114p.

Lose, Patrick. *Fun and Fancy Jackets and Vests: Folk Art Using No-Sew Appliqué.* New York: Sterling Pub., 1995. 144p.

Murrah, Judy. *Jacket Jazz Encore: Six More Great Looks—Over 30 Patchwork Techniques.* Bothell, WA: That Patchwork Place, 1994. 115p.

Rainwear for Men and Women. Extension Circular 1246. Corvallis, OR: Oregon State University, Extension Service, 1986. 7p.

Stephen Ballard & Co. *New Illustrated Price List . . . Sole New York Agents for the Ly-
coming Rubber Co's Boots and Shoes: Rubber Clothing, English Mackintosh Tweed
Coats, English Gossamer Rubber Garments, American Gossamer Rubber Clothing,
Oiled Clothing, &c.* New York: The Company, 1886. 88p.

W. S. Nott Company. *Rain Coats, Mackintoshes, Rubber Clothing, Oiled Clothing: For
Men, Women, Boys, Misses.* Minneapolis: The Company, 1906. 47p.

————. *Stormy Weather Outerwear for the Entire Family: Including Comforts for Driving
and Automobiling and Protection for the Animals and Vehicles.* Minneapolis: The
Company, 1907. 27p.

Underwear

Underwear has elicited much interest. The variety of undergarments
also helps add to the volume of the literature. And although there continues to be some interest in handsewing, the sewing guides are less represented in this group. Catalogs are included in the mix of publications,
such as the 1880 Kalamazoo Corset Company catalog of *American Beauty
Corsets* (1880), which would stand in stark contrast with garments featured
in a contemporary Victoria's Secret (London/Columbus, Ohio) catalog.
Examples of the making of underclothes include Flora Klickmann's *Popular Knitting Book* (1922), which included knitted underwear and many
other garments, and Eileen Collard's *Guide to Dressmaking and Fancy Work*
(1977), which contained instructions for "cutting and making ladies underclothing." Early quilting appears in a paper by Tandy Hersh, "Quilted
Petticoats," presented at the 1988 symposium sponsored by the Oral Tradition Project of the Union County Historical Society in Pennsylvania.

Histories on the subject have appeared frequently. Willett C. Cunnington's original 1951 work, *The History of Underclothes*, was revised in 1981 by
A. D. and V. Mansfield and was reprinted in 1992. Crawford and Guernsey
wrote *The History of Corsets* (1951), which was followed in 1952 by their *The
History of Lingerie in Pictures.* Norah Waugh's *Corsets and Crinolines* (1954)
concentrates on Western Europe, with many quotations on the topic from
European journals. Peggy Ott's "Survey of American Women's Underwear
and Foundation Garments from 1875 to 1950" was completed in 1958.

In the 1970s Elizabeth Ewing borrowed her title, *Dress and Undress*, from
an earlier work by Iris Brooke.[1] Brooke used "dress" to note formal attire
and "undress" to signify casual at-home wear. Ewing's 1978 work implies
a slightly different use of the word "undress." She refers to nylon as the
"most important innovation in the whole history of underwear." The
work includes separate bibliographies for U.K. and U.S. materials. Her
last chapter, "The Youth Revolution. Today's Invisible Underwear and
Underwear That Goes Everywhere," discusses the period 1960 to 1978 and
seems to suggest a freer display and use of underwear. Michael Colmer's
Whalebone to See-Through: A History of Body Packaging (1979) also seems to

imply an "undress" fashion; he focuses on the period 1855–1979 for both Britain and the United States. Corset advertisements from 1855 to about 1910, the girdle belt of the 1930s, "Warner's Merry Widow" of 1951, and the unstructured "body garment" of the 1970s are some of the popular items included.

In the 1980s Deborah Brunson researched *The Lingerie Look in America, 1901–1908,* while Christina Probert continued coverage to 1980 with a mostly visual account, *Lingerie in Vogue since 1910.* Carol Ramsdell concentrated on the "Development of the Brassiere in the United States, 1929–1938" (1980). David Kunzle (1982) looked at "body-sculpture" by the "corset, tight-lacing, and other forms," with a bibliography. Alexander, Herring, Holt, and Cockrell researched underwear for their master's theses in the late 1980s. Nancy Van Brunt wrote "A Concise History of Underwear from Ancient Times to 1918" for her 1990 thesis.

Men's underwear is the focus for Gary Griffin (1991). Popular items included the BVD, boxer, briefs, and t-shirts. "Mail Order Sources" indicates that the Vermont Country Store still sells union suits. Griffin discusses radio, advertising, movies, and movie stars who have attracted attention using underwear: Tom Cruise in *Risky Business* wearing cotton briefs and Richard Gere in *Looking for Mr. Goodbar* wearing a jockstrap. Joe Boxer offers a humorous look at shorts in 1995. Alison Carter's 1992 *Underwear: The Fashion History* covers garments for men, women, and children from the sixteenth through the twentieth centuries and is well illustrated. Underwear has also been the focal point for several exhibits, including the Fashion Institute of Technology's 1983 *Undercover Story* and the 1993 Metropolitan Museum of Art, Costume Institute's *Infra-Apparel* whose catalog was written by curators Richard Martin and Harold Koda, with a bibliography. Though three centuries are covered, the emphasis illustrated the "evolution from private, intimate apparel to street wear."[2]

As Martin and Koda and several other writers have indicated, underwear has been "uncovered," redesigned, and promoted for a new role as outerwear. This can be seen in contemporary sales catalogs—for example: *Victoria's Secret Fall Preview* 1995 catalog showing the "new empire slip-dress," the ankle-length slipdress, and the "elegant evening dress . . . lingerie-inspired slipdress." L. L. Bean's thermal underwear or sleepwear-type shirts are advertised in several colors for casual outerwear in the *Christmas 1995* catalog. Even the "Tartan intimates" flannel underwear bra and bikini presented by the *J. Crew Winter 1995* catalog looks very much like beach attire, differentiated only by fabric and construction.

Alexander, Nancy. "Bra Style and Silhouette, 1945 through 1970: 'What Came First, Barbie or the Bra?' " Master's thesis, Colorado State University, 1985.

Boxer, Joe. *A Brief History of Shorts: The Ultimate Guide to Understanding Your Underwear.* San Francisco, CA: Chronicle Books, 1995. [n.p.]

Brunson, Deborah L. "The Lingerie Look in America, 1901–1908." Master's thesis, University of Texas, 1980.

Carter, Alison. *Underwear: The Fashion History*. New York: Drama Book Publishers, 1992. 161p.

Cockrell, Rachel H. "Underneath It All: A Material Costume Study of the Historical Underclothing in the Collection of the McKissick Museum, Columbia, South Carolina." Master's thesis, University of South Carolina, 1989.

Collard, Eileen. *Guide to Dressmaking and Fancy Work: Containing . . . Complete Instructions for Cutting and Making Ladies Underclothing*. Burlington, Ontario: E. Collard, 1977.

Colmer, Michael. *Whalebone to See-Through: A History of Body Packaging*. Stanmore, N. S. W.: Cassell Australia, 1979. [94]p.

Crawford, Morris De Camp, and Elizabeth G. Crawford. *The History of Lingerie in Pictures*. New York: Fairchild, 1952. 81p.

Crawford, Morris De Camp, and E. Guernsey. *The History of Corsets*. New York: Fairchild, 1951. 41p.

Cunnington, C. Willett, and Phillis Cunnington. *The History of Underclothes*. New York: Dover, 1951. Revised 1981. 266p.

Ewing, Elizabeth. *Dress and Undress: A History of Women's Underwear*. New York: Drama Book Specialists Publishers, 1978. 191p.

Fashion Institute of Technology. *The Undercover Story*. New York: Fashion Institute of Technology, 1983. 118p.

Griffin, Gary M. *The History of Men's Underwear: From Union Suits to Bikini Briefs*. Los Angeles: Added Dimensions, 1991. 64p.

Herring, Margaret T. "Dating Criteria for Women's Undergarments: 1897 to 1914." Master's thesis, University of Alabama, 1985.

Hersh, Tandy. "Quilted Petticoats." In *Pieced by Mother: Symposium Papers*, 4–11. Lewisburg, PA: Oral Traditions Project of the Union County Historical Society, 1988. 119p.

Holt, Karen R. "Women's Undergarments of the 1920s and 1930s." Master's thesis, University of North Carolina, 1988. 155p.

Kalamazoo Corset Co. *American Beauty Corsets: The Most Popular of All Medium Price Corsets Made*. Kalamazoo, MI: The Company, 1880. [10]p.

Klickmann, Flora, ed. *The Popular Knitting Book, Showing the Newest Designs for . . . Underwear*. New York: Frederick A. Stokes Company, 1922.

Kunzle, David. *Fashion and Fetishism: A Social History of the Corset, Tight-Lacing, and Other Forms of Body-Sculpture in the West*. Totowa, NJ: Rowman and Littlefield, 1982. 359p.

Martin, Richard, and Harold Koda. *Infra-Apparel*. New York: Metropolitan Museum of Art, 1993. 130p. Catalog of exhibition, Costume Institute April 1–August 8, 1993.

Ott, Peggy S. "A Survey of American Women's Underwear and Foundation Garments from 1875 to 1950." Master's thesis, University of North Carolina, 1958.

Probert, Christina. *Lingerie in Vogue since 1910*. New York: Abbeville Press, 1981. 95p.

Ramsdell, Carol E. "The Development of the Brassiere in the United States, 1929–1930." Master's thesis. University of Texas, 1980.

Van Brunt, Nancy K. "A Concise History of Underwear from Ancient Times to 1918." Master's thesis, Morehead State University, 1990.

Waugh, Norah. *Corsets and Crinolines.* London: Batsford, 1954. 176p. Reprinted 1972.

Fur Garments

The literature concerned with fur garments consists of company catalogs, gallery or auction catalogs, instructions for sewing and making these garments, as well as advice books on purchasing and care of furs. Company catalogs include the Ellsworth & Thayer Mfg. Co. (Wisconsin) 1910 catalog with "Great Western Fur Coat" on the cover and *Alaska Furs and Fur Garments* from Chas. Goldstein & Co. in 1984. Two catalogs that were located focus on fur garments connected with the automobile: Saks, New York, in 1906 and Plymouth Fur Co., Minneapolis, in 1907. The latter also produced catalogs for *Men's Fur Garments* and *Plymouth Furs for Christmas.* More specialized gallery auction catalogs offered furs designed by specific furriers: by Frank Somper, 1968, Parke-Bernet Galleries and by G. Michael Hennessy in 1969 at PB Eighty-Four in New York. Company catalogs for fur coats during the late nineteenth and early twentieth centuries can be located for many companies from New York and Ohio west to Iowa and Minnesota: for example, from Minnesota, Haynie & Co, St. Paul 1893; Ranson & Horton, St. Paul, 1894; Harris Furs, St. Paul, 1913–1914; B. B. Menzel & Co., E. E. Atkinson & Co., L. S. Donaldson Co., and Dayton Co., all in Minneapolis in the 1920s; and H. B. Mackle Fur Coat & Robe Co., Meson City, Iowa, in 1914.

The handcraft of sewing or making fur garments is represented by several works. Faye Arnim told how to "glamourize" with fur in 1964. Phyllis Schwebke provided an amateurs' manual *How to Sew Leather, Suede, Fur* (1966, revised 1970). Butterick's Everything about Sewing series, included a volume on sewing, *Fur and Fur-Like Fabrics, from Vogue Patterns* (1971). As one might expect the Alaska Cooperative Extension Service continued in the Extension Service tradition by offering construction information: *The Fur Parka* (1973), written by Jane Windsor. A more formal and extensive *Handbook of Fur Craftsmanship* was written in 1985 by Sam Serter, with a bibliography. The remaking aspects were discussed by Helen Turner in 1985.

Purchasing and caring for furs is covered in publications by Melissa Simmons (1986), Viola Sylbert (1986), and Leslie Goldin (1986). The story of furs and fur-bearing animals is represented by works such as the *Romance of Furs* (1936), by the Higbee Co. in Ohio and by Helen Hall (1936). *The Mode in Furs* (1951), which covers world styles historically, is accompanied by many line drawings. Author Ruth Wilcox included an extensive glossary and a bibliography. A more specialized history was the topic of Lynne Kotlarczyk's thesis in 1988; she researched the fur industry and garments in Ohio from 1900 to the 1980s.

Arnim, Faye. *Fur Craft: How to Glamourize Your Wardrobe with Fur.* New York: Key Pub. Co., 1964. 78p.

Butterick Fashion Marketing Co. *Fur and Fur-Like Fabrics, from Vogue Patterns.* New York: The Company, 1971. 48p.

Chas. Goldstein & Company. *Alaska Furs and Fur Garments.* Juneau, Alaska: The Company, 1984. [22]p.

Ellsworth & Thayer Mfg. Co. *Fur Coats.* Milwaukee, WI, 1910. 30p.

Goldin, Leslie. *How to Buy and Maintain a Fur Coat: A Practical Guide to Luxury.* New York: Harmony Books, 1986. 139p.

Hall, Helen F. *The Romance of Furs.* New York: Cramer-Tobias, 1936. 30p.

Higbee Co. *Romance of Furs.* Cleveland, OH: The Company, 1936. 30p.

Kotlarczyk, Lynne M. "The Northwest Ohio Fur Industry: 1900 to the Present." Master's thesis, Bowling Green State University, 1988.

Parke-Bernet Galleries. *Fur Fashions: Designed by Frank Somper: Exhibition . . . Sale.* New York: The Gallery, 1968. 50p.

PB Eighty-Four. *Designer Furs by G. Michael Hennessy: Exhibition.* New York: PB 84, 1969. 39p.

Plymouth Fur Company. *Fur Automobile Garments.* Minneapolis: The Company, 1907. 75p. Also *Men's Fur Garments.* 1907. 32p. *Plymouth Furs for Christmas.* 1910.

Saks & Company. *Fur Automobile Garments and Requisites: Exclusive Models for Men, Women, and Children.* New York: The Company, 1906. 87p.

Schwebke, Phyllis W. *How to Sew Leather, Suede, Fur.* Rev. ed. New York: Bruce/ London: Collier-Macmillan, 1970. 151p. 1966 edition by Margaret B. Krohn and P. W. Schwebke.

Serter, Sam. *A Handbook of Fur Craftsmanship.* London: Hutchinson, 1985. 304p.

Simmons, Melissa A. *Buying and Caring for Your Fabulous Fur.* New York: Fawcett Columbine, 1986, 1987. 223p.

Sylbert, Viola. *How to Buy a Fur That Makes You Look Like a Million: Expert Advice for Finding the Best Fur Value.* New York: Villard Books, 1986. 148p.

Turner, Helen. *Turner Design Fun with Fur.* Perdue, Sask.: H. Turner, 1985. 31p.

Wilcox, Ruth T. *The Mode in Furs.* New York: Charles Scribner's Sons, 1951. 257p.

Windsor, Jane W. *The Fur Parka.* Publication 71. Fairbanks, AK: University of Alaska, Cooperative Extension Service, 1973. 16p.

Sports Clothes

Histories of sports clothes range from Elaine Durst's 1959 thesis on bathing suits for women, 1900–1958, with emphasis on their functional aspect, to a very general account in the *Ciba Review* of 1965. Although the focus is Europe, some major points are relevant to the United States. The last section, "Sports and the Common Man," contains a discussion of camping and vacationing in general as popular pastimes possible because of labor agreements and the car.

Claudia Kidwell's *Women's Bathing and Swimming Costume in the United States* (1968) includes a section entitled "Cultural Environment," which reviews bathing and its customs for medical purposes in the eighteenth century to the development of swimming as a sport in the nineteenth century. Kidwell points out several "swimming personalities" of the 1920s, such as Johnny Weissmuller, Annette Kellerman, and Gertrude Ederle, who focused attention on the sport through movies, instruction books, and swimming the English Channel, respectively. "Early Bathing Gown," "Bifurcated Bathing Dress," "Princess Style Bathing Dress," and "Early Swimming Suits" are described and discussed. Other histories are by Terrie Rust (1977) and *Dressing and Undressing for the Seaside* (1983) by Irina Lindsay, with a bibliography. Skating costume history has also been the topic of a single volume by Lois and Richard Stephenson (1970), with a bibliography.

Charlie Lee-Potter's *Sportswear in Vogue since 1910* (1984) presents a visual history for women's "fashionable" sports attire. He writes that "golf was the originator of the first 'casual' to filter into mainstream fashion: the sweater, first seen in 1919." A 1985 Fashion Institute of Technology exhibit, *All-American: A Sportswear Tradition,* showcased popular interests in sports clothing. Judith Leslie (1985) studied sports fashions as a reflection of society, 1850–1920. Another 1987 thesis offers further insights concerning the differences in women's clothing for "private" physical education/gynmastic activities and the more "public" or formal participation in sports games themselves. Patricia Warner concluded that "by about 1940" clothing now called "sportswear" emerged with the coming together of the two styles (the former freer in design and more functional, with the latter "highly fashion-oriented").[3] Judy Grossbard (1990) concentrated her research on women's bicycling, riding, and swimming clothes, 1881–1910. Her focus is on style changes for the different sports. In keeping with Warner's earlier findings, Grossbard shows that most change occurred for bicycling attire (a "public" sport) and that it reflected "street dress fashions."[4] Juliana Albrecht (1986) concentrated her study on women's riding clothes and the differences between fashion and what was actually worn.

The bloomer as a historical women's garment has been discussed by Elizabeth Miller (1968) in a work focusing on U.S. feminism, which can be contrasted with a 1983 volume by Barbara Ricca using photography, cycling, and the bloomer for her student project (with a bibliography) and a thoroughly different type of publication, *Bloomers* (1993), by Rhoda Blumberg. This illustrated work, for young people, relates the story of Amelia Bloomer, her friends, and the development of the bloomer costume in the mid-nineteenth century.

Many of the theses on sports clothes are concerned with the choices made in purchasing the clothes. Even the Gallup Organization did a market survey in 1986 on mothers' choices for daughter's sportswear.

More popular works are the variety of company catalogs selling sports clothing. The advertising ephemera of labels, tags, and other promotional material abound as well, though they are not easily documented. A 1930 Cheney Brothers (New York) advertising folder shows its " 'Debonair' sports fabric" used in women's sports clothing. Ford Motorsport/PMI Ltd. in Alabama produced a gift catalog in 1990 offering "high performance sportswear." A Land's End sports clothing catalog features *Denim: The World's Friendliest Fabric for Men, Women and Children* (1993). R. J. Reynolds Tobacco Co. published *Smokin' Joe's Racing: High Performance Sportswear and Accessories* in 1994.

To see a collection of promotional material with tennis as a theme, consult Gary Schwartz's *The Art of Tennis, 1874–1940* (1990). It provides a colorful history of tennis as presented by magazine illustrations and covers, postcards, and advertising. The International Tennis Hall of Fame (Rhode Island) provides a 1995 catalog of tennis clothing and accessories, including its "Hall of Fame Grounds Crew" t-shirt. *Tennis Week* of June 8, 1995, featured an advertisement for Chris Evert Charities, Inc. that would provide donors with a "Chris Evert/Ellesse Pro-Celebrity T-Shirt," proving that the team of personalities and sport clothes is a winning combination in fund raising.

One of the more popular publicity events concerned with sports clothes is the *Sports Illustrated* swimsuit issue, which began in 1963 with a cover and feature article on travel.[5] By 1988 the "SI s.i." (as it is called in the 1989 article) consisted of some thirty-four pages of swimsuit photos and had become a tradition for other publications as well. The combination of attractive young women in bathing suits and the journalistic background was also deemed of enough popular interest to produce *The Making of the Swimsuit Issue*, for airing on HBO February 9, 1989, commemorating the twenty-five-year history.[6]

Albrecht, Juliana K. "Women's Riding Clothing in the Central United States: Ideal Fashion and Actual Practice, 1880–1930." Master's thesis, Iowa State University, 1986.

Blumberg, Rhoda. *Bloomers*. Illustrated by Mary Morgan. New York: Bradbury Press, 1993. [32]p.

Cheney Brothers. *A Summer Sportswear Idea*. New York: The Company, ? 1930, 1939. Folder with 18 leaves.

Clements, Patricia S. "Merchandising Active Sportswear for Women." Master's thesis, Washington University, 1951.

Compton, Norma H. "Factors Influencing Female Customers' Choices of Blouses, Sweaters, Skirts and Slacks in the Junior Sized Sportswear Department of a Washington, D.C. Specialty Store." Master's thesis, University of Maryland, 1957.

Durst, Elaine A. "The Functional Aspect of One Type of Women's Sportswear from 1900 to 1958 in the United States." Master's thesis, Michigan State University, 1959.

Fashion Institute of Technology. *All-American: A Sportswear Tradition.* New York: The Institute, 1985. 64p. Based on exhibition April 4–June 22, 1985.

Ford Motorsport/PMI, Ltd. *Ford Motorsport: The Official Ford Motorsport Catalog, High Performance Sportswear and Accessories for 1990.* Birmingham, AL: The Company, 1990. 63p.

Gallup Organization. *Attitudes and Behavior of Mothers in Purchasing Their Daughter's Sportswear: Summary Report: A Custom Study.* Princeton, NJ: The Organization, 1986. GO 86144.

Grossbard, Judy. "Style Changes in American Women's Sportswear from 1881–1910." Ph.D. diss., Florida State University, 1990.

International Tennis Hall of Fame Museum Gift Shop. Newport, RI: International Tennis Hall of Fame, [1995?]. 4p. Catalog with price list insert.

Kidwell, Claudia B. *Women's Bathing and Swimming Costume in the United States.* United States National Museum Bulletin 250. Washington, D.C.: Smithsonian Institution Press, 1968. 32p. SI 3.3:250.

Lands' End, Inc. *Lands' End Presents Denim: The World's Friendliest Fabric for Men, Women and Children.* Dodgeville, WI: Lands' End, 1993. 115p.

Lee-Potter, Charlie. *Sportswear in Vogue since 1910.* London: Thames and Hudson, 1984. 96p.

Leslie, Judith E. "Sports Fashions as a Reflection of the American Woman in Society from 1850 to 1920." Ph.D. diss., University of North Carolina at Greensboro, 1985.

Lindsay, Irina. *Dressing and Undressing for the Seaside.* Hornchurch, Essex: I. Henry, 1983. 67p.

Miller, Elizabeth S. "On the Bloomer Costume." In *Up from the Pedestal: Selected Writings in the History of American Feminism,* 123–124. Edited by Aileen S. Kraditor. Chicago: Quadrangle Books, 1968. 372p.

Miller, Mary G. "Preferences of a Group of College Women for Certain Standard Features of Selected Categories of Female Sportswear." Master's thesis, University of North Carolina, 1969.

Miller, Maryann T. "Relationship of Factors Influencing Purchase and Satisfaction with Sportswear by College Women." Master's thesis, Southern Illinois University, 1977.

Ricca, Barbara L. *The Camera, Bikes and Bloomers.* Tempe, AZ: School of Art, Arizona State University, 1983. [24]p.

R. J. Reynolds Tobacco Company. *Smokin' Joe's Sportswear and Accessories.* Winston Salem, NC: The Company, 1994. 16p.

Rust, Terrie E. "A History of Swimwear Reflecting Some Sociological and Technological Changes." Master's thesis, San Jose State University, 1977.

Schwartz, Gary H. *The Art of Tennis, 1874–1940: Timeless, Enchanting Illustrations and Narrative of Tennis' Formative Years.* Tiburon, CA: Wood River Publishing, 1990. 171p.

Snyder, Linda A. "The Effect of Sex, Ethnic Group and the Endorsement of Masculine/Feminine Personality Traits on the Perception, Use and Ownership of Selected Sportswear Apparel." Ph.D. diss., University of North Carolina, 1984.

"Sportswear." *Ciba Review,* no. 4 (1965): 2–34.

Stephenson, Lois, and Richard Stephenson. *A History and Annotated Bibliography of Skating Costume.* Meriden, CT: Bayberry Hill Press, 1970. 101p.

Warner, Patricia C. "Clothing the American Woman for Sport and Physical Education, 1860 to 1940: Public and Private." Ph.D. diss., University of Minnesota, 1987.

Weitz, John. *Sports Clothes for Your Sports Car.* New York: Sports Car Press, 1958. 120p.

Skirts

Most of the monographs on skirts are concerned with the making of the garment. Even the special kilt books discuss making and sewing or how to wear the skirt. Several other publications were located, including "Pleated Skirts Worn by High School Girls" (1962), by Dora Lockard. Also in 1962, style cycles as reflected in fashion magazines, 1925–1961, were researched by Nadine Hackler. A report by the University of Minnesota Agricultural Experiment Station in 1965 evaluated the performance characteristics of adolescent girls' skirts. Elizabeth Bundy researched the history and construction in "Farthingales, Paniers, Crinolines, and Bustles," her thesis in 1970. Skirts as advertised in *Vogue* and Sears catalogs from 1947 to 1972 were studied by Mary Ellen Brigham in 1988 and related to women's social position.

Some examples of books on making skirts include Patricia Riley's *Skirtmaking Book* (1979), on tailoring techniques; Nancy Pfeiffer's *Easy-to-Make Patchwork Skirts* (1980); and Nancy Zieman's *Just Skirts* (1994), which was related to her television program *Sewing with Nancy.*

Adolescent Girls Skirts. Bulletin 479. St. Paul, MN: University of Minnesota, Agricultural Experiment Station, 1965. 27p.

Brigham, Mary Ellen K. S. "*Vogue* Magazine and Sears, Roebuck & Co. Catalogues: Barometers of Women's Social Position, as Seen Through Skirts Advertised, 1947–1972." Master's thesis, University of Connecticut, 1988.

Bundy, Elizabeth. "Farthingales, Paniers, Crinolines, and Bustles: A Study of Their History and Guide to Their Construction." Master's thesis, University of Georgia, 1970.

Hackler, Nadine. "A Study of Fashion Cycles in Style, Fabric and Design of Women's Skirts in Four Fashion Magazines from 1925–1961." Master's thesis, Oklahoma State University, 1962.

Lockard, Dora M. "Pleated Skirts Worn by High School Girls." Master's thesis, Colorado State University, 1962.

Pfeiffer, Nancy. *Easy-to-Make Patchwork Skirts: Step-by-Step Instructions and Full-Size Templates for 12 Skirts and 2 Aprons.* New York: Dover, 1980. 25p.

Riley, Patricia. *The Skirtmaking Book.* London: Batsford, 1979. 120p.

Zieman, Nancy L. *Just Skirts*. Beaver Dam, WI: Nancy's Notions, 1994. 19p. *Sewing with Nancy* (television program).

Work Clothes/Trousers

Work clothes, trousers, and other occupation-related clothing in the United States have not received much attention in the monographic literature. Most information is found in sales catalogs, related business statistics, a few histories, and the ever-present guides to making and decorating.

Two histories are British in emphasis: *Occupational Costume* (1977) by Avril Lansdell and *Dressed for the Job* (1982) by Christobel Williams-Mitchell. Williams-Mitchell mentions that the European colonists thought Indian moccasins were comfortable for working. Clothing items from the index include apron, breeches, cap, hats, shirt, and trousers. Peter Copeland produced in 1977 an American equivalent for the colonial and Revolutionary periods. Arrangement is by occupation, with a brief background followed by documented drawings and discussions of the clothing. He includes a glossary. Another history, this one written for children, by Miriam Moss (1989), includes a discussion of protective clothing and clothing worn by entertainers.

Contemporary interest in reenacting historical events has prompted several costume histories, including *The Frontier Rifleman* (1989) by Richard La Crosse. This volume includes careful drawings of clothing and equipment, a bibliography of primary and secondary sources, and lists six periodicals of the 1770s. It mentions the hunting shirt, blanket coat, and breeches, trousers, and overalls. Two centuries later a very different frontier is reflected in Lillian Kozloski's *U.S. Space Gear: Outfitting the Astronaut* (1994). This work by the Smithsonian Institution is considered an introduction for a general audience to the history of the space suit, technical developments, and the collection of the National Air and Space Museum; a bibliography is included.

Popular interests in work clothes can be seen in the 1942 U.S. Department of Agriculture's *Work Clothes for Women* by Clarice Scott. It pictures and describes various clothes with the advisory, "Know your job and dress for it," and assures readers that the clothing is "simple to make and easy to wash and iron." Clothing includes the field suit, jumper-slack suit, food-preparation dress, divided-skirt dress, nurse's uniform and several special aprons (belted coverall, surplice coverall, princess coverall, and utility aprons "for carrying clothespins or seed packets"). "The Evolution of Pants ... for Women" (1969) by Margaret Watts indicates acceptance of this style by 1940.[7] *Slacks for Boys and Young Men* is a 1951 North Carolina Extension Service pamphlet. Several manufacturers' publications were noted—for example, a 1907 Rockford Overalls Mfg. Co. catalog and from

Sweet-Orr, Inc. the *Diamond Jubilee* volume celebrating seventy-five years of production of overalls and other work clothes. A report published in 1963 by the American Apparel Manufacturers Association, *Work Clothing Cyclical Analysis* (1947–1962), mentions men's work shirts, men's dungarees, and men's waistband overalls.

Making Work Pants by Apparel Manufacturer and the Apparel Institute and *The 20-Minute Trouser* (1960) by Robert Bonapfel are examples of the many books on making pants, slacks, and trousers. Others followed in the 1970s by Irene Kleeberg, Joyce LeClaire, and Jackie Halversen, with the latter two concentrating on sewing with knit fabrics. The decorating of overalls described by Sherry Britton (1976) also reflects popular interests. The overalls style has recently appeared in more fashionable attire, as evidenced by the "overall dress" in pale yellow advertised in *Victoria's Secret Fall Preview* 1995 catalog. The overall dress, however, is not as commonly worn as is the dungaree, blue jean, or jean, which, although it has been worn for work for a long period of time, is now worn for just about any occasion.

American Apparel Manufacturers Association. Compiled by Lionel D. Edie & Company. *Work Clothing Cyclical Analysis.* Washington, DC: The Association, 1963. 21p.

Apparel Manufacturer in cooperation with Apparel Institute. *Making Work Pants.* New York: Kogos International Corp., ? 1950, 1959. 24p.

Bonapfel, Robert H. *The 20-Minute Trouser.* New York: Kogos International Corp., 1960. 20p.

Britton, Sherry. *The Great Overall Coverup.* Palo Alto, CA: Hidden House, Flash Books, 1976. 144p.

Copeland, Peter F. *Working Dress in Colonial and Revolutionary America.* Westport, CT: Greenwood Press, 1977. 224p.

Halversen, Jackie F. *Men's Knit Slacks and Jackets.* Spokane, WA: Halversen, 1975. 168p.

Kleeberg, Irene C. *Make Your Own Pants and Skirts.* Rev. ed. New York: Bantam Books, 1971. 96p.

Kozloski, Lillian D. *U.S. Space Gear: Outfitting the Astronaut.* Washington, D.C.: Smithsonian Institution Press, 1994. 238p.

La Crosse, Richard B. *The Frontier Rifleman: His Arms, Clothing, and Equipment during the Era of the American Revolution, 1760–1800.* Union City, TN: Pioneer Press, 1989. 183p.

Lansdell, Avril. *Occupational Costume and Working Clothes, 1776–1976.* Aylesbury, Bucks., England: Shire, 1977. 32p.

LeClaire, Joyce. *Guide to Sew Knit Slacks for Men.* Minneapolis: Standard Fabrics, 1971. 51p.

Moss, Miriam. *Work Clothes.* New York: Marshall Cavendish, 1989. 31p.

Rockford Overalls Mfg. Co. *Rockford Overalls Mfg. Co. . . . Wholesale Manufacturers of Overalls, Pants, Jackets.* Rockford, IL: The Company, 1907. 32p.

Scott, Clarice L. *Work Clothes for Woman.* Washington, D.C.: U.S. Department of Agriculture, 1942. 16p. *Farmers' Bulletin* 1905. A 1.9: 1905.

Slacks for Boys and Young Men. Raleigh, NC: North Carolina Agricultural Extension Service, 1957. 4p. folded sheet.

Sweet-Orr, Inc. *Diamond Jubilee, 1871–1946.* New York: The Company, 1946. [47]p.

Watts, Margaret W. "The Evolution of Pants as an Outerwear Garment for Women." Master's thesis, University of Missouri, 1969.

Williams-Mitchell, Christobel. *Dressed for the Job: The Story of Occupational Costume.* Poole, Dorset: Blandford Press, 1982. 143p.

Jeans

Home economists in the 1950s took an early interest in advising on the serviceability of jeans, (University of Wisconsin Agricultural Experiment Station, 1959) and studying buying practices (Ohio Agricultural Experiment Station, 1961). The home sewing of jeans is also seen in works by Barbara Corrigan in 1978 emphasizing "fit," several publications by Peggy Layton for designer jeans during the 1980s, and Jean McBride on her *Jeanie's Jeans* (1981). Even in 1991 one sees the Union Special Corporation in Illinois producing *A Guide to Sewing Blue Jeans.*

In addition to making jeans, people have been interested in decorating and personalizing them. Eve Harlow explained how to "decorate to differentiate" in her 1973 book on techniques using trims, appliqué, gilding, junk, embroidery, patchwork, paint, dyes, and other techniques. Donna Lawson's *Superjeans* (1974) is a rather cheaply produced volume discussing decoration and the "recycling" of jeans into bags, hats, and skirts. In 1974 Levi Strauss & Co. held a contest with some 2,000 entrants. Color photographs of the winning decorated jeans were produced in *Levi's Denim Art Contest: Catalogue of Winners.* In another contest, sponsored by the American Denim Council and Levi Strauss, decoration met the theme "the literal matter of America, the worn, gritty artifacts of our lives."[8] Winning entries appeared in *American Denim: A New Folk Art* (1975). In 1991 Andra Rowland repeated the recycling idea with *Upside Down Vests to Make and Paint,* while Sharon McCoy focused her attention on girls in her *50 Nifty Ways to Jazz Up Your Jeans and Other Things* (1994).

Youngsters are also the target for several educational volumes where Levi Strauss and his jeans are the attention-gaining device. Manufacturing processes are covered in 1976 books by Jonathan Rosenbloom and by Alice Edmunds and John Greeman, who explore various jobs in the clothing industry. Both Sondra Henry and Maryann Weidt in 1990 concentrated on the biography of Strauss. And in 1995 Regine van Damme wrote *Jeans: The Stuff of American History* for the History Through Objects series by Puffin in London.

The popular culture of the jean and its related jacket and denim fabric has been explored in *Yankee Denim Dandies* (1974) by Barbara Fehr. Although it is written for a general audience and not footnoted, she includes a bibliography of some fifty-eight sources. Her focus is the phenomenon and its impact on youth. In contrast, Iain Finlayson's *Denim: An American Legend* (1990) offers a somewhat deeper analysis. Three sections are included: "From the Klondyke to Klein" on history, "The Hype" on advertising, and "Denim and Sex," where jeans and denim connections with sex and the homosexual world are made. The work is accompanied by black and white photographs, all credited. Jeans as a symbol of the depression "dirtpoor," of rebellion and freedom from the "sedate culture of . . . parents," and the sexual undercurrents evident to the author in the swinging pelvis, tight fit, "zippable crotch" seen through this garment and the companion denim jacket are discussed. Denim itself is presented as "the universal medium" and the "universal ideology of the post-war world." Although there are no footnotes or bibliography, many sources are documented within the text. In 1991 Beverly Gordon, also using the phrase "American Denim," contributed a chapter to *Dress and Popular Culture.* She includes a bibliography.

Several theses touch on a popular aspect of the jean: its advertisements. Roxanne Branch (1981) studied designer jean advertisement nudity and brand recall, while Angella Pace (1994) researched jean advertisements from the 1940s through the 1980s for their themes. She concluded that they generally fostered "equality" of men and women and the "dignity of manual labor."[9]

The mail order catalog can be used to document the ever-expanding variety of jeans, jean jackets, and other clothing made with denim. Name fashion designer wear capitalizes on the popularity of denim (*LIZ, LIZ claiborne* 1995 advertising booklet from Filene's in Boston included the "LIZ Denim" jumper dress and denim romper) as do specialty clothing outfitters (*Miller Stockman Western Wear Spring Catalog 1995* in Colorado shows the "Denim Tux and Tails" for women).

In addition to works on the jean itself—its popularity, history, and analysis—some of the material revealed in this search illustrates the collectibility of jean and denim-related ephemera. A single folded sheet written in 1966 by Helen Church is titled *Why Rip That Levi Leg to Mend It?* Hystrom Fibers Inc. produced nineteen plates, in case, of photographs by Bert Stern entitled *America in Levi's.* The Western Writers of America provided copies of *Levi's* (a poem) by S. Omar Barker to its members in 1977 as a souvenir. *Calvin Klein Jeans,* photographed by Bruce Weber and published by CRK Advertising in 1991, has become a collectible. Other manufacturers' and designer information, sales tags, and labels could be collected, as well as advertisements, posters, cartoons, and other ephemera. Literary reference to jeans in quotations, poems, short stories, and novels could be documented and collected using standard library reference tools in combination with electronic and/or full-text database.

American Denim: A New Folk Art. Presented by Richard Owens and Tony Lane. Text by Peter Beagle. Photos by Baron Wolman. New York: H. N. Abrams, 1975. 156p.

Barker, S. Omar. *Levi's* (poem). North Platte, NE: Western Writers of America, 1977. [8]p. 350 copies distributed to WWA members. Also 50 copies bound in Levi's denim, numbered and signed by the author.

Branch, Roxanne M. " 'Blue' Designer Jeans Advertisements: The Effect of Advertising Nudity on Brand Recall." Master's thesis, University of Kansas, 1981.

Calvin Klein Jeans. Photographed by Bruce Weber. New York: CRK Advertising, 1991. [n.p.]

Church, Helen L. *Why Rip That Levi Leg to Mend It?* Tucson, AZ: Cooperative Extension Service, University of Arizona, in cooperation with the U.S. Department of Agriculture, 1966. 1 folded sheet. In English and Spanish. AES 2.3:F 55/120.

Corrigan, Barbara. *How to Make Pants and Jeans That Really Fit.* Garden City, NY: Doubleday, 1978. 166p.

Damme, Regine van. *Jeans: The Stuff of American History.* London: Puffin, 1995. 47p.

Edmunds, Alice, and John Greeman. *Who Puts the Blue in the Jeans?* New York: Random House, 1976. 73p.

Fehr, Barbara. *Yankee Denim Dandies.* Blue Earth, MN: Piper, 1974. 96p.

Finlayson, Iain. *Denim: An American Legend.* New York: Simon & Schuster, 1990. 126p.

Gordon, Beverly. "American Denim: Blue Jeans and Their Multiple Layers of Meaning." In *Dress and Popular Culture,* 31–45. Edited by Patricia A. Cunningham and Susan V. Lab. Bowling Green, OH: Bowling Green State University Popular Press, 1991. 165p.

Harlow, Eve. *The Jeans Scene.* New York: Drake Publishers, 1973. 117p.

Henry, Sondra. *Everyone Wears His Name: A Biography of Levi Strauss.* Minneapolis, MN: Dillon Press, 1990. 128p.

Lawson, Donna. *Superjeans: Easy Ways to Recycle and Decorate Your Jeans.* Illustrated by Jeanne Kovalak. New York: Scholastic Book Services, 1974. 96p.

Layton, Peggy D. *Make Your Own Designer Jeans Book I, The Basics.* Rev. and updated. Layton, UT: Designer Jeans, 1983. 105p.

———. *Peggy Dianne Layton's Designer Jeans Made Easy.* Layton, UT: Designer Jeans, 1980. 103p.

———. *The Slip-Fit Method of Pattern Making: For Jeans and Dress Pants, with Solutions to All Your Fitting Problems.* Manit, UT: Designer Jeans, 1983. 64p.

Layton, Peggy D., with Julie S. Jennings. *Designer Jeans II: Beyond the Basics.* Layton, UT: Designer Jeans, 1983. 86p.

Levi Strauss and Company. *Levi's Denim Art Contest: Catalogue of Winners.* Mill Valley, CA: B. Wolman/Squarebooks, 1974. [54]p.

McBride, Jean E. *Jeanie's Jeans: Making Your Own Blue Jeans.* Hooper, UT: Jeanies Jeans, 1981. 45p.

McCoy, Sharon. *50 Nifty Ways to Jazz Up Your Jeans and Other Things.* Los Angeles: Lowell House Juvenile, and Chicago: Contemporary Books, 1994. 64p.

Ohio Agricultural Experiment Station. *Mother's Preferences and Buying Practices for Boys' Shirts, Jeans and Slacks.* Research Bulletin 873. Wooster, OH, 1961. 55p.

Pace, Angella M. "Denim Advertising: Society's Fabric (Blue Jeans)." Ph.D. diss., City University of New York, 1994.

Rosenbloom, Jonathan. *Blue Jeans.* New York: Messner, 1976. 63p.

Rowland, Andra. *Upside Down Vests to Make and Paint: Vests Made from Recycled Denim Jeans.* Norcross, GA: Plaid Enterprises, 1991. 23p.

Stern, Bert. *America in Levi's.* New York: Hystron Fibers Incorporated, 1972. 19 plates, issued in case.

Union Special Corporation. *A Guide to Sewing Blue Jeans.* Huntley, IL, 1991. 11p.

University of Wisconsin. Agricultural Experiment Station. *Serviceability of Boy's Shirts and Jeans.* Research Bulletin 212. Madison, 1959. 40p.

Weidt, Maryann N. *Mr. Blue Jeans: A Story about Levi Strauss.* Minneapolis: Carolrhoda Books, 1990. 64p.

Leather Garments

Most of the leather garment monographs emphasize how to sew, tailor, and craft with leather. Some publications include leather selection and preparation information as well. Most of this material was published from the late 1960s to the late 1980s. The introduction of synthetic leathers and furlike fabrics also is represented in works by Butterick, *Leather and Leather-Like Fabrics* and *Fur and Fur-Like Fabrics* (both 1971); by Krestine Corbin, *Ultrasuede Fabric Sewing Guide* (1973); by Pati Palmer and Susan Pletsch (1974) also on ultrasuede; and by Shirley Adams in her *Suave as Suede—But Better* (1983). Roberta Moss focuses on *Makin' Buckskin Clothes* (1982), while Harriet Jennings advises on *Caring for Natural and Man-Made Leathers, Suedes, and Furs* (1988).

The leather garment fashions themselves are singled out by several authors. *Suede and Leather Wear* (1972) is a brief piece with color illustrations by Helen Organ. Jeanne Argent honors *Imaginative Leatherwork* (1976), and David Holman, Billie Persons, and Pat Massey emphasize interest in the pioneer with *Buckskin and Homespun: Frontier Texas Clothing, 1820–1879* (1979). "The Inuit Parka" (1983), Bernadette Driscoll's research, highlights a leather garment outstanding enough to gain respect and to inspire.

Catalogs of leather garment manufacturers and retailers can be documented historically. Some examples from the early twentieth century include the Edes Robe Tanning Co., Berlin Glove Co., H. B. Mickie Fur Coat and Robe Co., and the Albert Lea Hide & Fur Co.

One of the more popular leather garments is the leather jacket. Usually seen in contemporary men's and women's clothing catalogs, it is also seen in advertisements in publications reaching a wide audience. For example, the "Merit Leather Jacket" is a promotional brown leather jacket for men or women and is advertised as a "Merit [cigarette] Awards" offered by Philip Morris Co. in *Parade Magazine*'s September 3, 1995, issue. Appealing to another audience, "The 50th Anniversary Limited-Edition Official A-2

Flying Jacket" is offered by Willabee & Ward of Norwalk, Connecticut, and made by Cooper Sportswear, the original military supplier of the jacket. This "piece of American History . . . on sale" is advertised, described, and pictured in *Smithsonian* (March 1995).

It is the black leather jacket, however, that has a whole book devoted to its personality. Mick Farren's *The Black Leather Jacket* (1985) contains many photographs and has chapters devoted to "Legendary Leather," "German Influence," "Golden Idols," "Teenage Dreams," "Smut by Numbers," "Swinging Singles," "The New Barbarians," and "Savage Skins." Farren writes, "There can be no doubt that western culture does perceive the black leather jacket as something *bad*." "Leathermen in San Francisco" were researched by Gayle Rubin for her 1994 thesis; here also the black leather jacket is a significant garment.

Adams, Shirley. *Suave as Suede—But Better.* Mentor(?), OH: S. Adams, 1983. 321p.

Albert Lea Hide & Fur Co. *Furs—America's Leading Fur Line: Season, 1918–1919.* Albert Lea, MN: The Company, 1918. 34p.

Argent, Jeanne. *Imaginative Leatherwork.* South Brunswick, NJ: A. S. Barnes, 1976. 172p.

Berlin Glove Company. *Mid-Western Leather Garments.* Berlin, WI: The Company, ? 1910, 1919. 1 sheet folded.

Butterick Fashion Marketing Co. *Fur and Fur-Like Fabrics, from Vogue Patterns.* New York: The Company, 1971. 48p.

———. *Leather and Leather-Like Fabrics, from Vogue Patterns.* New York: The Company, 1971. 48p.

Corbin, Krestine. *Ultrasuede Fabric Sewing Guide: Sew as High Fashion Designers Do.* Sacramento, CA: Creative Sewing, 1973. 39p.

Driscoll, Bernadette. "The Inuit Parka: A Preliminary Study." Master's thesis, Carleton University, 1983.

Edes Robe Tanning Co. *Every Product Guaranteed.* Dubuque, IA: The Company, 1910. 25p.

Farren, Mick. *The Black Leather Jacket.* London: Plexus, 1985. 96p.

H. B. Mickie Fur Coat and Robe Co. *Custom Price List: Galloway Coats, Robes, Gloves, Mittens.* Mason City, IA: The Company, 1914. 20p.

Holman, David, Billie Persons, and Pat Massey. *Buckskin and Homespun: Frontier Texas Clothing, 1820–1870.* Austin: Wind River Press, 1979. 130p.

Jennings, Harriet T. *Caring for Natural and Man-Made Leathers, Suedes, and Furs.* Raleigh, NC: North Carolina Agricultural Extension Service, 1988. 1 folded sheet (6p.).

Moss, Roberta. *Makin' Buckskin Clothes.* Union City, TN: Pioneer Press, 1982. 36p.

Organ, Helen D. *Suede and Leather Wear.* Leicester, Harbor City, CA: Dryad Press, 1972. 25p.

Palmer, Pati, and Susan Pletsch. *Sewing Skinner Ultrasuede Fabric.* Portland, OR: Printed by Metropolitan Printing Co., 1974. 79p.

Rubin, Gayle S. "The Valley of the Kings: Leathermen in San Francisco, 1960–1990." Ph.D. diss., University of Michigan, 1994.

T-Shirts

Although various shirts are popular clothing items, such as the button-down oxford shirt, the dress shirt, the flannel plaid shirt, and the chamois shirt, whole monographs devoted to them have not been located. They can be seen in catalogs and advertisements as commonly worn and advertised garments. *The Hawaiian Shirt* has been documented by H. Thomas Steele. His 1984 work covers the history of the shirt from its beginnings in the 1920s to the end of its classic quality in the 1950s. The color photographs throughout illustrate how the designs reflected the culture and natural history of the Hawaiians and their islands. Steele praises these shirts as fine folk art.

However, the t-shirt has the largest literature. The majority of titles deal with various methods of decorating the shirt, such as transfers for (Jeffery Feinman, Ed Sibbett, Laura Torbet, Parsons School of Design); painting on (Susan Figliulo, Ray Gibson and Vicki Rhodes' *Painted of Course!: Perfect Patchwork*); airbrushing of (Diana Martin, Cliff Stieglitz); and printing of (Scott Fresener, Rosalie Grattaroti) with a special American Entrepreneurs Association handbook, *T-Shirt Screen Printing* (1994). Most recently Linda Klopp has written *Computer T-Shirts: Make T-Shirts with Any Computer Printer* (1995). The general method of making the t-shirt and why many are made from cotton are the topics of two juvenile books by H. I. Peeples (1989) and Mary Schoeser (1994).

A second major group of publications simply exhibits the t-shirt as part of a selected group or as a result of a contest. The California t-shirt is shown in Bruce Levenstein's *A Few T-Shirts* (1976). The Last Gasp catalog provides a different view about ten years later, in 1985. *T-Shirt Graphics* (1992) "showcases 700 outstanding t-shirts . . . selected from more than 2000 submissions" from around the world, including "London, Los Angeles, New York and Tokyo." Another representation of international t-shirt design is *Graphis T-Shirt 1* (1994). *Print* magazine sponsored a commercial art t-shirt contest with many designs published in the 1995 *Print's Best T-Shirt Promotions 2*.

A smaller group of publications are concerned with the t-shirt and its history. John Neff wrote the brief *T-Shirt Essay* (1975) to accompany a Detroit Institute of Arts exhibit. Ken Kneitel, Bill Maloney, and Andrea Quinn wrote *The Great American T-Shirt* (1976). Also in 1976, Cal Kowal produced *Tee Shirts are Tacky,* a "limited edition commemorative book" of artistic photography. Victoria O'Donnell spoke about "How Films Function as Persuasion for the Mass Audience" (1983) including "spin-off" t-shirts sold later. Scott Fresener, not the only author to use the title *The T-Shirt Book* (1995), has contributed a historical account.

American Entrepreneurs Association. *T-Shirt Screen Printing.* 3d ed. Irvine, CA: Entrepreneur, 1994. 232 leaves.

Decorative T-Shirts and Sweats Made Easy. Lincolnwood, IL: Publications International, 1994. 96p.

Feinman, Jeffery, with Oscar Jordan. *The T-Shirt Book.* Garden City, NY: Doubleday, 1974. [n.p.]

Figliulo, Susan. *Decorate Your T-Shirts and Sweats.* Lincolnwood, IL: Publications International, 1991. 48p.

Fresener, Scott, with Pat Fresener. *How to Print T-Shirts—For Fun and Profit.* Ridgefield, NJ: Union Ink Co., 1991. 176p. (also 1994. 260p.)

Fresener, Scott, with Nancy Hall. *The T-Shirt Book.* Illustrated by Earl Smith. Salt Lake City, UT: Gibbs Smith Publisher, 1995. 96p.

Gibson, Ray. *Decorating T-Shirts.* London: Usborne and Tulsa, OK: EDC, 1995, 1994. 32p.

Graphis T-Shirt 1: An International Compilation of the Best in T-Shirt Design. Zurich, Switzerland: Graphis Press Corp., 1994. 216p.

Grattaroti, Rosalie. *Great T-Shirt Graphics.* Rockport, MA: Rockport Publishers, 1993. 157p.

Klopp, Linda, with Bernie Klopp. *Computer T-Shirts: Make T-Shirts with Any Computer Printer.* Baltimore, MD: Brainstorm Communications, 1995. 126p.

Kneitel, Ken, Bill Maloney, and Andrea Quinn. *The Great American T-Shirt.* New York: New American Library, 1976. 95p.

Kowal, Cal. *Tee Shirts Are Tacky.* N.p.: N.p., 1976. [46]p. "Limited edition commemorative book."

Last Gasp Tease Shirt Catalog. Text by Bill Maloney and Andrea Quinn. San Francisco: Last Gasp, 1985. 13p.

Levenstein, Bruce. *A Few T-Shirts.* Studio-City, CA: Levenstein, 1976. [22]p.

Martin, Diana, with Ed White. *How to Airbrush T-Shirts and Other Clothing.* Cincinnati, OH: North Light Books, 1994. 120p.

Neff, John H. *T-Shirt Essay.* Detroit: Detroit Institute of Arts, 1975. 71. Exhibition essay and glossary.

O'Donnell, Victoria. "How Films Function as Persuasion for the Mass Audience." 1983. 20p. Paper presented at the Annual Meeting of the International Communication Association, Dallas, TX, May 26–30, 1983. ED232227.

Parsons School of Design. *The Parsons Iron-on-Book.* New York: Pantheon Books, 1977. [n.p.]

Peeples, H. I. *T-Shirt.* Chicago: Contemporary Books, 1989. 23p.

Print's Best T-Shirt Promotions 2: Winning Designs from Print Magazine's National Competition. New York: RC Publications, 1995. 151p.

Rhodes, Vicki. *Painted of Course! Perfect Patchwork.* Provo, UT: Provo Craft, 1994. 30p.

Schoeser, Mary. *Why T-Shirts Are Cotton.* Harlow: Longman, 1994. 24p.

Sibbett, Ed. *Iron-On T-Shirt Transfers for Hand Coloring.* New York: Dover, 1976. [50]p.

Steele, H. Thomas. *The Hawaiian Shirt: Its Art and History.* New York: Abbeville Press, 1984. 96p.

Stieglitz, Cliff. Sara Day Graphic Design. *T-Shirt Airbrushing: The Step-by-Step Guide and Showcase.* Rockport, MA: Rockport Publishers, 1994. 144p.

Torbet, Laura. *The T-Shirt Book.* Indianapolis: Bobbs-Merrill, 1976. 127p.

T-Shirt Graphics. Tokyo, Japan: P-I-E Books, 1992. 221p.

T-Shirts in Education

In addition to the books that are about the t-shirt itself, a rather substantial volume of works in the field of education illustrates how the shirt's popularity is used to capture students' attention or to reward them. It may be used to promote reading and writing activities (Mary McCool, *Reap Around the State*, R. G. Schwab et al.), or it can be used to help promote learning in general (Aline Riquier). It has been found helpful in promoting better attendance and recruiting dropouts (Sigmund Boloz and Dorothea Lincoln, Beverly Gifford, Betty Nyangoni, Walter Oden) and self-esteem (*Elementary Youth, I Gotta be Me*). The t-shirt has been used to promote community/school interests (Judson Morris) as well as pride and as a way to stop vandalism (Glenn Borland).

Causes such as women's liberation (*High School Women's Liberation*), the environment (*Connections*), and fitness (Peter Saccone) all have benefited by using t-shirts as an advertisement or a unifying gift. Colleges have used them as recruitment incentives or souvenirs (Bob Flores and Bill Kellogg).

Very often decorating the t-shirt is part of the school activity. Even the computer has entered the mix, with the Hutinger et al. report on making a t-shirt on a computer (1992) as an activity for disabled students. T-shirt messages can be used in language study, according to C. Schon and J. Ferrell's "T-shirt Communication" (1983). The message and its "comment provoking potential" are researched by Christopher Spicer (1981). Even the federal government, *DOD Service Academies,* has shown concern for possible "harassing" or "offensive" messages on t-shirts worn by men at military academies.

The following references are from the ERIC (Educational Resources Information Service) database and are designated by ERIC document or ED numbers. Libraries that purchase this microfiche collection of education documents or reports house them by the ED numbers. Most ERIC documents are not commercially published. The ED number is essential in locating the full-text document easily.

Boloz, Sigmund A., and Dorothea C. Lincoln. *Combating Student Absenteeism: Strategies for Raising Attendance and Achievement.* 1982. 10p. ED224664. ("Ganado Attendance Star" t-shirt)

Borland, Glenn F. *LaFollette High School Student Vandalism Committee.* [1978]. 25p. ED181017. (t-shirts as promotions to build school support)

Connections: Life Cycle Kinesthetic Learning. 1993. 122p. ED372953. ("A T-Shirt Talks" activity to promote environmental concerns)

Department of Defense. *DOD Service Academies. More Actions Needed to Eliminate Sexual Harassment.* Report to Congressional Requesters. 1994. 66p. ED366803. (concern for t-shirt messages that might offend)

Elementary Youth. Alcohol, Tobacco, and Other Drugs Resource Guide. 1993. 29p. ED376425. (t-shirts to gain attention of troubled youth)

Flores, Bob, and Bill Kellogg. *26-Hours at Cal Poly* 1989. 7p. ED314633. (recruitment gift of stenciled t-shirts)

Gifford, Beverly. *Back on the Track: A Campaign to Recruit Dropouts Back into the Columbus Public Schools.* 1987. 11p. ED285247. (t-shirts as promotional device)

High School Women's Liberation. 1976. 85p. ED129648. (t-shirts used to promote cause)

Hutinger, Patricia, et al. *The Best of ACTTion News 1989–1992.* 1992. 66p. ED376940. (making t-shirts on computer as activity for the disabled)

I Gotta Be Me . . . You Gotta Be You: A Moderately Challenging Awareness Unit. 1977. 19p. ED151454. ("Me and My T-Shirt" activity to improve self-esteem)

McCool, Mary. *Reading with a Special Touch.* 1982. 11p. ED220798. (writing messages on t-shirts activity)

Morris, Judson H. Jr. *Run for the Gold: Small Town Fun(ding) Runs.* 1988. 31p. ED309904. (t-shirt's importance to fund raising)

Nyangoni, Betty. *The Media Is the Message: Using the Media to Improve School Attendance.* 1978. 11p. ED183683.

Oden, Walter E. *A Plan for Improving Student Attendance at Brownsville Junior High School.* 1978. 21p. ED155807.

Reap Around the State: "Best of Reap" Activities. 1991. 30p. ED348651. (t-shirt design contest to encourage reading)

Riquier, Aline. *The Cotton in Your T-Shirt.* 1993. 41p. ED362436. (learning about cotton production)

Saccone, Peter R. *It's "Funner" to Be a Runner Physical Education/Classroom Program.* 1984. 31p. ED242660. ("It's Funner to Be a Runner" t-shirt design to promote fitness)

Schon, C., and J. Ferrell. "T-Shirt Communication." In *Teaching Language Creatively.* 1983. 157p. ED276026.

Schwab, R. G. Jerry, et al. *Implementing Innovative Elementary Literacy Programs. Program Report.* 1992. 84p. ED350696.

Spicer, Christopher H. *Comment-Provoking Potential of T-Shirts: A Nonverbal Dimension of Communication Apprehension.* 1981. 28p. ED199778.

Wedding Dress

Although the dress itself is not one of the top ten clothing-specific items, there are still types of dresses that have been part of our general experience: the "day" dress (Karen Basralian, Heidi Montroll, Diane Vachon) and the evening dress or gown (Marco Tosa, Esther Nystrom) are examples. Even doll dresses (LeeWards Creative Crafts Center) are of interest to collectors. However, it is the wedding dress that seems to illustrate the strong link with generally observed ceremony. Works that focus on this type of dress in the U.S. experience are featured, although many works concern British, European, or other geographic areas and cultures. The literature located concerns historical analysis and customs associated with the wedding dress, illustrations of the fashions, and a few sources on the making of the dress.

Betty Mills in 1969 researched the dress for the period 1865 to 1965 covering the social, historical, and cultural influences. The "white wedding" was Ann Monsarrat's topic in 1973. Her work concentrates on manners and customs historically; she uses quotations from primary sources to amplify her discussion. Although the United States is not the major focus, the material is valuable. Her bibliography includes ten periodicals. Monsarrat indicates that the white wedding began in the mid-nineteenth century. Mary Eagon researched a lace wedding dress of 1910 for her 1984 thesis. Christina Probert's *Brides in Vogue since 1910* (1984) and Catherine Zimmerman's *The Bride's Book* (1985) are pictorial histories. Zimmerman's work covers early America, the nineteenth century, and the twentieth century. Illustrations are documented, and there is a bibliography. "The Pioneer Bride," "Wedding Fashions in Paintings and Illustrations," "Underclothing," and "The Military Bride" are some of the sections included. Donna Felger's *Bridal Fashions: Victorian Era* (1986) shows adult costumes but was produced for the doll collector. In 1990 Melissa Harmel researched fashion cycles for the period 1969–1988.

Books that focus on the dress as an attractive fashion or that glorify the art, design, and construction of the dress and its workmanship have appeared as well. Examples include Pauline Stevenson's *Bridal Fashions* (1978), the Better Homes and Gardens *Brides Book,* published annually from 1980 to 1987; Jules Schwerin's *Wedding Styles: The Ultimate Bride's Companion* (1985); Catherine Woram's *Wedding Dress Style* (1993); Larry Goldman's *Dressing the Bride* (1993); and Jo Packham's *Wedding Gowns and Other Bridal Apparel: Looking Beautiful on Your Special Day* (1994). Random House refers to its *The Wedding Dress* (1993) by Maria McBride-Mellinger as "the ultimate source book, . . . perfect for dreaming, planning, designing, and celebrating the dress of a lifetime."[10] The hand sewing of the wedding dress as a cultural practice is reflected not only in the patterns available for purchase but also in books, such as Nicholas Bullen's *Making Classic Wedding Dresses* (1981), Ann Ladbury's *The Bride's Sewing Book* (1985), and *Sewing for Special Occasions: Bridal, Prom and Evening Dresses* (1994).

Because of special interests in the wedding ceremony and the wedding dress, museums often collect these dresses, exhibiting them periodically. Some museums have produced catalogs as permanent records. Wedding photographs have been featured by Barbara Norfleet's *Wedding* exhibit at the Carpenter Center for the Visual Arts, Harvard University, 1975, and Vincent Cianni's *Wedding Photographs* at the Dutchess County Arts Association, Poughkeepsie, New York, in 1987. Other exhibits contain materials that may include costumes, while others are specifically costume exhibitions. Exhibitions documented include those held at the Hallmark Gallery, New York, in 1900; Yeshiva University Museum, 1977; the Balch Institute, Philadelphia, 1987; the Goldstein Gallery at the University of Minnesota, 1990; and the Museums at Stony Brook, New York, in 1991.

Balch Institute for Ethnic Studies. *Something Old, Something New: Ethnic Weddings in America: A Traveling Exhibition.* Philadelphia, PA: The Institute, 1987. 35p.

Basralian, Karen M. "American Women's Day Dress, 1890 through 1900, as Reflected in the American Fashion Magazines." Master's thesis, University of Maryland, 1969.

Bullen, Nicholas. *Making Classic Wedding Dresses.* London: Bell & Hyman, 1981. 80p.

Cianni, Vincent. *Wedding Photographs.* Poughkeepsie, NY: Dutchess County Arts Association, 1987. 8p.

Eagon, Mary Ann. "A Lace Wedding Dress 1910." Master's thesis, University of Wisconsin, 1984.

Felger, Donna H. *Bridal Fashions: Victorian Era.* Cumberland, MD: Hobby House Press, 1986. 166p.

Goldman, Larry. *Dressing the Bride.* New York: Crown, 1993. 208p.

Goldstein Gallery, University of Minnesota. *Here Comes the Bride, Then and Now: An Exhibition of Wedding Gowns from 1880 to 1990: April 1–June 10, 1990.* By M. A. Madson. St. Paul, MN: The Gallery, 1990. 18p.

Hallmark Gallery. *The Art of the Wedding.* New York: The Gallery, 1900. 16p.

Harmel, Melissa. "The Fashion Cycles of Bridal Gown Styles from 1969–1988: Predicting Future Trends." Master's thesis, Texas Tech University, 1990.

Ladbury, Ann. *The Bride's Sewing Book.* London: Stanley Paul, 1985. 126p.

LeeWards Creative Crafts Center. *Patterns: Art no. 33-13160, Set of 6 Patterns for a 16" Doll: Sunday Dress, Play Dress and Pinafore, Party Dress, Undergarments and Body.* Elgin, IL: The Center, 1977. Envelope format.

McBride-Mellinger, Maria. *The Wedding Dress.* New York: Random House, 1993. 160p.

Mills, Betty J. "Reflection of Social, Historical, and Cultural Influences on the Modes of Wedding Dress and Customs for 100 Years in America, 1865–1965." Master's thesis, Texas Technological College, 1969.

Monsarrat, Ann. *And the Bride Wore . . . The Story of the White Wedding.* New York: Dodd, Mead, 1973. 252p.

Montroll, Heidi S. "Women's Everyday Dress in the United States during World War I: An Analysis of Style Change." Master's thesis, George Washington University, 1974.

Museums at Stony Brook. *To Love and to Cherish: The Great American Wedding.* "Interpretive essay on the occasion of an exhibition . . . April 21–July 21, 1991 at the Margaret Melville Blackwell History Museum." By Amy McKune. New York: Museums at Stony Brook, 1991. 21p.

Norfleet, Barbara P. *Wedding: March 22 to May 2, 1976, The Carpenter Center for the Visual Arts, Harvard University.* Cambridge, MA: The Center, 1975. [64]p.

Nystrom, Esther. *Evening Elegance. Bulletin 351.* Moscow, ID: University of Idaho, College of Agriculture, 1961. 10p.

Packham, Jo. *Wedding Gowns and Other Bridal Apparel: Looking Beautiful on Your Special Day.* New York: Sterling Pub., 1994. 96p.

Probert, Christina. *Brides in Vogue since 1910.* London: Thames and Hudson, 1984. 84p.

Schwerin, Jules V. *Wedding Styles: The Ultimate Bride's Companion.* New York: W. Morrow, 1985. 160p.

Sewing for Special Occasions: Bridal, Prom and Evening Dresses. Minnetonka, MN: Cy DeCrosse, 1994. 128p.

Stevenson, Pauline. *Bridal Fashions.* London: I. Alan, 1978. 128p.

Tosa, Marco. *Evening Dresses, 1900–1940.* Modena, Italy: ZanfiEditori, 1988. 127p.

Vachon, Diane L. "Documentation Guidelines for Women's Day Dress, 1850–1949." Thesis, University of Kentucky, 1976.

Woram, Catherine. *Wedding Dress Style: The Indispensable Style-File for Brides-to-Be and Designers.* London: Apple, 1993. 128p.

Yeshiva University Museum. *The Jewish Wedding.* Shlomo Pappenheim. Exhibition opening October 30, 1977. New York: The Museum, 1977. 88p.

Zimmerman, Catherine S. *The Bride's Book: Pictorial History of American Bridal Dress.* New York: Arbor House, 1985. 289p.

ACCESSORIES

Jewelry

Because the literature of jewelry is so vast, consisting of a wide variety of types of publications—general histories, business materials on companies and jewelers, sale catalogs, how to make jewelry; jewelry lore, collector guides—a small selection of titles will be mentioned here to illustrate jewelry's presence in the popular culture. Marcus Baerwald and Tom Mahoney's *Story of Jewelry* (1960), was written to enhance appreciation for its tradition and history. The contents is by type of gemstone and for specific popular topics, such as birthstones, bridal and other rings, and jewelry for men. Popular aspects include the birthstone as a good-luck charm; various types of rings: wedding, signet, token, religious, fraternal, and for special occasions; watches; and the use of sport motifs in jewelry, belt buckles, key chains, and other objects for men or any sports enthusiast.[11] Joan Dickinson's *Book of Pearls* (1968) includes the story of pearls and the popularity of the string of pearls, often seen in celebrity photographs but affordable for all. A glossary and chapter bibliographies are included. *American and European Jewelry, 1830–1914* (1975), by Charlotte Gere, contains an excellent bibliography, as well as a review of nineteenth-century international design exhibitions where new jewelry designs were presented to promote trade. She indicates that large-scale American jewelry manufacture did not begin until the early 1840s and that the Philadelphia Centennial Exhibition of 1876 signaled interest in establishing an "American personality" in jewelry style.

Some publications focus on individual designers or companies, such as Laurence Krashes' *Harry Winston: The Ultimate Jeweler* (1993) and Janet Zapata's *The Jewelry and Enamels of Louis Comfort Tiffany* (1993). The former includes biographical and business information, as well as descriptions and stories about specific diamonds owned at one time by Winston; the latter concentrates on Tiffany's jewelry designs and artistic career. *Tiffany,*

150 Years of Gems and Jewelry (1987), written by Peter Schneirla and Penny Proddow, serves as a collectors' item itself; it was published on the 150th anniversary of the 1837 founding of Tiffany & Co. *Magical Art* in (1986) features the designs of Heyoehkah Merrifield, who is part Cherokee; his work symbolizes his philosophy of life and is prized by collectors. Other books are written for the collector and usually include price guides. From this category are books by Lillian Baker, Joanne Ball, Roseann Ettinger, J. L. Lynlee, and Lynn Sallee, who cover costume jewelry, while Dorothy Rainwater's *American Jewelry Manufacturers,* (1988) is a reference work providing manufacturers' marks, trade names, a glossary, and other information for identification for jewelry made from 1840 to the late 1980s.

The work of Penny Proddow and Debra Healy truly synthesizes the American popular culture aspects of jewelry. Together they wrote *American Jewelry Glamour and Tradition* (1987). In Ralph Esmerian's introduction, the impact of a jewelry gift as a symbol of a relationship and jewelry as a symbol of wealth or power is mentioned, in addition to its reflection of the designer's feelings. Here again the importance of international design expositions and world fairs is discussed. The authors mention Tiffany & Company's award at the 1889 Paris Exposition; the company borrowed Native American materials, design forms, images, and colors to create its collection of jewelry. The use of colorful semiprecious stones in jewelry with nature themes, jewelry with sport themes, Hollywood's use of expensive jewels, and the development of seasonal collections by manufacturers and designers are several other popular aspects of jewelry discussed by the authors. Proddow, Healy, and Fasel, in *Hollywood Jewels: Movies, Jewelry, Stars* (1992), illuminate the fascinating relationship between American movies and jewelry from the silent films in 1912 to the movies of Elizabeth Taylor. Here one can see the use of jewelry in costuming, as promotion for jewelry designers and manufacturers, as part of the advertised image of a star, and as the subject of movie conversation and themes. Some of the popular jewelry items and practices mentioned include the vanity case, giving charms and the charm bracelet, the "dancing flowers" from *Fantasia,* patriotic items such as American flags, pins, and other insignia, turquoise jewelry reflecting interests in semiprecious stones in the late 1950s and early 1960s, and the Tiffany "blue book" catalog. A bibliography, index, and illustration credits conclude the volume.

The mail order catalog can serve to document popular jewelry as well. In the Tiffany "blue book," expensive watches are illustrated in elegant simplicity ("Tiffany Classics Watch Collection," *Tiffany & Co. Winter Selections 1995* catalog). Also, the TAG Heuer watch collection is featured in a collectible booklet printed in Switzerland and entitled, *"A Sports Watch Is Not a Piece of Jewelry."* Here are described and pictured the "advanced timepieces . . . designed to time competitive sports rather than the silences at dinner parties." Many other general sales catalogs feature quite the opposite in watches. For example, the general *Seasons Halloween 1995* gift catalog offers no fewer than seven rather wild watches: the "Color Chip Watch," with a red band and color chips in place of numerals on the face; the "Anodized Swirls Watch," with wristband of twisted aluminum in a rainbow of colors; the "Glass Bean Bangle Watch," with hand-blown glass beads for the band; the "Hearts Toggle Watch," with sterling hearts and venetian beads; the "Many Faces Watch," with "millefiori clay beads" with painted faces as the band; the "New Moon Watch," strung with sterling charms; and the "Pencil Watch," with "#2 yellow pencil hands."

Exhibition catalogs during the past ten years have appeared on jewelry, such as the American Craft Museum's *American Jewelry Now* (1985); *Inspired by Tradition* (1987), an exhibition of the collection of Claire V. Bersani; *Gioie de Hollywood: American Designers of Fashion Jewelry, 1920–1960,* a 1987 exhibit in Venice; *Ascots to Zoot Suits* (1989), on wearable art; and *Brilliant Stories: American Narrative Jewelry* (1994). Other catalogs focus on individual designers, such as Tom Manhart's *William Harper: Artist as Alchemist* (1989); Harper's *William Harper: Jasper's Variations and Faberge's Seeds* (1994); William Spratling's silver jewelry by Sandy Cederwall and Hal Riney (1991); and *Albert Paley: Sculptoral Adornment* (1991), by Deborah Norton. The Artwear gallery in New York began an exhibition catalog series in 1992 featuring the works of contemporary designers. *Origins,* a gallery exhibit of works by Artwear founder Robert L. Morris, contained pieces showing influences from science fiction and anthropology such as "brass virtual-reality goggles" and "fanciful visors."[12] His gallery catalogs and exhibits in 1992 commemorated the fifteenth birthday of Artwear. These and other gallery catalogs also serve as part of the record of American art jewelry. Several theses appear on popular jewelry themes—for example, Shelly Foote's "Egypt in America: The Popularization of Egypt and Its Influence on American Jewelry 1869 to 1925" (1985) and Susan Hosking's thesis (1988) on hair jewelry in the United States.

American Craft Museum, New York. *American Jewelry Now.* New York: The Museum, 1985. 72p. [traveling exhibit]

Ascots to Zoot Suits: The Child's ABC's of Art to Wear. A National Invitational Exhibition of Contemporary Artwear by 25 Artists from Alaska to New England and Several Points Between, June 18, 1989 to May 20, 1990. By David Edlefsen. Anchorage: Anchorage Museum of History and Art, 1989.

Baerwald, Marcus, and Tom Mahoney. *The Story of Jewelry: A Popular Account of the Lure, Lore, Science, and Value of Gems and Noble Metals in the Modern World.* London: Abelard-Schuman, 1960. 221p.

Baker, Lillian. *Fifty Years of Collectible Fashion Jewelry, 1925–1975.* Paducah, KY: Collector Books, 1986, 1989. 191p.

———. *100 Years of Collectible Jewelry, 1850–1950.* Paducah, KY: Collector Books, 1978, 1995. 169p.

Ball, Joanne D. *Costume Jewelers: The Golden Age of Design.* West Chester, PA: Schiffer, 1990. 208p.

Blauer, Ettagale. *Contemporary American Jewelry Design*. New York: Van Nostrand Reinhold, 1991. 198p.

Bodine, Sarah. *Modern American Jewelry: 1940–1970*. New York: Rizzoli, 1990. [n.p.]

Brilliant Stories: American Narrative Jewelry. By Lloyd E. Herman. Washington, D.C.: International Sculpture Center, 1994. 30p. Catalog of a traveling exhibition first held at the Charles and Emma Frye Museum of Art, Seattle, WA.

Cederwall, Sandraline, and Hal Riney. *Spratling Silver*. San Francisco: Chronicle Books, 1991. 128p.

Dickinson, Joan Y. *The Book of Pearls: Their History and Romance from Antiquity to Modern Times*. New York: Crown, 1968. 248p.

Ettinger, Roseann. *Forties and Fifties Popular Jewelry: With Price Guide*. Atglen, PA: Schiffer, 1994. 159p.

———. *Popular Jewelry, 1840–1940*. West Chester, PA: Schiffer, 1990. 193p.

Foote, Shelly J. "Egypt in America: The Popularization of Ancient Egypt and Its Influence on American Jewelry, 1869 to 1925." Master's thesis, George Washington University, 1985.

Gere, Charlotte. *American and European Jewelry, 1830–1914*. New York: Crown, 1975. 240p.

Gioie de Hollywood: American Designers of Fashion Jewelry, 1920–1960. By Piero Mainardis de Campo. Venezia: Venice Design Art Gallery, 1987. 79p.

Harper, William. *William Harper: Jasper's Variations and Faberge's Seeds*. Essay by Arthur C. Danto. New York: Peter Joseph Gallery, 1994. [34]p.

Hosking, Susan L. "I Have a Piece of Thee Here: A Material Cultural Study of the Wearing and Production of Hair Jewelry in the United States during the Late Eighteenth and Nineteenth Centuries." Master's thesis, University of South Carolina, 1988.

Inspired by Traditions: Gems and Jewelry from a Private Collection, Created by Claire V. Bersani. Exhibition presented at the Walters Art Gallery, 1987. Baltimore, MD: Trustees of the Walters Art Gallery, 1987. 47p.

Krashes, Laurence S. *Harry Winston: The Ultimate Jeweler*. 4th ed. rev. New York: H. Winston and Gemological Institute of America, 1993. 236p.

Lynnlee, J. L. *All That Glitters*. West Chester, PA: Schiffer, 1986. 128p.

Manhart, Tom. *William Harper: Artist as Alchemist*. Orlando, FL: Orlando Museum of Art, 1989. 117p.

Merrifield, Heyoehkah. *Magical Art*. Inchelium, WA: Rain Bird Publishers, 1986. 60p.

Morris, Robert L. *Origins*. Exhibition catalog 1. Artwear (New York) Exhibition, April 1992.

Norton, Deborah L., and Matthew Drutt. *Albert Paley: Sculptural Adornment*. Washington, D.C.: Renwick Gallery of the National Museum of American Art, Smithsonian Institution, in association with the University of Washington Press, 1991. 79p.

Proddow, Penny, and Debra Healy. *American Jewelry Glamour and Tradition*. New York: Rizzoli, 1987. 208p.

Proddow, Penny, Debra Healy, and Marion Fasel. *Hollywood Jewels: Movies, Jewelry, Stars*. Photography by David Behl. New York: H. N. Abrams, 1992. 200p.

Rainwater, Dorothy T. *American Jewelry Manufacturers*. West Chester, PA: Schiffer, 1988. 296p.

Sallee, Lynn. *Old Costume Jewelry, 1870–1945*. Florence, AL: Books Americana, 1979. 130p.

Schneirla, Peter, and Penny Proddow. *Tiffany, 150 Years of Gems and Jewelry*. New York: Tiffany, 1987. 10p. [27]p. plates.

TAG Heuer. *"A Sports Watch Is Not a Piece of Jewelry."* N.p.: TAG Heuer, 1994(?). 20p.

Zapata, Janet. *The Jewelry and Enamels of Louis Comfort Tiffany*. New York: H. N. Abrams, 1993. 176p.

Shoes, Boots, and Footwear

Shoes, boots, and footwear histories have been published throughout this century. Manufacturing histories extend through the 1980s and include the histories of several shoe manufacturers. The books mentioned here concentrate on design and style history and include specific sources on the cowboy boot as an example of popular culture footwear. Edwin Clapp & Sons contributed an early history in 1923, *Three Score Years and Ten: A Romance in the History of Footwear*. Wohl Shoe Co. produced a small booklet, *Pageant of Progress in Shoe Styling, 1916–1941* (1941). Ruth Wilcox's *Mode in Footwear* (1948) features black and white drawings and covers the subject from ancient Egypt to the twentieth century. The last plate is entitled "Twentieth Century—Ageless Footwear." A "Glossary of Shoe Leathers" appears in the book. Harold Quimby's *Story of Footwear* (1949) contains a bibliography. A 1954 thesis by John Hall focused on the craft of the Yankee shoeman; shoe fashions were the subject for Eunice Wilson (1968). The *Book Review Digest*, 1971, indicates that although Wilson's volume covers the Western history of the shoe, it does not mention Mary Janes or Buster Browns. Women's shoes from the colonial period to 1930 were studied by Jo Ann Tammen (1973). A more popular and visual account is Christina Probert's *Shoes in Vogue since 1910* (1981); colorful advertisements and fashion photographs tell the story. June Swann's *Shoes* (1982), part of the Batsford Costume Accessories series, covers the period 1600 to the 1960s with a British focus.

The popular *Shoes Never Lie* appeared in 1985, written by Mimi Pond. L.L. Bean, Inc. published *"Old Friends," Our Customers' Favorites for over 50 Years* (1987); featured first is the "Bean's Maine Hunting Shoe Introduced in Our Original Fall 1912 Circular." Other footwear noted in the pamphlet are the woman's Maine hunting shoe and various moccasins. Interest in athletic performance is reflected in B. Segesser and W. Pforringer's *The Shoe in Sport* (1989). Although technical in nature it includes photographs and drawings of running, tennis, court, and soccer shoes, as well as ski, skating, hockey, and cross-country boots and children's athletic shoes. Pegged footwear during gold rush days was discussed by Julia Huddleson and Mitsun Watanabe in 1990. More recent histories have been published by the Essex Institute, *Step Forward, Step Back: Three Centuries of American Footwear Fashion* (1991) and by Bata Ltd., *All About Shoes: Footwear Through the Ages* (1994). Both of these institutions have strong shoe connections: the Peabody Essex Museum, Salem, Massachusetts, and the Bata Shoe Museum Foundation, Don Mills, Ontario, Canada.

All About Shoes: Footwear through the Ages. Toronto: Bata Limited, 1994. [n.p.]

Brooke, Iris. *Footwear: A Short History of European and American Shoes.* New York: Theatre Arts Books, 1971, 1972. 131p.

Edwin Clapp & Son. *Three Score Years and Ten: A Romance in the History of Footwear.* East Weymouth, MA, 1923. 63p.

Hall, John P. "The Gentle Craft: A Narrative of Yankee Shoemakers." Ph.D. diss., Columbia University, 1954.

Huddleson, Julia E., and Mitsuru S. Watanabe. "Pegged Footwear from 1851 San Francisco." In *The Hoff Store Site and Gold Rush Merchandise from San Francisco, California,* 94–100. Edited by Allen G. Pastron and Eugene M. Hattori. Pleasant Hill, CA: Society for Historical Archaeology, 1990. 115p.

Old Friends, Our Customers' Favorites for over 50 Years. Freeport, ME: L. L. Bean, 1987. 12p.

Pond, Mimi. *Shoes Never Lie.* New York: Berkley Books, 1985. 127p.

Probert, Christina. *Shoes in Vogue since 1910.* New York: Abbeville Press, 1981. 96p.

Quimby, Harold R. *The Story of Footwear.* New York: National Shoe Manufacturers Association, 1949. 40p.

Segesser, B., and W. Pforringer, eds., in collaboration with E. Stussi and A. Stacoff. *The Shoe in Sport.* Translated by Thomas J. DeKornfeld. Chicago: Year Book Medical Publishers/London: Wolfe, 1989. 271p.

Step Forward, Step Back: Three Centuries of American Footwear Fashion. Salem, MA: Essex Institute, 1991. 184p.

Swann, June. *Shoes.* Costume Accessories Series. London: Batsford, 1982. 96p.

Tammen, Jo Ann. "An Historical Tracing of American Women's Shoes from Colonial Days with Identification Criteria for the Years 1890 to 1930." Master's thesis, Oklahoma State University, 1973.

Wilcox, Ruth T. *The Mode in Footwear.* New York: C. Scribner's Sons, 1948. 190p.

Wilson, Eunice. *A History of Shoe Fashions: A Study of Shoe Design in Relation to Costume for Shoe Designers, Pattern Cutters, Manufacturers, Fashion Students and Dress Designers.* Shoe drawings by Gay Lloyd. New York: Theatre Arts Books, 1970, 1968. 334p.

Wohl Shoe Company. *Pageant of Progress in Shoe Styling, Nineteen Hundred and Sixteen [to] Nineteen Hundred Forty-One.* St. Louis, 1941. [20]p.

Cowboy Boots

One of the more popular footwear styles is the cowboy boot. It is represented in company sales catalogs from Colorado, Kansas, and Texas from the early 1900s to the 1940s (see Denver Dry Goods, C. H. Hyer & Sons, H. J. Justin & Sons, Tony Lama, and White & Davis as examples). Several volumes have been published on this type of boot. D. W. Fromer's *Western Boot Making: An American Tradition* (1988) is a reprint of articles from the periodical *Shoe Service*. Sharon DeLano and David Rieff's *Texas Boots* (1981) contains color photographs of boot styles, sections on bootmakers and their works, a listing of where to buy boots, and a glossary. Tyler Beard's *The Cowboy Boot Book* (1992) includes some color illustrations. An exhibition catalog, *Cowboy Boots: The Kansas Story*, written by Barbara Brackman was produced by the Kansas State Historical Society in 1994 and includes several essays on the subject.

Beard, Tyler. *The Cowboy Boot Book*. Salt Lake City: Peregrine Smith Books, 1992. 152p.

Brackman, Barbara. *Cowboy Boots: The Kansas Story*. Topeka: Kansas State Historical Society, 1994. 43p. Developed in conjunction with the traveling exhibit.

DeLano, Sharon, and David Rieff. *Texas Boots*. Photographs by Star Black. New York: Viking, 1981. 173p.

Denver Dry Goods Co. *The Stockman's Store for Stockman's Supplies*. Denver, 1931. 64p.

———. *Stockman's Store: Western Outfitters to the Nation*. Denver, 1947. 56p.

Frommer, D. W. *Western Bootmaking: An American Tradition*. Baltimore, MD: Shoe Service Magazine, 1988, 1989. Various pagings.

C. H. Hyer & Sons. *Olathe Cowboy Boots and Shoes: Handmade by C. H. Hyer & Sons, Olathe, Kansas*. Olathe, 1915. 44p.

Justin, H. J. *H. J. Justin & Sons: Manufacturers of Justin's Celebrated Cowboy Boots*. Nocona, TX: Justin Boots, 1923. 48p.

H. J. Justin & Sons. *Justin Cowboy Boots, 1940–41*. Fort Worth, TX, 1941. 32p.

Tony Lama (Firm). *Dealers Price List as of July 25th, 1939: De Luxe Line of Hand-Made Cowboy Boots & Shoes*. El Paso, TX, 1939. 12p.

———. *Tony Lama Catalogue no. 1*. El Paso, TX, ?1940, 1949. [n.p.]

White & Davis: The West's Own Store . . . since 1889. Pueblo, CO, 1937. 35p. "A Catalog of Western Supplies."

Hats and Millinery

Hats and hat making are represented by general histories, such as *The Mode in Hats and Headdresses* (1945) by Ruth Wilcox; Fiona Clark's *Hats* (1982); and the Philadelphia Museum of Art's *Ahead of Fashion: Hats of the 20th Century* (1993). More specific histories include Katherine Shawer's 1940 *Research Report on Eighteenth Century Milliners and Fashions;* Wendy Gamber's 1990 work on milliners, 1860–1930; Anna Binder's 1983 work on women's hats, 1750–1800; and Vonnie Alto's work on milliners, 1620–1920, written in 1992. Christina Probert's colorful *Hats in Vogue since 1910*, (1981) covers the fashionable hat for women by decade for the general audience. Several works focus on the art of hat making: Anna Ben-Yusuf's 1909 (reprinted 1992) work contains an extensive glossary of millinery and dry goods terms, and Denise Dreher's 1981 book provides a more contemporary source, also with a glossary and a bibliography. Even doll hat making, 1855–1916, has a separate volume, edited by Clare Blau (1979).

Popular customs and stories are provided in William Severn's *Here's Your Hat* (1963) for a young audience. The cowboy hat as an example of a specific type of hat is discussed by Martha Hartzog with "Manny" Gummage in "The Art of the Cowboy Hat" (1985). Five sources are listed in the bibliography. Contemporary clothing mail order catalogs often contain cowboy-type hats—for example, the "Saturday Night" classic "worn by working cowboys when they weren't working," offered by *The J. Peterman Co., Summer Sale 1995* catalog. The hat is described as "flattering" for both women and men in "Cheyenne or Manhattan." In the *Miller Stockman Western Wear Spring Catalog 1995,* a white cowboy-style "Wedding Hat" is shown of straw with lace hatband, bow, and a tulle veil. Although not associated as much with the United States as with Europe, the bowler has its own volume. Fred M. Robinson's *The Man in the Bowler Hat: His History and Iconography* (1993) includes its connections with art, literature, movies, theatre, advertisements, postcards, and cartoons.

Alto, Vonnie R. "The Business of Female Fripperies and the Fashionable Lady: Women's Millinery in America (1620–1920) and the Oregon Experience, a Proprietorship Study of Hats and Hatmaking." Master's thesis, University of Portland, 1992.

Ben-Yusuf, Anna. *Edwardian Hats: The Art of Millinery* (1909). Enlarged and edited by R. L. Shep. Mendocino, CA: R. L. Shep, 1992. 256p.

Binder, Anna L. "A Glossary and Catalog of Women's Hats, 1750–1800." Master's thesis, California State University, 1983.

Blau, Clare, ed. *Hat Making for Dolls, 1855–1916.* Reprinted from the Old Books and periodicals in Our Collection with additional patterns and instructions by Sandy Williams. Cumberland, MD: Hobby House Press, 1979. 31p.

Clark, Fiona. *Hats.* Costume Accessories Series. London: R. T. Batsford, 1982, 96p.

Dreher, Denise. *From the Neck Up: An Illustrated Guide to Hatmaking.* Minneapolis, MN: Madhatter Press, 1981. 199p.

Gamber, Wendy. "The Female Economy: The Millinery and Dressmaking Trades, 1860–1930." Ph.D. diss., Brandeis University, 1990.

Hartzog, Martha, with M. E. "Manny" Gummage. "The Art of the Cowboy Hat." In *Folk Art in Texas,* 94–103. By Francis E. Abernethy. Dallas: Southern Methodist University Press, 1985. 204p.

Philadelphia Museum of Art. *Ahead of Fashion: Hats of the 20th Century.* Edited by Dilys E. Blum. Philadelphia: The Museum, 1993. 48p.

Probert, Christina. *Hats in Vogue since 1910.* New York: Abbeville Press, 1981. 96p.

Robinson, Fred M. *The Man in the Bowler Hat: His History and Iconography.* Chapel Hill: University of North Carolina Press, 1993. 198p.

Severn, William. *Here's Your Hat.* Illustrated by Vana Earle. New York: D. McKay, 1963. 209p.

Shawer, Katherine. *Research Report on Eighteenth Century Milliners and Fashions.* Colonial Williamsburg Foundation Library, ? 1940, 1990. 601 leaves. RR-157.

Wilcox, Ruth T. *The Mode in Hats and Headdresses.* New York: C. Scribner's Sons, 1945. 332p. (also printed in 1948, 1952, 1959)

Eyeglasses

Eyeglasses have grown in popularity. Interests extend from the sight-saving issues and invention to the objects as collectibles. John H. Curtis wrote in 1844 about the choices of "spectacles" and "reading glasses." Their invention was also discussed by Edward Rosen in 1956. Justine Randers-Pehrson wrote *Notes . . . on the Early History of Spectacles* for an exhibit in 1956 at the Armed Forces Medical Library in Washington, D.C. The fashionable aspects of glasses were noticed by Richard Corson in his *Fashions in Eyeglasses* (1967), with a bibliography. The young reader is the audience for Alberta Kelley's 1978 work, including both a history of eyewear and discussion of the work of various eye care professionals.

Doris Hamblin's "What a Spectacle" (1983) is worth mentioning; she includes several popular "glasses" personalities: Steve Garroway's tortoise-shells in the 1950s, John Lennon's grannys, Elton John's "hard-sell specs," and Gloria Steinem's " 'aviator' lenses." The American Optometric Association produced a booklet, *Eyecare Then and Now,* in 1984. Shire Publications devotes one of its characteristic small volumes to the subject, authored by Derek Davidson in 1989. The collectible interests can be seen in L. D. Bronson's *Early American Specs* (1974), with a bibliography, and J. Rosenthal's *Spectacles and Other Vision Aids* (1995), with a bibliography and index. "FunSpecs™," an eyeglasses collectible, were advertised in the *Seasons to Celebrate and Remember: Gifts that Last for Times That Change, Halloween 1995* catalog. They are multicolored and come with a thirty-inch beaded eyeglass leash in coordinating colors. Whole mail order catalogs are devoted to glasses, such as the Winter 1995 *Sunglass Hut International Official Oakley Catalog,* featuring many "red iridium" and "blue iridium" lenses.

American Optometric Association, Communications Division. *Eyewear Then and Now: News Backgrounder.* St. Louis: The Association, 1984. 12p.

Bronson, L. D. *Early American Specs: An Exciting Collectible.* Glendale, CA: Occidental Pub. Co., 1974. 189p.

Corson, Richard. *Fashions in Eyeglasses.* London: Peter Owen, 1967. 288p.

Curtis, John H. *Curtis Observations on the Preservation of Sight: The Diseases of the Eye, and the Use, Abuse and Choice of Spectacles, Reading-Glasses, etc.* New York: Burgess and Stringer, 1844. 48p.

Davidson, Derek C. *Spectacles, Lorgnettes and Monocles.* Shire, 1989. [32]p.

Hamblin, Dora J. "What a Spectacle! Eyeglasses, and How They Evolved." *Smithsonian* 13 (March 1983): 100–102, 104, 106–108, 110–111.

Kelly, Alberta. *Lenses, Spectacles, Eyeglasses, and Contacts: The Story of Vision Aids.* New York: Elsevier/Nelson Books, 1978. 98p.

Randers-Pehrson, Justine D. *Notes to Accompany an Exhibit on the Early History of Spectacles, July–August 1956.* Washington D.C.: Armed Forces Medical Library, Reference Division, 1956. 10p.

Rosen, Edward. "The Invention of Eyeglasses." *Journal of the History of Medicine and Allied Sciences* 11 (1956): 183–218.

Rosenthal, J. William. *Spectacles and Other Vision Aids: A History and Guide to Collecting.* San Francisco: Norman Publ, 1995. [n.p.]

Sunglass Hut International. Official Oakley Catalog. Winter 1995/1996. Boulder, CO, 1995. 24p.

Hosiery

Hosiery, socks, stockings, and the others known as argyles, knee socks, bobby socks, tube socks, wool socks, and tights, have received some special attention in the literature. Milton E. Grass published his *History of Hosiery* in 1955, covering the subject from ancient Greece to "nylons in America." Johannis Dirk de Haan (1957) wrote on the history of the hosiery industry in the United States, with a bibliography. The subject also became part of the Batsford Costume Accessories Series in 1992 with work by Jeremy Farrell. Although a British focus, the work presents valuable information with many illustrations, 1600–1990, and with a glossary, a bibliography, and an index. Rosemary Hawthorne has also contributed with her *Stockings and Suspenders: A Quick Flash* (1993). To further document popular culture aspects of hosiery, one can consult the variety of mail order catalogs—for example, "foot warmers" with "embossed pattern of garden tools" are sold in one size for men and women in the *Gardeners Eden 1995 January* catalog. Mail order catalogs typically contain socks and stockings designed as Christmas stockings and produced for that purpose alone.

Farrell, Jeremy. *Socks and Stockings.* Costume Accessories Series. London: B. T. Batsford, 1992. 96p.

Grass, Milton E. *History of Hosiery from the Piloi of Ancient Greece to the Nylons of Modern America.* New York: Fairchild, 1955 [1956]. 283p.

Haan, Johannis Dirk de. *The Full-Fashioned Hosiery Industry in the U.S.A.* The Hague: Mouton, 1957. 188p.

Hawthorne, Rosemary. *Stockings and Suspenders: A Quick Flash.* London: Souvenir, 1993. 128p.

Buttons

Buttons as fastening devices are and have been used as a decoration and even as advertisements on clothing. Button collecting is reflected in the literature. *Button Barage* (1942) by Dorothy F. Brown focuses on the button itself; it includes a button glossary, a bibliography, and a classification of button types. She also illustrated the *Backs of Buttons* for collectors in 1946. *Buttons and Sundries,* part of the Twentieth Century History of Fashion series by ZanfiEditori in Italy, is written by Vittoria de Buzzaccarini. This 1990 volume contains a glossary, a polyglot dictionary, and a bibliography, which lists books, catalogs, and magazines. The high-quality production and text with many colored illustrations and photographs serves to present all the various ways buttons have contributed to fashion (or detracted from it, according to one's opinion); 237 button plates are described and documented throughout the volume. Even the buttonhole receives proper attention. Here we also see the use of company logos on jeans and jean jacket buttons, a decorative touch adding dimension to the cult of denim.

Brown, Dorothy F. *Button Barage: A Book of Button Groupings Drawn and Described by* . . . 2d ed. Chicago: Lightner Pub. Co., 1942. 111p.

————, and George E. Adams. *Backs of Buttons: Drawings by* . . . Glocester, RI: G. E. Adams, 1946. 42p.

Buzzaccarini, Vittoria de. *Buttons and Sundries.* Twentieth Century Histories of Fashion. Modena, Italy: ZanfiEditori, 1990. 143p.

Gloves

Glove monographic literature is sparse. S. William Beck provides the history and lore for pre–twentieth century gloves in his *Gloves, Their Annals and Associations* (1883) and an article in *Cosmopolitan* in 1892, "The Romance of Gloves." A few authors move the story into the twentieth century: C. Cody Collins with *Love of a Glove,* published in 1945 when gloves in the United States were a popular accessory; Eeba Adams and Edith Hummel, both with instructions on making gloves in 1946; and Valerie Cumming with *Gloves* (1982), as part of the Costume Accessories Series. Here the story is presented from 1600 to 1980, with a glossary and a bibliography.

Cumming states that today gloves are worn more for their protective qualities than as a statement of fashion. This can be seen in work settings where gloves may be required, such as in health care or construction; for leisure-time activities such as gardening; and for sports, such as riding, golf, football, baseball, hunting, other outdoor sports, winter sports, and race car driving. For example, the *Gardeners Eden 1995 January* catalog offers "French Garden Gloves" of washable cowhide in red, yellow, green, or blue. "The Evolution of Baseball Catchers' Equipment in the United States of America" was researched by Ralph Holding in his 1971 thesis. Even cyclists have special protective gloves, such as the "Blob City Cycling Glove for Women," sold through the *Title Nine Sports Spring 1995 Catalog;* these gloves contain a gel padding to reduce vibration.

Hand-made (and commercially knit) mittens and gloves represent a continually colorful scene where the wide variety of old and new knitting pattern books reflects styles. The hand-knit mitten has often been a staple of the New England church fair. Robin Hansen has helped to foster the custom of hand knitting traditional Maine mittens with her record of patterns and instructions together with photographs for *Fox and Geese and*

Fences (1983). Here she documents for the first time patterns for unique Maine double-knit, wrister, fleece-stuffed, and fisherman's wet mittens.

Adams, Eeba. *Gloves. Leather Glovemaking*. U.S. Department of Agriculture, Extension Service. Washington, D.C.: GPO, February 1946. 7p. A 43.2: G51.

Beck, S. William. *Gloves, Their Annals and Associations: A Chapter of Trade and Social History*. London: Hamilton, Adams, 1883. 263p.

———. "The Romance of Gloves." *Cosmopolitan* 13, no. 4 (August 1892): 450–457.

Collins, C. Cody. *Love of a Glove*. New York: Fairchild, 1945. 128p.

Cumming, Valerie. *Gloves*. Costume Accessories Series. London: Batsford, 1982. 96p.

Hansen, Robin. *Fox and Geese and Fences: A Collection of Traditional Maine Mittens*. Camden, ME: Down East Books, 1983. 69p.

Holding, Ralph O. "The Evolution of Baseball Catchers' Equipment in the United States of America." Master's thesis, San Jose State College, 1971.

Hummel, Edith M. *You Can Make Your Own Gloves*. New York: Fairchild, 1946. 63p.

CLOTHING AND ACCESSORIES IN PERFORMANCE

Dance

Although dancing is an activity that can be performed by ordinary people as well as professionals, there is very little monographic literature on the clothing worn for general participation by the public in dance. Costume design for formal dance performances or programs can be seen in works by Betty Joiner (1937), Treva Folkers for modern dance (1967), Phyllis Watson's *Designed for Applause* (1972), Lorna Brusstar for modern dance (1978), and Mary Clarke for ballet (1978). The costume and its relation to modern dance has been studied by Martin Prelle-Tworek (1983), while L. F. Hofsess included costume in his 1986 comparison of Kabuki with American jazz dance.

Many schools include some instruction in dance, exemplified by the 1978 *Teacher Training Program: Folk, Square, Social Dance,* with some discussion of costume. *Dance: A Very Social History,* covering Europe and the United States during the eighteenth, nineteenth, and twentieth centuries, was the subject of Diana Vreeland's fifteenth costume exhibition at the Metropolitan Museum of Art, New York, in 1986. Many colorful photographs and drawings highlight the exhibition catalog, which contains a chapter by Jean Druesedow entitled "The Fabric of Dance: Whalebone and Swirling Silk." Druesedow states that although "light and airy" fabrics in "pale pastels and white" were often used throughout the nineteenth century, it is the "black gown" that "has come to dominate the twentieth century and to represent a high degree of sophistication."[13] She focuses on the ball gown and elegant evening clothes of the wealthy, ending her review with the 1960s when "rock and roll entered the ballroom," bringing many changes in dress.

While the urban ball or party invited the wealthy to dance, the town hall, school gym, or barn often invited those interested in square or western dancing to assemble. In *Square Dances of Today* (1950), Richard Kraus pointed out that if dancers became overly concerned with "exhibition— concentrating on costumes" and perfecting intricate steps "they may lose the pleasure they once experienced in the dances." Indeed the drawings in this book show dancers in ordinary street clothing. In contrast, *Cowboy Dances* (1952) by Lloyd Shaw, although it does not discuss costume specifically, contains many photographs of dancers obviously dressed in specific costume for the occasion. In Jessie Flood and Cornelia Putney's *Square Dance U.S.A.* (1955) the full cultural impact of square dancing at that time is noted in the section on how to organize a square dance festival. "Classes, Clinics, Dances, Jamborees, Festivals, Dance Camps and callers, professional and amateur:—this is *Square Dancing U.S.A.*" Highlights of the festivals would be exhibitions by experienced dancers, undoubtedly in costume. In fact the general use of a costume for both men and women in western square dancing has been noted and studied by James LaVita. His 1987 paper describes the clothing and its relation to the dance, as well as his understanding of the sexual elements of the dress.

Brusstar, Lorna T. "Designing and Constructing Costumes for Modern Dance." Ph.D. diss., Texas Woman's University, 1978.

Clarke, Mary, with Clement Crisp. *Design for Ballet.* New York: Hawthorn Books, 1978. 288p.

Dance: A Very Social History. New York: Metropolitan Museum of Art: Rizzoli, 1986. 128p.

Dreusedow, Jean L. "The Fabric of Dance: Whalebone and Swirling Silk." In *Dance: A Very Social History,* 80–105. New York: Metropolitan Museum of Art: Rizzoli, 1986. 128p.

Flood, Jessie B., and Cornelia F. Putney. *Square Dance U.S.A.* Dubuque, IA: Wm. C. Brown Co., 1955. 110p.

Folkers, Treva A. "Mayfair for the Modern Dance (A Guide for Costume Design)." Master's thesis, University of Iowa, 1967.

Hofsess, L. F. "A Comparison of the Vernacular Dance of Two Countries: Japanese Kabuki and American Jazz." In *Mind and Body: East Meets West,* 113–119. Edited by S. Kleinman. Champaign, IL: Human Kinetics Publishers, 1986.

Joiner, Betty. *Costumes for the Dance.* New York: A. S. Barnes, 1937. 82p.

Kraus, Richard G. *Square Dances of Today and How to Teach and Call Them.* New York: A. S. Barnes, 1950. 130p.

LaVita, James. "The Study of Costumes in Square Dancing." In *A Spectrum of World Dance: Tradition, Transition, and Innovation. Selected Papers from the 1982 and 1983 CORD Conferences,* 99–109. Edited by Lynn A. Wallen and Joan Acocella. *Dance Research Annual* XVI. CORD, 1987. 159p.

Prelle-Tworek, Martin E. "Borders: A Choreographic Exploration of the Interrelationship of Costume and Movement." Master's thesis, University of Oregon, 1983.

Shaw, Lloyd. *Cowboy Dances: A Collection of Western Square Dances.* Rev. ed. Caldwell, ID: Caxton Printers, 1952. 417p.

Teacher Training Program: Folk, Square, Social Dance . . . Merritt College, Oakland, California. San Francisco(?): The Federation? 1978. 80p. Cosponsored by Folk Dance Federation of California.

Watson, Phyllis. *Designed for Applause.* Winter Park, FL: Performing Arts, 1972. 159p.

Film

Literature on costume in film productions concentrates on presenting the history as well as the designers, and their careers and creations. *Hollywood Costume Design* (1976) by David Chierichetti presents the history of the costume designers and departments at Hollywood movie studios from 1915 to the 1960s. Arrangement is by studio: MGM, Paramount, Warner Brothers, Fox, RKO and Columbia/Universal/and the Independents. "Designers Filmographies," arranged by designer name, offer information on studio name(s) and dates of films. The foreword is by Edith Head. In contrast to emphasis on the studio and its use of costume designers, *Costume Design in the Movies* (1976) by Elizabeth Lesse arranges information by designer's name and provides biographical information and historical background, followed by chronological lists of film credits. This major reference work features an index for over 6,000 film titles and appendixes for awards given by the Society of Film and Television in England, 1964–1975, and Oscar nominations (with winners noted), 1948–1975. Julie Harris writes in the foreword that costume designers were not formally recognized with their own Oscar nomination until 1948. A designer herself she points out that it is often very difficult to design for "films that require dressing down." Lesse discusses the difficulty in documenting costume design work and indicates that for the silent films "film magazines are the only reliable source."

Robert LaVine's *In a Glamorous Fashion: The Fabulous Years of Hollywood Costume Design* (1980) sets forth a history of the film industry, early twentieth century to the 1970s, and provides information on ten leading designers. The photographs, as in the other works, add interest and a better understanding of the impact of the clothes. Some of these images are classic not only because of the star but because of the combination of star and costume—for example: "Judy Garland in Summer Stock (MGM, 1950)" with a costume designed by Walter Plunkett who "dared to dress a star in such a starkly mannish outfit" (tailored jacket, mannish hat, dark stockings, and heels). Cecil Beaton states in the foreword, "Cinema will always be a dramatic force," with costuming contributing its strength to the total impact. LaVine includes a bibliography and lists the Academy Awards for costume, 1948–1979. Margaret Bailey's *Those Glorious Glamour*

Years (1982), concentrates on the 1930s, with arrangement by type of "glamorous" clothing—for example, "evening glamour," "daytime glamour," "glamour at home," "glamour at play," "epic glamour," and "wedding glamour." As Bailey points out, the movies of the 1930s were seen by many more women than those able to see fashion shows in Paris or New York or who were able to look at *Vogue*. The "glamorous" lifestyles and clothes appearing in the depression-years movies had the power of both attracting and distracting the population. The techniques used by Irene Sharaff to design four key productions were studied by Arlene Grauch for her 1988 Ph.D. dissertation. Sybil DelGaudio has also contributed to the Hollywood costume history scene with *Dressing the Part: Sternberg, Dietrich and Costume* (1993), with a bibliography.

Several exhibits have reflected continued interests in Hollywood costume: *Romantic and Glamorous Hollywood Design* mounted by the Costume Institute, Metropolitan Museum of Art, in 1974–1975; *Hollywood Film Costume* at the Whitworth Art Gallery in Manchester, England, in 1977; and *Hollywood and History: Costume Design in Film* at the Los Angeles County Museum of Art in 1987–1988.

Bailey, Margaret J. *Those Glorious Glamour Years*. Secaucus, NJ: Citadel Press, 1982. 384p.

Chierichetti, David. *Hollywood Costume Design*. New York: Harmony Books, 1976. 192p.

DelGaudio, Sybil. *Dressing the Part: Sternberg, Dietrich and Costume*. Rutherford, London, Cranbury, NJ: Fairleigh Dickinson University Press, Associated University Presses, 1993. 195p.

Grauch, Arlene E. "A Comparison of Four Stage and Motion Picture Productions Costumes Designed by Irene Sharaff." Ph.D. diss., University of Michigan, 1988.

Hollywood and History: Costume Design in Film. By Edward Maeder et al. Thames and Hudson: Los Angeles County Museum of Art, 1987. 256p.

Hollywood Film Costume. By Michael Regan. Manchester, England: University of Manchester, Whitworth Art Gallery 1977. 48p.

LaVine, W. Robert. *In a Glamorous Fashion: The Fabulous Years of Hollywood Costume Design*. Photo Consultant, Allen Florio. New York: Scribner, 1980. 259p.

Lesse, Elizabeth. *Costume Design in the Movies*. Isle of Wright: BCW Publishing Ltd., 1976. 168p.

Romantic and Glamorous Hollywood Design. Catalog of an exhibition at the Costume Institute, Metropolitan Museum of Art. By Diana Vreeland. New York: Metropolitan Museum of Art, 1974. 44p.

Sports and Nonmilitary Uniforms

Professional sports as a performance occupation displays many types of clothing, costumes, and uniforms; their planning, design, hand construction or manufacture, and ultimate impact on the audience, whether at the sporting event or in print or electronic media and advertising, are collectively part of our popular culture. Jewelry, such as the Superbowl ring, is a major symbol of success. *Sports Illustrated,* published since 1954, is an excellent primary source for color photographs of sports clothing and uniforms. Few books on sports uniforms were located. Some provide drawings or photographs of players in their gear, such as *Rules of the Game* (1974). Recently entire businesses have developed by marketing team jackets, t-shirts, or caps to the general public. The sales catalogs of these type of outfitters help to document the phenomenon.

As a major world celebration, the Olympics is full of fashion images. Clothing connected with the Olympics can be purchased by the public to raise money for the U.S. Olympic Committee, as is evidenced by *U.S. Olympic Spirit: Official Catalog of the U.S. Olympic Committee,* with a look to the 1996 games in Atlanta. Here are featured the "Atlanta Flame Cap," "Dream Team T-Shirt," the "Stars 'n' Stripes Tote Bag," and many other popular items, including the "Runner Pendant." Another example is the "Olympic Games Collection" of key fobs for the 1996 Atlanta and 1886 Athens games offered by the *American Express Coach Holiday 1995* catalog. In addition, histories of the Olympics, if well illustrated, and promotional materials produced for the games historically might document costume and fashion, even if the subjects are not discussed specifically. Sporting event programs usually contain promotional photographs of the athletes. The few monographs that could be located on nonmilitary uniforms worn for performing a specific job or activity are also included here.

Curran, Mary J. "Women in White: The Development of the American Nurses Uniforms, 1860–1915." Master's thesis, University of Massachusetts, 1994.

Dalzell, Frederick A. B. *The Evolution of the Seals, Flags, and Uniforms of the United States Customs Service.* Germantown, MD: History Associates, [1985]. 83 leaves.

Dean, Tammera S. H. "History of the 4-H Uniform for Females in Texas." Master's thesis, Texas Women's University, 1985.

Information on Uniforms: A Guide for Commissioned Officers of the Public Health Service. Rockville, MD: The Service, [1990]. [n.p.]

Kuennen, Catherine M. "School Uniforms and Social Groups." Master's thesis, Bowling Green State University, 1991.

Okkonen, Marc. *Baseball Uniforms of the 20th Century: The Official Major League Baseball Guide.* New York: Sterling Pub. Co., 1991. 274p.

Reis, Mitch. *A Guide to Dating Boy Scouts of America Badges, Uniforms and Insignia.* Windsor, CT: M. Reis, 1988. 57p.

Rules of the Game: The Complete Illustrated Encyclopedia of All Sports of the World. Diagram Group. New York: Paddington Press, 1974. 320p. (also New York: St. Martin's, 1990)

Singletary, Betty L. "Contemporary Designs of Athletic Uniforms of Women." Master's thesis, Texas Women's University, 1985.

U.S. Olympic Spirit: Official Catalog of the U.S. Olympic Committee. Colorado Springs, CO: The Committee, [1995?]. 24p.

Stage

Many of the books on costume and the stage deal with designing and making the costumes. In the earlier titles, the audience seems to be those costuming locally produced plays or pageants. Rose Kerr's *Interpretive Costume Design,* part 3, covered American costume, 1620–1860, with third and fourth editions in 1925–1926. The work consists of the author's drawings with a brief description of the clothing (e.g., plate 2, "Puritan Maiden, 1620"). Margaret Mackey and Louise Sooy's *Early California Costumes, 1769–1847* (1932) contains costume plates arranged by type of person (e.g., "A Ranch Owner," "The Father President of All the Missions") and is designed to answer the "continued requests for information concerning authentic costume in Spanish and Mexican California" and for those who are "interested in reconstructing the fiesta and siesta days of California." Lucy Barton's *Historic Costume for the Stage* (1935), revised in 1963, is directed to the stage costumer but does not focus on U.S. historic clothing. A bibliography, periodical list, and index are included. Each chapter contains historical background, clothing for men, women, and children, and related aspects of materials, colors, decoration, jewelry, garment construction techniques, and so forth from Egyptian times to about 1914. Mary Evans (1942) emphasized American costumes for use in children's plays. The book presents eighty-two illustrations (e.g., "Cape of Puritan Woman," "Men's Breeches, 1770," "Woman's Dress, 1847"). Coverage extends to the Civil War with information on materials, dyeing, construction, and patterns. Estelle Worrell's *Early American Costume* (1975), covering about 1580–1850, provides many illustrations and advice for the costumer.

Background and more specific types of stage performances are represented by several volumes. James Laver's *Drama: Its Costume and Decor* (1952) highlighted the collections of the Victoria and Albert Museum in England from the Greeks to the mid-twentieth century. Costume practices can be seen in work for 1751–1901 (Genevieve Richardson), for work by R. E. Jones, N. B. Geddes, L. Simonson, and A. Bernstein for 1915–1935 (Donald Stowell), and for the living theater, open theater, and performance group (Eleanor Patton). American fashions, 1915–1960, and adaptations for the stage are presented by Shirley O'Donnol (1969), while the influence of fashionable dress on theatrical costume, 1760–1860, was studied by Eunice Glosson (1985). "Female Costume and Accessories of the Early Twentieth Century American Stage" is the title of Dorothy Haven's 1970 thesis. John Hirsch discussed the American revue costume at a conference on Musical Theatre in America in 1984. In 1987 Bobbi Owen completed a major reference work, *Costume Design on Broadway: Designers and Their Credits, 1915–1985.* Here, some one hundred illustrations complement the text, which is arranged by costume designer and gives biographical information, play title, date, and type of costume(s) designed. Appendixes list Tony Award winners, 1947–1986, Marharam Awards, 1964/5–1985/6, and Donaldson Awards, 1943–1954/5. An index of plays is provided. In 1988 John Hirsch completed his thesis, "Glorifying the American Showgirl: A History of Revue Costume in the United States from 1866 to the Present," which examined "movie house revues, ice shows, cabaret, and circus productions."[14] More recently the costumemaker's art has been recognized by editor Thom Boswell in his 1992 publication.

In 1993 on a possibly more "popular" stage performance, that of the Miss America Pageant and its competition, Marian Maiwiejczyk-Munigumery has analyzed swimsuits and evening gowns worn from 1921 to 1987.

Barton, Lucy. *Costume for the Stage.* Boston: Walter H. Baker Co., 1935. (1961 new materials added, reprinted 1963).

Boswell, Thom, ed. *The Costumemaker's Art: Cloaks of Fantasy, Masks of Revelation.* Asheville, NC: Lark Books, 1992. 144p.

Evans, Mary. *How to Make Historic American Costumes.* New York: A. S. Barnes, 1942. 178p.

Glosson, Eunice A. "Influence of Fashionable Dress on Theatrical Costume as Seen in Theatrical Portrait Engravings of Actresses Who Performed on American Stages, 1760–1860." Master's thesis, University of Rhode Island, 1985.

Haven, Dorothy C. "Female Costume and Accessories of the Early Twentieth Century American Stage." Master's thesis, San Diego State College, 1970.

Hirsch, John E. "American Revue Costume." In *Musical Theatre in America: Papers and Proceedings of the Conference* 155–177. Edited by Glenn Loney. Westport, CT: Greenwood Press, 1984. 441p.

———. "Glorifying the American Showgirl: A History of Revue Costume in the United States from 1866 to the Present." Ph.D. diss., New York University, 1988.

Kerr, Rose H. *Interpretive Costume Design.* 3d and 4th ed. New York: Fairbairn Art Co., 1925–1926. 3v. Part III: *American Costume, 1620–1860.*

Laver, James. *Drama: Its Costume and Decor.* New York: Studio Publications, 1952. 276p.

Mackey, Margaret G., and Louise P. Sooy. *Early California Costume, 1769–1847, and Historic Flags of California.* Stanford, CA: Stanford University Press; London: Humphrey Milford, Oxford University Press, 1932. 136p.

Maiwiejczyk-Munigumery, Marion A. "Concepts of Fashion, 1921–1987: A Study of Garments Worn by Selected Winners of the Miss America Pageant." Ph.D. diss., New York University, 1993.

O'Donnol, Shirley M. "A Stage Costumer's Guidebook to American Fashions, 1915–1960." Ed.D. diss., Columbia University, 1969.

Owen, Bobbi. *Costume Design on Broadway: Designers and Their Credits, 1915–1985.* Westport, CT: Greenwood Press, 1987. [368]p.

Patton, Eleanor N. "Costuming Practices of the Living Theatre, the Open Theatre, and the Performance Group: Theory, Form, and Function." Ph.D. diss., University of Kansas, 1984.

Richardson, Genevieve. "Costuming on the American Stage, 1751–1901: A Study of the Major Developments in Wardrobe Practice and Costume Style." Ph.D. diss., University of Illinois, 1953.

Stowell, Donald Charles, Jr. "New Costuming in America: The Ideas and Practices of Robert Edmond Jones, Norman Bel Geddes, Lee Simonson and Aline Bernstein, 1915–1935." Ph.D. diss., University of Texas at Austin, 1972.

Worrell, Estelle A. *Early American Costume.* Harrisburg, PA: Stackpole Books, 1975. 183p.

Television

The most recent and pervasive performance media, although full of costumes and fashions in the programming, the advertisements, programming specifically designed to sell or showcase clothing, or occasionally in programs about costume or fashion itself, has not been the subject of many monographs dealing with clothing. Most material located is student research conducted for graduate degrees. Work in 1953 by Elsie Williams and in 1968 by the Alabama Educational TV Network is concerned not with the commercial television programs but with the value of television as a medium for teaching sewing. The influences of fashions seen on television were studied by Linda Pecotte in 1987 for their impact on adolescent girls, by Elliot Bloom in 1988 for "Women's Perceptions of Fashion Comparing Viewers and Non-Viewers of Evening Soap Operas," and by Theresa Manento in 1991 for the impact of music videos on adolescent fashion. Also, the influence of "fashion leadership" on actual purchase of items advertised on television shopping chanels was studied by Liza Leggett in 1990.

At least one program on clothing history was documented in book form by Elizabeth Wilson and BBC Books in 1991. Kristina Seitz wrote "Historic Fashion Cycles of Women's Daywear in Television Sitcoms: 1952–1992" (1993). And again we see the popular interest in collecting reflected in *Entertainment Memorabilia,* a 1994 sales catalog of the Western Costume company's collection, which included costume and television program collectibles.

Alabama Educational Television Network. *Shortcuts to Fashion Television Guide.* By Alfred Bach. Auburn, AL, 1968. 24p.

Bloom, Elliot P. "Women's Perception of Fashion Comparing Viewers and Non-Viewers of Evening Soap Operas: The Cultivation Effect, A Thesis." Master's thesis, University of the Pacific, 1988.

Entertainment Memorabilia and Highlights from the Western Costume "Star Collection" *Part III.* San Francisco: Butterfield & Butterfield, 1994. 167p.

Leggett, Liza. "An Analysis of Fashion Opinion Leadership: As an Indicator of Buying Behavior among Subscribers to Cable Television Shopping Channels." Master's thesis, Texas Tech University, 1990.

Manento, Theresa M. "A Study of the Effects Music Videos Have on Adolescent Fashion and Hair Styles." Master's thesis, Kutztown University of Pennsylvania, 1991.

Pecotte, Linda S. "Conformity in Judgements of Fashionability by Adolescent Girls." Master's thesis, New Mexico State University, 1987.

Seitz, Kristina N. "Historic Fashion Cycles of Women's Daywear in Television Sitcoms: 1952–1992." Master's thesis, Auburn University, 1993.

Williams, Elsie K. "Effectiveness of Television as a Teaching Medium for Clothing Construction." Master's thesis, Iowa State College, 1953.

Wilson, Elizabeth. *Through the Looking Glass: A History of Dress from 1860 to the Present Day.* New York: Parkwest; London: BBC Books, 1991. 240p. Accompanied the BBC television series.

COLLECTING CLOTHING AND ACCESSORIES

Although individuals have been collecting clothing and accessories for a long time, with some special collections making their way into museums, the business of treating them like other antique objects has come into its own during the latter part of the twentieth century and is known as the vintage clothing/textile/accessory business. Literature using the term "vintage clothing" first appeared in the 1980s. Most of the books are identification guides with illustrations, descriptions, and price information. Many include historical background and bibliographies. Harriet Love's 1982 *Guide to Vintage Chic* was followed in 1983 by Frances Kennett's *Collector's Book of Twentieth-Century Fashion,* with a bibliography, and Tina Irick-Nauer's *First Price Guide to Antique and Vintage Clothes: Fashions for Women, 1840–1940* (1983). Naomi Tarrant, a costume curator in Scotland, offered authoritative care, storage, and display information in her 1983 publication, *Collecting Costume.* Other price guides in the 1980s were by Maryanne Dolan (for 1880–1960) in 1984 and by Cynthia Giles. Diane McGee wrote *A Passion for Fashion* in 1987, containing photographs of her collection. Terry McCormick, Kathleen La Barre, and Roselyn Gerson have contributed with a consumers' guide, reference series on women's and men's twentieth-century styles, and handbags, respectively. Fashions for adults and children from the 1950s have been set forth with photographs by Roseann Ettinger (1995). And in 1995 the title *Vintage Denim* was claimed by David Little and Larry Bond.

The use of vintage clothing in community festivals and ceremonies is exemplified by a 1985 Victorian Week celebration in Cape May, New Jersey, designed to attract tourists and highlight the area's heritage. It included the modeling of vintage fashions at several events, as well as a Victorian dinner where guests were invited to wear vintage clothing.[15] The booklet *Modeling the Past* (1994) by Marian Mills-Godfrey documents fashion shows held to promote the annual Hollenberg Pony Express Festival in Kansas. For reenacting historical events, attending costume parties and dances, creating vintage styles rather than wearing actual antique garments is recommended. Thus sewing, repairing, and embroidering for the vintage collector is represented by a growing number of books. Eileen MacIntosh wrote *Sewing and Collecting Vintage Fashions* in 1988 and included a bibliography. French machine sewing is featured in all Martha Pullen's 1990s publications and by Frances Grimble (1993), who also advises how to wear vintage styles. Wendy Shoen (1994) discusses *Heirloom Embroidery for Boys.*

Exhibitions are also being held featuring vintage clothing. The first, in 1984, organized by Molly Turner and entitled *Molly's Manhattan Show and Sale of Vintage Fashion and Antique Textiles,* continues twice a year.[16] Promotional literature, catalogs, and other paper ephemera connected with such sales or auctions form a part of the primary literature.

Dolan, Maryanne. *Vintage Clothing: 1880–1960: Identification and Value Guide.* Florence, AL: Books Americana, 1984. 201p. (2d ed., 1987. 219p)

———. *Vintage Clothing: 1880–1980: Identification and Value Guide.* Florence, AL: Books Americana, 1995. 296p.

Ettinger, Roseann. *50s Popular Fashions for Men, Women, Boys, and Girls.* Atglen, PA: Schiffer Publ. Co., 1995. 158p.

Gerson, Roselyn. *Vintage Vanity Bags and Purses.* Paducah, KY: Collector Books, 1994. 270p.

Giles, Cynthia. *The Official Identification and Price Guide to Vintage Clothing.* New York: House of Collectibles, 1989. 320p.

Grimble, Frances. *After a Fashion: How to Reproduce, Restore, and Wear Vintage Styles.* Illustrated by Deborah Kuhn. San Francisco, CA: Lavolta Press, 1993. 337p.

Irick-Nauer, Tina. *The First Price Guide to Antique and Vintage Clothes: Fashions for Women, 1840–1940.* New York: E. P. Dutton, 1983. 128p.

Kennett, Frances. *The Collector's Book of Twentieth-Century Fashion.* London: Granada, 1983. 256p.

La Barre, Kathleen M. *Reference Book of Men's Vintage Clothing: 1900–1919.* Portland, OR: La Barre Books, 1992. 323p.

———. *Reference Book of Women's Vintage Clothing, 1900–1919.* Portland, OR: La Barre Books, 1990. 364p.

———. *Reference Book of Women's Vintage Clothing, 1920–1929.* Portland, OR: La Barre Books, 1994. 472p.

Little, David, and Larry Bond. *Vintage Denim.* Salt Lake City, UT: Gibbs Smith, Publisher, 1995. [n.p.]

Love, Harriet. *Harriet Love's Guide to Vintage Chic.* New York: Holt, Rinehart and Winston, 1982. 209p.

MacIntosh, Eileen. *Sewing and Collecting Vintage Fashions.* Radnor, PA: Chilton, 1988. 176p.

McCormick, Terry. *A Consumer's Guide to Vintage Clothing.* New York: Dembner Books, 1987. 248p.

McGee, Diane. *A Passion for Fashion: Antique, Collectible, and Retro Clothes.* Omaha, NE: Simmons-Boardman Books, 1987. 208p.

Mills-Godfrey, Marian. *Modeling the Past . . . Washington County Historic Fashion Group*

Present Fashion Shows across the State to Promote the Annual Hollenberg Pony Express Festival near Hanover. Topeka, KA: Kansas Department of Commerce and Housing, 1994. 11p.

Pullen, Martha C. *Antique Clothing: French Sewing by Machine.* Huntsville, AL: Martha Pullen Co., 1990. 303p.

————. *Grandmother's Hope Chest: French Sewing by Machine, Smocking, Shadowwork Embroidery, Embroidery.* Huntsville, AL: M. Pullen Co., 1992. 352p.

————. *Heirloom Sewing for Women: French Sewing by Machine, Machine Embellishment Techniques, New French Sewing Techniques, Heirloom Blouse Designs, Shadow Embroidery, Antique Clothing, Embroidery.* Huntsville, AL: M. Pullen Co., 1993. 384p.

Schoen, Wendy P. *Heirloom Embroidery for Boys.* New Orleans, LA: Wendy Schoen Design, 1994. 87p.

Tarrant, Naomi E. A. *Collecting Costume: The Care and Display of Clothes and Accessories.* London, Boston; Allen & Unwin, 1983. 146p.

5 ─────

Psychological, Sociological, and Cultural Aspects

MONOGRAPHS

This chapter looks at the body of literature that focuses not so specifically on clothing itself but on its meanings as described from a variety of perspectives. Terms repeated throughout this literature include *psychology, psychological, behavior, attitude, identity, image, perception, gender, sex, personality, society, sociology, sociological, socioeconomic, sociopsychological, sociocultural, culture, cultural, democracy, democratization, consumer,* and *consumerism.* "Interdisciplinary" perhaps describes this body of work as it reflects the research and thinking of people from the fields of costume, clothing, and textiles as well as the behavioral sciences, sociology, business, history, and anthropology. And although most of the monographs were written by academicians, several have been contributed by others whose work, vocation, or interests prompted them to write on the topic. Works range from critical analyses, personal opinion, and research studies to advice books. Some cover a broad and often historical perspective, while others focus on a specific topic or represent the thinking of an emerging field such as feminist or cultural studies.

The Psychology of Dress (1923) by Frank A. Parsons was written for a general audience and covers medieval Europe to the early twentieth century.

America is included for the eighteenth through twentieth centuries. Parsons notes in his preface a recent general interest in "man and his works, between the mind and its expression in material objects."[1] The volume then shows how religion, politics, and social life have influenced styles in clothes and allied arts. A second *Psychology of Dress* was written by Elizabeth B. Hurlock in 1929. Her goal was to coordinate the various theories and opinions on fashion motive and add her own interpretation. She suggests that because fashion interests persist in each generation, a human trait or tendency might be involved. One special feature of this book is "Broadcasting Fashion News," which outlines the variety of methods available for advertising a new fashion (e.g., fashion dolls, pantines, cut-out figures, papyrotamia, pin-pricked figures, wax figures, mannequins, fashion shows).

With a slight variation in title, *The Psychology of Clothes* (1930) sets forth John C. Flugel's theories. His preface credits a few psychologists, anthropologists, and social scientists who have contributed to the field. Flugel felt that the most "fundamental fact" in the psychology of clothing was the interplay between decoration and modesty. Competition was seen as the "why" of fashion. His discussion of the evolution of garments is presented as if the clothes were living plants or animals. Other topics are individual and sex differences and ethics. *Recurring Cycles of Fashion, 1760–1937* (1937) by Agnes Young identifies typical fashions for the various periods and indicates that "fashion in dress depends for its very existence on the freedom of choice of individuals." Mildred G. Ryan's *Your Clothes and Personality* (1937) provided advice for young girls on how to achieve a "well-balanced pleasure in appearing suitably and attractively gowned at all times." *Fashion Is Spinach* (1938) by Elizabeth Hawes was also a popular approach presenting advice on how American women should dress for "complete individual satisfaction." *It's Still Spinach* followed in 1954. Quentin Bell analyzed current clothing theories in *On Human Finery* in 1947 (revised, 1976). Another critic, Bernard Rudofsky, expressed himself sarcastically in *Are Clothes Modern?* in 1947. He complained of the lack of a costume library and his inability to get permission to use photos from *Vogue*. Praise for fashion and the fashion industry was shown by the *City of New York Golden Anniversary of Fashion* commemorating New York's fashion industry, 1898–1948. Text, many advertisements from manufacturers and retailers, cartoons on fashion by Vertes, a foldout on collections at the Metropolitan Museum of Art, a glossary, and other features make this a collectible item.

As quite a departure in focus, Edmund Bergler uses his clinical psychoanalytic cases in *Fashion and the Unconscious* (1953). His discussion of colors provides quotations from literature on red, green, blue, and yellow. His theory of the "fantastic fashion hoax" concerned the fact that many women's clothes were designed by male homosexuals who dislike women and thus have control over them in this way. In 1959 another viewpoint, clothes as inventions, was offered by Lawrence Langner, who at that time was an inventor of clothing-related devices as well as a founder of the American Shakespeare Festival. His *The Importance of Wearing Clothes* offered, on a popular note, that the striptease was one of "America's lesser contributions to world culture" and that there appeared to be a "cult of the brassiere" represented by the plethora of bra advertisements.

By 1965 Mary E. Roach and Joanne B. Eicher edited a collection of essays, *Dress, Adornment, and the Social Order,* for which they selected pieces that included cross-cultural comparisons. Many of the essays had been previously published. The book's annotated bibliography lists general and classic monographs, articles, and some theses on the sociocultural aspects of dress and adornment; arranged by author, it is an excellent feature of the book. Two new texts for students appeared in the 1960s: Mary S. Ryan's *Clothing, A Study of Human Behavior* (1966) and Marilyn J. Horn's *Second Skin* (1968). Although Ryan's book emphasizes culture and the cultural role, Horn's work, a collective effort by the Home Economics Education Board of the U.S. Department of Health, Education and Welfare, reflects an effort to change the way clothing and textile courses were taught in the United States. The preface discusses the history of the college clothing course and concludes that clothing and the individual/family/culture should be studied from an interdisciplinary (health, management, aesthetic, psychological, socioanthropological, and economic) perspective.[2] *The Why of Fashion* (1967) by Karlyne Anspach examines social and economic factors as well as the ways popular fashions reflect American life ("conservatism," "youth," and "casual"); specific clothes and "looks" are covered, with an excellent index. "The Relations of Women's Fashions to Women's Status," in Aileen S. Kraditor's *Up from the Pedestal: Selected Writings in the History of American Feminism* (1968) contains selections from nineteenth-century writings by S. M. Grimké, E. S. Miller, G. Smith, E. C. Stanton, T. C. Claflin, and T. Veblen. *New People: Desexualization* in *American Life* (1968) by Charles Winick contains the essay "Costume and Customs: The Vanishing Difference."

In the 1970s at least two textbooks were produced reflecting the new approach to the study of clothes. Mary L. Rosencrantz's *Clothing Concepts: A Social-Psychological Approach* (1972) contains many quotations from various theorists as well as sections containing tests or measures of clothing awareness, symbols, and role. "Clothing Cartoons" are shown as used in one study of individual awareness. Roach and Eicher collaborated again on *The Visible Self: Perspectives of Dress* (1973), which discusses sources for studying clothing from the artifact, its depiction and description, to sources seeking to moralize, satirize, reform, prescribe, or analyze. Several chapters focus on art and society (folk, agrarian, urban, industrial, and mass).

Ann Hollander's *Seeing through Clothes* (1978) asserts that the most important aspect of clothing is how it looks, a factor dependent on not only the design and construction but also on how it is perceived "through a filter of artistic convention."[3] She states that in Western culture, dress has the status of a visual art and should be studied not simply as a "cultural by-product" but as "connected links in a creative tradition of image-making."[4] Nudity and the use of mirrors in art works are analyzed, among other topics. Also in 1975 an edited volume of essays appeared, *Dimensions of Dress and Adornment.* Most of the pieces are reprints of earlier material. Both editors, Lois M. Gurel and Marianne S. Beeson, are represented by nine and seven papers, respectively. The fifty-nine essays are grouped under broad topics: "Anthropological Perspectives," "Historical Influences," "Clothing Behavior," and "Apparel as an Economic Good." Some popular clothes receive attention—for example, the gray flannel suit by Moira Johnston and Marianne S. Beeson; the shirt by Judith Hennessee and Joan Nicholson; street fashion by Sheldon Zalaznick; t-shirts by Maria J. Schoolman; and fake fur by Phyllis Feldkamp. Joseph Dispenza's *Advertising the American Woman* (1975) analyzed advertisements in the popular press to see how women's roles were being interpreted. One of six categories of advertisements was for foundation garments and fashion.[5]

Advice books appear again, as exemplified by Joan T. Molloy's *Woman's Dress for Success Book* (1977). Prudence Glynn's *In Fashion: Dress in the Twentieth Century* (1978) discusses fashion as an art, special clothes (e.g., for children and sporting dress), and fashion as a trade. Written with a British focus, it includes a bibliography and an index. Glynn wonders if the twentieth-century idea of being in fashion (a "phenomenon" allowed because of leisure, wealth, cheap labor, and technology) might be coming to an end, and if so what will follow.[6] "Icons of Popular Fashion" (1978) by Valerie Carnes concentrates on the 1960s and early 1970s when "the dominance of Hollywood as icon-maker was over." She discusses the screen heroine, pinup girl, Playboy foldout, fashion models, rock stars, fashion groupies, consumers, and women themselves as popular icons and mentions ideas from Gore Vidal, Thomas Wolfe, Walter Weisskopf, and others.

During the 1980s more books analyzing clothing began to include popular themes. Stewart and Elizabeth Ewen's scholarly *Channels of Desire* (1982, 1992) provides a historical look at mass images in American society. The section "Fashion and Democracy" consists of several essays on clothing and its connections with social history. Included are "Images of Democracy," on ready-to-wear clothing's wide availability; "Avenues of Display," on advertising, department stores, and catalogs; "New Patterns," on the idea of fashion's reflecting common people's life; and "Sirens of Style," discussing how people set the styles. "Commerce of Choice" reflects the variety of style choices available at one time, and "History and Clothes Consciousness" points out fashion as a reflection of people's desires, a "perpetual vernacular of critical, popular expression."[7] The index lists specific terms—among them, *business suit, bustles, corsets, dresses, flapper style, jeans, lingerie, hobble skirts, high heels, overalls, paper dolls,* and *plain-style clothing*—that are popular or significant enough to have elicited comment by the authors. Also in 1982, Loretta Carrillo contributed "Fashion" to M. Thomas Inge's collection, *Concise Histories of American Popular Culture.* She covers the seventeenth century to the 1950s. Many specific clothes are mentioned, such as trunk hose, knickerbockers, farthingales, hunting smock, homespun fabric, cloche hats, "slave" bracelets, shoulder pads, and bermuda shorts.

Not to be overlooked, Lois Alexander produced *Blacks in the History of Fashion* in 1982. The journalistic history includes many photographs. In addition to focusing on the fashion designers, she emphasizes the history of the Black Fashion Museum founded in 1979 and its exhibition and other fashion-related social and fund-raising events. The Harlem Institute of Fashion, founded in 1966, also reflected popular social practices by providing sewing and fashion design lessons. This unique source includes a bibliography, with radio and television programs mentioned. Ted Polhemus's *Pop Styles* (1984) covers another "alternative fashion force," especially in England during the 1960s, when ideas and styles came from the young (noncouture) designers, musician designers, and the street. The major second part of the volume provides a discussion with illustrations of popular styles (e.g., baggy trousers, bullet belts, ties, transex, winklepickers, zips). Another book commenting on music and fashion is *Zootsuits and Second-Hand Dress* (1989), edited by Angela McRobbie. *Fashion and Eroticism: Ideals of Feminine Beauty from the Victorian Era to the Jazz Age* (1985), reflected in upper- and middle-class dress, is Valerie Steele's theme in this work, covering 1820–1928. France and England, the fashion leaders of that time, are the main focus. Undergarments are used to illustrate erotic expression and feelings of the time, an era much less "antisexual" than previously thought.[8] The fashions are seen in their relation to "culture, socioeconomic development . . . group behavior, and individual psychology, particularly the female sexual psychology."[9] "The Foundations of Fashion" uses underwear, lingerie, petticoats, corsets, the tea gown, and "Attractions of Underclothes" to exemplify the author's ideas. Other theories of fashion are reviewed in the light of her research; the historical overview ends with "Into the Twentieth Century." The bibliography is an excellent feature, with primary sources including store catalogs and advertising pamphlets, and secondary sources including exhibition catalogs.

Another behavioral study that examines sexual and moral connotations is Aileen Ribeiro's *Dress and Morality* (1986), which provides a documented history of the criticism of clothing based on its immorality. One example given is the ability of a government to "enforce sartorial morality" by requiring uniforms of its prisoners.[10] An example from American popular culture is the idea of the Hollywood femme fatale as a "sexually predatory woman."[11] Ribeiro states that her book is "just one approach to the many-faceted subject of the history of dress."[12] The extensive criticism of female clothing over time extends even today as often women are admired for their beauty as well as "denounced for it."[13]

Throughout the 1980s, more texts were produced analyzing the meanings of fashion. Alison Lurie used her background as an English professor and novelist to present meanings communicated by clothing in terms of English grammar and its vocabulary. In *Language of Clothes* (1981), for instance, she mentions that accessories are the adverbs and adjectives while casual or "loose" clothing could be the slang or vulgar words of the language. She includes a selected bibliography but no index. In 1981, Jeannette and Robert Lauer published *Fashion Power, The Changing Meaning of Fashion*. Their discussion of meaning is focused on "Nature of Clothes and Fashion," "Fashion and Social Life," and "Theory of Fashion" in America. The introduction reviews in academic terms various fashion meanings; the rest of the book exposes American opinions from the popular literature, including a review of articles from *Poole's Index, Readers' Guide to Periodical Literature*, and the *New York Times*. There are chapter conclusions and bibliographies, as well as an index, which is basically for analytical terms rather than names of clothing items. In 1985 Susan B. Kaiser's *Social Psychology of Clothing and Personal Adornment* focused on the "social meaning of appearance." This book includes a discussion of the "cultural studies movement that emerged in the 1970s."[14] A list of references and author and subject indexes add to the value of the book. The subject index includes "popular culture," which leads to discussions of the affordability of clothing in the twentieth century; the corset; eclecticism; fashion retailing effects; gender differences; music videos and rock music; romance novels; and television shows. Clothing types with the most page references in the index are uniforms (twenty-two), undergarments (ten), white collar (ten), t-shirts (eight), folk costume (eight), shoes (seven), and men's clothing (seven).

The issue of uniforms is the focus of Nathan Joseph's *Uniforms and Nonuniforms: Communication through Clothing* (1986). This sociological approach provides background information followed by "Uniforms," covering issues of control, nonconformity, and perceptions, and "Nonuniforms," covering issues of nonbureaucratic dress, occupational clothing, leisure-time clothing, and costumes. The section on costumes discusses costume symbolism with several popular examples (e.g., the town of Metropolis, Illinois, dedicated to Superman, has seen increased tourism and Disney characters on adult clothing help to satisfy fantasies). The cowboy as an "ideological symbol" is included, as well as the notion that children may often be "personal symbol bearers" for their parents who control what clothing the child wears. In this way, the children might be dressed to advertise parental views of "patriotism, ethnic pride, and religious piety in pageants and parades."[15] Popular terms listed in the index include baseball caps, bell-bottoms, cowboys, folk clothing, hunting shirt, jeans, redcaps, sports clothing, urban cowboy, and the Philadelphia Mummers.

In 1987 several student textbooks were published. Marilyn R. DeLong wrote *The Way We Look*, which emphasizes how to be an educated "viewer" of clothing. Penny Storm's *Functions of Dress* emphasizes all cultures and their use of clothing for adornment and protection, its intrinsic values, roles, and ways of communicating status; and its sociological and psychological considerations. There is an extensive bibliography. Inge's three-volume *Handbook of American Popular Culture* appeared in 1989 in its second edition. Here a section on fashion appears by Vicki Berger, along with many other popular culture topics. The idea of *Selling Culture: Bloomingdale's, Diana Vreeland, and the New Aristocracy of Taste in Reagan's America* (1986) is analyzed and criticized by Debora Silverman. The "politics and culture of wish-fullfillment" she observes are exemplified by the "aristocratic invocation" seen in the 1980s connections between "the museum," "department store" "fashion design," and "media." The fashion designer, nineteenth century to the 1980s, is featured in Caroline Milbank's *New York Fashion: The Evolution of American Style* (1989). The introduction and the nineteenth-century chapter are followed by information on each decade. Milbank indicates that the Gibson girl shirtwaist and skirt of about 1899 typified an American style easily manufactured for all classes. Although American fashion began in the nineteenth century as a "blend of hand and machine work, with the distinction between retailer, manufacturer, and designer blurred," individual designers did emerge. Biographies are included, with a bibliography and photo credits.

The 1990s literature brings attention to the feminist perspective in *Fabrications: Costume and the Female Body* (1990), edited by Jane Gaines and Charlotte Herzog. Again, as in many other titles, we see clever use of clothing, textile, and related terminology to send a message about the content of the book. "Fabrications" immediately brings to mind the crafting of an object (the costume, the female character), the falseness of the image, and the fabric of possibly both the costume and the story being told. The introductory essay by Gaines provides an overview of feminist thought on female images, especially in fashion magazines and movies. Gaines in this essay uses "fictions for the eye" and "cinematic illusionism" to explain the impact of the work of the costumers and seamstresses.[16] The "fabrication" of females into advertising statements or visual images, where the individual person is lost under layers of cosmetics, clothing, and pose, is a startling theme illustrated by these writers—how women are both the "target" audience and the "raw material of the culture of the body."[17] The twelve essays, some reprinted, are documented and cover the period from 1900 to the 1950s. The bibliography is extensive and lists articles as well as books in three sections: "Hollywood Costumes," "Fashion/Body/Consumer Culture," and "Feminism and Cultural Studies."

Other edited volumes include *Dress and Popular Culture* (1991) by Patricia A. Cunningham and Susan V. Lab. The eleven essays cover themes of Barbie doll clothing, jeans, clothing symbolism as expressed by black fraternal groups, popular music, punks, paper clothes, senior cords, dress reform, and the folklore clothing image of the witch. *Dress and Gender: Making and Meaning in Cultural Contexts* (1992), edited by Ruth Barnes and Joanne Eicher, features sixteen essays presented at a workshop sponsored by the Centre for Cross-Cultural Research on Women, Oxford. The essays on American culture include C. Cerny's study of quilted apparel and gender identity and R. Bailey's study of maternity clothing in the United States from 1850 to 1990. Cerny notes that a popular practice was the use of the quilted vest as a gift. "Made with love" and "especially for you" were frequent feelings expressed with the presentation of handmade quilted gifts.

Fred Davis provides a sociological perspective in *Fashion, Culture, and Identity* (1992). The index includes the entry "Public Opinion and Influence," which leads to mention of middle-class America's relation to economic success of the fashion industry; jeans; the mass adoption of trousers by women in the 1960s; unisex styles; public influence on new designs to be first modified and then manufactured; the change in the fashion show to a media event for the ready-to-wear industry; and the influence of street fashion. Davis's general focus is on fashion codes, ambiguity, ambivalence, the process from fashion creation to consumption, and antifashion. In the conclusion he discusses two methods of studying fashion: the "fashion system model" and the "populist model."

Two other edited volumes—*Dress in American Culture* (1993) by Cunningham and Lab and *On Fashion* (1994) by Sheri Benstock and Suzanne Ferriss—contain essays touching on some popular themes. From Cunningham and Lab we see ethnic clothing, the cowboy, the pioneer, costumed dressing in the nineteenth century, the sport gymsuit, simplicity in dress, and the impact of World War I shortages on clothes, which included the appearance of "denim 'Overalls Clubs.' "[18] The Benstock and Ferriss book touches on the Barbie doll and its magazine, fashion magazines, silent film fashions, and popular music personality Madonna's use of fashion. The essays focus on "photography, cinema, and video" and their impact on "consumerism, postmodernism and feminism."[19]

Understanding the power of fashion in society is the focus of *Empire of Fashion: Dressing Modern Democracy* (1994), by Gilles Lipovetsky, a scholarly volume that is part of the Princeton University Press series New French Thought. The translation is by Catherine Porter, with a foreword by Richard Sennett. Lipovetsky's views question current and historical thinking about fashion and its impact. According to the foreword, Lipovetsky theorizes that "democracy works better the more superficial the social relations between people," and fashion helps achieve this "indifference" as does its advertising, since by experiencing the "fantasy" of the advertisement, one almost seems to possess the object, thus lessening expressions of anger at those who actually own the item.[20] The larger issue is his concern with the decline of the "soulful" individual to one who is content to simply "taste, own, consume."[21] The author uses charged language to label the two sections of the book: "The Enchantment of Appearances" and "Consummate Fashion." In his introduction, he indicates that he is seeking to understand the "central, unprecedented place it [fashion] occupies in democracies that have set out along the path of consumerism and mass communications."[22] The epilogue explains the development of his theories; chapter notes and works cited are included. The index includes such terms as *advertising, clothing, consummate fashion, democracy, fashion, individual, individualism, mass culture, novelty, seduction, taste, tradition, youth,* and many more terms with subheadings; also included are names of people. A second French work, *The Culture of Clothing* (1994) by Daniel Roche concentrates on the seventeenth and eighteenth centuries in France. Shelley Budgeon writes about fashion magazine advertising and femininity in a 1994 essay.

In contrast, Ruth P. Rubinstein's *Dress Codes: Meanings and Messages in American Culture* (1995) offers the sociological view in a presentation for both academic and general readers. She brings her considerable experience at the Fashion Institute of Technology to her work. The outline includes discussions of dress and society; nineteenth-century clothing theories; private and public images; power, gender and seduction; beauty, leisure, youth, and health; tie signs and symbols; the presidency and contemporary fashion, and the individual. Other 1995 volumes are Christopher Bernard's *Culture of Fashion,* Patty Fox's *Star Style: Hollywood Legends as Fashion Icons,* and Dodie Kazanjian's *Icons.* Popular fads have also been outlined and described with the British *Fads, Fashions and Cults* by Tony Thorne (1993) and *Fashion and Merchandising Fads* (1994) by Frank Hoffmann and William Bailey.

Alexander, Lois K. *Blacks in the History of Fashion.* New York: Harlem Institute of Fashion, 1982. 152p.

Anspach, Karlyne A. *The Why of Fashion.* Ames, IA: Iowa State University Press, 1967. 378p.

Barnes, Ruth, and Joanne B. Eicher, eds. *Dress and Gender: Making and Meaning in Cultural Contexts.* New York: St. Martin's Press, 1992. 293p.

Bell, Quentin. *On Human Finery.* 2d ed., rev. and enl. New York: Schocken Books, 1976. 239p. (1st ed. 1947)

Benstock, Sheri, and Suzanne Ferriss, eds. *On Fashion.* New Brunswick, NJ: Rutgers University Press, 1994. 317p.

Berger, Vicki L. "Fashion." In *Handbook of American Popular Culture,* 1: 417–443.

Edited by M. Thomas Inge. 2d ed. Westport, CT: Greenwood Press, 1989. 3v.

Bergler, Edmund. *Fashion and the Unconscious.* New York: Robert Brunner, 1953. Reprint with new foreword, Madison, CT: International Universities Press, 1987. 305p.

Bernard, Christopher. *The Culture of Fashion: A New History of Fashionable Dress.* Manchester: Manchester University Press, 1995. 244p.

Budgeon, Shelley. "Fashion Magazine Advertising: Constructing Femininity in the Postfeminist Era." In *Gender and Utopia in Advertising: A Critical Reader.* Edited by Luigi Manca and Alessandra Manca. Lisle, IL: Procopian Press, 1994. 168p.

Carnes, Valerie. "Icons of Popular Fashion." In *Icons of America,* 228–240. Edited by Ray B. Brown and Marshall Fishwick. Bowling Green, OH: Popular Press, 1978. 301p.

Carrillo, Loretta. "Fashion." In *Concise Histories of American Popular Culture,* 129–135. Edited by M. Thomas Inge. Westport, CT: Greenwood Press, 1982.

City of New York. Golden Anniversary of Fashion, 1898–1948. Official Jubilee ed. New York: Official Publication of the Mayor's Committee for the Commemoration of the Golden Anniversary of the City of New York, 1948. 196p.

Cunningham, Patricia A., and Susan V. Lab, eds. *Dress and Popular Culture.* Bowling Green, OH: Bowling Green State University Popular Press, 1991. 165p.

———. *Dress in American Culture.* Bowling Green, OH: Bowling Green University Popular Press, 1993. 221p.

Davis, Fred. *Fashion, Culture, and Identity.* Chicago: University of Chicago Press, 1992. 226p.

DeLong, Marilyn R. *The Way We Look: A Framework for Visual Analysis of Dress.* Ames, IA: Iowa State University Press, 1987.

Dispenza, Joseph E. *Advertising the American Woman.* Dayton, OH: Pfaum Pub., 1975. 181p.

Ewen, Stuart, and Elizabeth Ewen. *Channels of Desire: Mass Images and the Shaping of American Consciousness.* New York: McGraw-Hill, 1982. 312p. (2d ed. 1992. 247p.)

Flugel, John C. *The Psychology of Clothes.* London: Hogarth Press, 1930. 257p.

Fox, Patty. *Star Style: Hollywood Legends as Fashion Icons.* Santa Monica, CA: Angel City Press, 1995. 128p.

Gaines, Jane, and Charlotte Herzog, eds. *Fabrications: Costume and the Female Body.* New York: Routledge, 1990. 295p.

Glynn, Prudence. *In Fashion.* Illustrated by Madeleine Ginsburg. New York: Oxford University Press, 1978. 243p.

Grimké, Sarah M., et al. "The Relation of Women's Fashions to Women's Status." In *Up from the Pedestal: Selected Writings in the History of American Feminism,* 122–136. Edited by Aileen S. Kraditor. Chicago: Quadrangle Books, 1968.

Gurel, Lois M., and Marianne S. Beeson, comps. *Dimensions of Dress and Adornment: A Book of Readings.* 3d ed. Dubuque, IA: Kendall/Hunt Pub. Co., 1979. 219p. (1st ed. 1975, 2d ed. 1977).

Hawes, Elizabeth. *Fashion Is Spinach.* New York: Random House, 1938. 223p.

———. *It's Still Spinach.* Boston: Little, Brown, 1954. 233p.

Hoffmann, Frank W., and William G. Bailey. *Fashion and Merchandising Fads.* New York: Haworth Press, 1994. 317p.

Hollander, Anne. *Seeing through Clothes.* New York: Viking Press, 1978. 504p.

Horn, Marilyn J. *Second Skin: An Interdisciplinary Study of Clothing.* Boston: Houghton Mifflin, 1968. 435p.

Hurlock, Elizabeth B. *The Psychology of Dress: An Analysis of Fashion and Its Motive.* New York: Ronald Press, 1929. 244p.

Inge, M. Thomas, ed. *Handbook of American Popular Culture.* 2d ed., rev. and enlarged. Westport, CT: Greenwood Press, 1989. 3v.

Joseph, Nathan. *Uniforms and Nonuniforms: Communication through Clothing.* Westport, CT: Greenwood Press, 1986. 249p.

Kaiser, Susan B. *The Social Psychology of Clothing and Personal Adornment.* New York: Macmillan, 1985. 500p. (*The Social Psychology of Clothing: Symbolic Appearances in Context.* 2d ed. New York: Macmillan, 1990. 590p.)

Kazanjian, Dodie. *Icons.* New York: St. Martin's Press, 1995.

Kraditor, Aileen S., ed. *Up from the Pedestal: Selected Writings in the History of American Feminism.* Chicago: Quadrangle Books, 1968. 373p.

Langner, Lawrence. *The Importance of Wearing Clothes.* New York: Hastings House, 1959. 349p.

Lauer, Jeanette C., and Robert H. Lauer. *Fashion Power: The Meaning of Fashion in American Society.* Englewood Cliffs, NJ: Prentice-Hall, 1981. 275p.

Lipovetsky, Gilles. *The Empire of Fashion: Dressing Modern Democracy.* Translated by Catherine Porter, with a foreword by Richard Sennett. Princeton, NJ: Princeton University Press, 1994. 276p.

Lurie, Alison. *The Language of Clothes.* New York: Random House, 1981. 272p.

McRobbie, Angela, ed. *Zootsuits and Second-Hand Dresses: An Anthology of Fashion and Music.* New York: Routledge Chapman & Hall, 1989. 288p.

Milbank, Caroline R. *New York Fashion: The Evolution of American Style.* New York: Harry N. Abrams, 1989. 303p.

Molloy, John T. *Woman's Dress for Success Book.* Chicago: Follett Pub. Co., 1977. 189p.

Parsons, Frank A. *The Psychology of Dress.* Garden City, NY: Doubleday Page & Co., 1923. 358p.

Polhemus, Ted, and Lynn Procter. *Pop Styles.* London: Vermilion, 1984. 144p.

Ribeiro, Aileen. *Dress and Morality.* New York: Holmes & Meier, 1986. 192p.

Roach, Mary E., and Joanne B. Eicher, eds. *Dress, Adornment, and the Social Order.* New York: Wiley, 1965. 429p.

———. *The Visible Self: Perspectives of Dress.* Englewood Cliffs, NJ: Prentice-Hall, 1973. 246p.

Roche, Daniel. *The Culture of Clothing: Dress and Fashion in the "Ancien Regime."* Translated by Jean Dirrell. New York: Cambridge University Press, 1994. 537p.

Rosencranz, Mary L. *Clothing Concepts: A Social-Psychological Approach.* New York: Macmillan, 1972. 339p.

Rubenstein, Ruth P. *Dress Codes: Meanings and Messages in American Culture.* Boulder, CO: Westview Press, 1995. 314p.

Rudofsky, Bernard. *Are Clothes Modern? An Essay on Contemporary Apparel.* Chicago: Paul Theobald, 1947. 241p.

Ryan, Mary S. *Clothing, A Study in Human Behavior.* New York: Holt, Rinehart & Winston, 1966. 341p.

Ryan, Mildred G. *Your Clothes and Personality.* New York: Appleton-Century Co., 1937. 367p. (rev. ed., 1942)

Silverman, Debora. *Selling Culture: Bloomingdale's, Diana Vreeland, and the New Aristocracy of Taste in Reagan's America.* New York: Pantheon Books, 1986. 175p.

Steele, Valerie. *Fashion and Eroticism: Ideals of Feminine Beauty from the Victorian Era to the Jazz Age.* New York: Oxford University Press, 1985. 327p.

Storm, Penny. *Functions of Dress: Tool of Culture and the Individual.* Englewood Cliffs, NJ: Prentice-Hall, 1987. 358p.

Thorne, Tony. *Fads, Fashions and Cults: From Acid House to Zoot Suit, via Existentialism and Political Correctness, the Definitive Guide to (Post-) Modern Culture.* London: Bloomsbury, 1993. 310p.

Winick, Charles. "Costume and Custom: The Vanishing Difference." In *New People: Desexualization in American Life,* 223–271. New York: Pegasus, 1968. 384p. (also as *Desexualization in American Life,* 1995. 402p.)

Young, Agnes B. *Recurring Cycles of Fashion, 1760–1937.* New York: Cooper Square, 1966, c. 1937. 216p.

THESES

Master's and Ph.D. theses concerned with the psychological, sociological, and cultural aspects of clothing are numerous. By their very nature, they represent specific research projects where a well-defined topic is analyzed, with results reflecting outcomes rather than personal opinions. Although women and teenage girls receive most attention, there is work on men, boys, children, the elderly, the disabled, and fashion leaders or innovators. Much of the work covers consumer behavior—the selecting and purchasing of clothes. Related to this are those referring to terms such as *clothing behavior, practice,* or *preference* and *clothing attitudes* and *acceptance.* Perceptions, interests, needs, and general awareness, as well as self-concept, esteem, and worth, are also mentioned frequently. The impact of color and the use of words such as *appearance* and *culture* are seen a little less frequently. Specific clothing is mentioned in many titles, with the student reflecting historically or, more often, looking at a clothing practice contemporary with the research project.

The studies selected for discussion represent three groups: insights into special people (men, boys, children, and fashion leaders) special clothes popular enough to receive attention, and psychological, sociological, and cultural research projects that touch the more popular topics of consumerism, brand name, impact of color, home sewing, and used clothing, as well as those with a general cultural focus and those focused on the media as a specific cultural influence.

Men, Boys, Children, and Fashion Leaders

Theses focused on men include concerns with social status (Hoolt, 1952), scientists' dress (Lundeen, 1958), and fashion leaders among fraternity men (Sohn, 1959). "External Influence Affecting Clothing Worn by High School and College Men" (Lokken, 1961) begins a trend in study of outside information and inducements to purchase clothing. "Clothing acceptance" related to "clothing norms" and personality of "black college men" is the subject of Adams's 1972 Ph.D. dissertation. "Novelty as a style attribute" is featured by Lyla Stolz (1977), while two studies of elderly men—their clothing preferences (Giorgi, 1977) and their clothing in relation to self-esteem and independence (Simpson, 1982)—illustrate interests in an aging population. "Male Fashion Innovators: Sex-Role Type and Life-Style Characteristics" (Havasy, 1985) and "Male Role and Lifestyle" (Oliver, 1989) stand in contrast to John Jacob's interest reflected in "Stylistic Change in Men's Business Suits Related to Changes in the Masculine Role . . . 1950–1988." (1990).

Adams, Amelia E. "Clothing Acceptance for the Self and for Others, and Adherence to Selected Clothing Norms as Related to Selected Aspects of Personality in a Sample of Black College Males." Ph.D. diss., Pennsylvania State University, 1972.

Giorgi, Sue T. "Selected Clothing Practices and Preferences of Elderly Men in Tallahassee, Florida." Master's thesis, Florida State University, 1977.

Havasy, Jamie. "Male Fashion Innovators: Sex-role Type and Lifestyle Characteristics." Ph.D. diss., Ohio State University, 1985.

Hoolt, Thomas. "Clothing as a Factor in the Social Status Rating of Men." Ph.D. diss., University of Southern California, 1952.

Jacob, John B. "Stylistic Change in Men's Business Suits Related to Changes in the Masculine Roles in the United States, 1950–1988." Master's thesis, Virginia Polytechnic Institute, 1990.

Lokken, Doris E. "External Influence Affecting Clothing Worn by High School and College Men." Master's thesis, Oregon State University, 1961.

Lundeen, Shirley M. "The Dress of Scientists as Viewed by Scientists and Nonscientists." Master's thesis, Pennsylvania State University, 1958.

Oliver, Nancy A. "Male Role and Lifestyle: Clothing Selection Attitudes for the Professional and Social Environment." Ph.D. diss., University of Tennessee, 1989.

Simpson, Mary M. "Association between the Attitudes toward Dress and the Physical Independence, Role Involvement, and Self-Esteem of Elderly Men." Master's thesis, Iowa State University, 1982.

Sohn, Marjorie A. "Personal and Social Characteristics of Clothing Fashion Leaders among Fraternity Men." Master's thesis, Pennsylvania State University, 1959.

Stolz, Lyla J. M. "Assessment of Novelty as a Style Attribute and Its Relationship to Fashion Adoption." Master's thesis, University of Nevada, 1977.

Boys have been of interest to several students. Clothing leadership is covered by Albert Glickman (1952) while slack and shirt selection by boys and their mothers was researched by Agatha Huepenbecker (1956). Choice of cotton clothing by high school boys is reflected by Mamie Hardy (1957). Clothing interests, preferences, and problems were studied by Bessie Forbes (1957), Hazel Lawrence (1958), and Lois Baldwin (1960), respectively. Appearance and peer acceptance, for girls and boys, is the subject of M. Young's 1967 study.

Baldwin, Lois M. "A Study of Clothing Problems of the Teen-Age Boy." Master's thesis, Virginia Polytechnic Institute, 1960.

Forbes, Bessie B. "A Study Designed to Find Out the Interests in Clothing of Boys in Booker T. Washington High School." Master's thesis, Cornell University, 1957.

Glickman, Albert S. "Clothing Leadership among Boys." Ph.D. diss., Ohio State University, 1952.

Hardy, Mamie L. "Choices of Cotton Clothing for Boys in a Rural Area of Iowa." Master's thesis, Iowa State College, 1957.

Huepenbecker, Agatha L. "Factors Which Influence Mothers and Sons in the Selection of Boy's Slacks and Shirts." Master's thesis, Iowa State College, 1956.

Lawrence, Hazel M. "Preferences of Mothers and Sons for Clothing of Eighth Grade Boys." Master's thesis, Iowa State University, 1958.

Young, Mary J. "Relationship of Clothing to Peer Acceptance and to Personal Appearance of Adolescents." Master's thesis, Michigan State University, 1967.

Children in general have received more attention than boys alone. During the 1950s, the majority of theses dealt with clothing preferences with six studying the mother or parent's preferences for the children (Cassidy, 1954; Mitchell, 1955; Pahopin, 1955, 1958; Williams, 1958; Margaret Warning, 1956; Terasawa, 1956). Three studies concentrated on the preferences of the children themselves (Terasawa; Hunt, 1956; Morris, 1958). Girl's clothing practices versus their social class was studied by Mary Roach in 1960. Preferences of deaf girls and for textures among preschoolers and their mothers were studied by Dorothy King (1961) and Mary Burton (1961), respectively. Other theses in the 1960s included influences on selection of outerwear for children by (Willett, 1962) and age and gender related to children's awareness of clothing and appearance (Hodgkins, 1962).

Low-income mothers and their first-grade children were questioned about their feelings of acceptance and/or rejection by Mary Bolton (1970). Choice, selection, and purchases were studied for different age groups by Ann Stephens (fourth and seventh graders), Beverly Keenan (sixth graders), and Linda Simpson (preschoolers). The issue of conformity in middle school children was reported by Anita May (1982), while clothing and school behavior were studied by Carolyn Jones (1983).

Bolton, Mary J. "Study of the Clothing of First Grade Children in a Low Income Situation." Master's thesis, University of Tennessee, 1970.

Burton, Mary E. "Texture Preferences of a Selected Group of Preschool Children and Their Mothers." Master's thesis, Iowa State University of Science and Technology, 1961.

Cassidy, Louise. "Clothing Preferences of One Hundred Fifty Pre-Adolescent Girls and Fifty of Their Mothers." Master's thesis, Ohio State University, 1954.

Hodgkins, Betty J. "Preadolescent Awareness of Clothing and Appearance as Related to Age and Sex." Ph.D. diss., Florida State University, 1969.

Hunt, Lucille A. "Factors Related to Children's Clothing Preferences." Ph.D. diss., Purdue University, 1956.

Jones, Carolyn A. C. "Relationships between Clothing and School Behavior of Third-Grade Students." Master's thesis, Texas Woman's University, 1983.

Keenen, Beverly D. "Factors That Influence Clothing Choices of Sixth Grade Students." Master's thesis, University of Arkansas, 1986.

King, Dorothy W. "Clothing Preference of a Group of Six-to-Ten-Year-Old Deaf Girls in a Residential School in Knoxville, Tennessee." Master's thesis, University of Tennessee, 1961.

May, Anita. "Effects of Instruction on Clothing Conformity at the Middle School Level." Master's thesis, University of Nevada, 1982.

Mitchell, Roberta. "A Study of Mothers' Preferences of Play Clothing for Children Ages Two to Four." Master's thesis, Ohio State University, 1955.

Morris, Katherine. "Study of the Clothing Preferences and Buying Practices of 788 Junior High School Students in Austin, Texas." Master's thesis, University of Texas, 1958.

Pahopin, Jo S. "Exploratory Study of Techniques for Determining Consumer Preferences in Children's Wear." Ph.D. diss., Ohio State University, 1958.

———. "Factors which Influence the Selection of Jeans, Slacks, and Other Specified Ready-to-Wear Garments for Children." Master's thesis, Ohio State University, 1955.

Roach, Mary E. "Influence of Social Class on Clothing Practices and Orientation at Early Adolescence: A Study of Clothing Related Behavior of Seventh Grade Girls." Ph.D. diss., Michigan State University, 1960.

Simpson, Linda D. "Influences, Parental Selection Factors, and Parents' Feelings on Preschool Children's Clothing." Master's thesis, Eastern Illinois University, 1989.

Stephens, Anne C. "Clothing Purchasing Practices; A Comparison of Fourth and Seventh Grade Children." Master's thesis, Virginia Polytechnic Institute, 1982.

Terasawa, Haruko. "Relationship between Selected Factors of Fourth Grade Girls' Clothing Preferences, Their Mothers' Clothing Preferences, and the Girls' Wardrobe." Master's thesis, Pennsylvania State University, 1956.

Warning, Margaret C. "Implications of Social Class for Clothing Behavior: The Acquisition and Use of Apparel for Girls Seven, Eight and Nine Years of Age in Three Social Classes in Des Moines, Iowa." Ph.D. diss., Michigan State University, 1956.

Willett, Ann M. "Factors Influencing the Selection of Outer Apparel for Pre-School Children 2–6 Years." Master's thesis, University of Georgia, 1962.

Williams, Iona S. "Preferences of Fifty Mothers in the Selection of Designs and Fabric for Their Six to Nine Year Old Daughters." Master's thesis, Ohio State University, 1955.

Fashion leader studies include Kathleen Moore's look at teenage girls (1962), and comparisons between fashion leaders and innovators versus nonleaders by Mary Pasnak (1968) and Helen Allen (1971). Carol Meyers (1971) relates fashion leadership to social participation and "favorableness" to new styles, while Tami Hall (1993) relates fashion leadership to "social values of adolescents."

Allen, Helen H. "Adolescent Fad and Fashion Leaders Compared with Fad and Fashion Non-Leaders on Selected Personality Factors and Social Participation." Master's thesis, University of Tennessee, 1971.

Hall, Tami W. "Relationship between Fashion Leadership and Social Values of Adolescents." Master's thesis, Florida State University, 1993.

Meyers, Carol A. "Fashion Opinion Leadership and Fashion Adoption in Relation to Social Participation and Favorableness toward New Styles in University Women's Clothing." Master's thesis, Michigan State University, 1971.

Moore, Kathleen A. "Fashion Leadership Designation and Other Related Factors among a Group of Adolescent Girls." Master's thesis, Pennsylvania State University, 1962.

Pasnak, Mary F. D. "Fashion Innovators Compared with Non-Innovators on Clothing Attitudes, Self-Actualization, and Tolerance of Ambiguity." Ph.D. diss., Pennsylvania State University, 1968.

Specific Clothing Types

Specific clothing is featured in many behavioral studies of clothing and dress. Dresses and skirts were studied especially during the 1950s and 1960s. Again preferences and selection criteria predominate. Winter skirts are featured by Eleanor Gradwohl (1956) and Margaret Reed (1961). Skirt length and silhouette and skirts related to social status, 1947–1972, were studied by Barbara Goings (1971) and Mary Brigham (1988), respectively. Brigham used *Vogue* and Sears catalog advertisements as primary sources in her research. The house dress (Hamilton, 1956), the school dress (Showalter, 1959), and the party dress (Hurst, 1961) have received attention. Preference for dress designs among college students in the early 1950s was reported by Mary Lyle (1953), while preferences for the knitted (straight cut) versus the woven (bias cut) were explored by Leora Duce (1993).

Brigham, Mary E. "*Vogue* Magazine and Sears, Roebuck & Co. Catalogues: Barometers of Women's Social Position, as Seen through Skirts Advertised, 1947–1972." Master's thesis, University of Connecticut, 1988.

Duce, Leora L. G. "Consumer Preference for Dress Designs in Woven Bias or Knit Fabric." Ph.D. diss., Texas Woman's University, 1993.

Goings, Barbara D. "Changes in Fashion Preference for Skirt Length and Silhouette." Master's thesis, Iowa State University, 1971.

Gradwohl, Eleanor. "An Appraisal of the Qualities Available in Moderate-Price Winter Skirts in Light of Satisfaction Desired by College Women." Master's thesis, Ohio State University, 1956.

Hamilton, Coradel. "Criteria Used by Homemakers Purchasing Low-Priced, Cotton House Dresses in Two Lafayette, Indiana, Stores." Ph.D. diss., Purdue University, 1956.

Hartung, Sara J. "Problems of the Young Teenage Girl in Buying Ready-Made Skirts and Dresses." Master's thesis, Ohio State University, 1959.

Hurst, Marie J. "Comparison of Mothers' and Daughters' Preferences and Areas of Agreement and Disagreement in the Choice of a Dress-Up or Party Dress." Master's thesis, Ohio State University, 1961.

Lyle, Mary F. "College Students' Choice of Dress Designs When Matched to People's Faces and Drawings of Those Faces." Master's thesis, Iowa State College, 1953.

Miller, Martha S. "Comparison of Mother's and Daughter's Values Concerning the Relative Importance of Certain Components of Satisfaction with School Dresses." Master's thesis, Cornell University, 1959.

Reed, Margaret D. "Study of the Influences Affecting the Selection of Winter Skirts by Certain College Freshman Women." Master's thesis, Michigan State University, 1961.

Rowland, Rachel. "Development of an Instrument for Determining Women's Attitudes toward Dresses of a Specified Type." Master's thesis, Ohio State University, 1958.

Showalter, Martha. "A Comparison of Mother's and Daughter's Values Concerning the Relative Importance of Certain Components of Satisfaction with School Dresses." Master's thesis, Cornell University, 1959.

Stoten, Mary R. "Influence of Selected Factors in Choice of Cotton Daytime Dresses." Master's thesis. Purdue University, 1961.

Outerwear preferences were reported by Dorma Johnson (1954) and Dorothy Runbeck (1956). Suit and coat preferences for college women were studied by Minnie Pender (1962). Product attributes and sources used in the decision to purchase parkas were studied by Roxanne Stell (1983). A market analysis for women's suiting in southern states was conducted by Anne Redwine (1991). The sweater is represented by several theses. Kay Gipson (1986) and Jo Anne Surerus (1989) cover label issues—"country-of-origin" and "Crafted with Pride in USA"—while Charlotte Swanson (1959), Bliss Finlayson (1959), and Shari Stout (1988) cover satisfaction and selection concerns.

Blouses, shoes, and underwear also receive attention. Labeling preferences are seen in Mary Brown's work in 1959 on blouses. Shoes selection was reported by Virginia Foster and Edna Akers in 1958 and by Angelene Phillips in 1961. The white slip purchased by college women was studied by Lois Korslund in 1956, and the relationship between self-esteem and underwear selection was researched by Jin-kook Lee in 1989.

Behavioral studies on clothing for the specific period of pregnancy and for sports appear as student interests. Maternity career clothing and the issues of self-esteem/worth and body image appear in research by Alison Pikin (1989), Margaret Keeney (1990), and Janine Manley (1991). Among the few theses concentrating on sportswear, Judith Leslie (1985) related the sports fashions themselves to the changing role of women, 1850–1920, and Anne Hieronymus (1955) and Norma Compton (1957) considered preferences.

Akers, Edna. "An Analysis of Factors Contributing to the Selection, Purchase and Use of Women's Shoes." Master's thesis, Ohio State University, 1958.

Brown, Mary L. "Labeling Preferences of Consumers of Blouses." Master's thesis, Iowa State University, 1959.

Cochran, Mary F. "Satisfactions and Dissatisfactions Experience with Blouses by Home Economics Students and Home Economists." Master's thesis, Ohio State University, 1956.

Compton, Norma H. "Factors Influencing Female Customers' Choices of Blouses, Sweaters, Skirts and Slacks in the Junior Sized Sportswear Department of a Washington, D.C. Specialty Store." Master's thesis, University of Maryland, 1957.

Finlayson, Bliss B. "Investigation of Consumer Motivation in the Selection of Sweaters as Related to General Personal Values." Master's thesis, Cornell University, 1959.

Foster, Virginia B. "Criteria Used by College Girls in the Selection of Shoes." Master's thesis, Ohio State University, 1958.

Gipson, Kay G. "Importance of Country-of-Origin at Point of Purchase in Women's Decisions to Purchase Sweaters." Master's thesis, Oregon State University, 1986.

Greer, Rebecca W. "Apparel-Buying Practices of Pregnant Women and Their Reported Satisfaction with Available Maternity Wear." Ph.D. diss., Texas Woman's University, 1988.

Hieronymus, Anne K. "Women's Preferences in Certain Active Sportwear in Sizes 18, 20, 40, and 42." Master's thesis, Colorado A&M College, 1955.

Horning, Priscilla. "Observed Activity of Women Shopping for Blouses." Master's thesis, Cornell University, 1961.

Johnson, Dorma L. "Practices of Corvallis High School Graduates in Selecting Women's Outer Garments as a Basis for High School and Adult Clothing Courses." Master's thesis, Oregon State University, 1954.

Keeney, Margaret A. "Body Image, Maternal Attitudes, and Appearance Management in Pregnancy." Master's thesis, Ohio State University, 1990.

Korslund, Lois N. "Preference and Buying Practices among College Women for Selected White Slips." Master's thesis, Michigan State University, 1956.

Lee, Jin-kook. "Relationship between One's Self-Esteem and Evaluative Criteria in Underwear Selection." Master's thesis, Ohio State University, 1989.

Leslie, Judith E. "Sports Fashions as a Reflection of the Changing Role of American Women in Society from 1850 to 1920" (Riding Habits, Swim Wear, Bicycle, Golf, Tennis Dresses). Ph.D. diss., University of North Carolina, 1985.

Manley, Janine W. "Self-Worth, Body Cathexis, and Satisfaction with Available Selection for Those Who Wear Different-Size Maternity Clothing." Ph.D. diss., Virginia Polytechnic Institute and State University, 1991.

Miller, Kimberly A. "Clothing Preferences for Maternity Career Apparel and Its Relationship to Perceived Job Effectiveness." Master's thesis, Louisiana State University, 1985.

Pender, Minnie L. "Preferences and Practices in the Purchase of Coats and Suits by Two Selected Groups of Women at Texas College, Tyler Texas." Master's thesis, University of Texas, 1962.

Phillips, Angelene C. "Consumer's Preferences and Satisfactions in the Selection, Purchase, and Utilization of Shoes for Boys, Age Ten and Eleven Years." Master's thesis, Ohio State University, 1961.

Pipkin, Alison L. "Store Patronage of Pregnant Consumers: Effects of Shopping Motivations, Career Orientation, and Choice Set Formation." Master's thesis, Louisiana State University, 1989.

Redwine, Ann E. "Women's Suiting: A Market Study of Warm-Weather States." Master's thesis, Auburn University, 1991.

Runbeck, Dorothy C. "Values Given Importance in the Selection of Outer Garments by a Random Sample of Stephens College Women." Master's thesis, Kansas State College, 1956.

Stell, Roxanne. "Product Attributes and Informal Sources Preferred in the Purchase Decisions for a Parka." Master's thesis, Oklahoma State University, 1983.

Stout, Shari A. "Ramie/Cotton and Cotton Sweaters: An Exploration of Wearer Satisfaction." Master's thesis, Iowa State University, 1988.

Surerus, Jo Anne M. "Effect of 'Crafted with Pride in the USA' Cues on Evaluations of Sweaters Made in the USA, a Developed Country, and a Developing Country." Master's thesis, Oregon State University, 1989.

Swanson, Charlotte L. "Interrelationships among Factors Related to Satisfaction in Sweaters." Master's thesis, Cornell University, 1959.

Consumer Issues

The following discussion covers selected theses that focus on typical consumer issues and those of a popular nature. Consumer studies often focus on the actual expenditures related to given factors or the impact of the clothing itself on the purchase. Expenditures were studied by Norma Walker in relation to self-actualization (1968); to socioeconomic status (Flint, 1973); to lifestyle of black and white women (Edmonds, 1979); and in relation to race (Hodges, 1982). Looking at the clothing itself, Felicia Cornwell (1959) studied preference for natural versus synthetic fabrics in clothing; Rosalie Bivin (1970), analyzed workmanship; price and scarcity as influences on the value of fashions were researched by George Szybillo (1973); and clothing attributes as a concern for the consumer versus the retail buyer were reported by D. White (1976). Joyce Johnson presented a different perspective in her 1989 study of users and nonusers of customized clothing services.

Bivin, Rosalie J. "An Investigation of Consumer Appraisal of Workmanship in Ready-to-Wear Street Dresses as Related to Level of Training in Clothing Construction." Masters' thesis, University of Missouri, 1970.

Cornwell, Felicia M. "Use and Preference for Natural and Man-Made Fibers in Clothing by a Selected Group of Homemakers in Christiansburg, Virginia." Master's thesis, Virginia Polytechnic Institute, 1959.

Edmonds, Linda L. "Clothing Buying Practices and Life Style Differentials between Employed Black and White Women." Ph.D. diss., Virginia Polytechnic Institute, 1979.

Flint, M. Elaine S. "Clothing Expenditures as Related to Socio-Economic Status and Other Selected Family Characteristics." Ph.D. diss., Pennsylvania State University, 1973.

Hodges, Lloyd C. "Clothing and Race; An Examination of the Effects of Race on Consumption." Ph.D. diss., University of Illinois, 1982.

Johnson, Joyce S. "Profiles of Users and Non-Users of Customized Clothing Services." Master's thesis, Iowa State University, 1989.

Szybillo, George J. "Effects of Price and Scarcity on the Valuation of Fashions by Fashion Opinion Leaders and Nonopinion Leaders." Ph.D. diss., Purdue University, 1973.

Walker, Norma P. "Clothing Expenditures as Related to Selected Values, Self-Actualization, and Buying Practices: An Exploratory Study." Ph.D. diss., Pennsylvania State University, 1968.

White, D. Douglass. "Importance of Selected Clothing Attributes to Consumers Compared to Retail Buyers' Perception of This Importance." Ph.D. diss., Pennsylvania State University, 1976.

Related to these studies of consumerism is the role that color plays in choice and why. Studies here cover personality issues, first impressions, attraction, and status and include men, women, preschool children, and the elderly. One historical study (Thackeray, 1960) discusses "Factors Affecting Changes in Color of Men's Dress in France from the 16th through the 19th Centuries," which may provide insights on color used in American clothes as well.

Bowser, Debra J. "Clothing Color Preferences of the Elderly in Washington County, Arkansas." Master's thesis, University of Arkansas, 1985.

Duntley, Linda K. "Color of Dress as It Relates to First Impressions of Personality Traits." Master's thesis, San Francisco State University, 1981.

Elliott, Shirley D. "Availability on the Market of Colors Preferred by High School and Freshman College Girls." Master's thesis, Texas Woman's University, 1962.

Lopez, Nylda N. "Relationship among Color Preferences, the Use of Color in Dress, and Extroversion and Introversion." Master's thesis, Pennsylvania State University, 1958.

McGruder, Diana Lynn. "Clothing Color Preferences of Preschool Children Attending the New School, Fayetteville, Arkansas." Master's thesis, University of Arkansas, 1984.

Reynolds, Jeannette. "Choice of Color for Apparel by High School and College

Students in Relation to Academic Level and Family Socio-Economic Status.''
Master's thesis, Texas Woman's University, 1962.

Smith, Loretta J. H. "Comparison of Color Preferences for Apparel with Person-
ality Types, Body Types, Complexion Types and Eye Coloring of High
School and University Freshman Girls." Master's thesis, Texas Woman's
University, 1962.

Thackeray, Renee. "Factors Affecting Changes in Color of Men's Dress in France
from the 16th through the 19th Centuries." Master's thesis, Oregon State
University, 1960.

Yener, Barbara A. V. "Influence of Clothing Color on Attraction and Impression
Formation." Ph.D. diss., Purdue University, 1982.

One interesting specific consumer interest is in brand names. Issues of
brand name awareness, selection, and consumer attitude predominate,
and again we see the "Crafted with Pride in USA" issue and country-of-
origin label reappear with work by Annette Devitt (1985), Janet Khachaturian (1988), and Jo Anne Surerus (1989). "The Effect of Music in
Fashion Video Advertisements on Attitudes toward Apparel Brand" by
Karen Hennessy in 1989 reflects popular culture influences, while brand-
name casual apparel was the focus for Younhwa Chang in 1989. Even
children's demand for the brand name is studied (McCormick, 1988),
leading to a deeper reflection on American culture than simply how we
choose our clothing.

Calandro, Donna F. "Study of Consumers' Attitudes toward Price, Brand and
Trade Names, and Time of Care of Garments." Master's thesis, Louisiana
State University, 1982.

Chang, Younhwa. "Relative Importance of Attitudinal versus Normative Influence
Associated with Purchase of Brand Name Casual Apparel." Ph.D. diss., Ohio
State University, 1989.

Devitt, Annette. "Country of Origin Important Rating for Apparel: Effects of a
Crafted with Pride Educational Message." Master's thesis, Ohio State University, 1985.

Hennessy, Karen E. "Effect of Music in Fashion Video Advertisements on Attitudes
toward Apparel Brand." Master's thesis, Oregon State University, 1989.

Khachaturian, Janet L. "Influence of Country of Origin on Consumer Perception
of Store and Brand Quality." Master's thesis, University of Illinois, 1988.

McCormick, Kari L. "Incidence of Demand for Brand Name Clothing among a
Selected Group of Children." Master's thesis, Lamar University, 1988.

Penalis, Frances M. "Self-Esteem and Conformity in Clothing of Adolescent Girls
as Reflected by Brand Name Awareness and Preference." Ed.D. thesis,
Pennsylvania State University, 1968.

Surerus, Jo Anne M. "The Effect of Crafted with Pride in the USA Cues on Evaluations of Sweaters Made in the USA, A Developed Country, and A Developing Country." Master's thesis, Oregon State University, 1989.

White, Gerry S. "Relationship of the Knowledge and Use of Brand-Named Clothing with Certain Needs and Clothing Behaviors of a Selected Group of
College Women." Master's thesis, University of Tennessee, 1970.

Home sewing and sewers as a popular activity are represented by theses that also show how consumption issues seem to predominate as exemplified by Barbara Morales's (1989) work on the reasons for home sewing related to equipment owned. Another popular practice, of using hand-me-downs or second-hand clothing has been studied by Joan Hickman (1970), Susan Richardson (1981), and Phoebe Morrow (1986).

Baum, Shelley J. "Sources of Information Used and Information Sought by Southeast Idaho Home Sewers in Their Selection of Fabrics with Which They Are Familiar." Master's thesis, Utah State University, 1988.

Caldwell, Lark F. "Home Sewers' Clothing Values and Reasons for Sewing: A Comparison of Retail Fabric Customers." Ph.D. diss., Texas Woman's University, 1986.

Formanek, Janet L. "Buying Habits of Women Who Sew." Master's thesis, California State University, 1977.

Hickman, Joan T. "Factors Related to Acceptance or Rejection of Second-Owner Clothing for Preschool Children." Master's thesis, University of Missouri, 1970.

Morales, Barbara A. "Home Sewers: Reasons for Sewing, Sources of New Home Sewing Information, and Items Sewn in Relationship to Equipment Owned." Master's thesis, University of Idaho, 1989.

Morrow, Phoebe M. "Purchasers and Consignors of Secondhand Clothing in Consignment Stores." Master's thesis, Virginia Polytechnic Institute, 1986.

Richardson, Susan O. "Consumers of Used Clothing." Master's thesis, Oregon State University, 1981.

Shirley, Jeanne C. "Home Sewing: Procedures and Practices Which Contribute to Consumer Satisfaction." Master's thesis, University of Oklahoma, 1977.

Stewart, Marian G. "Study of the Clothing Practices of the White High School Girls in Copiah County, Mississippi: A Comparison of Buyer, Buyer Maker, and Maker Families." Master's thesis, Mississippi Southern College, 1955.

Wilgus, Virginia R. "Comparative Study of Selected Characteristics and Practices of Clothing Buyers, Buyer-Makers, and Makers in the Home Demonstration Clubs of Jones County, Mississippi, as of 1954." Master's thesis, Mississippi Southern College, 1955.

Williams, Joan. "Factors Influencing the Selection of Patterns by Home Sewers." Master's thesis, Cornell University, 1960.

York, Marjorie O. "Practices and Opinions of a Select Group of Homemakers with Regard to Home Sewing." Master's thesis, Oklahoma State University, 1961.

Culture

Studies where "culture" terminology is used or where cultural practice or experience seems to predominate include a variety of perspectives. Clothing fads and acceptance or rejection of some popular clothes, studied by Olive Perkins (1958), cross-cultural "communicative aspects" by Ruth Sherlock (1961), and "cultural influences" on clothing of "foreign" college women by Kathryn Orme (1961) represent some of the earlier work. Attitudes toward foreign influences on American dress around the time of the American Revolution by Saundra Steadman (1974) purport to place "dress of the late 18th century into the broader context of the total culture."[23] Fashion awareness related to popular culture is studied by Judith Orkus (1971) and Janice Patterson (1978). The practice of dressing for the occasion, 1770–1910, is explored by Marguerite Connolly (1987). Changes in American fashion, work, and culture from 1930 to 1955, a study of the fashion elite and their power and influence, were researched by Victoria Billings (1990). The common practice of gift giving, especially the risks perceived by husbands and wives in giving clothing gifts was highlighted by Lena Horne (1991). A biographical study was quite a departure; Susan Williams (1992) wrote about Alice Morse Earle, author of *Two Centuries of Costume in America, 1620–1820* (1903). Williams indicates that through her "domestic history" writings, Earle showed how clothing, among other material and social factors, was an "important vehicle for social and cultural continuity."[24] Also in the 1990s the role of dress in American Indian and white relations as a "symbol of contending cultures" was researched for the period 1834–1862 by David Trayte.

Billings, Victoria C. "Altered Forever: A Women's Elite and the Transformation of American Fashion Work and Culture, 1930–1955." Ph.D. diss., University of California, Los Angeles, 1990.

Connolly, Marguerite A. "Dressing for the Occasion: The Differentiation of Women's Costume in America, 1770–1910." Master's thesis, University of Delaware, 1987.

Horne, Lena. "Risks Perceived by Husbands and Wives in Giving Clothing Gifts within the Family." Ph.D. diss., Iowa State University, 1991.

Orkus, Judith O. "Fashion Awareness of Men as Related to Aspects of the Popular Culture." Thesis (not specified), Pennsylvania State University, 1971.

Orme, Kathryn. "Cultural Influence on Clothing Practices of Foreign Women at Oregon State University." Master's thesis, Oregon State University, 1961.

Patterson, Janice L. "Fashion Awareness as Related to Aspects of the Popular Culture." Master's thesis, Pennsylvania State University, 1978.

Perkins, Olive. "Investigation of the Clothing Fads and Fashions of a Group of Freshman College Women and the Reasons for Accepting or Rejecting Some Popular Clothes." Master's thesis, Cornell University, 1958.

Sherlock, Ruth. "Cross-Cultural Study of the Communicative Aspect of Clothing." Master's thesis, Cornell University, 1961.

Steadman, Saundra N. "Investigation of American Attitudes toward Foreign Influences on American Dress during and Immediately following the American Revolution." Master's thesis, Cornell University, 1974.

Trayte, David J. "The Role of Dress in Eastern Dakota and White Interaction, 1834–1862: A Symbol in Contending Cultures." Ph.D. diss., University of Minnesota, 1993.

Williams, Susan R. "In the Garden of New England: Alice Morse Earle and the History of Domestic Life." Ph.D. diss., University of Delaware, 1992.

The last selection of theses is concerned with the media, both print and electronic, as a specific popular cultural phenomenon. One of its major impacts, the eventual purchase of clothing and fashion or other items, is of critical importance to a consumer-oriented society where livelihoods and jobs depend on the collective and continual purchase of goods. Its use of and impact on clothing and fashion can be seen in a number of student projects. Several analyze the media and their use of clothing or fashion—for example, advertising trends related to social changes reflected in fashion (Noel, 1960), apparel's effects on retail television commercials (Harp, 1982), a cultural analysis of the Calvin Klein advertising campaigns (Clark, 1988), MTV ideology, where "clothing fetishism"[25] can appear (Wilson, 1992), and "a Marxist feminist analysis" of catalogs for "tall and large women" (Coulter, 1994), which focuses on "rhetoric." Jane Funderburk (1994) uses *New York Times* advertisements to study ready-to-wear women's clothes, 1865–1914.

Effects on the consumer are reflected for print media in fashion advertising (Ruiz, 1982; Gardner, 1993), fashion magazines (Krugs, 1991), and catalogs (Pietsch, Simabur and Kim, all 1991; Yang, 1995). Cartoons were used to analyze changes in the masculine image in the United States from 1880–1910 (Paoletti, 1980). Television studies include cable television shopping channels and buying behavior (Leggett, 1990) and its impact on low-income eleventh-grade girls (Mack-Keeles, 1986).

Clark, Lori J. "A Cultural Analysis of the Calvin Klein Advertising Campaigns." Master's thesis, University of Utah, 1988.

Coulter, Linda S. "The Rhetoric of Deviance; A Marxist Feminist Analysis of Mail-order Clothing Catalogs for Tall and Large Women." Master's thesis, Wichita State University, 1994.

Funderburk, Jane A. U. "The Development of Women's Ready-to-Wear, 1865 to 1914: Based on *New York Times* Advertisements." Ph.D. diss., University of Maryland, 1994.

Gardner, Linda V. "Consumer Attitudes toward Fashion Advertising and Factors That Make Fashion Advertisements Appealing or Offensive." Ph.D. diss., Texas Woman's University, 1993.

Harp, Shelley S. "Effect of Apparel on Retail Television Commercials." Ph.D. diss., Texas Woman's University, 1982.

Kim, Youn-Kyung. "Professional Women's Catalog Use and Its Relationships with Their Clothing Involvement and Lifestyle." Ph.D. diss., University of North Carolina, 1991.

Krugs, Melissa I. "Perceived Value of Fashion Magazines versus Other Types of Fashion Information Sources by Florida State University Women Graduates." Master's thesis, Florida State University, 1991.

Leggett, Liza. "An Analysis of Fashion Opinion Leadership as an Indicator of

Buying Behavior among Subscribers of Cable Television Shopping Channels." Master's thesis, Texas Tech University, 1990.

Lewis, Martha A. "Income, Interpersonal, and Media Influences on the Clothing Purchases of Female Adolescent Consumers." Ph.D. diss., University of Tennessee, 1991.

Mack-Keeles, Vermell. "Influence of Television on Eleventh Grade Low-Income Black Girls' Clothing Practices." Master's thesis, San Francisco State University, 1986.

Noel, Juanita M. "Nature of Advertising Trends in Relation to Changing Social Patterns as Emphasized in Fashion." Ph.D. diss., New York University, 1960.

Paoletti, Jo B. "Changes in the Masculine Image in the United States, 1880–1910: A Content Analysis of Popular Humor about Dress." Ph.D. diss., University of Maryland, 1980.

Pietsch, Jeanine M. "Market Segmentation of Petite Catalog Shoppers: Satisfaction and Shopping Behavior." Master's thesis, Colorado State University, 1991.

Ruiz, Joyce. "Teenage Girl's Attitudes toward Fashion Advertising." Master's thesis, North Texas State University, 1982.

Simabur, Djas W. "Effect of Country of Origin, Warranty, and Mail Order Image on Purchase of Apparel Products." Master's thesis, University of Alabama, 1991.

Wilson, Janelle L. "MTV Ideology: Rocking to a Different Beat?" Master's thesis, Western Michigan University, 1992.

Yang, Cheng-Yuan Y. "Development of a Scale to Measure Perceived Risk in Apparel Catalog Shopping." Master's thesis, Florida State University, 1995.

6

Dictionaries

Many monographs provide convenient glossaries of specialized terms for the topic under discussion; examples are noted in the index under "glossaries." The general English-language dictionaries, especially those that are unabridged, contain many costume, clothing, and fashion words. The classic *Oxford English Dictionary (OED)* does much more. It not only provides definitions, etymology, and pronunciation but also lists quotations from the literature chronologically, illustrating how the words have been used and how their meanings have changed over time. Each quotation is documented, with most sources listed in the bibliography at the end of the dictionary. For example, the information for the word *apron* includes quotations dating from 1307 to 1883. Additional terms are *aproned, aproneer, aproner, apronful, apronless,* and *apron-string.* A textile example is the word *tiffany,* containing quotations about the thin silk from 1601 to 1882. Electronic access to the 1989 edition is available via CD-ROM. The best discussion and bibliography of English-language and other language dictionaries is found in Sheehy's *Guide to Reference Books* (1986, with supplement in 1992).

"Language Dictionaries." In *Guide to Reference Books,* 146–208. Edited by Eugene P. Sheehy. 10th ed. Chicago: American Library Association, 1986.

———. In *Guide to Reference Books, Covering Materials from 1985–1990,* 39–54. Edited by Robert Balay, and E. P. Sheehy. Supplement to the 10th ed. Chicago: American Library Association, 1992.

Oxford English Dictionary. Prepared by J. A. Simpson and E. S. C. Weiner. 2d ed. Oxford: Clarendon Press, 1989. 20v. (1st ed. 1933. 12v. and supplement). Supplemented by: *Oxford English Dictionary Additions Series* v.1–2, 1993–. Biennial. Helpful: *A User's Guide to the Oxford English Dictionary.* Donna L. Berg. Oxford: Oxford University Press, 1991. 71p. For electronic access see: *OED2 on CD-ROM.* Oxford: Oxford University Press, 1992.

COSTUME, FASHION, CLOTHING, AND DRESS

To complement the *OED* and other dictionaries for English and other languages, specific costume, clothing, and fashion dictionaries are available. Obviously date of publication affects the word content, although some contemporary dictionaries concentrate on historical terminology. Alice M. Earle (1894) provided an early perspective with her *Costume of Colonial Times,* containing information and definitions predicated on data from letters, wills, newspapers, and other eighteenth-century primary sources. Costume and textile terms are included, and price information is contained in some entries. For the twentieth century several major contributors emerge: Mary B. Picken's *Language of Fashion* (1939) and *Fashion Dictionary* (1957); Cecil W. Cunnington, Phyllis Cunnington, and Charles Beard's *Dictionary of English Costume* (1960); Ruth T. Wilcox's *Dictionary of Costume* (1969, with bibliography) and Charlotte M. Calasibetta's *Fairchild's Dictionary of Fashion* (1975) and *Essential Terms of Fashion;* (1986). Several jewelry dictionaries (Mason, 1973; Newman, 1981; Robins, 1981) are noted, since jewelry is a major costume accessory.

Baclawski, Karen. *The Guide to Historical Costume.* New York: Drama Book Publishers, 1995. 239p.

Buck, Anne, Madeleine Delpierre, and Leonie von Wilckens. "Vocabulary of Basic Terms for Cataloguing Costume/Vocabulaire de Base pour les Fichiers de Costume." Reprinted from *Waffen und Kostumkunde* (1982): 119–151. English, French, and German vocabulary.

Calasibetta, Charlotte M. *Essential Terms of Fashion: A Collection of Definitions.* New York: Fairchild, 1986. 244p.

———. *Fairchild's Dictionary of Fashion.* New York: Fairchild, 1975. 693p. (2d ed., 1988. 749p.)

Clothing Terms and Definitions. 3d ed. London: Clothing & Footwear Institute, 1983. 32p.

Cunnington, Cecil W., Phyllis Cunnington, and Charles Beard. *A Dictionary of English Costume.* Philadelphia: DuFour Editions, 1960. 281p. Reprint, New York: Barnes & Noble, 1968; London: A&C Black, 1976. 284p. (includes a lace glossary)

Davies, Stephanie C. *Costume Language: A Dictionary of Dress Terms.* Malvern, England: Cressrelles, 1994. 183p.

Earle, Alice M. *Costume of Colonial Times.* New York: Charles Scribner's Sons, 1894. 264p.

Ironside, Janey. *A Fashion Alphabet.* London: Joseph, 1968. 262p.

McDowell, Colin. *McDowell's Directory of Twentieth Century Fashion.* 2d rev. ed. London: Muller, 1987. 320p.

Mason, Anita. *An Illustrated Dictionary of Jewellery.* Reading: Osprey Publishing, 1973. 390p.

Newman, Harold. *An Illustrated Dictionary of Jewelry.* New York: Thames and Hudson, 1981. 336p.

Picken, Mary B. *The Language of Fashion: A Dictionary and Digest of Fabric, Sewing and Dress.* New York: Funk & Wagnalls, 1939. 175p. Includes line drawings.

———. *The Fashion Dictionary: Fabric, Sewing, and Dress as Expressed in the Language of Fashion.* New York: Funk & Wagnalls, 1957. 397p. (based on her 1939 work) (Revised and enlarged 1975. 434p.)

Project Access: Clothing and Sewing Vocabulary, Dictionary. Springfield, IL: Illinois State Board of Education, Department of Adult, Vocational, and Technical Education, Research and Development Section, 1982. [19] leaves.

Roberts, Thelma A. *Dictionary of Style Terms (As Applied to the Present Mode).* New York: Fairchild News Service, 1929. 22p.

Robins, Bill. *An A–Z of Gems and Jewelry.* New York: Arco, 1981. 96p.

Takamura, Zeshu. *Fashion with Style: Ladies' Fashion Items.* Tokyo: Graphic-Sha, 1993. 163p.

Wilcox, Ruth T. *The Dictionary of Costume.* New York: Scribner's, 1969. 406p. Reprint, London: Batsford, 1970; NY: Macmillan, 1986, 1987; London: Batsford, 1992.

TEXTILES AND EMBROIDERY DICTIONARIES

Specialized dictionaries can be located using library collections by adding the word(s) *dictionary* or *dictionaries* or *glossary* or *glossaries* to a subject search of the catalog. Dictionaries on the subjects of textiles and needlework or embroidery might need to be consulted when studying the subject of costume or fashion. The following selection of textile dictionaries or glossaries represents works by Louis Harmuth for Fairchild in 1920 to the 1992 *Encyclopedia of Textiles* by Judith Jerde published in honor of the bicentennial of the "founding in 1792 of the first cotton mill in the United States . . . in Pawtucket, Rhode Island."

Textiles

"Dictionary of Textile Terms." In *Encyclopedia of Textiles,* 512–601. By the Editors of American Fabrics and Fashions Magazine. 3d ed. Englewood Cliffs, NJ: Prentice-Hall, 1980. 636p.

Fairchild's Dictionary of Textiles. Edited by Isabel B. Wingate. Rev. ed. New York: Fairchild, 1967. 662p.

"Glossary." In *The New Textiles: Trends and Traditions,* By Chloe Colchester, 188–189. New York: Rizzoli, 1991. 192p.

Harmuth, Louis. *Dictionary of Textiles.* 2d enl. ed. New York: Fairchild Publishing Co., 1920. 222p.

Jerde, Judith. *Encyclopedia of Textiles.* New York: Facts on File, 1992. 260p. Bibl.

Klapper, Marvin. *Fabric Almanac.* 2d ed. New York: Fairchild Publications, 1971. 191p.

Koester, Ardis W. *Fashion Terms: Apparel Fabric Glossary.* Corvallis, OR: Oregon State University Extension Service, 1992. [8]p.

Linton, George E. *Modern Textile and Apparel Dictionary.* 4th rev. enl. ed. Plainfield, NJ: Textile Book Service, 1973. 716p.

Montgomery, Florence M. *Textiles in America: 1650–1870. A Dictionary Based on Original Documents, Prints and Paintings, Commercial Records, American Merchants' Papers, Shopkeepers' Advertisements, and Pattern Books with Original Swatches of Cloth.* New York: W. W. Norton & Co., 1984. 412p.

Embroidery

Caulfield, Sophia F. A., and Blanche C. Saward. *The Dictionary of Needlework.* 2d ed. London: L. Upcott Gill, 1887. 3v. 535p. Reprint, *Encyclopedia of Victorian Needlework.* New York: Dover, 1972. 2v. 697p.

Clabburn, Pamela, and Helene Von Rosenstiel. *The Needleworker's Dictionary.* New York: Morrow, 1976. 296p. Bibl.

"Glossary." In *Plain and Fancy: American Women and Their Needlework, 1700–1850,* 221–234. By Susan B. Swan, New York: Holt, Rinehart and Winston, 1977. 240p. Bibl.

Glossary of Needlework and Textile Terms. Pittsburgh, PA: Center for the History of American Needlework, 1975. 24p.

Swift, Gay. *The Batsford Encyclopedia of Embroidery Techniques.* London: Batsford, 1984. 240p.

Thomas, Mary. *Mary Thomas's Dictionary of Embroidery Stitches.* London: Hodder & Staughton, 1934. 234p. (New ed. by Jan Eaton. 1989. 208p.)

BIOGRAPHICAL DICTIONARIES AND RELATED SOURCES

People involved with the fashion industry are featured in specific biographical dictionaries or directories, such as *The Fashion Guide, An International Designers Directory;* Fairchild's *Who's Who in Fashion,* currently written by Ann Stegemeyer and containing, in the 1996 edition, an appendix listing "Council of Fashion Designers of America (CFDA) Awards," "Coty American Fashion Critics' Awards," and "Neiman Marcus Awards"; *Who's Who in Fashion,* published in Zurich (1982), containing "prominent personalities in the fields of fashion, beauty and jewelry"; and *Who's Who in Designing: America's Foremost Clothing Designers* (of men's fashions) produced in 1986 as a vocational guidance source. The major fashion dictionary by Charlotte Calasibetta contains an excellent feature,

"Fashion Designers," including "Designer Portraits" and "Designer Styles."

In addition to these specialized biographical dictionaries and directories, several general biographical sources can be used, such as *Current Biography*, which provides information and photographs for people prominent in the news, and the *Biography Index*, which indexes books and articles on Americans for the most part; alphabetically arranged by individual name, there is also an index by occupation or profession. The *Guide to Reference Books* contains a "Biography" section fully describing biographical sources arranged by country.

More specific biographical material can be located by consulting several monographs. In M. D. C. Crawford's *The Ways of Fashion*, (1941), many people are mentioned, and their contributions to fashion, especially during World War II are noted. Many designers are included in chapter 4, "La Grande Couture," which has sections on millinery and fabrics. Another interesting feature is the chapter on museums, where the people and institutions involved in the first connections between museum collections and fashion designers are chronicled. In 1985 Caroline Milbank's glossy production, *Couture: The Great Designers*, was published. It provides biographical information with photographs and illustrations of the designers' work. Designers are grouped as follows: "The Founders," "Artists," "Purists," "Entertainers," "Extravagants," "Architects," and "The Realists." An index and an extensive bibliography conclude the volume. In 1985 Brenda Person wrote "Black Fashion Designers in the United States, 1945 through 1981," while in 1995 Richard Martin produced *Contemporary Fashion*, about designers and fashion houses after the end of World War II. Broadway costume designers received attention from Bobbi Owen in 1987. She researched biographical data and Broadway credit information for the period 1915–1985, thus providing convenient reference to this difficult-to-locate information.

Membership directories of associations and organizations provide names and addresses and often areas of interest and specialization of their members. Corporate and institution members may be listed as well. One example is the Costume Society of America's *Membership Directory*, which provides personal data as well as indexes for geographical area and professional affiliation plus other society information. The availability of other membership directories can be ascertained by consulting the *Encyclopedia of Associations*, a standard reference source.

"Biography." In *Guide to Reference Books*, 279–313. Edited by Eugene P. Sheehy. 10th ed. Chicago: American Library Association, 1986.

———. In *Guide to Reference Books, Covering Materials from 1985–1990*, 72–81. Edited by Robert Balay and E. P. Sheehy. Supplement to the 10th ed. Chicago: American Library Association, 1992.

Biography Index. v.1, 1946/1949–. New York: H. W. Wilson Co., 1949–. Quarterly, annual cumulation.

Calasibetta, Charlotte M. "Fashion Designers." In *Fairchild's Dictionary of Fashion,* 619–749. 2d ed. New York: Fairchild Publications, 1988. 749p.

Costume Society of America. *1995–1996 Membership Directory: The Costume Society of America.* Earleville, MD: The Society, 1995. 79p. Published periodically.

Crawford, M. D. C. *The Ways of Fashion.* New York: G. P. Putnam's Sons, 1941. 320p.

Current Biography. v.1, 1940–. New York: H. W. Wilson Co., 1940–. Monthly except December, annual cumulation. Cumulative index available for 1940–1990.

Encyclopedia of Associations. 28th ed. 1994. Detroit: Gale Research, 1993. 2v. in 4. Membership list availability is noted.

The Fashion Guide, 1994: International Designer Directory. New York: Fashion Guide International, 1994. 680p.

Martin, Richard. *Contemporary Fashion.* New York: St. James Press, 1995. 575p.

Milbank, Caroline R. *Couture: The Great Designers.* New York: Stewart, Tabori & Chang, 1985. 432p.

Owen, Bobbi. *Costume Design on Broadway: Designers and Their Credits, 1915–1985.* Westport, CT: Greenwood Press, 1987. 254p.

Person, Brenda E. "Black Fashion Designers in the United States, 1945 through 1981." Master's thesis, Florida State University, 1985.

Stegemeyer, Anne. *Who's Who in Fashion.* New York: Fairchild Publications, 1980. 179p. Bibl. Continuation of work by Josephine J. Watkins.

———. 2d ed. 1988. 243p. Bibl.

———. 3d ed. New York: Fairchild Publications, 1996. 300p. Bibl.

———. *Who's Who in Fashion.* 2d ed. New York: Fairchild Fashion & Merchandising Group, 1992. 61p.

Watkins, Josephine E. *Who's Who in Fashion.* 1st ed. rev. New York: Fairchild Publications, 1975. 295p.

Who's Who in Designing: America's Foremost Clothing Designers. New York: Apparel Institute, 1986. 71p. List of men's fashion designers.

Who's Who in Fashion. Edited by Karl Strute and Theodor Doelken. Zurich: Who's Who, the International Red Series Verlag GmbH, 1982. 3v in 2.

7

Specialized Bibliographies

GENERAL

Many of the special bibliographies on costume, clothing, and fashion topics are found in the monographic literature as lists of reference sources or bibliographies of materials used by the authors in their research. Many of these are noted in the subject index under "bibliographies." Of course, periodical articles also may contain excellent bibliographies. This chapter reviews separately published bibliographies on costume, clothing, and fashion. A major index to bibliographies, the *Bibliographic Index* (1937–), is published three times a year by the H. W. Wilson Company. Its indexing of substantial bibliographies (containing fifty or more citations) in both monographs and periodical articles allows the user to create a good picture of work that has been done on a particular subject. Electronic databases can be used to limit a subject search to bibliographies, and most databases also indicate the presence of a bibliography, often giving page numbers or number of citations, or both.

Interest in producing bibliographies on the subject of costume and fashion has been demonstrated continually during the twentieth century. Many bibliographies have been created due to interests of librarians and educators. Paul Nystrom's *Bibliography on Fashion* (1932) preceded two major works, the *Costume Index* (1937, supplement 1939) by Isabel Monro and the *Bibliography of Costume* (1939) by Hilaire and Meyer Hiler. While the Hiler volume covers some 8,400 books worldwide, Monroe provides a "List of Books Indexed" in both volumes. Just after World War II, the National Book League (Great Britain) produced a catalog, *The Literature of Fashion* (1947). In 1963 Joanne Eicher produced a bibliography on the sociocultural significance of dress. With the founding of the Costume Society in London came an annual publication, *Costume,* which began to include lists of new books with issue 4, in 1970; selected articles were included beginning in 1976. Although the focus is usually British, the articles and bibliographies are of interest. For example, "Straw Hats, a Bibliography," by John G. Dong (*Costume,* nos. 1–2 [1967–1968]: 10–11) focused on the English straw hat industry of the nineteenth century. Even the *Dictionary of Costume* (1969) by Ruth T. Wilcox contains a good bibliography.

Aesthetics and Clothing by the American Home Economics Association and the (British) Library Association's *Reader's Guide to Books on Costume* appeared in 1972. A brief bibliography by Zelma Weisfeld in 1975 made costume sources easily available to educators using the ERIC database and document collection. Also, the Costume Society of America began a newsletter in 1974 and its annual journal *Dress* in 1975. The *CSA News* regularly includes mention of new books, exhibitions, and exhibition catalogs. Although *Dress* does not have a separate annual bibliography, its articles often contain valuable bibliographic information; several book reviews have been included since volume 12, 1986. Adele Filene began the Costume Society of America's *Bibliography* in 1975; it was continued by Polly Willman, with the last issue in 1983. Pegaret Anthony and Janet Arnold's 1974 *Costume: A General Bibliography* contains classic works on Western European costume.

In 1981 Paul Parvis contributed "Historical Clothing Selected Bibliography" to a meeting sponsored by the Association of Living History Farms and Agricultural Museums. Also in the 1980s several library bibliographies were published by the Fashion Institute of Technology, University of Texas, and Valerie Oliver at the University of Connecticut. These most likely were prepared to meet the needs of students. A special bibliography "Costume in Canada" (1984), was written by Jacqueline Beaudion-Ross and Pamela Blackstock. In the 1990s interests have continued, with Valerie Oliver's *Databases for Costume Research* produced for the Costume Society of America's 1991 symposium. Doreen Yarwood's *Fashion in the Western World, 1500–1990* (1992) contains an excellent bibliography.

American Home Economics Association. Textiles and Clothing Section. *Aesthetics and Clothing: An Annotated Bibliography.* Washington D.C.: American Home Economics Association, 1972. 159p.

Anthony, Pegaret, and Janet Arnold. *Costume: A General Bibliography.* Rev. and enl.

ed. prepared by Janet Arnold. London: Costume Society and Victoria & Albert Museum, 1974. 42p.

Beaudion-Ross, Jacqueline, and Pamela Blackstock. "Costume in Canada: An Annotated Bibliography." *Material History Bulletin* 19 (Spring 1984): 59–92.

Bibliographic Index. 1937/1942–. Three times per year including annual cumulation.

Costume, no. 1–2 (1967/68–). Annual.

CSA News, The Newsletter of the Costume Society of America (title varies) 1, no. 1 (1974–). Currently published four times a year.

Dress 1 (1975–). Annual.

Eicher, Joanne B., comp. *An Annotated Bibliography on the Sociocultural Significance of Dress and Adornment.* East Lansing: Departments of Textiles, Clothing and Related Arts and Sociology and Anthropology, Michigan State University, 1963.

Fashion Institute of Technology. Library. *Fashion: A Bibliography.* New York, 1981. 11p.

Filene, Adele. *A Bibliography of Recent Books Relating to Costume, 1975.* N.p.: Costume Society of America, 1975. 18p.

———. *Costume Society of America Bibliography 1979.* N.p.: Costume Society of America, 1979. 61p.

———. *Costume Society of America Bibliography, 1974/1979.* Edited and indexed by Polly Willman. N.p.: Costume Society of America, n.d. 91p. Continued by Polly Willman.

Hiler, Hilaire and Meyer. *Bibliography of Costume.* Edited by Helen Grant Cushing and Adah V. Morris. New York: H. W. Wilson Co., 1939. 911p.

Library Association. County Libraries Group. *Reader's Guide to Books on Costume.* 2d ed. London, 1972. 30p.

Monro, Isabel, and Dorothy E. Cook, eds. "List of Books Indexed." In *Costume Index: A Subject Index to Plates and to Illustrated Text,* 296–338. New York: H. W. Wilson Co., 1937. 338p.

Monro, Isabel, and Kate M. Monro, eds. "List of Books Indexed." In *Costume Index Supplement,* 191–210. New York: H. W. Wilson Co., 1939. 210p.

National Book League (Great Britain). *The Literature of Fashion.* London: Cambridge University Press, 1947. 64p.

Nystrom, Paul H. *A Bibliography on Fashion, Costume, Domestic Architecture and Home Furnishings.* New York: Columbia University, 1932. 120p.

Oliver, Valerie B. *Databases for Costume Research.* Storrs, CT: Research and Information Services, Homer Babbidge Library, University of Connecticut, 1991. 18p. Prepared for the 17th Annual Meeting and Symposium of the Costume Society of America, American Dress as Social History, Boston, May 15–17, 1991.

———. *Textiles and Clothing: Selected Sources of Information.* Storrs: University of Connecticut Library, Reference Department, 1982. 15p.

Parvis, Paul. "Historical Clothing Selected Bibliography." In *Annual Proceedings of the Meetings Held at Ottawa, Santa Fe, and Old Sturbridge: 1978–1980,* 68–70. Edited by Virginia Briscoe. Washington, D.C.: Association for Living History Farms and Agricultural Museums, 1981. 129p.

University of Texas at Austin. General Libraries. *Clothing and Textiles.* Austin: University of Texas at Austin, 1983. 17p.

Weisfeld, Zelma H. *Selected Annotated Bibliography on Costume History.* ED 102639. 1975. 9p.
Wilcox, Ruth T. "Bibliography." In *Dictionary of Costume,* 405–406. New York: Charles Scribner's, 1969. 406p.
Willman, Polly. *Costume Society of America Bibliography, 1983.* New York: Costume Society of America, n.d. 94p.
Yarwood, Doreen. "Bibliography." In *Fashion in the Western World 1500–1990,* 170–171. New York: Drama Book Publishers, 1992. 176p.

CLOTHING FOR THE ELDERLY AND DISABLED

Several bibliographies have appeared reflecting society's interests in older individuals and the disabled. In the early 1960s Iva Bader and Adeline Hoffman both wrote works on clothing for the older woman; Audrey Newton wrote a bibliography in 1975. Naomi Reich, Patricia Otten, and Marie Carver's 1979 bibliography on clothing for the disabled includes a resource list. This work, done at the University of Arizona, was printed and distributed by the President's Committee on Employment of the Handicapped. Another group, the PRIDE Foundation, completed *Resources and Clothing for Special Needs* in 1989. This work was made more widely available by its appearance in the ERIC document collection.

Bader, Iva M. *The Social Science Aspects of Clothing with Implications for Older Women, a Comprehensive Bibliography.* Iowa City: State University of Iowa, 1962. 21p.
Hoffman, Adeline M. *Social Science Aspects of Clothing for Older Woman: An Annotated Bibliography.* Iowa City: State University of Iowa, 1964. 32p. (2d ed. 1977, 28p.)
Newton, Audrey. *Clothing for the Elderly: An Annotated Bibliography.* Lincoln: University of Nebraska, 1975. 18p.
PRIDE Foundation. *Resources and Clothing for Special Needs.* Groton, CT: The Foundation, 1989. ED311673. 27p.
Reich, Naomi, Patricia Otten, and Marie N. Carver. *Clothing for Handicapped People: An Annotated Bibliography and Resource List.* Washington, D.C.: President's Committee on Employment of the Handicapped, Washington DC, 1979. PrEx 1.10/9: C62.

CLOTHING AND ACCESSORIES

Bibliographies on specific clothing or accessories are rare in book-length form. The general histories of costume and fashion, as well as monographs, journal articles, and exhibition catalogs on specific types of clothing and accessories, offer a better opportunity for locating material. The leading scholarly journals, *Costume* and *Dress,* are obvious sources for good bibliographies. Although a complete review of *Costume* articles has not been made, an example might be an article entitled "Blazers" by Alan Mansfield in no. 5 (1971): 25–28, which focuses on the origin of the blazer and its name. Selected articles from *Dress* with good bibliographies have been noted as examples.

Accessories as the subject of bibliographies have often appeared from the business perspective. Bibliographies on footwear include the University of Illinois's *Books about Shoes* (1924); Eva Shively's *Footwear* (1927); Karen Gillespie's *Footwear* (1962); Rowena Dowlen's bibliography (1965) covering 1926–1964; and Charles Collazzo's three works dating from 1969 to 1988. Several jewelry bibliographies represent varied perspectives: *Jewelry Retailing* by Arthur Wienslaw for the Small Business Administration (1968), Hawaiian jewelry by Brian Leu (1988), and *Jewelry History . . . in Support of Preservation* (1992) by Christine Klein. Other clothing accessory topics include bibliographies on buttons (Dauterman, 1940; Adams, 1981), the motorcycle helmet (Carter, 1982), and accessories generally (Gillespie, 1965; Edelman, 1975; Fashion Institute of Technology, 1982).

Adams, Jane F. *All about Buttons, 1761–1980: A Descriptive and Annotated Bibliography of Publications Containing Information about the Making, Wearing, and Collecting of Buttons.* San Diego, CA: J. F. Adams, 1981. 53p.

Carter, Robert A. *Motorcycle Helmets, Bibliography.* Albany: Legislative and Governmental Services, New York State Library, 1982. [4] p.

———. *Motorcycle Helmets: NHSTA Studies.* Albany: Legislative and Governmental Services, New York State Library, 1982. [2] p.

Collazzo, Charles J. *Bibliography of Articles on Science and Learning in the Footwear Industry and Allied Professions or Trades.* Boston: Bureau of Business and Economic Research, Northeastern University, 1972. 39p.

———. *A Bibliography of Books, References, Works, and Research Studies Concerning the Footwear Industry and Allied Trades.* Amherst, MA: Commonwealth Technical Resource Service, School of Engineering, University of Massachusetts, 1969, 1983. 51p.

———. *The Foot and Shoe: A Bibliography.* Boston: Bata Shoe Museum Foundation, 1988. 254p. in various pagings.

Dauterman, C. C., and J. Lancour. "Buttons: A Bibliography." *Cooper Union Museum for the Arts and Decoration Chronicle* 1 (April 1940): 245–248.

Dowlen, Rowena P. *Annotated Bibliography on Feet and Shoes, 1926–1964.* Washington, DC: Clothing and Housing Research Division, Agricultural Research Service, U.S. Department of Agriculture, 1965. 23p.

Dress v.1, 1975– annual. Selected articles, with good bibliographies, on clothing and accessories:

Albrecht, Juliana, Jane Farrell-Beck, and Geitel Winakor. "Function, Fashion, and Convention in American Women's Riding Costume, 1880–1930." 14 (1988): 56–67.

Bartsch, Donna, and Patricia Trautman. "Skirts for the Nineteenth-Century American Equestrienne." 13 (1987): 21–32.

Brandt, Brenda M. "Arizona Clothing: A Frontier Perspective." 15 (1989): 65–78.

Cunningham, Patricia. "Swimwear in the Thirties: The B.V.D. Company in a Decade of Innovation." 12 (1986): 11–27.

Doering, Mary D. "American Red Cross Uniforms." 5 (1979): 33–48.

Kidwell, Claudia. "Short Gowns." 4 (1978): 30–65.

Morra, Marisa. "Silent Informers: Men's Coats from a 19th Century Period of Transition." 11 (1985): 68–76.

Palmer, Alexandra. "Form Follows Fashion: A Motorcoat Considered." 12 (1986): 5–10.

Paoletti, Jo B. "Clothes Make the Boy, 1860–1919." 9 (1983): 16–20.

Parker, Donna. "Made to Fit a Woman: Riding Uniforms of the Frontier Nursing Service." 20 (1993): 53–64.

Warner, Patricia C. "Mourning and Memorial Jewelry of the Victorian Age." 12 (1986): 55–60.

———. "Public and Private: Men's Influence on American Women's Dress for Sport and Physical Education." 14 (1988): 48–55.

Wass, Ann B., and Clarita Anderson. "What Did Women Wear to Run?" 17 (1990): 169–184.

Edelman, Phyllis C. *Apparel and Accessories for Women, Misses, and Children.* Revision. Washington, D.C.: U.S. Small Business Administration, 1975. 10p.

Fashion Institute of Technology. Library. *Accessories, A Bibliography.* New York: The Institute, 1982. 7p.

Gillespie, Karen R. *Apparel and Accessories for Women, Misses, and Children.* Revision. Washington, D.C.: U.S. Small Business Administration, 1965. 19p.

———. *Footwear.* U.S. Small Business Administration. Small Business Bibliography no. 63. Washington, D.C.: U.S. GPO, 1962. 12p. SBA 1.3:63; (Revised 1966 16p. SBA 1.3:63/2.)

Klein, Christine De Bow. *Jewelry History: A Core Bibliography in Support of Preservation.* Washington, D.C.: Commission on Preservation and Access, 1992. 18, [31] p.

Leu, Brian Y. N. *Lei Niho Palaoa: An Annotated Bibliography.* Prepared for Library Studies 693, School of Library and Information Studies, University of Hawaii, 1988. 19, [2] leaves.

Shively, Eva (Thayer), comp. *Footwear.* U.S. Bureau of Home Economics, Home Economics Bibliography 1. Washington, D.C., 1927. 29p.

University of Illinois. Bureau of Economic and Business Research. *Books about Shoes.* Bulletin no. 4. Urbana: University of Illinois, 1924. 19p.

Wienslaw, Arthur E. *Jewelry Retailing.* Revision. Small Business Bibliography, no. 36. Washington, D.C.: U.S. Small Business Administration, 1968. 8p.

POPULAR CULTURE AND PERFORMANCE

Some bibliographies have focused on a more popular view such as Arthur Wertheim's *American Popular Culture: A Historical Bibliography* (1984). This source is a reprint of popular culture citations, 1973–1980, from the *America: History and Life* database. "Fashion and Appearance" nos. 2250–2273 includes only twenty-four references. Other topics that might be checked are "Popular Arts" (theater, circus, etc.), "Mass Media and Communications" (print, television, film, photography, and advertising), and

"Customs, Behavior and Attitudes" (sports, celebrations and holidays, and youth). The 1991 "Forum: Gendered Appearances in Twentieth-Century Popular Media" with sections on television sitcoms, comic strips, and animated cartoons provides good bibliographic information and discussion. The *Journal of Women's History, Guide to Periodical Literature* complied by Gayle Fischer in 1992, contains three sections under the heading "Material and Popular Culture": "Fashion/Textiles/Beauty Culture," "Photographs/Paintings/Visual Images/Movies," and "Popular Culture/Mass Media/Advertising." Articles are covered from 1980 to 1990. Frank Hoffmann's *American Popular Culture* (1995) serves as a guide to the reference literature. Unfortunately there is no specific focus or emphasis for clothing. Two fashion Who's Who titles, one encyclopedia on fads, and two fashion periodicals are included. However, since much of the literature outlined and described covers activities where one could hardly ignore the impact of fashion, many sources might be of interest. Additionally several articles from *Dress* on popular aspects of clothes have been included as examples.

Performance activities of dance, film, and musical, all involving costuming of some kind, are represented by several bibliographies. The Wilson Company is responsible for an early bibliography for dance compiled by Paul Magriel in 1936; it contains "Accessories and Costume" and a list of periodicals. Serge Leslie's bibliography of his dance collection, published in two volumes in 1966 and 1968, has indexes in each volume for "Design: Costumes and Settings" and "Photographic Records and Illustrated Books," in addition to the indexing of specific dances, techniques, and so forth. Social, ballroom, and tap dancing are included. Dance is covered by the *Guide to Dance Periodicals* 1931/35–1961/62 and the New York Public Library's *Dictionary Catalog of the Dance Collection* (1975; CD-ROM, 1992). The Catalog is supplemented by the *Bibliographic Guide to Dance 1975* (1976–). *Theatrical Costume* (1979) by Jackson Kesler features books and their illustrations from 1957 to 1979, while *Film Costume* (1981) by Susan Prichard covers books, journal articles, and other relevant material for a seventy-year period. "American musical theater" is featured in a bibliography compiled by Paul Metzger in 1992. Although costume is not featured, the literature would contain much costume background and illustration. As a personal or group performance, skating, and specifically its costume, has received attention by Lois and Richard Stephenson in their *History and Annotated Bibliography of Skating Costume* (1970). Their considerable skating book collection was donated to Special Collections, Dodd Research Center, University of Connecticut.

Dance on Disc, the Complete Catalog of the Dance Collection of the New York Public Library on CDROM. 1992.

Dictionary Catalog of the Dance Collection. Research Libraries of the New York Public

Library Performing Arts Research Center. New York. Boston: G. K. Hall, 1974. 10v. Supplemented by the *Bibliographic Guide to Dance, 1975–*, published 1976–.

Dress v.1, 1975—Annual. Selected articles, with good bibliographies, on popular aspects of clothing:

    Connolly, Lois. "Recycling Feed Sacks and Flour Bags: Thrifty Housewives or Marketing Success Story?" 19 (1992):17–36.

    Farrell-Beck, Jane, and Joyce S. Johnson. "Remodeling and Renovating Clothes, 1870–1933." 19 (1992): 37–46.

    Gordon, Beverly. "Dress and Dress-Up at the Fundraising Fair." 12 (1986):61–72.

    Helvenston, Sally. "Advice to American Mothers on the Subject of Children's Dress: 1800–1920." 7 (1981): 30–46.

    Thompson, Elizabeth J., and Walter Konetschni. " 'Feetsie' Pajamas and White Fur Muffs: Recollections of Childhood Clothing." 13 (1987):72–81.

    Wehrle, Louise and Jo Paoletti. "What Do We Wear to the Wedding Now That the Funeral Is Over: A Look at Advice and Etiquette . . . 1880–1910 in America." 16 (1990): 81–88.

Fischer, Gayle V. *Journal of Women's History, Guide to Periodical Literature*. Bloomington and Indianapolis, IN: Indiana University Press, 1992. 501p.

"Forum: Gendered Appearances in Twentieth-Century Popular Media." *Dress* 18 (1991): 49–77. Papers on gendered appearances presented at the 1990 meeting of the Costume Society of America in Washington, D.C. Includes: "Appearance and Roles in Television Sitcoms," by Sharron J. Lennon; "Gender and Appearance in Daily Comic Strips," by Mary L. Damhorst; and "Damsels in Distress versus Superheroines: Changing Appearances and Roles of Women in Animated Cartoons," by Susan B. Kaiser.

Guide to Dance Periodicals: An Analytical Index of Articles v.1–10 (1931/35–1961/62).

Hoffmann, Frank W. *American Popular Culture: A Guide to the Reference Literature*. Englewood, CO: Libraries Unlimited, 1995. 286p.

Kesler, Jackson. *Theatrical Costume: A Guide to Information Sources*. Detroit: Gale Research Co., 1979. 308p.

Leslie, Serge. *A Bibliography of the Dance Collection of Doris Niles and Serge Leslie*. Annotated by Serge Leslie. Edited by Cyril Beaumont. London: C. W. Beaumont, 1966, 1968. 2v. v.1: A–K, 1966, 279p.; v.2: L–Z, 1968. 594p.

Magriel, Paul D., comp. *A Bibliography of Dancing: A List of Books and Articles on the Dance and Related Subjects*. New York: H. W. Wilson Co., 1936. 229p.

Metzger, Paul. "American Musical Theater: A Guide to Information Sources." *Bulletin of Bibliography* 49, no. 4 (December 1992):251–261.

Prichard, Susan P. *Film Costume: An Annotated Bibliography*. Metuchen, NJ: Scarecrow Press, 1981. 563p.

Stephenson, Lois, and Richard. *A History and Annotated Bibliography of Skating Costume*. Illustrated by Kathleen Stephenson. Meriden, CT: Bayberry Hill Press, 1970. 101p. Bibl.

Wertheim, Arthur F. *American Popular Culture: A Historical Bibliography*. Santa Barbara, CA: ABC-Clio Information Services, 1984. 246p.

TYPES OF PUBLICATIONS

The last group of special bibliographies covers types of publications, such as exhibition catalogs and museum publications, federal government publications, and theses. Exhibit catalogs and museum publications are represented by special bibliographies, such as the *Library Catalog of the Metropolitan Museum of Art, New York,* first published in 1960. This type of book catalog often included periodical articles in addition to monographs, journals, and other specialized materials in the library. In addition the *Annual Report* of the Metropolitan Museum of Art, which began publication in 1870/71, provides a history of the museum and for many years has included special listings of museum publications, exhibitions, and exhibition catalogs. Jane Clapp's *Museum Publications* (1962) includes material on the decorative arts, including costume and textiles, identified through surveys, from over 200 museums in the United States and Canada.

U.S. federal documents are well indexed over time through several special bibliographies. The *Document Catalog* indexes publications from 1893 to 1940 in twenty-five volumes. The *Monthly Catalog,* 1895–, is the major ongoing index, with its online counterpart entitled *GPO Monthly Catalog* 7/1976–. Several indexes allow for retrospective searching over time; the *CIS US Serial Set Index* provides a subject index for the period 1789–1969, and the *Cumulative Title Index* covers GPO publications (not *Serial Set* materials) for the period 1789–1976; the *Cumulative Subject Index to the Monthly Catalog, 1900–1971* provides convenient access to much twentieth-century material.

Since there is no organized bibliographic control of all theses in the United States, that work is often hidden. Several individuals have attempted to provide access to theses. Joanne Eicher (1963) and Sandra Hutton (1983) produced bibliographies; University Microfilms International (UMI) prepared lists in 1983 and in 1992.

CIS U.S. Serial Set Index [covering 1789–1969]. Washington, D.C.: CIS Congressional Information Service, 1975–1979. In 12 parts.

Clapp, Jane. *Museum Publications: A Classified List and Index of Books, Pamphlets and Other Monographs, and of Serial Reprints. Part 1: Anthropology, Archeology, and Art.* New York: Scarecrow, 1962. 434p.

Cumulative Subject Index to the Monthly Catalog of United States Government Publications 1900–1971. Washington, D.C.: Carrollton Press, 1973–1975. 15v.

Cumulative Title Index to United States Public Documents, 1789–1976. Arlington, VA: United States Historical Documents Institute, 1979–1982. 16v.

Document Catalog [covering 1893–1940]. Washington, D.C.: U.S. GPO, 1896–1945. 25 v.

Eicher, Joanne B. *Ph.D., M.A., and M.S. Theses Pertaining to the Sociocultural Significance of Dress and Adornment.* East Lansing: Michigan State University, 1963. 17p. Preliminary draft.

Hutton, Sandra S. *Thesis Index and Abstracts, 1978–1981: Clothing, Textiles and Interior Design from 12 Central Region Universities.* Lincoln, NE: University of Nebraska, College of Home Economics, 1983. 167p.

Metropolitan Museum of Art. New York. *Annual Report.* New York: Metropolitan Museum of Art, 1870/71–. Annual.

———. Library. *Library Catalog of the Metropolitan Museum of Art, New York.* 2d ed. Boston: G. K. Hall, 1980. 48v. Supplement, 1st, 1982–.

Monthly Catalog of United States Government Publications, 1895–. Monthly. Online database, *GPO Monthly Catalog,* 7/1976–.

University Microfilms International (UMI). *A Dissertation List on Fashion, 1861–1983: Prepared for Dr. Matern, Home Economics Department, New Mexico State University.* Ann Arbor, MI: UMI, 1983. 37 leaves.

———. *Dissertation Services: Costumes 1861–Oct. 1992.* Ann Arbor, MI: UMI, 1992.

8

Indexing and Abstracting Services

MONOGRAPHS AND PERIODICALS

Indexing of books published in the United States and of books held by major libraries in the United States can be seen historically in publications of the H. W. Wilson Company, Bronx, New York, and the Library of Congress (LC), Washington, D.C. The *United States Catalog* (now known as the *Cumulative Book Index*) was the first publication of the H. W. Wilson Company in its founding year, 1898.[1] It was an index to books published in the United States. Supplements were published from 1912 through 1925. In 1933 the title was changed to *Cumulative Book Index, World List of Books in the English Language,* covering books published from 1928 to 1932. This author, title, and subject index continues today as the *Cumulative Book Index (CBI)*. In 1946 the Library of Congress published a 167-volume set, *A Catalog of Books Reproduced by the Library of Congress Printed Cards Issued to July 31, 1942*. Halsey William Wilson himself would suggest in March 1946 that this catalog be continued in book form.[2] In January 1947 LC began its *Cumulative Catalog of Library of Congress Printed Cards,* which was continued in 1950 by its *Library of Congress Subject Catalog* and *Library of Congress Author Catalog*. Also in the 1940s the R. R. Bowker Company began to produce its *Books in Print (BIP)*, an annual index by author, title, and subject to books available from U.S. publishers. Both *CBI* and *BIP* include price and order information not available in the LC publications.

From 1968 through 1980 the monumental *National Union Catalog Pre 1956 Imprints* was published in 685 oversized volumes. This Catalog represented the book collections (and other monographic and serial publications) of the Library of Congress and other U.S. research libraries, which contributed their cataloging information. Although not a subject catalog, the author entries (both personal and corporate) and entries for title for works by four or more authors provided a major service for documenting various editions of books as well as locating titles in specific library collections. The catalog, together with its supplements, form the basis of the *OCLC Online Union Catalog*, a major bibliographic network known simply as *OCLC*. The OCLC Online Computer Library Center, established in Dublin, Ohio, in 1967 as a nonprofit company providing network services to member libraries, has provided online subject access to the *OCLC* database since the late 1980s (enhancing earlier author, title, and author/title combination searches). Recently newer service options have been designed. The EPIC Service allows access to some thirty-five other bibliographic indexing and abstracting services in addition to the *OCLC* database with flexible methods of online searching and continuous printing or downloading of search results. FirstSearch Catalog allows OCLC member libraries a more cost-effective system of providing users access to a variety of some forty bibliographic and directory-type databases in addition to the *OCLC* database itself. Both options continue to expand their database offerings to complement access to the important *OCLC Online Union Catalog*.

The *Research Libraries Information Network (RLIN)* is the second major network of book and monographic materials. *RLIN*, established in 1978, represents collections of Research Library Group member libraries. These collections contain much specialized humanities material—the *National Union Catalog of Manuscript Collections* and the *SCIPIO Art Sales Catalog* database, among others. Both *OCLC* and *RLIN* services are provided by many libraries through various service options. Personal access accounts can be obtained for *RLIN*. In addition to these large networks of book and other monographic materials held by libraries in North America, Internet connection allows access to hundreds of individual library online catalogs. Although individuals, through their professional institutional affiliations, are the largest users of the Internet, increasingly libraries are providing Internet access for their users. Thus many libraries now provide electronic access to information resources well beyond their own collections.

Exhibition catalogs may or may not be documented by the various book indexes and databases, although exhibition catalogs, if formally copyrighted in the United States or held by research libraries, should become part of the OCLC and/or RLIN databases. There have been two indexes specifically devoted to exhibition catalogs: *Worldwide Art Catalogue Bulletin,* published from 1963 to 1992 and describing both the exhibit itself and the catalog, and the *Art Exhibition Catalogs Subject Index* in computer output microfilm (COM), representing thousands of catalogs in the Arts Library at the University of California, Santa Barbara. Selected exhibition catalogs are also indexed by *ARTbibliographies Modern* (1969–), *Design and Applied Arts Index* (v. 1, 1987–), and *BHA: Bibliography of the History of Art* (1991–). A section entitled "Reviews of Exhibitions" has appeared in *Costume, the Journal of the Costume Society* annually since issue 16, 1982; selected exhibitions are announced with brief descriptions in the *CSA Newsletter* published quarterly by the Costume Society of America.

Book chapters have received some special indexing attention. The H. W. Wilson Company's *Essay and General Literature Index* provides author and subject indexing for chapters beginning with the period 1900–1933. The *MLA International Bibliography* has included the indexing of chapters in festschriften for many years; therefore clothing and costume concerns within the modern languages and literatures field are more fully revealed. *ARTbibliographies Modern* indexes essays in books and exhibit catalogs (1969–) while *PsycLIT* includes separate access to chapter information in the behavioral sciences since 1987. Some book chapters can also be identified through use of online library catalogs if the contents have been described.

Formal continuously published indexes to periodical literature began to appear in the United States around the beginning of the twentieth century. Although several scientific associations, such as the Association of Engineering Societies in 1892 and the American Chemical Society in 1907, recognized the importance of providing author and subject access to periodical literature, with abstracts or summaries, and were instrumental in supporting their production (*Descriptive Index of the Current Engineering Literature* v.1, 1884–1891–, and *Chemical Abstracts* v.1, 1907–), the indexing of periodicals for the laypublic was instituted by William F. Poole, who in 1848 published a 154-page index prepared while a student at Yale College.[3] A second expanded edition was produced in 1853. In October 1876 at the first American Library Association meeting, a proposal was made to continue and expand the index. *Poole's Index to Periodical Literature* was published in 1882 and covered 239 periodicals from 1802 to 1881. William F. Poole, then librarian of the Newberry Library in Chicago, and his associate editor, William I. Fletcher, librarian at Amherst College, worked with the American Library Association and fifty-one member libraries to accomplish the indexing task. This first volume was followed in 1887 through 1908 by supplementary volumes indexing the period from 1882 to January 1, 1907. In 1905 the *Readers' Guide to Periodical Literature* began publication by the H.W. Wilson Company, covering a selected list of periodicals by author and subject for the period 1900–1904. This index continues to be one of the most important reflections of our culture as represented by periodical articles written for the general public on a wide variety of topics.

The H. W. Wilson Company built a significant legacy for the United States, as is evidenced by its continual efforts at indexing a wide variety of subject areas. Within nine years it was also producing the *Industrial Arts Index* (1914) and the *International Index to Periodicals* (1916), indexing the professional periodicals of the applied sciences/business and the social sciences/humanities, respectively. In 1958 the *Industrial Arts Index* split into the *Business Periodicals Index* (1958–) and the *Applied Science and Technology Index* (1958–). And in 1965 the *International Index to Periodicals* became the *Social Sciences and Humanities Index,* which by 1974 had split into the *Social Science Index* and the *Humanities Index.* All these changes reflected increases in periodical publication, expansion and defining of subject fields, and the interest of the publisher in meeting the needs of library users.

In the 1920s two other professional organizations, the Modern Language Association and the American Psychological Association, began indexing efforts. The *MLA International Bibliography* in 1922 expanded the humanities coverage of the *International Index to Periodicals* and focused on modern languages and literatures, linguistics, and folklore. This indexing service provides strong access to clothing as reflected in literature, clothing terminology, symbols, and images. *Psychological Abstracts* in 1927 provided author and subject indexing with abstracts or summaries to publications on the behavioral sciences, including clothing and its relation to behavior. The *Cumulated Subject Index to Psychological Abstracts, 1927–1960* reveals under "Clothing" a modest output for the 1920s: two publications indexed in 1927, one in 1928, and three in 1929. Almost seventy years later, the CD-ROM version, *PsycLIT,* indicates forty-three articles with "clothing" as a subject word and a publication year of 1990.

By the 1930s the H. W. Wilson Company began several more indexes. The *Art Index,* first published in 1930 and covering materials back to 1929, appeared as a permanent three-volume cumulation in 1933 covering January 1929–September 1932 in one volume. This continuing index was initially a joint venture of the American Association of Museums, the Association of Art Museum Directors, and the H. W. Wilson Company. It includes the indexing of museum bulletins and annuals in addition to other periodicals. The index has included the decorative arts from its inception. *Education Index* appeared in 1932. Through this index, one can trace not only education efforts in the fields of home economics, clothing design and construction, and sewing but also clothing issues within the school setting, such as the use of uniforms, sports or gym clothing, academic regalia, and teacher/student clothing concerns. School plays, theatrical productions, and costume design are also reflected in this literature from the educator's point of view. In the September 1937 issue of *Wilson Bulletin for Librarians* the Wilson Company reported on its joint agreement with the American Library Association designed to serve the common bibliographical interests of both groups.[4] This formal agreement of cooperation has been significant in the continued publication of reference books and indexes for libraries.

By 1944 the company completed publication of the *Nineteenth Century Readers' Guide to Periodical Literature,* covering 1890–1922, thus extending the coverage provided by *Poole's Index* for the nineteenth century and continuing the indexing of periodicals up until coverage in the *Reader's Guide.* In 1949 the *Music Index* was introduced by Information Service in Detroit. Musical performances of all types are covered, including the costume and uniform issues related to them.

In 1953 the American Theological Library Association and the American Sociological Association began indexing efforts, resulting in the *Religion Index* and *Sociological Abstracts,* respectively. In 1961 the *Index to Selected Periodicals Received in the Hallie Q. Brown Library* (Central State University, Wilberforce, Ohio) was published by G. K. Hall of Boston, covering 1950–1959. The title continued as the *Index to Periodical Articles by and about Negroes* and the *Index to Periodical Articles by and about Blacks* until its current title, *Index to Black Periodicals,* (1984–). The New York Public Library's Schomburg Collection of Negro Literature and History participated in the project during the period 1960–1970.[5] The *Index* offers access to the topics of clothing and dress, cosmetics, fashion, and theater, as well as articles on other topics, such as museums and music, where fashion or costume could appear. It also represents periodicals where African Americans will be pictured and represented in advertisements. The *Cumulated Magazine Subject Index, 1907–1949: A Cumulation of the F. W. Faxon Company's Annual Magazine Subject Index* was published in 1964. It had been designed in 1907 to complement *Poole's Index* and the *Reader's Guide* by indexing additional periodicals from England, Canada, and the United States. It offers enhanced access to "United States local and state history" and "other serial publications of state historical societies" for that period.[6]

Both *America: History and Life* (1965–), which includes books and dissertations in addition to journal articles, and the *International Bibliography of Research in Marriage and the Family* (1967), covering periodical literature, 1900–1964, and continued by the *Inventory of Marriage and Family Literature,* represent the appearance of more specialized indexes within the fields of history and the social sciences generally. The former provide access to fashion and costume materials in the North American history literature, and the latter reveal writings on the impact of clothing issues in the family setting: economic issues, individual preferences, and social importance, to mention a few. The federal government initiated the *ERIC* (Educational Resources Information Center) database in the early 1970s, corresponding to the print *Resources in Education* and *Current Index to Journal in Education*. It promoted access to education report literature and enhanced access to education periodical literature. Also by 1966, the Institute for Scientific Information (ISI) in Philadelphia was producing its unique citation indexes (e.g., *Social Sciences Citation Index*), to allow not only author and title word subject searching but also citation searching. This new feature allows users to learn where a citation has been footnoted since its original publication. The well-known technique of using footnotes to locate prior related material can now be used in reverse. A known citation published, say, in 1982 could be traced forward in time to learn who was using it as a footnote. In 1969 a new art index appeared, *ARTbibliographies Modern*, for a variety of types of publications in addition to periodical articles. The focus of this index is on twentieth-century design, including design of fashions and accessories. The wedding dress and other specific types of clothes and costume receive special attention.

With the 1970s and 1980s came further specialization in indexes, such as *Women Studies Abstracts* (1972–), *Occupational Safety and Health* (1973–), and the *Film Literature Index* (1975–). While not containing great amounts of fashion or costume information, these indexes do provide, respectively, a feminist viewpoint; clothing, uniform, and related equipment safety issues in the workplace; and a detailed look at film and television periodicals for costume design, costume designers, and types of films and television productions where costume work could be compared (e.g., detective, musical, and western films, "doctors in film," and "youth in film"). General and popular periodicals not covered by the *Readers' Guide to Periodical Literature* were given their own index with the publication of *Access, the Supplementary Index to Periodicals* (1976–). This index allows for more complete scrutiny of contemporary fashion and clothing topics in the popular periodical literature, including such periodicals as *Women's Day, Elle,* and *Village Voice*. Coverage of the arts and humanities was expanded by special indexes such as the *Arts and Humanities Citation Index* (1977–), *Design and Applied Arts Index* (1987–), and *BHA: Bibliography of the History of Art* (1991–). These indexes allow, respectively, for citation searching from 1977; enhanced access to fashion design, fashion illustration, jewelry and its design, and textile, embroidery, illustration, photography, advertising, and exhibit design as well as design for the disabled; and for *BHA*, the art history topics of costume and material culture covering publications back to 1989. Expansion of indexing for periodicals of the eighteenth century was provided with the publication in 1986 of the two-volume *Index to American Periodicals of the 1700's*. This index represents a tremendous indexing achievement facilitated by the use of computer technology. It also exposes in detail for the first time individual articles, letters, marriage notices, marriage ceremonies, poems, other literary work, and opinion and information reflecting many aspects of American culture.

Over eighty eighteenth-century American periodicals are indexed for the period 1741–1799.

Newspapers as a special type of periodical provide a different reflection of culture through a narrative and often visual record of events, together with commercial advertisements containing product descriptions, often prices, and other clues to influences of the time period. Local and regional newspapers, especially from the past, have to be consulted in libraries or archives. However, some U.S. newspapers have published indexes—for example, the *New York Times Index* (September 1851–), *Los Angeles Times Index* (1972–), and *Wall Street Journal Index* (1958–). Five major U.S. newspapers—*New York Times, Wall Street Journal, Christian Science Monitor, Washington Post,* and the *Los Angeles Times*—are indexed by the *National Newspaper Index,* available online from 1979 or via the CD-ROM service Infotrac. Infotrac dates usually covered are the current three to four years. Selected newspapers from each state (usually two or three) are indexed by Newsbank. The *Newsbank* database is available in both print and electronically (1973–). Over fifty newspapers are included in the Dialog PAPERS full-text database. Descriptions can be found in the annual *DIALOG Database Catalogue* published by Knight-Ridder Information. Because these newspapers are likely to have news of industries and companies in their geographic areas, they are valuable sources of information. Examples from the 1994 catalog include the *San Francisco Examiner*'s coverage of the Gap Stores, *Los Angeles Times*'s entertainment industry, *Cincinnati Post/Kentucky Post*'s the Levi-Straus Company, and *Sun Sentinel*'s (Ft. Lauderdale) sports and recreation industries. Dates of coverage of each newspaper vary; most date back to the mid- to late 1980s. Many newspapers—national, regional, and trade, as well as business and trade journals—are available full text in the LEXIS/NEXIS online service. Full-text access allows for searching of the full text rather than just by author, title, or subject. Most periodicals or trade journals included in LEXIS/NEXIS date from the 1980s.

THESES AND DISSERTATIONS

Interest in fashion and costume is also reflected in the body of research completed by graduate students. Some of the indexing and abstracting services already mentioned include selected theses and dissertations. *ARTbibliographies Modern* and *Sport* (or *Sport Discus*) index theses and Ph.D. dissertations. *America: History and Life, BHA,* and *Sociological Abstracts* include Ph.D. dissertations. However, the best coverage of Ph.D. dissertations and master's theses is provided by *Dissertation Abstracts Online* (1861–) or *Dissertation Abstracts OnDisc* (1861–) and *Dissertation Abstracts International (DAI)* (1938–) and *Comprehensive Dissertation Index* (1861–). Abstracts of dissertations have been included in the electronic database since July 1980. A growing number of U.S. colleges and universities are cooperating with the publisher, University Microfilms International, to have their master's theses included in the database. Currently over 100 schools participate. These theses also appear in the print *Masters Abstracts* (1962–1968) and *Masters Abstracts International* (1968–).

Because all U.S. master's theses are not adequately indexed, other bibliographies or indexes are important as well. For the 1952–1962 period the U.S. Department of Agriculture provided *Titles of Completed Theses in Home Economics and Related Fields in Colleges and Universities in the United States. Titles of Theses: Home Economics and Related Fields* (1962–1978) and *Home Economics Research Abstracts* (1966–1978) were produced by the American Home Economics Association. Coverage is continued by an annual feature of the *Home Economics Research Journal* beginning with lists of 1982 theses in the June 1983 issue. Another index, *Masters Theses in the Arts and Social Sciences in the United States and Canada,* began publication in 1976. Arrangement is by broad subject category, with subject index added in 1989.

As indexes have grown more specialized to reflect society's interests and developing subject disciplines during this century, they have also experienced several revolutionary changes in technology. During the mid-1960s computer technology began to have an impact on the ways indexes were published and used. Not only did computers speed up the indexing process, making coverage of the print index more timely, they also allowed for direct online access to the information. No longer was consultation of the print index necessary to conduct the literature search. The scientific areas and their associations, especially chemistry and the American Chemical Society's Chemical Abstracts Service, pioneered in these efforts, but the social science and humanities fields were not far behind. Most of the print indexes now have online database counterparts. Although the H. W. Wilson Company, so critical for supplying access with print indexes during the first half of the twentieth century, was later than other producers in providing online access, it is now providing as many service or product options as others in this competitive industry. Because the technology came into use in the mid-1960s most of the online access does not cover material prior to that time, although there are exceptions.

Just as libraries and researchers were getting used to the new online environment, a further technological advance, compact disc–read only memory (CD-ROM) came into general library use in 1985. With this technology, libraries could purchase the index in CD-ROM format as a subscription, paying one fee and allowing for unlimited use. Most of the online databases are now available in CD-ROM. Since this technology arrived in the mid-1980s the CD–ROM versions of the databases often extend only back to that time; again there are exceptions.

The online and CD-ROM database phenomenon has created an information industry that, in addition to producing the information or creating the index or abstracting service itself, now includes companies that contract with various producers to provide public access to their databases and companies that create software programs to be used for CD-ROM products. The *Information Industry Directory* is an excellent source of information for learning about databases by subject and the companies that produce and provide access to them.[7]

As technology evolves, more access options emerge: local area networks allow access to selected files or databases by many users at once; dial-up end user services allow connection via telephone to remote online databases; locally mounted computer tapes of databases allow for the development of specialized services within an institution or group for example. All of these forces, including libraries, are working bit by bit, alone and in concert, to place growing numbers of information sources and formats conveniently into the user's lap. One example of a network information service is the UnCover service owned by Knight-Ridder Information. It offers daily updated table of contents information for over 17,000 periodicals with access by periodical title word(s), author name(s), and subject word(s) from article titles. Access is through a library service or direct dial. Full articles can be ordered over the network using credit card, and specific journal titles or search strategies can be automatically marked or "revealed" so that contents or search results are automatically sent to patrons' email address. This service includes popular as well as scientific and scholarly journals.

FASHION AND COSTUME

Specific indexes to the subjects of fashion and costume mirror these same pathways and technologies. Since all general subject or popular indexes and many of those in the social sciences and humanities reflect various fashion and costume interests, they are valuable resources for locating much fashion and costume material. It was again the H. W. Wilson Company, in the 1930s, that supported the publication of two major costume book reference indexes. The first was the *Costume Index, a Subject Index to Plates and to Illustrated Text* (1937). According to the preface, as early as the 1920s, needs for such an index were recognized especially by librarians of the Art Reference Round Table of the American Library Association (ALA). In 1921 Anne M. Boyd and Mabel V. Miller at the University of Illinois Library also recognized a need by publishing a list of "inexpensive, illustrated books" to assist high schools with "costume design, color combinations, dramatic groupings, and stage settings."[8] In fact a project to create an index to costume plates (full-page illustrations) in books was suggested to the H. W. Wilson Company in 1927.[9] The preface of the *Costume Index* states that in 1930, a formal needs study was con-

ducted by the Art Reference Round Table under the chairmanship of
Dorothy Breen, chief of the Art Department at the St. Louis Public Library. Thirty-seven libraries and art museums participated. To make the
index more useful to libraries, several lists of books on the subjects of
costume, travel, and history were developed by Minnie E. Sears, the first
editor, and sent to fifty-seven libraries around the country and in England.
Those titles receiving the most votes plus other titles were then selected
to be indexed. This endeavor over several years illustrates the cooperation
that existed between the H. W. Wilson Company and librarians prior to
the signing of the formal agreement between the company and ALA in
1937. In addition to the Wilson Company editors, the librarians most
closely allied with the project were Dorothy Breen and Ruth Wilcox of the
ALA Art Reference Round Table and Margaret Green and Jean Murphy
of the Queens Borough Public Library, Jamaica, New York, who cooper-
ated by lending some one hundred volumes of the Hiler Costume Collection to facilitate indexing. The editors, Isabelle Monro and Dorothy E.
Cook, who took over the work after the death of Minnie E. Sears, indicated in the preface that they "hoped the Index may prove a useful tool
in general costume reference work in libraries, a source for theatrical and
moving picture costumers, and an aid to illustrators."

By 1957 renewed interest in the subject by the Reference Librarians
Section of the Association of College and Research Libraries prompted
the preparation of a supplement volume. Together the 1937 and 1957
volumes provide a subject index to full-page illustrations (plates) and to
selected other illustrations with and some without text in some 962 books.
Costume worldwide is covered. It is interesting to note from the *Supplement:*

As in the original volume, costumes of the 19th and 20th centuries have been
indexed under the centuries, not under separate countries, since it is assumed that
style was much the same in all countries during those periods. However, some
entries have been made under the United States for the 19th century, because in
the earlier part of the century at least, America did not always follow European
fashions and because some books devote sections to distinctively American costume.[10]

The *Costume Index* therefore supplemented existing book indexes of the
1930s through the 1950s, and even today it provides access to illustrations
unavailable through electronic indexes. Individual clothing is indexed
when separate illustrations appear for those items. The influence of popular culture was evident then, as the preface to the *Supplement* notes: "In
the earlier volume, the compilers thought it unnecessary to index books
on dolls . . . but because of widespread interest and requests for such information, this class of books has been indexed, though for character dolls

only." One popular periodical, the *National Geographic,* was also indexed for the period 1905–1954.

The second major costume book index produced by the H. W. Wilson Company in the 1930s was the *Bibliography of Costume* (1939), compiled by Hilaire and Meyer Hiler and edited by Helen Grant Cushing and Adah V. Morris. According to the preface, the bibliography was compiled at the New York Public Library and at libraries in Paris, Berlin, London, Madrid, and other European cities over many years. During 1937 and 1938 it was also checked against the Colas bibliography[11] and the *Costume Index*. It indexes some 8,400 works in one alphabet by author, title, subject, illustrator, and engraver and provides full bibliographical descriptions. "The compilers believe that this is by far the most extensive and complete bibliography of costume ever offered, covering every period and country from prehistoric times to the present day, as well as every specialized phase of the subject."[12] In addition to books, it also provides lists of fashion periodicals under "Periodicals" arranged by century; under country name where "Periodicals" follow the book entries, which are arranged by century; and with more specific information and descriptions given under individual periodical titles alphabetically.

Hilaire Hiler was an artist, painter, and theatrical designer, an associate of the literary group in France during the 1920s and 1930s composed of such people as Ernest Hemingway, F. Scott Fitzgerald, and Sinclair Lewis, and a costume book collector.[13] He "had one of the world's best libraries on costume" according to his obituary in the *New York Times* on January 21, 1966. In 1929, he had finished his *From Nudity to Raiment, an Introduction to the Study of Costume*. In the foreword to this volume, he mentions his "eight wooden boxes," each with about "eight hundred to a thousand cards" representing "books having to do with clothing or adornment."[14] He further comments, "The stream of books while relatively thin is steady and unbroken . . . yet recent researches and methods have developed a novel point of view and the newer sciences of anthropology, ethnology, and psychology permit of an approach quite different from the almost purely historical one employed practically without exception in the past." In Hilaire Hiler's "Costumes and Ideologies" section in the front of the *Bibliography,* he notes his father Meyer Hiler's *Catalogue of the Hiler Costume Library,* which was privately printed in 1927. The entry in the *National Union Catalog Pre 1956 Imprints* notes that the collection was formed by both men and sold by them to the Queens Borough Public Library in about 1931. It was this collection that formed the basis for the *Bibliography of Costume*. Hilaire Hiler writes about the "Compilation of the Bibliography" in the front of the *Bibliography of Costume* and indicates that even the best library catalogs and bibliographies of that time were inadequate at covering all the materials or providing adequate access to the subject of costume.

The announcement of the publication by H. W. Wilson in the *Wilson Bulletin for Librarians* (February 1939) points out its thirty-six pages of materials on uniforms and states that the "baggy breeches" worn by sixteenth-century mercenaries established men's fashion in Europe. On an even more popular theme, it mentions that among the over 300 journals listed is included "the famous American *Godey's Ladys Book* whose color plates have furnished designs and decoration for numerous Christmas cards and lamp shades."[15]

Interest in the subject of fashion and costume has resulted in the establishment of several organizations and associations, including: the Costume Society, founded in London in 1965, and the Costume Society of America (CSA), founded in 1974 in the United States. Both organizations have made contributions to indexing or highlighting the literature. The Costume Society, in its annual publication *Costume,* has included a "New Books" section beginning with issue 4, 1970. This literature section has been expanded over the years to include book reviews, (from issue 6, 1972) and a selective list of articles from periodicals published in that year (from issue 10, 1976, listing articles from 1975). This feature has been compiled by Naomi E. A. Tarrant. With issue 16 (1982) reviews of exhibitions were included in most issues. The Costume Society of America has produced four editions of a *Bibliography* covering books for the period 1975–1983. Initiated in 1975 by Adele B. Filene, designer, lecturer, and author, the last two editions have been edited, indexed, and in the case of the 1983 edition compiled by Polly Willman of the National Museum of American History, Smithsonian Institution.

In the early 1980s a separate, ongoing index to periodicals devoted to the subject began to be produced by Sandra S. Hutton, then in the Department of Textiles, Clothing and Design, University of Nebraska–Lincoln. The effort began as the *Clothing Behavior Index, an Index to Periodical Literature, January 1975–December 1979,* published circa 1980. In 1982 the title was changed to the *Clothing Index, an Index to Periodical Literature January 1970–December 1979.* This edition included all the citations (1975–1979) from the earlier work. This title continued annually with a cumulation for the period 1980–1984 published in 1986 under the current title: *The Clothing and Textile Arts Index, an Index to Periodical Literature,* with editor Sandra S. Hutton, then at the Department of Textiles and Clothing, Colorado State University, Fort Collins. The title change indicated, according to prefatory material, a "broadened scope" concerned with "behavioral and artistic use of clothing and textile items." The *Index* continues with materials for 1985 and 1986 published separately in 1988; 1987 published in 1989; 1988 published in 1990; 1989 published in 1991; 1990 published in 1992; and 1991 published in 1993. For the 1988 articles, arrangement and indexing were improved so that information could be searched first by century, then by specific subject (e.g., "capes," "ceremonies," "jackets," "satisfaction"), and then by author. A scan of the key terms listed in the 1991 volume reveals some engaging popular culture interests: "disposable," "eyeglasses," "fads," "fashion dolls," "fashion shows," "jeans," "miniatures" (for toys), "patchwork," "recycling," and "t-shirts."

This index represents a tremendous amount of work because the editor consults each article directly prior to its placement in the database; thus the Interlibrary Loan Office at the Colorado State University Library has been acknowledged. As indicated in the prefatory materials for the 1991 volume, the *Index* has evolved from indexing 3,619 articles in the ten years 1970–1979 to 8,065 articles for the five-year period 1980–1984. Individual year coverage shows growth in the literature from 1,940 citations for 1985 up to 2,617 in 1989, a peak year, with a slight drop to 2,375 items indexed in 1990 and 2,465 items in 1991. Some nineteen different indexing or abstracting services are regularly reviewed, in addition to selectively indexing articles from over fifty periodical publications. Fashion and costume periodical literature is also available electronically; in 1993 Hutton produced *The Clothing and Textile Arts CD-ROM* covering the twenty-two years, 1970–1991, on one disc.

SELECTED BIBLIOGRAPHY

Arrangement is alphabetical by title, usually of print source, with online and CD-ROM equivalents included. Online and CD-ROM citations include place and producer if different from the publisher of the print source or if the online or CD-ROM version is listed first. Although electronic databases are usually more convenient to use, they may not be available at all libraries. Just as print indexing or abstracting services can cease publication, electronic products and their access can change as well.

Access: The Supplementary Index to Periodicals. 1976–. Evanston, IL: John Gordon Burke Publishers, 1976–. Three per year, including annual cumulation.

Access [online]. (current material unavailable in print). Available: Publisher's Electronic Information Service. Contact a librarian.

America: History and Life. v.0, 1954–1963; v.1, 1964–. Santa Barbara, CA: ABC-CLIO, 1972; 1965–. Quarterly, plus annual index.

America: History and Life [online]. (1964–). Available: DIALOG file: 38.

America: History and Life [CD-ROM]. (1987–). Available: ABC-CLIO.

Art Index. January 1929–September 1932–. New York: H. W. Wilson Company, 1933–. Quarterly, cumulated annually.

Art Index [online]. (1984–). Available: OVID and OCLC's EPIC and FirstSearch Catalog.

Art Index [CD-ROM]. (9/1984–). Available: WILSONDISC.

ARTbibliographies Modern: Abstracts of the Current Literature of Modern Art, Photography, and Design. v.1, 1969–. Santa Barbara, CA: ABC-CLIO, 1969–. Semiannual.

ARTbibliographies Modern [online]. (1974–). Available: DIALOG file: 56.

ARTbibliographies Modern [CD-ROM]. (1984–). Available: ABC-CLIO.

Arts and Humanities Citation Index. 1977–. Philadelphia, PA: Institute for Scientific Information, 1977–. Semiannual.

Arts and Humanities Search [online]. (1980–). Available: DIALOG file: 439.

Arts and Humanities Citation Index Compact Disc Edition [CD-ROM]. (1991–). Available: ISI.

BHA: Bibliography on the History of Art. v.1, 1991–. Santa Monica, CA: INIST/CNRS, France and the Getty Art History Information Program, J. Paul Getty Trust, 1991–. Quarterly, cumulated index. Successor to *RILA, International Repertory of the Literature of Art,* and *RRA, Repertoire d'Art et d'Archeologie.*

Art Literature International (RILA) [online]. (1973–). Williamstown, MA: RILA, J. Paul Getty Trust. Available: DIALOG file: 191. Contains the *BHA* database.

Bibliography of Costume: A Dictionary Catalog of about Eight Thousand Books and Periodicals. Compiled by Hilaire and Meyer Hiler. Edited by Helen Grant Cushing and Adah V. Morris. New York: H. W. Wilson Company, 1939.

Bibliography of Recent Books Relating to Costume, 1975. By Adele Filene. Earlville, MD: Costume Society of America, 1975. Continued by: *Costume Society of America: Bibliography 1979.* Compiled by Adele B. Filene. Costume Society of America, Spring 1979. Cumulated by: *Costume Society of America: Bibliography 1974–1979.* Compiled by Adele B. Filene. Second printing edited and indexed by Polly Willman. Costume Society of America, [n.d.]. Continued by: *Costume Society of America: Bibliography 1983.* Compiled by Polly Willman. Costume Society of America, [1983?].

"Book Reviews." Section in *Costume, the Journal of the Costume Society,* no. 6, 1972–. Annual.

Books in Print. 1947–. New Providence, NJ: R. R. Bowker, Reed Reference Publishing, 1947–. Annual.

Books in Print [online]. (current). Available: DIALOG file: 470.

Books in Print Plus [CD-ROM]. (current). Available: Bowker Electronic Publishing.

Business Periodicals Index. 1958–. New York: H. W. Wilson Company, 1958–. Monthly, cumulated annually.

Business Periodicals Index [online]. (7/1982–). Available: OVID and OCLC's EPIC and FirstSearch Catalog.

Wilson Business Abstracts [CD-ROM]. (7/1982– with abstracts included, 6/1990–). Available: WILSONDISC.

Clothing and Textile Arts Index: An Index to Periodical Literature 1980–1984; 1985–. Edited by Sandra S. Hutton. Monument, CO: Sandra S. Hutton, 1986, 1988–. Annual.

Clothing and Textile Arts CD-ROM [CD-ROM]. (1970–1991–). Available: Hutech.

Clothing Behavior Index: An Index to Periodical Literature, January 1975–December 1979. Edited by Sandra S. Hutton. Lincoln, NE: Micro Control Systems, [1980?]. Continued by: *Clothing Index.*

Clothing Index: An Index to Periodical Literature, January 1970–December 1979. Edited by Sandra S. Hutton. Lincoln, NE: Micro Control Systems, 1982. Continued by: *Clothing and Textile Arts Index.*

Comprehensive Dissertation Index. 37 vols., 1861–1972; 38 vols., 1973–1982; 1983–.

Ann Arbor, MI: University Microfilms International (UMI), 1973, 1984, 1984–. Annual.

Costume Index: A Subject Index to Plates and to Illustrated Text. Edited by Isabel Monro and Dorothy E. Cook. New York: H. W. Wilson Company, 1937.

———. *Supplement.* Edited by Isabel Monro and Kate M. Monro. New York: H. W. Wilson Company, 1957.

Cumulated Magazine Subject Index, 1907–1949: A Cumulation of the F. W. Faxon Company's Annual Magazine Subject Index. 2 vols. Boston: G. K. Hall, 1964.

Cumulative Book Index. 1928–1932–. New York: H. W. Wilson Company, 1933–. Eleven per year, cumulated annually.

Cumulative Book Index [CD-ROM]. (1982–). Available: WILSONDISC.

Design and Applied Arts Index. v.1, 1987–. Burwash, England: Design Documentation, 1987–. Semiannual.

DIALOG Database Catalogue. Mountain View, CA: Knight-Ridder Information. Annual.

Dissertation Abstracts Online [online]. (1861–). Ann Arbor, MI: University Microfilms International (UMI). Available: OVID and DIALOG file: 35.

Dissertation Abstracts OnDisc [CD-ROM]. (1861–). Available: UMI ProQuest.

Education Index. 1929–1932–. New York: H. W. Wilson Company, 1932–. Ten per year, cumulated quarterly and annually.

Education Index. [online]. (1983–). Available: OCLC's EPIC and FirstSearch Catalog.

Education Index. [CD-ROM]. (6/1983–). Available: WILSONDISC.

ERIC [online]. (1966–ERIC documents; 1969–periodical articles). Washington, D.C.: U.S. Department of Education, Educational Resources Information Center (ERIC). Available: OVID, DIALOG file: 1, and OCLC's EPIC and FirstSearch Catalog.

ERIC [CD-ROM]. (1966–). Available: SilverPlatter. Both correspond to print *Resources in Education*, 1966–, and *Current Index to Journals in Education*, 1969–.

Essay and General Literature Index. 1900–1933–. New York: H. W. Wilson Company, 1934–. Two per year, with second issue a cumulation; cumulated every five years.

Essay and General Literature Index [online]. (1985–). Available: WILSONLINE.

Essay and General Literature Index [CD-ROM]. (1985–). Available: WILSONDISC.

Film Literature Index. 1973–. Albany, NY: State University of New York at Albany, Film and Television Documentation Center, 1975–. Quarterly, cumulated annually.

Home Economics Research Abstracts. 18 vols., 1966–1978. Washington, D.C.: American Home Economics Association, 1867–1981. Information continued by: "Theses and Dissertations Completed in Home Economics."

Humanities Index. v.1, 1974–. New York: H. W. Wilson Company, 1974–. Monthly, cumulated annually.

Humanities Index [online]. (1984–). Available: OVID and OCLC's EPIC and FirstSearch Catalog.

Humanities Index [CD-ROM]. (1984–). Available: WILSONDISC.

Index to American Periodicals of the 1700's: Keyed to University Microfilms APS 1. 2 vols. Indianapolis, IN: Computer Indexed Systems, 1986.

Index to Black Periodicals. 1984–. Boston: G. K. Hall, 1988–. Annual.

Index to Periodical Articles by and about Blacks. 11 vols., 1973–1983. Boston: G. K. Hall, 1978–1986. Continued by: *Index to Black Periodicals.*

Index to Periodical Articles by and about Negroes (formerly *Index to Selected Periodicals*): *Cumulated 1960–1970.* Boston: G. K. Hall, 1971. Continued by: *Index to Periodical Articles by and about Negroes.*

Index to Periodical Articles by and about Negroes. 2 vols., 1971–1972. Boston: G. K. Hall, 1973–1974. Continued by: *Index to Periodical Articles by and about Blacks.*

Index to Selected Periodicals Received in the Hallie Q. Brown Library: Decennial Cumulation 1950–1959. Boston: G. K. Hall, 1961. Continued by: *Index to Periodical Articles by and about Negroes.*

Industrial Arts Index. 45 vols., 1913–1958. New York: H. W. Wilson Company, 1914–1958. Continued in part by: *Business Periodicals Index.*

InfoTrac [CD-ROM] (current three to four years). Foster City, CA: Information Access Company (IAC). Available: IAC various service options.

International Bibliography of Research in Marriage and the Family. 2 vols., 1900–1964, 1965–1972. University of Minnesota Press in association with the Minnesota Family Life Study Center and the Institute of Life Insurance, 1967, 1974. Continued by *Inventory of Marriage and Family Literature.*

International Index to Periodicals. v.1–18, 1907–1965. New York: H. W. Wilson Company, 1916–1965. Continued by the *Social Sciences and Humanities Index.*

Inventory of Marriage and Family Literature. 1973–1974–. St. Paul, MN: National Council on Family Relations, 1975–. Annual.

Family Resources [online]. (1970– for journals; 1970–1990 for other media). Available: OVID (books and journal articles only) and DIALOG file: 291: 1970–1993 only.

LEXIS-NEXIS [online]. Dates of coverage vary per file. Updated daily. Available: LEXIS, Dayton, OH. Online information system consisting of full-text legal (LEXIS) materials and business, trade, and news information (NEXIS). Excellent source for full-text local, regional, national, and international fashion news; exhibition news and descriptions; biographical information and other information on clothing business and social issues. No graphic or illustrative material, although the presence of such material is noted.

Los Angeles Times Index. 1972–. Ann Arbor, MI: University Microfilms International, 1972–. Eight per year plus quarterly and annual cumulations.

Electronic access, see *National Newspaper Index.*

Masters Abstracts. v.1–23, 1962–1985. Ann Arbor, MI: University Microfilms International, 1962–1985. Continued by: *Masters Abstracts International.*

Masters Abstracts International. v.24, 1986–. Ann Arbor, MI: University Microfilms International, 1986–. Quarterly. See *Dissertation Abstracts Online* for electronic access.

Masters Theses in the Arts and Social Sciences in the United States and Canada. no. 1, 1976–. Cedar Falls, IA: Masters Theses Directories, 1977–. Annual.

MLA International Bibliography of Books and Articles on the Modern Languages and Literatures. (title varies) 1921–. New York: Modern Language Association, 1921–. Annual. (Earliest volumes for period 1921–1968 have been reprinted.) Subject indexing improved with 1981 volume; optimum access for costume and clothing research is via the online or CD-ROM versions.

MLA Bibliography Database [online]. (1963–). Available: OCLC's EPIC and FirstSearch Catalog.

MLA Bibliography Database [CD-ROM]. (1963–). Available: SilverPlatter.

Music Index: A Subject-Author Guide to Music Periodical Literature. 1949–. Warren, MI: Harmonie Park Press, 1949–. Monthly, including annual cumulation.

Music Index on CD-ROM [CD-ROM]. (1981–1989–). London: Chadwyck-Healey. Available: Chadwyck-Healey.

National Newspaper Index [online]. (1979–; 1982–for *Los Angeles Times* and *Washington Post*). Foster City, CA: Information Access Company. Available: DIALOG file: 111. Index to the *New York Times, Wall Street Journal, Christian Science Monitor, Washington Post,* and *Los Angeles Times.*

National Newspaper Index [CD-ROM]. (current three to four years). Available: Infotrac.

National Union Catalog Pre 1965 Imprints. 685 vols. London: Mansell Information Publishing, 1968–1980.

"New Books." Section in *Costume, the Journal of the Costume Society,* no. 4, 1970–. Annual. Section title changed to "New Books and Articles" with issue 10, 1976; see "Selected List of Articles for Periodicals Published in [year]." Annual feature.

New York Times Index. v.1, 1913–. New York: New York Times Company, 1913–. Semimonthly, cumulated quarterly and annually.

———. *Prior Series.* 15 vols., September 1851–December 1912 to 1907–1912. New York: Bowker, 1966–1976.

New York Times Index OnDisc [CD-ROM]. (1989–). Available: UMI. See also *National Newspaper Index.*

The *New York Times* is also available for full-text searching (6/1980–). Available: LEXIS/NEXIS: NEWS library, NYT file.

Newsbank. New Canaan, CT: Newsbank, 1974–. Monthly, cumulated annually. Selectively indexes over 450 city newspapers from 1970 and provides microfiche collections of the full-text articles. Offer various services, including *Review of the Arts.*

Newsbank [CD-ROM]. (1970–). Available: Newsbank, various service options.

Nineteenth Century Readers' Guide to Periodical Literature, 1890–1899, with supplementary indexing, 1900–1922. 2 vols. New York: H. W. Wilson Company, 1944.

Occupational Safety and Health [online]. (1973–). Cincinnati, OH: U.S. National Institute for Occupational Safety and Health. Available: DIALOG file: 161.

OCLC Online Union Catalog (OCLC) [online]. (pre-1900–). Dublin, OH: OCLC On-line Computer Library Center. Available: Various OCLC service options such as EPIC Service, FirstSearch Catalog.

Papers [online]. (varies per title). Provided by individual newspaper publishers. Available: DIALOG file: PAPERS. Allows for full-text access to a collection of newspapers from around the United States; most date from mid- to late 1980s.

Poole's Index to Periodical Literature. 1v. in 2 parts, 1802–1881. Rev. ed. 1891. Reprint, New York: Peter Smith, 1938; Gloucester, MA: Peter Smith, 1963.

———. *Supplements.* 5 vols. January 1882–January 1, 1907. Boston: Houghton, 1887–1908.

Psychological Abstracts. 1927–. Washington, D.C.: American Psychological Association, 1927–. Monthly, cumulated twice a year.

PsycINFO [online]. (1967–). Available: OVID and DIALOG file: 11.

PsycLIT [CD-ROM]. (1967–). Available: Silverplatter.

Readers' Guide Abstracts [online]. (1983–). Available: OVID and OCLC's EPIC and FirstSearch Catalog; and WILSONLINE. Contains abstracts.

Readers' Guide Abstracts [CD-ROM]. (1983–). Available: WILSONDISC. Contains abstracts.

Readers' Guide to Periodical Literature. 1900–1904–. New York: H. W. Wilson Company, 1905–. Seventeen per year with quarterly and annual cumulations.

Readers' Guide to Periodical Literature [online]. (1983–). Available: OVID and OCLC's EPIC and FirstSearch Catalog.

Readers' Guide to Periodical Literature [CD-ROM]. (1983–). Available: WILSONLINE.

Religion Index [online]. (1949–). Evanston, IL: American Theological Library Association. Available: DIALOG file: 190. Corresponds to print: *Index to Religious Periodical Literature, 1949–1977, Religion Index One, Periodicals,* 1949–, *Religion Index Two: Multi-Author Works,* 1960–, *Religion Index Two: Festschriften,* and several other indexes.

Research Libraries Information Network (RLIN) [online]. (pre-1900–). Mountain View, CA: Research Libraries Group. Available: various RLIN service options.

"Selective List of Articles from Periodicals Published in 1975." Section in *Costume, the Journal of the Costume Society,* no. 10, 1976–. Annual. Compiled by Naomi E. A. Tarrant; articles arranged in chronological order of subject matter.

Social Sciences and Humanities Index. v.19–27, 1965–1974. New York: H. W. Wilson Company, 1966–1974. Continued by: *Humanities Index* and *Social Sciences Index.*

Social Sciences Citation Index. 1966–. Philadelphia, PA: Institute for Scientific Information (ISI), 1966–. Three per year, cumulated annually.

Social SciSearch [online]. (1972–). Available: DIALOG file: 7.

Social Sciences Citation Index Compact Disc Edition [CD-ROM]. (1981–). Available: ISI.

Social Sciences Index. v.1, 1974–. New York: H. W. Wilson Company, 1975–. Monthly, cumulated annually.

Social Sciences Index [online]. (1983–). Available: OVID and OCLC's EPIC and FirstSearch Catalog; WILSONLINE.

Social Sciences Index [CD-ROM]. (1983–). Available: WILSONDISC.

Sociological Abstracts. v.1, 1953–. San Diego, CA: Sociological Abstracts, 1953–. Five per year, indexes cumulated annually.

Sociological Abstracts [online]. (1963–). Available: OVID and DIALOG file: 37.

Sociofile [CD-ROM]. (1974–). Available: SilverPlatter.

Sport [online]. (1949–, monographs and theses; 1975–, periodical articles). Ottawa, Ontario, Canada: Sport Information Resource Centre. Available: OVID and DIALOG file: 48.

Sport Discus [CD-ROM]. (1949–, monographs and theses; 1975–, periodical articles). Available: SilverPlatter.

"Theses and Dissertations Completed in Home Economics" [for 1982]. In *Home*

Economics Research Journal 11, no. 4 (June 1983–). Annual feature; issue number and feature title may vary.

Titles of Completed Theses in Home Economics and Related Fields in Colleges and Universities in the United States. 9 parts, 1952/53–1961/62. Washington, D.C.: GPO, U.S. Department of Agriculture, Agricultural Research Service, 1953–1963.

UnCover [online]. (1988–, for most journals). Denver, CO: UnCover Company. Available: libraries with *UnCover* service. Contents of some 17,000 journals; updated daily with access by author, article title word(s), and journal title.

Wall Street Journal Index. 1958–. Princeton, NJ: Dow Jones & Company, 1958–. Monthly, annual cumulation. Electronic access, see *National Newspaper Index* and LEXIS/NEXIS.

Women Studies Abstracts. v.1, 1972–. Littleton, MA: Rush Publishing Company, 1972–. Quarterly, annual index.

WorldCat, online service option through OCLC FirstSearch service. See *OCLC Online Union Catalog.*

Worldwide Art Catalogue Bulletin. v.1–23, 1963–1987. Ithaca, NY: Worldwide Books, 1963–1987.

9

Media

When looking at the *WorldCat* database for clothing publications, searches can be limited to media publication types (film, microfilm, slides, video-cassettes, and other nonprint formats). A search was conducted on July 6, 1995, using a variety of clothing and accessory subject terms. When sorted for count by media format in the English language, the general subject headings of "clothing and dress," "children's clothing," and "men's clothing" were included in the top ten. Disregarding these general terms, the specific clothing and accessory terms receiving the most results were "jewelry," 240; "hats," 103; "shoes," 90; "eyeglasses," 66; "gloves," 63; "coats," 49; "skirts," 43; "color in clothing," 42; "t-shirts," 40; and "trousers," 37. These counts may include duplicate entries because different editions are reflected, and sometimes different cataloging input by libraries leads to duplicate citations. Nevertheless, the relative counts collectively for all the terms form an interesting view of the publications. (Consult the Appendix to see the full range of terms and search counts.) Photograph collections not specifically identified as photos or other illustrations can be located by conducting general literature searches; specific photograph collections in libraries can be consulted as well. Following is a brief overview and analysis of the subjects of the various media concerned with the top ten specific clothing and accessory terms.

Then general fashion and costume media concerned with U.S. history are discussed, followed by a section on advertising and clothing.

SPECIFIC CLOTHING AND ACCESSORY PUBLICATIONS

Jewelry

About half of the jewelry media publications are devoted to jewelry making: instructions for beginners and the experienced and exhibitions of professional jewelry designers. The non–jewelry making media publications concern such topics as jewelry collecting and related issues of identification and collection protection, as well as advice on the wearing of jewelry.

American Craftsman John Satterfield. Robert Rasch. Cinemasonics Production, 1974. Film, 23 min.

Antique and Collectible Jewelry Video Series. Pittsburgh, PA: Antique Images, 1994. Videocassette.

Artsmart. Lincoln, NE: Great Plains National Instructional Television Library, 1990. Videocassette, 30 min. Lost-wax cast jewelry technique, other alternative casting methods.

Basics for Beginners: 3 Standard Rings. Bradenton, FL: Universal Wirecraft Co., 1988. Videocassette, 110 min.

Carolee Outrageous Faux Jewelry Presents How, Why and When to Wear Jewelry. New York: Carolee Designs, 1992. Videocassette, 30 min.

Clay: Beads. Fresno, CA: Scope Productions, 1965. Film, 4 min.

Comprehensive Bead Stringing. Albuquerque, NM: Rio Grande Video Library, 1992. Three videocassettes, 248 min.

Contemporary Jewelry: Six American Craftsmen. Art Council Aids [distributor], 1952. Thirty-six slides and guide.

Creating Cloisonné Enameling. Felicia Liban. Albuquerque, NM: Rio Grande [distributor], 1988. Videocassette.

Edwardian, Art Nouveau, and Art Deco Jewelry, Circa 1887–1930's. Pittsburgh, PA: Antique Images. Videocassette, 60 min.

Handcrafted Jewelry. Narrated by Lee Martin. Beaumont, CA: A. Goodman, 1988. Videocassette.

In the Beginning: Who, When, Where, Why, How of Making Beautiful, Original Jewelry with Friendly Plastic. Pro Media Video Production. Coeur d'Alene, ID: Elizabeth Ann, 1992. Videocassette, 60 min.

Jewelry and Musical Instruments. WXXXI (TV station Rochester, NY) Alexander, VA: Distributed by PBS Video, 1988. Videocassette, 60 min. Features jewelry artists Barry Merritt, Frances Wells, and Gary Griffin.

Protect the Family Jewels: How to Make a Video Inventory of Your Valuables. Shelton, WA: Harstine Gold Video Production, 1994. Videocassette, 37 min.

Hats

Hats seen in media format reflect safety interests at work and at school. Hats are also used as a very visual way to attract attention and enhance the teaching process. The *Career Hat Set* uses actual hats to educate and suggests many other possibilities. Videos are also made exhibiting the creative talents of hat designers.

Don't Knock It Until You Try One On. Washington, DC: U.S. Department of Transportation, National Highway Traffic Safety Administration. Poster, "Motorcycle safety, there's a lot riding on it."

A Feather in the Cap. British Broadcasting Corp, Vedo Films. 1972. Film, 14 min. Puppet in feathered cap helps children with imaginative and verbal skills.

Hard Hats, Hard Heads. LaPorte, TX: Safety Short Production, 1989. Videocassette, 5 min.

Heads Up. Virginia Beach, VA: Coastal Video Communications Corp., 1994. Hard Hat Safety Series. Videocassette, 19 min.

[*Occupation Hats Puzzle.*] Decatur, GA: Puzzle People, 1984. Puzzle, depicting several hats, designed to enhance children's motor learning.

Police Hat. Edison, NJ: Childcraft, 1980 (?). Career Hat Set. Hat.

There's No One Like You! Don Baylor, Larry Green, and First Image (firm). Denver, CO: HEADstrong Coalition, 1994. Videocassette and guide. To help youngsters value wearing recreational safety helmets.

Wearable Art from California: Ellen Hauptli and Candace King. Davis and Berkeley, CA: Instructional Media, University of California, 1986. Videocassette, 40 min.

Wedding Finery: A Step-by-Step Approach to Creative Bridal Headwear. Kathy Lamancusa. North Canton, OH: Visual Design Concepts, 1990. Videocassette, 58 min.

Shoes

The making of shoes, including the making of doll shoes, is featured in videos. Shoe manufacturer Thomas Bata is the subject of the video *One Man's Multinational.* A few sources focus on shoe styles; others use shoes to educate. Health and safety issues are also reflected in the media sources.

The Better Step. Buffalo, NY: Sherwin Greenberg Productions, 1984. Videocassette, 16 min. On proper shoes for industrial settings.

Chic Design by Fran Shoes. Fran Peterson. Sunnyvale, CA: Chic Designs by Fran, 1992. Videocassette, 105 min. On changing old shoes into fashionable shoes.

Footloose in History. Wilton, CT: Reading & O'Reilly, 1985. Four filmstrips, 35 min.; four sound cassettes and guide. History using the shoe as "linking device."

How Are Tennis Shoes Made? NBC Educational Enterprises. 1991. Film (?), 5 min. Features Jonathan Winters, Jo Anne Worley, and Woody Allen; for elementary grades.

How a Shoe Is Made. Jay Friedman. Bamberger's Customer Merchandising Services, 1980. Videocassette, 60 min.

Making Doll Shoes. Greta Smith. Culver City, CA: Victory Audio Video Services, 1991. Videocassette, 80 min.

One Man's Multinational. New York: LCA Video/Films, 1981. Videocassette, 29 min. About Thomas Bata, shoe manufacturer.

Shoe Fashions—Today and Through the Ages. Thom McAn Shoe Co. New York: Audio-Visual School Service, 1958. Fifty-eight slides and manual.

Wearable Art from California: Gaza Bowen, Shoemaker. Davis and Berkeley, CA: Instructional Media University of California, 1985. Videocassette.

Eyeglasses

Safety and eye protection are the emphasis in most of these media sources. Professional interests in technical aspects of eyeglass lenses are apparent in videos on sunglasses, ophthalmic lenses, and lenses for the computer user.

Eye and Safety Protection. Van Nuys, CA: AIMS Media, 1989. Videocassette, 10 min.

Eye Protection, A New Approach. Orange, CA: Don Brown Productions, 1992. Videocassette, 16 min.

Eyeglass Lenses for the Computer User. Buffalo, NY: American Optical Corp., 1993. Videocassette, 21 min.

The Sunglass Story. A-V Scientific Aids, 1954. Audiovisual, 7 min.

Take Your Choice. Detroit Society for the Prevention of Blindness. Detroit, MI: The Society, 1950. Film, 14 min. On high school student safety eyewear.

VIP GOLD: The Impossible Just Became Possible. Sola Optical USA. CA: SOLA Optical, 1992. Videocassette, 5 min. On ophthalmic lenses.

Gloves

The glove media sources almost exclusively deal with surgical, medical, or dental uses and concerns. *How to Wear and Carry Gloves* apparently was a concern in 1970 for adults, but the younger person might have been more interested in *How Do They Make Baseball Gloves?* Playtex gloves also promoted hand protection on film in 1980.

For Lovelier Hands. International Latex Corp., Playtex Glove Division. International Latex Corp., Audio-Visual School Service, 1980. Filmstrip and guide.

How Do They Make Baseball Gloves? NBC Educational Enterprises. Hot Dog series. 1971. Film (?), 4 min. Features Jonathan Winters.

How to Wear and Carry Gloves. Bobbi Ray Bowler. Milady Publishing Corp. 1970. Eighteen slides and guide. Based on a book by Ruth Tolman.

Safety Gear: Hand and Arm Protection. Van Nuys, CA: AIMS Media, 1989. Videocassette, 11 min.

Coats, Skirts, and T-Shirts

The media publications of the top three specific clothing terms—coats, skirts, and t-shirts—reflect popular interest in making the garments and, in the case of the t-shirt, decorating as well. These publications provide instructions for beginners, for professional tailoring, and for quick and speedy methods. The latter seems in itself to reflect another aspect of our culture. Promotional pieces are seen for individual t-shirts; individual garment patterns appear in the media sources as well, although patterns as a format are not featured in this discussion.

California Car Design with Larry Alvarez. Cliff Stieglitz and Jim Dotson. Lakewood, NJ: Airbrush Action, 1993. Videocassette, 52 min. Airbrushing cars onto t-shirts.

Coat Craze. Paulette Durfee. Salt Lake City, UT: Learn by Video, 1984. Videocassette, 120 min.

Comparative Quality of Men's Tailored Suits. Peyton B. Hudson. Greensboro, NC: MEDIApparel, 1992. Videocassette, 120 min.

Frostline Kits. Arthur L. Higbee and Ellie Copley. [Logon]: Utah State University Extension Service, 1980. Videocassette, 28 min.

Hassle-Free Designer Jackets. Sandra B. Webster. New York: Practicality Press, 1993. Videocassette, 62 min.

I Dialed "H" for Hero. Len Wein. n.p.: DC Comics, 1983. T-shirt (illustration), a reward for having submission accepted for printing in Adventure Comics "Dial 'H' for Hero" promotion.

Indian's Gym, Dartmouth College [tank top shirt]. Dartmouth Review (firm). 1990. Tank-top shirt in box; shirt depicts "muscular Indian holding a barbell between his teeth."

Introduction to Tailoring a Simple Coat. Anne Darlington. Owings Mills, MD: Maryland Center for Public Broadcasting, 1970. Videocassette, 30 min.

Just Skirts. Nancy L. Zieman. Beaver Dam, WI: Nancy's Notions, 1994. Videocassette, 60 min.

[Peace Tweety] Looney Tunes. Queens, NY: Changes, 1988. T-shirt illustration with picture of Tweety depicted as a nuclear-disarmament supporter.

Print Black T-Shirts with Opaque Cover Power Screen Printing Ink. Raymond S. Topple and Carol Winters. Passaic, NJ: Crown Art Video, 1990. Videocassette, 35 min.

Sewing Knits. Bonnie Buys. Salt Lake City, UT: Learn by Video, 1984. Videocassette, 87 min. On t-shirts.

Tailoring a Coat. Edna B. Bishop. 1962. Film, 35 min. Based on a book by Edna Bishop.

Tailoring Blazers. Nancy L. Zieman. Beaver Dam, WI: Nancy's Notions, 1985. Videocassette, 60 min.

Color in Clothing

The issue of color in clothing appears in the top ten group of specific clothing and accessory terms. Here the major subject seems to be providing advice on color choices and on how to create an integrated or color-coordinated wardrobe. Additionally, an exhibition entitled *In Black and White* was produced on videocassette in 1992 at Ohio State University.

Color and You. Kansas City, MO: McIntyre Productions, ? 1980, 1988. Videocassette, 13 min.

The Color Craze. Public Video ed. New York: Videofashion, 1988. Videocassette, 30 min.

Color Me Beautiful: Discover Your Natural Beauty through Color. Irwindale, CA: KVC

Home Video, Distributed by Barr Entertainment, 1984. Videocassette, 60 min.

Dressing by Design: Program 5: Color and Wardrobe. Produced by Harry Ratner. University of California Agricultural Extension Service, Extension Media Center, 1968. Film, 24 min.

In Black and White: Dress from the 1920s to Today. Eric C. Todd, producer, and Charles Kleibacker, executive producer/writer. Columbus, OH: Wexner Center for the Arts, Ohio State University, 1992. Videocassette. Based on exhibit and features workroom and designer studio scenes.

Jeans: The Popular Trouser

As a popular trouser type, blue jeans are the focus of the last group of specific clothing media publications. Audiovisuals date from the early 1970s and have continued steadily. Making and manufacturing are the predominant themes, with educational works included, such as using the jean to teach about economics (*Clothing: A Pair of Blue Jeans,* 1971). Titles on making jeans include *How Do They Make Blue Jeans?* (1971), *Designer Jeans* (1984), *The Jeans Story* (1988), *Foolproof Pants Fitting* (1993), and *From Fabric to 501's* (1993). In many of these sources, the popular attention-getting ability of the jean is used to teach much more than simply how to make or manufacture one pair. The life of Levi Strauss, *The First Blue Jeans,* was produced in 1979 as an educational film for children.

Another group of videos is concerned with the history and phenomenon of the jean and related garments. *Levi's: Not by Jeans Alone* (1981), a WGBH-TV production, was narrated by Eric Sevareid and concerned the company's efforts at marketing other "jean"-type products. *Current Trends in Jeans* (1983) is a short video produced with students at William Rainey Harper College, Palatine, Illinois. A possibly more accessible film, *"Jean"-ealogy,* was produced in 1983 by the Men's Fashion Association of America and Jeanswear Communications; it documents the history of the garment whose "popularity [is] unprecedented in the history of fashion." Marketing competition is featured in *The Jeans Battles* (1984). Another student project, this time at Iowa State University, resulted in an award by Levi Strauss to the students for their creation of a marketing campaign for the company. The video documents the winner's advertising campaign. Consumer advice on buying jeans is also represented on film, as might be expected.

Clothing: A Pair of Blue Jeans. International Cinemedia Center, Learning Corporation of America. 1971. Film, 15 min.

Current Trends in Jeans. William Rainey Harper College, Palatine, IL. 1983. Videocassette.

Designer Jeans. Salt Lake City, UT: Learn by Video, 1984. Videocassette, 87 min.

The First Blue Jeans. Chicago: Coronet, 1979. Filmstrip, 11 min., workbook, guide, and poster. About Levi Strauss.

Foolproof Pants Fitting. Shirley Davalos, voiceover. New York: Practicality Press, 1993. Videocassette, 75 min.

From Fabric to 501's: Levi Strauss & Co. Lubbock, TX: Creative Educational Video, 1993. Videocassette, 19 min.

How Americans Buy Jeans. Charlotte, NC: Walter J. Klein Co., 1978. Film, 14 min.

How Do They Make Blue Jeans? NBC Educational Enterprises, 1971. Film, 6 min. Hot Dog series. For elementary grades.

"Jean"ealogy. New York: Men's Fashion Association of America, 1983. Filmstrip, 35 min.

The Jeans Battles. Consulting authors: Ben M. Enis, Philip Kotler, and Stephen A. Greyser. Englewood Cliffs, NJ: Produced by the Burton Kaplan Company for Prentice-Hall Media, 1984. Videocassette, 19 min.

The Jeans Story: Added Resources, Added Value. San Francisco, CA: Foundation for Teaching Economics, 1988. Videocassette, 14 min. Our Economy: How It Works series.

Levi's: Not by Jeans Alone. New York: Learning Corporation of America, 1981. Videocassette, 29 min.

1986 AAF NSAC. Iowa State University for Levi Strauss & Company. Washington, D.C.: American Advertising Federation, 1986. Videocassette, 24 min. Winning entrant: Iowa State University's advertising campaign for Levi Strauss.

FASHION AND COSTUME HISTORY

Unlike the media publications on specific clothing and accessories, many similar sources on the more general subject of fashion or costume history have been produced by or in conjunction with museums. They may have been created as a result of a significant exhibition or for educational purposes. Other groups have undertaken similar projects for their educational value. Examples include the 1968 *American Theatre: Costume and Stage Design* from Sandak and a student project in California, *Period Costumes,* 1890s–1960s, produced in 1973. Butterick Publications contributed two series of slides covering "two hundred years of authentic fashion": *American Woman* and *American Man.* Slides and filmstrip have been produced on *Costume, 1750–1880* (1975) as part of the Index of Early American Crafts and Folk Art series. *Early American Textiles* (1975) is part of the same series. Colonial Williamsburg Foundation produced *Colonial Clothing, 1760–1770* (1976), focusing on the clothing of an upper-class couple. Focusing more on "everyone," the Smithsonian Institution's National Museum of History and Technology, Division of Costume and Furnishings, produced a slide set to accompany the exhibition *Suiting Everyone* (1975, 1976, 1978). The *Index of American Design,* with a section, *Textiles, Costume and Jewelry,* was produced in microfiche in 1978. The paintings of objects for this index had been done through the Works Progress Administration efforts during the depression years; production of the microfiche was done in conjunction with the National Gallery of Art.

In the 1980s more media publications appeared, including a student thesis, "American Fashion, 1776–1980" (1982), by Shianne Fleetwood, with 64 slides. The Smithsonian produced a slide set, *First Ladies' Gowns,* in 1982. Bi-Folkal Productions created *In Agony and Ecstacy: Reflections on Fashion* (1986) as entertainment for senior citizens. The Brooklyn Museum produced, in 1986 and 1987, 657 slides and a microfiche collection as a result of their exhibition, *New York and Hollywood Fashion and Costume Design.* A recent student journalism project resulted in a video, *Framing Lesbian Fashion* (1992), by Karen Everett.

American Man, Two Hundred Years of Authentic Fashion. New York: Butterick Publishing, 1977. 2 filmstrips, sound cassettes, poster, and guide.

American Theatre: Costume and Stage Design. Stamford, CT: Sandak, 1968. 25 slides.

American Woman, Two Hundred Years of Authentic Fashion. New York: Butterick Publishing, 1974. 173 slides with sound cassettes.

Colonial Clothing, 1760–1770. Produced by Arthur L. Smith, written and directed by Gene Bjerke. Williamsburg, VA: Colonial Williamsburg Foundation, 1976. Videocassette, 17 min.

Costume, 1750–1880. Washington, D.C.: Photo Lab, 1975. 45 slides, sound cassette and guide; also used as filmstrip.

Early American Textiles. Washington, D.C.: Photo Lab, 1975. Audiovisual, 22 min.

Everett, Karen. *Framing Lesbian Fashion.* Berkeley, CA: Graduate School of Journalism, University of California, 1992. Videocassette.

First Ladies' Gowns. Washington, D.C.: Smithsonian Institution, 1975. 41 slides and guide. (1982. 44 slides and guide.)

Fleetwood, Shianne. "American Fashion, 1776–1980." Master's thesis, Ball State University, 1982. Contains 64 slides and sound cassette.

In Agony and Ecstacy: Reflections on Fashion. Madison, WI: Bi-Folkal Productions, 1986. 80 slides, sound cassettes, and manual. (reproduced in 1989 as *Remembering the Fashion.*)

Index of American Design. Part 1: *Textiles, Costume and Jewelry.* Teaneck, NJ: Cambridge and Somerset House, Chadwyck Healy, 1978. Microfiche. (*Costume.* 1985. 27 slides and script.)

New York and Hollywood Fashion and Costume Design from the Brooklyn Museum Collection. New York: Clearwater Publishing Co., 1986. 28 microfiche and guide. (1987. 657 slides and guide.)

Period Costumes. Chico, CA: Instructional Media Center, California State University, Chico, 1973. Videocassette, 15 min.

Suiting Everyone. Washington, D.C.: Smithsonian Institution, 1975, 1976, 1978. 80 slides and guide.

ADVERTISING AND CLOTHING

Advertisements represent a more plentiful and constantly changing media type. Advertisements for clothing and accessories, as well as for the clothing used in advertising other products and services, can be fairly easily located and studied through print collections of periodicals and newspapers, both current and historical. Research collections specializing in advertising itself offer excellent opportunities for study. Several awards for clothing advertisements appear, including the *Advertising Age* annual award for the best TV commercials in twelve categories, presented first in 1982.[1] The Association of Fashion, Advertising and Editorial Photographers (AFAEP), founded in Britain in 1970, began presenting awards for advertising photography with the fifth award given in 1987. The World Institute of Black Communications has sponsored the CEBA Awards (Communications Excellence to Black Audiences) since 1978.[2] Other awards can be documented in the reference work *Awards, Honors and Prizes*. Advertisements and their related ephemera are highly collectible, as evidenced by the 1990 publication, *Labels and Tags: An International Collection of Great Label and Tag Designs*.

Advertising Age. Best TV Commercials (in twelve categories). 1982–.

The AFAEP Awards. London: Association of Fashion, Advertising and Editorial Photographers, n.d.

Awards, Honors and Prizes. Edited by Gita Siegman. 8th ed. Detroit, MI: Gale Research, 1989. 2v.

Labels and Tags: An International Collection of Great Label and Tag Designs. Kazuo Abe. Tokyo: P. I. E. Books, 1990. In English and Japanese.

World Institute of Black Communications. *CEBA Awards.* 1978–. For 1990, four videocassettes documented.

The following discussion covers the general subject term "clothing and dress" linked with "advertisements" or "advertising." The examples selected reflect much student interest in the topic. Ruth Nassau researched the "Effect of War Conditions on the Advertising of Certain Clothing" in 1943. Advertising trends were studied by Juanita Noel in 1960, closely related to the later 1985 video, *Sound and Vision: 1950s and 1960s,* which looks at advertising history. Verna Ball compared fashion advertising in New York and Texas in her 1969 thesis. A professional text was written by Arthur Winters: *Fashion Sales Promotion* (1972).

The impact of advertising on teenagers (Rego, 1981) and the effect of apparel on retail television commercials (Harp, 1982) exemplify opposite analyses: one for the clothing ad impact, the other for the clothing impact on the ad. Lori Clark introduces the word *cultural* into her 1988 analysis of Calvin Klein advertising campaigns. The same year, the fashion show, also an advertising medium, was reviewed in *Creative Fashion Show Productions*. Advertisements in the *New York Times,* 1865–1914, were used by Jane Funderburk in 1994 to show the history of ready-to-wear clothing. Her Ph.D. dissertation contains an extensive bibliography.

Ball, Verna D. B. "A Comparison of Fashion Advertising of New York, New York, Dallas, Texas, and Lubbock, Texas." Master's thesis, Texas Technological College, 1969.

Clark, Lori J. "A Cultural Analysis of the Calvin Klein Advertising Campaigns."
    Master's thesis, University of Utah, 1988.
Creative Fashion Show Productions. Polly Guerin. New York: Fairchild Visuals [distrib-
    utor], 1988. Videocassette, 24 min.
Funderburk, Jane A. U. "The Development of Women's Ready-to-Wear, 1865 to
    1914: Based on *New York Times* Advertisements." Ph.D. diss., University of
    Maryland, College Park, 1994.
Harp, Shelley S. "Effect of Apparel on Retail Television Commercials." Ph.D. diss.,
    Texas Women's University, 1982.
Nassau, Ruth S. "Effect of War Conditions on the Advertising of Certain Clothing
    and Household Textiles in Four National Magazines." Master's thesis, Iowa
    State College, 1943.
Noel, Juanita M. "The Nature of Advertising Trends in Relation to Changing So-
    cial Patterns as Emphasized in Fashion." Ph.D. diss., New York University
    School of Education, 1960.
Rego, Antoinette D. "Impact of Clothing Advertising on Teenage Consumers."
    Master's thesis, San Francisco State University, 1981.
Sound and Vision: 1950s and 1960s Fashion. New York: Video Catalogue Co., 1985.
    Videocassette, 60 min.
Winters, Arthur A. *Fashion Sales Promotion: Promoting the Business of Fashion.* 4th ed.
    Dubuque, IA: Kendall/Hunt, 1972. 139p.

The subject heading "men's clothing" and "advertisements" or "advertising" is reflected in several studies. There were no significant works
located linking children, clothing, and advertising. Interests in men's
clothing ads date back to 1926 with a work by Allen Sinsheimer for the
Harvard Social History project, *Retail Advertising of Men's and Boy's Wear.*
Selling Men's Apparel through Advertising (1939) by Myron Lebensburger
showed continued interest. Fairchild Publications produced Neal Fahy's
256 Tested Promotion Ideas for Men's Wear Retailers in 1959, reprinted from
the *Daily News Record.*

In 1969 business suit advertisements, 1901–1950, were analyzed by
Linda Matthews. Advertising media and mass media were studied by Jer-
deen Harper and Jane Fuller, both in 1972, for effects on men and their
clothing choices. Even the elderly man's connection with fashion ads was
researched by Lucinda Francis in 1982. Sears catalog ads were used to
analyze men's boxer shorts, 1946–1988, in work by Bernadette Tatarka
(1990), while Joe Hill (1991) looked at postmodern culture and its "consuming aesthetics and gender in men's fashion advertising."

Fahy, Neal. *256 Tested Promotion Ideas for Men's Wear Retailers.* New York: Fairchild
    Publications, 1959. 48p.
Francis, Lucinda F. "Elderly Men's Use of and Satisfaction with Fashion Advertise-
    ments as Related to Their Fashion Awareness and Shopping Practices."
    Master's thesis, University of Alabama, 1982.
Fuller, Jane M. "The Mass Media Impact on Male Fashion Awareness." Master's
    thesis, Ohio University, 1972.

Harper, Jereleen H. "The Use of Advertising Media as Related to Factors Affecting Masculine Apparel." Master's thesis, Texas Woman's University, 1972.

Hill, Joe M. "Theorizing the Subject in Postmodern Culture: Consuming Aesthetics and Gender in Men's Fashion Advertising." A. B. honors thesis, Harvard University, 1991.

Lebensburger, Myron M. *Selling Men's Apparel through Advertising.* New York: McGraw-Hill, 1939. 310p.

Matthews, Linda M. "Change in Men's Business Suit as Reflected in Fashion Advertisements, 1901 through 1950." Master's thesis, University of Maryland, 1969.

Sinsheimer, Allen. *Retail Advertising of Men's and Boy's Wear.* New York: Harper & Bros., 1926.

Tatarka, Bernadette. "A Study of Fashion Change Related to Men's Boxer Undershorts as Depicted in Sears Annual Merchandise Catalogs (1946–1988)." Master's thesis, Oregon State University, 1990.

10

Research Centers

DIRECTORIES

Because of the pervasive nature of costume, clothing and dress, and fashion in our society, research can usually be started by investigating local library and museum resources. Electronic databases and networks, as well as Internet, may help to reduce time spent traveling long distances. Most of the research centers located are library collections. A few university centers are included from the *Research Centers Directory*, which describes university centers and other not-for-profit institutions in the United States and Canada. Companies doing product-related research in their own research group settings can also be located. In the *Directory of American Research and Technology*, much of the research is scientific and technical, and thus not within the scope of this work. However, some possible popular culture links can be seen in the fact that Levi Strauss conducts research on garment finishing, a serious factor for many when considering purchase of their next pair of jeans. Also, the current craze in athletic footwear is reflected in research done by Interco's Converse Inc., L.A. Gear, and Reebok International. But for the most part it is the library directories that reveal the research centers.

Several directories can be used to locate libraries with collections on costume or fashion or of other types of information and materials that might be used to research the subject of costume or fashion. Lee Ash and William Miller's *Subject Collections* is a standard reference source indexing by subject book and other collections in various types of libraries and museums in the United States and Canada. *Special Collections in College and University Libraries* (1989) is also indexed by specific subject terms. The *Directory of Popular Culture Collections* (1989) is arranged geographically; its subject index has twenty-one entries under "costume" and nine entries under "fashion." Most entries describe library and museum collections with popular culture materials. The *American Library Directory,* published annually, contains library descriptions with collection information arranged by state, city, and then library name. For many major libraries, the collection descriptions are quite detailed. All libraries in the following list were verified for address and inclusion in this source. Most of the museums listed in chapter 11 have libraries, naturally varying in size and subject emphasis; several are specifically noted in this list. There are many other more specialized library directories as well. Depending on the type of research, the *Directory of Historical Organizations in the United States and Canada* or the *Directory of Archives and Manuscript Repositories in the United States* might be helpful. Several periodicals and newsletters might be used to learn about collections being acquired by libraries as purchases, gifts, or bequests. *College and Research Libraries News* is one such source with a regular feature entitled "Grants and Acquisitions."

American Library Directory. 48th ed. New Providence, NJ: R. R. Bowker, 1995. 2v.

Ash, Lee, and William G. Miller, comps. *Subject Collections: A Guide to Special Book Collections and Subject Emphases as Reported by University, College, Public, and Special Libraries and Museums in the United States and Canada.* 7th ed. rev. and enl. New Providence, NJ: R. R. Bowker, 1993. 2v.

College and Research Library News (C&RL News). Association of Research Libraries, American Library Association. Eleven issues per year.

Directory of American Research and Technology 1995. Organizations Active in Product Development for Business. 29th ed. New Providence, NJ: R. R. Bowker, 1994.

Directory of Archives and Manuscript Repositories in the United States. U.S. National Historical Publications and Records Commission. Washington, D.C.: The Commission, 1978. 905p.

Directory of Historical Organizations in the United States and Canada. 14th ed. Edited by Mary B. Wheeler. Nashville, TN; American Association for State and Local History, 1990.

Directory of Popular Culture Collections. Edited by Christopher D. Geist et al. Phoenix, AZ: Oryx Press, 1989. 234p.

Research Centers Directory. 20th ed. Detroit, MI: Gale Research, 1995. 2v.

Special Collections in College and University Libraries. Compiled by MODOC Press. New York: Macmillan, 1989.

RESEARCH CENTERS

Research centers are arranged by state and have been chosen because the directories consulted indicated collections in costume, fashion, or related popular topics such as advertising or commercial art, cowboys, or sports. A few centers are noted for research on popular culture generally. Many other subject collections (e.g., dance, dolls, posters, moving pictures, theater, television, rock music) could serve the researcher but have not been included due to space considerations. Research center and address are followed by source notation. If the center or library was noted as having collections on a related topic, that topic follows the source notation. If the related materials are in addition to costume or fashion collections, the word *also* is included. Following are the sources consulted and notation used:

A   Ash and Miller, *Subject Collections*, 1993.

ALD   *American Library Directory*, 48th ed., 1995.

RCD   *Research Centers Directory*, 20th ed, 1995.

SC   *Special Collections in College and University Libraries*, 1989.

Arizona

Arizona Historical Society, Southern Arizona Division Library, 949 East Second St., Tucson, AZ 85719. A (cowboys).

California

Academy of Motion Picture Arts and Sciences, Margaret Herrick Library, 333 South La Cienega Blvd., Beverly Hills, CA 90211. A, ALD.

Burbank Public Library, 110 North Glenoaks Blvd., Burbank, CA 91502. A, ALD.

California State University, Sacramento, Library, 2000 Jed Smith Drive, Sacramento, CA 95819-6039. SC, ALD.

Carlsbad City Library, 1250 Carlsbad Village Dr., Carlsbad, CA 92008-1991. A, ALD.

Columbia College–Hollywood, Joseph E. Bluth Memorial Library, 925 North La Brea Ave., Hollywood, CA 90038. SC, ALD.

Fashion Institute of Design and Merchandising, Resource and Research Center, 919 South Grand Ave., Los Angeles, CA 90015. SC.

Los Angeles County Museum of Art, Art Research Library, 5905 Wilshire Blvd., Los Angeles, CA 90036. A, ALD.

Los Angeles Public Library, Arts and Recreation Department, 630 West Fifth St., Los Angeles, CA 90017-2097. A (sports), ALD.

University of California, Davis, General Library, Special Collections, Davis, CA 95616-5292. A (posters, counterculture), ALD.

University of California, Irvine, Library, PO Box 19557, Irvine, CA 92713-9557. SC, ALD.

University of California, Los Angeles, Library, Special Collections, 405 Hilgard Ave., Los Angeles, CA 90024-1575. A (also advertising).

————. Arts Library, University Research Library, Los Angeles, CA 90024. A (posters, film), ALD.

University of Southern California, Edward L. Doheny Memorial Library, Cinema Collection, University Park, Los Angeles, CA 90089-0182. A (posters, film), ALD.

Western Costume Company, Research Library, 11041 Vanowen St., North Hollywood, CA 91605. A, ALD.

Colorado

Colorado Historical Society, Stephen H. Hart Library, 1300 Broadway, Denver, CO 80203. A (cowboys), ALD.

Colorado State University, Wm. E. Morgan Library, Fort Collins, CO 80523-0002. A (cowboys, western American literature), ALD.

————. Historic Costume and Textile Collection and the Gustafson Gallery, 314 Gifford Bldg., Fort Collins, CO 80523. RCD.

Pro Rodeo Hall of Fame Library, 101 Pro Rodeo Dr., Colorado Springs, CO 80919. A (cowboys), ALD.

United States Figure Skating Association, 20 First St., Colorado Springs, CO 80906. A (sports, maintains World Figure Skating Hall of Fame and Museum).

Connecticut

Barnum Museum and Library, 820 Main St., Bridgeport, CT 06604. (commercial art).

University of Connecticut Libraries, Thomas J. Dodd Research Center, Special Collections, Storrs, CT 06269-1005. ALD (Stephenson Skating Collection).

Wadsworth Atheneum, Auberach Art Library, 600 Main St., Hartford, CT 06103. A, ALD.

Yale University Library, 120 High St., PO Box 208204, New Haven, CT 06520-8240. A (also advertising, trade cards, sports).

District of Columbia

Competitive Enterprise Institute, 1001 Connecticut Ave., NW, Suite 1250, Washington, D.C, 20036. RCD (popular culture).

Library of Congress, Prints and Photographs Division, Washington, D.C. 20540. A (also cowboys, frontier life), ALD.

Florida

International Swimming Hall of Fame, Henning Library, One Hall of Fame Dr., Fort Lauderdale, FL 33316. A (sports), ALD.

University of Florida Libraries, George A. Smathers Libraries, 204 Library W, PO Box 117001, Gainesville, FL 32611. SC, ALD.

Georgia

University of Georgia Libraries, Hargrett Rare Book and Manuscript Library, Athens, GA 30602. A, SC, ALD.

Hawaii

University of Hawaii at Manoa, Maurice J. Sullivan Training and Research Laboratory, College of Business Administration, 2402 Maile Way, Honolulu, HI 96822. RCD (advertising, consumer, logos).

Illinois

Chicago Public Library, 400 South State St., Chicago, IL 60605. A, ALD.
Newberry Library, 60 West Walton St., Chicago, IL 60610-3394. A (cowboys), ALD.
Parkland College Library, 2400 West Bradley Ave., Champaign, IL 61821. A (advertising), ALD.
University of Illinois at Chicago, University Libraries, 801 South Morgan St., PO Box 8198, Chicago, IL 60680. A (commercial art), ALD.
University of Illinois Urbana–Champaign Library, 1408 West Gregory Dr., Urbana, IL 61801. A (also advertising), SC, ALD.
———. Applied Life Studies, 146 Main Library. A (sports), ALD.
———. Home Economics Library, 314 Bevier Hall. A, ALD.
Wheaton College, Buswell Memorial Library, Wheaton, IL 60187-5593. SC (television commercials, Betsy Palmer Collection), ALD.

Indiana

Allen County Public Library, P.O. Box 2270, Fort Wayne, IN 46801. A, ALD.
Eiteljorg Museum of American Indian and Western Art, White River State Park, 500 West Washington St., Indianapolis, IN 46204-2707. A (cowboys).
Indiana University Bloomington, Research Center for Language and Semiotic Studies, 2805 East 10th St., Bloomington, IN 47408-2601. RCD (advertising).
Purdue University Libraries, Consumer and Family Sciences Library, Stone Hall, West Lafayette, IN 47907-1002. A, ALD.
University of Notre Dame, Libraries, Notre Dame, IN 46556. A (sports), ALD.

Iowa

Iowa State University Library, Ames, IA 50011. A, ALD.

Kansas

Kansas State University, Farrell Library, Manhattan, KA 66506-1002. A (also consumer), SC, ALD.

Kentucky

Hopkinsville Community College Library, P.O. Box 2110, Hopkinsville, KY 42241-2100, A, ALD.

University of Kentucky Libraries, Margaret I. King Library, Special Collections, Lexington, KY 40506. A (sports), ALD.

Louisiana

New Orleans Public Library, Louisiana History Collection, 219 Loyola Ave., New Orleans, LA 70140-1016. A, ALD.

Maryland

Goucher College, Julia Rogers Library, Dulaney Valley Rd., Towson, MD 21204. A.

Lacrosse Foundation National Headquarters and Hall of Fame Museum, 113 West University Pkwy., Baltimore, MD 21210. A (sports).

Massachusetts

American Antiquarian Society, 185 Salisbury St., Worcester, MA 01609-1634. A (advertising cards).

Harvard University Library, Widener Memorial Library, Cambridge, MA 02138. A (also sports), ALD.

Northeastern University, Center for the Study of Sport in Society, 360 Huntington Ave., 161CP, Boston, MA 02115. RCD (sports).

Old Sturbridge Village, Research Library, Sturbridge, MA 01566. A, ALD.

Peabody Essex Museum, Phillips Library, East India Sq., Salem, MA 01970-3773. A, ALD.

Project Save Archives, 46 Elton Ave., Watertown, MA 02172-4116. A, ALD. (Armenian ethnic photos).

University of Massachusetts at Amherst, W. E. B. DuBois Library, Amherst, MA 01003. A (sports), ALD.

Wenham Museum, Timothy Pickering Library, 132 Main St., Wenham, MA 01984. A.

Michigan

Detroit Public Library, Art and Literature Department, 5201 Woodward Ave., Detroit, MI 48202-4007. A, ALD.

Henry Ford Museum and Greenfield Village, Research Center, 20900 Oakland Blvd., P.O. Box 1970, Dearborn, MI 48121-1970. RCD (advertising).

Michigan State University Library, East Lansing, MI 48824-1048. A, ALD.

University of Michigan, University Libraries, Special Collections Library, 711 Hatcher South, Ann Arbor, MI 48109-1205. A, ALD.

Minnesota

Minneapolis College of Art and Design Library, 2501 Stevens Ave. South, Minneapolis, MN 55404-3593. A, ALD.

Saint Paul Public Library, 90 West Fourth St., Saint Paul, MN 55102-1668. A, ALD.

Missouri

Saint Louis Public Library, 1301 Olive St., Saint Louis, MO 63103. A, ALD.

Washington University Libraries, Art and Architecture Library, Saint Louis, MO 63130-4899. A, ALD.

Montana

Montana Historical Society Library and Archives Program, 225 North Roberts St., Helena, MT 59601-1201. A (cowboys, range life), ALD.

Montana State University–Bozeman, Home Economics Research Program, Herrick Hall, Bozeman, MT 59717. RCD.

Nebraska

University of Nebraska–Lincoln, University Libraries, Archives and Special Collections, Lincoln, NE 68588. A (cowboy art, C. M. Russell).

New Jersey

College of Saint Elizabeth, Mahoney Library, 2 Convent Rd., Morristown, NJ 07960. SC, ALD.

U.S. Golf Association Library, Golf House, Far Hills, NJ 07931. A (sports), ALD.

New Mexico

Museum of New Mexico, Museum of International Folk Art Library, PO Box 2087, Santa Fe, NM 87504-2087. A, ALD.

New York

Advertising Research Foundation, 641 Lexington Ave., 11th Fl., New York, NY 10022. RCD (advertising).

Brooklyn Museum, Art Reference Library, 200 Eastern Pkwy., Brooklyn, NY 11238. A, ALD.

Brooklyn Public Library, Grand Army Plaza, Brooklyn, NY 11238. A (also advertising), ALD.

City College of the City University of New York, Morris Raphael Cohen Library, North Academic Center, 138th and Convent Ave., New York, NY 10031. SC, ALD.

Columbia University, University Libraries, Avery Architectural and Fine Arts Library, 535 West 114th St., New York, NY 10027. A, ALD.

————. Rare Book and Manuscript Library. A (sports), ALD.

Cornell University, Agricultural Experiment Station, 245 Roberts Hall, Ithaca, NY 14853. RCD.

Fashion Institute of Technology, Shirley Goodman Research Center, Glaydes Marcus Library and Special Collections Library, 7th Ave. at 27th St., New York, NY 10001-5992. A, SC, ALD (Edward C. Blum Design Laboratory, collections of clothing and textiles).

Laboratory Institute of Merchandising Library, 12 East 53d St., New York, NY 10022. SC, ALD.

Marymount College, Gloria Gaines Memorial Library, Tarrytown, NY 10591-3796. A, ALD.

Metropolitan Museum of Art, Costume Institute, Irene Lewisohn Costume Reference Library, 1000 Fifth Ave., New York, NY 10028-0198. A, ALD.

Museum of the City of New York, Theatre Collection, 1220 Fifth Ave., New York, NY 10029. A, ALD.

Museum of Television and Radio Library, 25 West 52d St., New York, NY 10019. ALD (on-site use only).

National Baseball Hall of Fame and Museum, Library and Archives, PO Box 590, Cooperstown, NY 13326-0590. A (sports), ALD.

National Museum of Racing and Hall of Fame International, 191 Union Ave., Saratoga Springs, NY 12866. A (sports), ALD.

New Rochelle Public Library, One Library Plaza, New Rochelle, NY 10801. A, ALD.

New York Public Library Research Libraries, Fifth Ave. and 42 St., New York, NY 10018.

————. Miriam and Ira D. Wallach Division of Art, Prints, and Photographs. A (also advertising, commercial art), A, ALD.

————. General Research Division. A (sports), ALD.

————. Performing Arts Research Center, 40 Lincoln Center Plaza, New York, NY 10023. A, ALD.

Parsons School of Design, New School for Social Research, Adam and Sophie Gimbel Design Library, Two West 13th St., New York, NY 10011. A, ALD.

Pratt Institute Library, 200 Willoughby Ave., Brooklyn, NY 11205-3897 A (also commercial art), ALD.

Racquet and Tennis Club Library, 370 Park Ave., New York, NY 10022. A (sports), ALD.

North Carolina

Duke University, John W. Hartman Center for Sales, Advertising and Marketing History, Special Collections Library, Box 90185, Durham, NC 27708-0185. RCD (advertising).

——. William R. Perkins Library, Special Collections Department, Durham, NC 27706-0190. A (advertising), ALD.

University of North Carolina at Chapel Hill, Walter Royal Davis Library, Chapel Hill, NC 27514-8890. A, SC, ALD.

Ohio

Bowling Green State University, Center for Study of Popular Culture, Popular Culture Center, Bowling Green, OH 43402. RCD (popular culture).

Cleveland Public Library, Social Sciences Department, 325 Superior Ave., Cleveland, OH 44114-1271. A, ALD.

Ohio State University, Human Ecology Library, Campbell Hall, 1787 Neil Ave., Columbus, OH 43210-1295. A, ALD.

Pro Football Hall of Fame Library Research Center, 2121 George Halas Dr., NW, Canton, OH 44708. A (sports), ALD.

Public Library of Cincinnati and Hamilton County, Art and Music Department, 800 Vine St., Cincinnati, OH 45202-2071. A, ALD.

Oklahoma

National Cowboy Hall of Fame, Western Heritage Center Library, 1700 Northeast 63d St., Oklahoma City, OK 73111. A (cowboys), ALD.

Will Rogers Memorial Library, 1720 West Will Rogers Blvd., Claremore, OK 74018. A (cowboys), ALD.

Oregon

Bassist College Library, 2000 Southwest Fifth Ave., Portland, OR 97201-4972. A (also advertising), SC, ALD.

Oregon State University, Oregon Agricultural Experiment Station, Strand Hall 138, Corvallis, OR 97331-2201. RCD.

University of Oregon, International Institute for Sport and Human Performance, Bowerman Bldg., Eugene, OR 97403-1243. RCD (arts and humanities aspects of sports).

Pennsylvania

Drexel University, W. W. Hagerty Library, 32d and Chestnut Sts., Philadelphia, PA 19104-2884. A, ALD.

Marywood College, Learning Resources Center, 2300 Adams Ave., Scranton, PA 18509-1598. SC, ALD.

Philadelphia College of Textiles and Science, Textile and Apparel Research, Schoolhouse Ln. and Henry Ave., Philadelphia, PA 19144. RCD.

Rhode Island

International Tennis Hall of Fame and Tennis Museum Library, 194 Bellevue Ave., Newport, RI 02840-3515. A (sports), ALD.

Rhode Island School of Design Library, Two College St., Providence, RI 02903-2785. A (also commercial art), ALD.

Tennessee

University of Tennessee, Knoxville, Tennessee Agricultural Experiment Station, 103 Morgan Hall, P.O. Box 1071, Knoxville, TN 37901-1071. RCD.

Texas

Amarillo Public Library, 413 East Fourth St., PO Box 2171 Amarillo, TX 79189-2171. A (Southwest, cowboys), ALD.

Amon Carter Museum Library, 3501 Camp Bowie Blvd., PO Box 2365, Fort Worth, TX 76113-2365. A (western American art, Remington, Russell), ALD.

Panhandle-Plains Historical Museum, Research Center, Box 967, WTAMU Sta., Canyon, TX 79106. A (also American West), RCD.

Texas Tech University, Advertising Research Center, PO Box 43082, Lubbock, TX 79409-3082. RCD (advertising).

Texas Woman's University, Mary Evelyn Blagg-Huey Library, PO Box 23715, TWU Station, Denton, TX 76204. A, SC, ALD.

Trinity University Library, 715 Stadium Dr., San Antonio, TX 78212. SC, ALD.

University of Texas Libraries, General Libraries, Humanities Research Center, Austin, TX 78713. A (also cowboys), ALD.

Utah

Utah State University, Merrill Library, Special Collections, Logan, UT 84322-3000. A (cowboys), ALD.

Virginia

George Mason University Libraries, Special Collections Department, 4400 University Dr., Fairfax, VA 22030-4444. A, ALD.

Virginia Polytechnic Institute and State University Libraries, PO Box 90001, Blacksburg, VA 24062-9001. A (cowboys), ALD.

Washington

University of Washington, Plestcheef Institute for the Decorative Arts, 814 Highland Dr., Seattle, WA 98102. RCD.

University of Washington Libraries, Costume and Textile Collection, Seattle, WA 98195-0001. A (drama library), A, ALD.

Washington State University, College of Agriculture and Home Economics Research Center, Pullman, WA 99164-6240. RCD.

Wisconsin

Milwaukee Public Library, 814 West Wisconsin Ave., Milwaukee, WI 53233-2385. A (sports), ALD.

State Historical Society of Wisconsin Library, 816 State St., Madison, WI 53706. A (advertising, media), ALD.

University of Wisconsin–Madison, General Library System and Memorial Library, Madison, WI 53706. A (sports), ALD.

School of Journalism Reading Room, Madison, WI 53706. A (advertising).

University of Wisconsin–Milwaukee, Center for Twentieth Century Studies, P.O. Box 413, Milwaukee, WI 53201. RCD (popular culture).

University of Wisconsin–Stout, Library Learning Center, Menomonie, WI 54751-0790. A, ALD.

11

Costume Museums and Collections

The Official Museum Directory (OMD), published since 1971, provides a wealth of information about all types of museums in the United States; the 1995 edition lists over 7,300 museums and notes 45 museums under the specialized category of "Costume Museums." Other types of museums typically have costume, clothing, or related objects such as illustrations or photographs in their collections (e.g., museums specializing in history or performance activities such as the circus, sports, theater, or allied interests of toys and dolls). In fact in the "Index to Institutions by Collection," costumes and textiles account for some 1,076 entries, or almost 15 percent, illustrating their popularity in museum collections.

An earlier *Museums Directory of the United States and Canada*, also produced by the American Association of Museums and edited by Erwin O. Christensen in 1961, indexed museums by category, listing five as "costume museums": Campbell House Museum, Missouri; Metropolitan Museum of Art, Costume Institute, New York; Texas Women's University, Collection of Household Arts and Sciences, Museum of Historic Costumes, Texas (with the Museum of Motoring Memories, Virginia, and the Traphagen School of Fashion, Museum Collection, New York, being the only two not currently listed in the 1995 *OMD*). This directory surveyed some 4,500 institutions and also provided a subject index with fifteen entries under "costume" adding twelve museums to those noted above. Thus this directory notes seventeen U.S. museums with costume collections. Other categories of interest were sports museums (four), textile museums (four) with subject indexing for doll collections (thirty), and jewelry (six), for example.

The 1985 *Directory of Unique Museums* compiled by Bill Truesdell is a possible source, although "costume" is not in the index. Entries of potential interest are "cowboys" (two), "cartoons" (one), "bullfighting" (one), "dolls and doll houses" (eight), and "fans" (one). Name, address, and brief descriptions are provided.

It is through the various editions of the *OMD* that one can see the development of costume museums and collections. The 1971–1978 editions were published biennially and included Canadian museums. In 1980, publication became annual, and Canadian listings were omitted beginning in 1986. The number of museums listed has increased from some 5,000 in the early 1970s to over 7,300 in 1995. Comparing the numbers of U.S. museums listed under the "Costume Museum" category from Christensen's 1961 directory (five) to the 1995 *OMD* (forty-five) one sees an 800 percent increase in the thirty-four years. Although it was only in the 1995 edition that an index was provided for collections, an overview of sorts can be pieced together.

Ann A. Lafferty identified 252 institutions from Christensen's 1961 *Museums Directory of the United States and Canada* as having costumes.[1] This allows a comparison to be made. The *OMD*'s 1995 listing of 1,076 costume and textiles collections represents over four times as many as noted by Lafferty in the 1961 directory.

The *1995–1996 Membership Directory, The Costume Society of America,* lists 213 members under the "Museum" category with forty-four specific U.S. museums as institution members; an additional five are listed under the "Restored Historic Site" category and one under "State/National Parks." In addition four individual members represent the "Theme Park" category: Busch Entertainment Corp., Virginia; Dollywood, Tennessee; Fiesta Texas, Texas; and Old Tucson Studios, Arizona.

Although there is no definitive number of costume museums, the fact that their numbers have been growing is evident. From analyzing the data in the list of 175 institutions provided at the end of this chapter, one can see that forty-four states are represented, with the largest numbers of institutions coming from New York (nineteen), Massachusetts (fourteen), Ohio (ten), Connecticut (eight), California and Missouri (each seven), and Alabama, Pennsylvania, and Wisconsin (each with six). The type of museum most noted with costume collections is in the area of history, historical society, historic site, historic house or building (seventy-two), followed by college or university collections (twenty-eight) and art museums (twenty-three). Looking at the founding dates, ten institutions were established between 1799 and 1849, twenty-five from 1850 to 1899, sixty-six from 1900 to 1949, and fifty-six since 1950. All founding dates and museum types were those noted in the 1995 edition of the *OMD;* no founding dates were located for nineteen of the institutions.

COSTUME COLLECTION SURVEYS

There are several surveys of costume collections. Irene P. Huenefeld, Louisiana State University, completed the *International Directory of Historical Clothing* in 1967. It lists collections separately from the United States, Canada, and Europe, as well as by clothing categories, century, and institution. Two thousand institutions were surveyed during a six-year period, including museums, art galleries, historic societies, libraries, and churches. Although she does not indicate how she determined her initial list of institutions, quite a bit of preliminary evaluation must have been done since Christensen's 1961 directory covered some 4,500. She lists 265 institutions in her U.S. section. In addition to the geographical lists, Huenefeld provides access by clothing type and clothing accessory.

During the same period Ann A. Lafferty, Texas Women's University, was conducting a survey of collections in the United States. Of the 252 surveyed 161 returned usable data, which she analyzed in her 1968 thesis. Unfortunately, the list of 161 institutions is not provided, but the analysis reveals that about 50 percent of the collections were started prior to 1925,[2] and 53.3 percent were founded by individual collectors.[3] States with the most museum costume collections were Massachusetts and New York (each sixteen), Pennsylvania (ten), and Ohio (eight).[4] Twenty-two costume collections were noted as having two thousand or more items in their collections, with sixteen of these located in cities of over 100,000 population.[5] It is unfortunate that these twenty-two collections are not listed.

In 1976 Cecil Lubell's *Textile Collections of the World* was published in three volumes. Volume 1, *United States and Canada,* contains an index entry for "costume." Collection data can be scanned easily by consulting the geographical list, which includes the number of items in the collection. In this list no distinction is made between costume or textile holdings. Seventy museums in the United States and Canada contain collections where holdings emphasize American textile history.[6] The main body of the work is arranged by museum name, first for the United States and then for Canada. Additional materials cover textile subjects.

In 1979, Frances J. Duffield, Auburn University, conducted a survey of costumes, accessories, textiles, and slides in college and university collections. Her survey contains a graphic presentation of the results with types of clothes indicated for each school. For the study 141 departments of home economics were surveyed, with about 93 to 95 returns used for analysis.[7] Of this number, 80 appear in the "Costume Collections" section. An article describing the survey project appeared in 1980 in *Theatre Design and Technology*.[8]

Jean L. Druesedow, then assistant curator, Costume Institute, Metropolitan Museum of Art, wrote a short article in 1981, "Major East Coast Costume Collections Accessible for Study." It provides a brief note on the strength of each collection. Also costume collections are featured in Pieter Bach's *Textile, Costume, and Doll Collections, in the United States and Canada* (1981). The directory was designed to be useful for travelers and for creating mailing lists. Costume collections are listed by state, and then city, with name and address; 834 U.S. collections are listed.

In 1990 Meredith Wright included costume in museum collections in her *Put on Thy Beautiful Garments*, focusing on New England clothing, 1760–1937. The list of some nineteen institutions can be seen in an index by specific type of clothing. Another publication of the 1990s was the special 1993 issue of *Museum International* devoted to fashion and costume museums. The editorial by Marcia Lord notes that "museums have long recognized that fashion is a serious subject of study" and that over one hundred museums in the world concentrate on "clothing and dress," not considering the many other related specialties, such as accessories, textiles, and cosmetics. Although there is no list of these museums, the twelve articles coordinated by Elizabeth Ann Coleman, Museum of Fine Arts, Houston, Texas, offer insights into the functions and importance of the costume museum. "Preserving Human Packaging" by Coleman, serves as the introduction. Several articles emphasize popular issues reflected by museum costume collections. "Bringing Costumes to Life: An Exercise in Media Documentation" by Aagot Noss describes the filming of interviews with owners of costumes and the various processes (dying, sewing, embroidering, etc.) as a method of enhancing the knowledge of the clothes and of furthering the education process not only for museum visitors but for those who might borrow the film as well. "Costumes as Indicators of Community" by Mariliina Perkko highlights costume as "one of the main assets of a historical museum" and uses the wedding costume to illustrate her points.[9] Even the "Viewpoint" article, which is not technically part of the group of costume museum articles, offers insight into the importance of the participative museum. Dan Bernfeld discusses involving the public and the relationship between the visitor and the museum staff. His examples of visitors being able to view restorative artists at work might suggest that costume restoration work on view could add to the educational experience for museum visitors and that the living history museums where costumed interpreters perform daily tasks are of value to the public and the museum.

Recently the Costume Society of America has shown an interest in creating a costume collection directory; data have been gathered but not published as of this writing. Region VI has produced a guide to collections, *Costume Collections Directory of the Southeast Region, Costume Society of America, 1994–1995*. It is edited by Frances B. Loba of Colonial Williamsburg, Costume Design Center. The most accessible and comprehensive way to look at U.S. costume museums or specialized museums with costume or clothing collections is still to consult *The Official Museum Directory*. Museum descriptions and information are arranged by state, with indexes for name of institution, personnel, category of museum (such as art, general, history, specialized including sports museums and theater museums), and by collections (such as audiovisual and film, costumes and textiles, decorative arts, folk arts and culture, photographs, prints, graphic arts, recreational artifacts, and personal artifacts).

Several students have surveyed costume collections. Ann Lafferty's 1963–1964 survey of U.S. museum costume collections, completed in 1967, concluded that there was a need for better communication of costume information and a need to increase the scope of costume collections used for education.[10] Sixty-five Arizona costume and textile collections were analyzed by Vickie Raison in 1970. Kyle Hennings surveyed historical costume collections in Ohio museums in 1980, while Kathleen McCarney described the costume and textile collections in California museums in 1981. Most of the other theses dealing with costume collections discuss aspects of specific collection(s), such as collection development, storage and display issues, identification of certain types of garments or patterns in a collection or collections, or the management of collection information.

MUSEUM HISTORIES

Although no history of the costume museum has been written, several histories of U.S. museums in general point out important costume connections. *The Museum and Popular Culture* (1939) by Thomas R. Adam provides a history of museums in the United States showing their early establishment as promoting the social good and challenges them to continue to have an impact in popular education and more specifically in continuing education for adults.[11] The 1937 traveling Neighborhood Exhibits of the Metropolitan Museum of Art, New York, are mentioned by Adam as an example of community outreach. Adam mentions that the effective transmission of museum research to the general public requires staff dedication, which might include the use of museum publications such as the *Smithsonian* or *National Geographic* and museum shop items such as coloring books and calendars. He points to the nation's interest in history and collecting old objects as another popular pursuit that museums can use in their continuing-education efforts.

Herbert and Marjorie Katz prepared *Museums U.S.A.: A History and Guide*

(1965), focusing on art, science, history, and children's museums. Although "costume" and "clothing" do not appear in the index, they are briefly noted in the "Art" section: remodeling of the Costume Institute, Metropolitan Museum of Art is noted, and fashion displays at the Brooklyn Museum are termed "exciting." Museums in the section titled "An Infinite Variety" contain costume: Circus World Museum, Baraboo, Wisconsin, which participated in an annual parade; Ringling Circus Museum, Sarasota, Florida; dolls at the Shelburne Museum, Shelburne, Vermont; National Cowboy Hall of Fame and Western Heritage Center, Oklahoma City, Oklahoma; the Panhandle-Plains Historical Museum, Canyon, Texas; Will Rogers Memorial, Claremore, Oklahoma; and the Buffalo Bill Museum, Cody, Wyoming. The Katzs conclude that "there is no end to collecting . . . to the impulse to leave something behind—a souvenir or a whole heritage—for a future generation."[12] A directory of some 2,500 museums with brief collection notes concludes the volume. The "Acknowledgments and Bibliographic Notes" is an excellent feature.

Kenneth Hudson's *Museums of Influence* (1987) discusses thirty-seven museums around the world. These museums he considers to have been so innovative in their programs or presentations that they have made an impact on other museums, causing them to reconsider or to change their practices. Three of the thirty-seven are U.S. museums. Interestingly it is in this highly selective work that costume receives its recognition, for Colonial Williamsburg receives attention as the site museum of influence. To give visitors a true impression of eighteenth-century American life, it uses costumed interpreters and has created an Interpretation Department, which is sensitive to the contribution of all the people in the society, including black slaves. Training craftsmen over the years to provide live demonstrations has resulted in a growing group of "historical archaeologists," another innovation that fosters citizen education and appreciation for historical methods of making various objects.[13] The museum is also noted for its innovative use of conferences, films, publications, and interests in sharing information with other museum professionals. Hudson admits that dressing guides in period clothes was not original to Williamsburg, but its efforts have influenced other sites, such as Mystic Seaport, Connecticut; Plimouth Plantation, Massachusetts; Old Sturbridge Village, Massachusetts; and Farmers' Village, Cooperstown, New York. He discusses earlier examples, including tableaux at the 1876 Centennial Exhibition in Philadelphia, George F. Dow's interpreters at the seventeenth-century John Ward House, Essex Institute, Salem, Massachusetts, in 1909, and the costume celebrations at Henry Ford's Wayside Inn, Sudbury, Massachusetts, in 1926.

Although there is little written on the costume or fashion museum generally and its impact on our popular culture, costume is evident in the advertisements for many exhibitions. For example in a recent *CSA* (*Cos-*

tume Society of America) News a picture of Seminole costume dolls was chosen to attract attention to the announcement of an exhibit, *All the World Arrayed,* at the Cincinnati Art Museum.[14] Current promotional booklets for the Publick House Historic Resort, Sturbridge, Massachusetts, show colored photographs of costumed resort staff, and in addition to promoting the inn and resort, mention is made of nearby Old Sturbridge Village with "period-costumed interpreters." Even state tourism agencies recognize the impact of costume, as evidenced by the advertisement in April 1995 *Travel and Leisure* for "See History Come to Life in Philadelphia." Here the colored photo shows costumed children washing potatoes and an adult cooking over an open fire with text informing the reader about Philadelphia museums, hotels, tours, and free Pennsylvania visitor guides. Costume and fashion are also used to advantage in promotional museum publications themselves or publications produced for museums—for example, the New York Metropolitan Museum of Art's *Women in White: Addresses,* published in 1989 by Bullfinch Press.[15] The address book features nineteenth- and twentieth-century photographs and paintings of women wearing white dresses. All works are from their collections. The pairings show similarities in costume and pose and serve to educate and delight the reader, about both the artists and their works and about costume history as well. Notecards were also produced using these images. The visual and entertainment aspects of costume and fashion in connection with the educational goals and more practical financial needs of museums are evident.

SELECTED BIBLIOGRAPHY

Adam, Thomas R. *The Museum and Popular Culture.* New York: American Association for Adult Education, 1939. 177p.

Bach, Pieter, ed. *Textile, Costume and Doll Collections in the United States and Canada.* Lopez, WA: R. L. Shep, 1981. 69p.

Christensen, Erwin O., ed. *Museums Directory of the United States and Canada.* Washington, D.C.: American Association of Museums, 1961. 567p. (2d ed. 1965).

Costume Society of America. *1995–1996 Membership Directory: Costume Society of America.* Earleville, MD, 1995. 79p.

Druesedow, Jean L. "Major East Coast Costume Collections Accessible for Study." *Theatre Design and Technology* 16 (Winter 1980): 17.

Duffield, Frances J. *Resources in the Form of Historic Costumes, Accessories, Textiles and Slides Located in Universities and Colleges. A Bibliography.* N.p: n.p., 1979. 86p.

"Fashion and Costume Museums." *Museum International* 45, no. 3 (1993): 3–49.

Hudson, Kenneth. *Museums of Influence.* Cambridge: Cambridge University Press, 1987. 220p.

Huenefeld, Irene P. *International Directory of Historical Clothing.* Metuchen, NJ: Scarecrow Press, 1967. 175p.

Katz, Herbert, and Marjorie. *Museums, U.S.A.: A History and Guide.* Garden City, NY: Doubleday, 1965. 395p.

Loba, Frances Burroughs, ed. *Costume Collections Directory of the Southwest Region, Costume Society of America, 1994–1995.* 30p.

Lubell, Cecil, ed. *Textile Collections of the World.* v.1: *United States and Canada.* New York: Van Nostrand Reinhold, 1976. 336p. (v.2: *United Kingdom and Ireland;* v.3: *France*)

The Official Museum Directory. American Association of Museums. New Providence, NJ: Reed Elsevier, 1971–1978 biennial; 1980–annual. (25th ed. 1995, published 1994, 2040p.)

Truesdell, Bill. *Directory of Unique Museums.* Phoenix, AZ: Oryx Press, 1985. 165p.

Wright, Meredith. "Costume in Museum Collections." In *Put on Thy Beautiful Garments,* 112–113. East Montpelier, VT: Clothes Press, 1990.

Theses

Hennings, Kyle L. "A Survey of Historical Costume Collections in Ohio Museums." Master's thesis, Ohio University, 1980.

Lafferty, Ann A. "Contents and Services of Museum Costume Collections in the United States, 1963–1964." Master's thesis, Texas Women's University, 1968.

McCarney, Kathleen. "A Descriptive Survey and Catalog of Costume and Textile Collections in California Museums, Universities and Colleges." Master's thesis, San Francisco State University, 1981.

Raison, Vicki L. "A Descriptive Survey of Textile and Costume Collections in Museums in Arizona." Master's thesis, University of Arizona, 1970.

THE MUSEUMS AND COLLECTIONS

This list of 175 U.S. institutions has been derived from a number of directories and lists. Included are the forty-five museums in the 1995 edition of the *Official Museum Directory* (OMD) listed under the category of "Costume Museums," seven museums designated as costume museums or indexed under "costume" in the 1961 Christensen *Museums Directory of the United States and Canada* (Chr), which still appear in the OMD with costume noted, fifty museums which have institution memberships in the Costume Society of America per the *1995–96 Membership Directory* (CSA), nine eastern museums identified by Duresedow (Dru) in her 1981 article, nineteen collections of over 499 items as identified by Duffield (Duf) in her 1979 survey of college and university collections (number of items listed in parentheses after notation), and seventy-two collections from the 1967 Huenefeld survey (Hue), which also indicates costume or a closely related accessory or topic in the 1995 OMD collection's statement. Information provided is name, state, founding date, brief costume collection note (+ [plus] indicates other materials in the collection), position of costume curator, and notation for appearance in the above lists. The initial list notation indicates where the institution was first noted.

Allen Memorial Art Museum, Oberlin College, Ohio. 1917, costumes+. Hue, OMD.

Allentown Art Museum, Pennsylvania, 1934, costumes+. CSA, OMD.

Allyn County–Fort Wayne Historical Society Museum, Indiana, 1921, nineteenth- and twentieth-century clothing, dolls+. Hue, OMD.

American Museum of Natural History, New York, 1869. Dru.

Amherst Historical Society, Strong House Museum, Massachusetts, 1889, costumes+. OMD.

Armenian Library and Museum of America, Massachusetts, 1971, Armenian folk arts, textiles+. CSA, OMD.

Battersea (Petersburg Museums), Virginia, 1985, eighteenth-century decorative arts. CSA, OMD.

Beauchamp Newman Museum, Elizabeth, West Virginia, 1950, costumes+. OMD.

Birmingham Museum of Art, Alabama, 1951, American decorative arts+. CSA, OMD.

Braintree Historical Society, Massachusetts, 1930, military records, photos+. OMD.

Brick Store Museum, Maine, 1936, costumes+. Hue, OMD.

Brooklyn Museum, New York, 1823, American and European costumes+. Dru, OMD.

Brooks Academy Museum, Massachusetts, 1963, wedding gowns, lace+. OMD.

Brunswick Railroad Museum, Maryland, 1974, railroad history. OMD.

Campbell House Museum, Montana, 1943, costumes+. Chr, OMD, Hue.

Carpenter Home Museum, Washington, 1990, miners, farmers, ethnic costumes+. OMD.

Chester County Historical Society, South Carolina, 1959, Indian artifacts+. OMD.

Cincinnati Art Museum, Ohio, 1881, costumes+, costume and textile curator. CSA, OMD, Hue.

City Island Museum, New York, 1964, yachting industry, artifacts, photos+. OMD.

Clown Hall of Fame and Research Center, Wisconsin, 1986, clown history, photos, art. OMD.

Colonial Williamsburg, Virginia, 1926, seventeenth- and eighteenth-century costumes+. Hue, OMD.

Colorado State University. *See* Gustafson Gallery.

Concordia Historical Museum, Montana, 1847, Lutheran costume+. Hue, OMD.

Connecticut Historical Society, Connecticut, 1825, costumes+. Hue, OMD.

Cooper-Hewitt National Museum of Design, Smithsonian Institution, New York, 1897, decorative arts, all periods+. Dru, Hue, OMD.

Country Music Hall of Fame and Museum, Tennessee, 1964, costumes, sight/sound exhibits+. OMD.

Craft and Folk Art Museum, California, 1973, Japanese, East Indian, Central American folk arts. CSA, OMD.

Cultural Heritage Center, Texas, 1976, ethnic and dance costumes+. OMD.

Cumberland County Historical Society, New Jersey, 1908, costumes+. OMD.

Dallas Historical Society, Texas, 1922, costumes+, costume curator. Hue, OMD.

Danbury Scott-Fanton Museum and Historical Society, Connecticut, 1942, hat-making artifacts, costumes+. Hue, OMD.

DAR Museum–First Ladies of Texas Historic Costumes Collection, Texas Women's University, Texas, 1940, inaugural ball gowns+. OMD, Chr, Hue.

Daughters of the American Revolution Museum, Washington, D.C., 1890, costumes+, associate curator of costumes. Hue, OMD.

Delaware State Museums, Delaware, 1938, costumes+. Chr, OMD, Hue.

Denver Art Museum, Colorado, 1893, costumes+. Hue, OMD.

Detroit Historical Museum, Michigan, 1928, costumes+. Hue, OMD.

Detroit Institute of Arts, Michigan, 1885, puppetry, textiles+. Hue, OMD.

Deutschheim State Historic Site, Montana, 1979, nineteenth-century German immigrant artifacts. CSA, OMD.

Dupage County Historical Museum, Illinois, 1967, nineteenth- and twentieth-century material culture, coverlets+. CSA, OMD.

Elizabeth Sage Historic Costume Collection, Indiana University, Indiana, 1935, nineteenth- and twentieth-century American and European clothing and accessories, curator, assistant curator. OMD, Duf (5,000 items).

Fashion Institute of Technology, New York, 1944, costumes seventeenth century to date (over 1 million items), curator of costumes. OMD, Dru.

First White House of the Confederacy, Alabama, 1900, costumes, President Davis items+. Chr, OMD Hue.

Florida State University, Florida, costumes+. Duf (1,000 items).

Fort Nisqually Historic Site, Washington, 1937, fort complex artifacts. CSA, OMD.

Fort Ticonderoga, New York, 1908, uniforms+. Hue, OMD.

Goldstein Gallery, University of Minnesota, Minnesota, 1976, 9,000 costumes and accessories, curator of costumes. OMD, Duf.

Graceland, Tennessee, 1982, clothing, costumes, jewelry+. OMD.

Grand Encampment Museum, Wyoming, 1965, mining history, costumes, uniforms, hat shop+. OMD.

Gustafson Gallery, Colorado State University, Colorado, 1986, costumes 1850–date, accessories+. OMD, Duf (3,000 items).

Hackettstown Historical Society Museum and Library, New Jersey, 1975, costumes, photos+. OMD.

Henry Ford Museum and Greenfield Village, Michigan, 1929, American artifacts, photos+. CSA, OMD.

Henry Francis Du Pont Winterthur Museum, Delaware, 1930, American decorative arts seventeenth to nineteenth century+. Dru, CSA, OMD, Hue.

Henry M. Flagler Museum, Whitehall Mansion, Florida, 1959, costumes, laces+. CSA, OMD.

Higgins Armory Museum, Massachusetts, 1928, arms, armor. OMD.

Hillwood Museum, District of Columbia, 1976, Russian decorative arts+. CSA, OMD.

Historic Mobile Preservation Society, Alabama, 1935, costumes+. Hue, OMD.

Historic St. Mary's City, Maryland, 1966, costumes, photos+, costume coordinator. CSA, OMD.

Historical Museum of the Gunn Memorial Library, Connecticut, 1899, dolls+. Hue, OMD.

Historical Society of Oak Park and River Forest, Illinois, 1968, local costumes+. OMD.

Hoard Historical Museum and National Dairy Shrine, Wisconsin, 1933, local history, crafts. CSA, OMD.

Illinois State Museum, Illinois, 1877, decorative arts+. CSA, OMD.

Indiana University. *See* Elizabeth Sage Historic Costume Collection.

Iowa State University, Iowa, costumes. Duf (5,000 items).

John and Mable Ringling Museum, Florida, 1928, circus costumes+. Chr, Hue, OMD.

John E. and Walter D. Webb Museum of Vintage Fashion, Maine, 1983, mid-nineteenth- through mid-twentieth-century clothing for men and women. OMD.

John Paul Jones House Museum, New Hampshire, 1920, costumes; docents wear costumes. Hue, OMD.

Kansas City Museum, Montana, 1939, costumes+. CSA, OMD, Hue.

Kansas Museum of History, Kansas, 1875, costumes+. CSA, OMD.

Kansas State University, Kansas, costumes. Duf (1,300 items).

Kelton House Museum and Garden, Ohio, 1976, Victorian clothes and toys. OMD.

Kent State University Museum, Ohio, 1981, western dress 1750–date. OMD.

Kentucky Historical Society, Kentucky, 1836, Kentucky decorative arts, material culture+. CSA, OMD.

Lace Museum, California, 1980, lace articles, trimmed clothing+. OMD.

Lake County Museum, Illinois, 1976, clothing+. CSA, OMD.

Lancaster County Historical Society, Pennsylvania, 1886, costumes+. Hue, OMD.

Liberace Museum, California, 1979, costumes+. OMD.

Liberty Memorial Museum and Archives, Montana, World War I insignia, memorabilia+. Hue, OMD.

Linn County Historical Museum and Moyer House, Oregon, 1962, local history, photos+. OMD.

Lockwood-Mathews Mansion Museum, Connecticut, 1966, costumes+. CSA, OMD.

Los Angeles County Museum of Art, California, 1910, North and South American, Asian and European costumes+, curator of costumes and textiles. CSA, OMD.

Loudoun Mansion, Pennsylvania, eighteenth-century costumes+. OMD.

Louisiana State Museum, Louisiana, 1906, costumes+, curator of costumes and textiles. Hue, OMD.

Lyman Allyn Art Museum, Connecticut, 1930, nineteenth- and twentieth-century costumes+. Hue, OMD.

Madison Historical Society, Connecticut, 1917, costumes, dolls+. Hue, OMD.

Maidenform Museum, New York, lingerie, underwear. CSA.

Mary Ball Washington Museum, Virginia, 1958, costumes, accessories+. CSA, OMD.

Maryland Historical Society, Maryland, 1844, costumes+. Hue, OMD.

Mattye Reed African Heritage Center, North Carolina Agricultural and Technical State University, North Carolina, 1968, arts, crafts of Africa, Haiti, New Guinea+. OMD.

Metropolitan Museum of Art (MMA), Costume Institute (CI) (New York University), New York, 1870 MMA; 1946 CI, costumes+, associate curator, Costume Inst. Chr, OMD, Dru, Hue.

Michigan State University Museum, Michigan, 1857, popular culture, decorative arts+. Hue, OMD, Duf (1,716 items).

Milan Historical Museum, Ohio, 1930, costumes, dolls+. OMD.

Mississippi County Historical Society, Mississippi, 1966, costumes+. OMD.

Mississippi State Historical Museum, Mississippi, 1902, needlework, decorative arts+. CSA, OMD.

Missouri Historical Society, Missouri, 1866, costumes+. Hue, OMD.

Monroe County Heritage Museum, Alabama, 1900–1950 clothing+. Hue, OMD.

Mount Mary College, Wisconsin, 1928, costume 1750s–date with emphasis on American and European designers. OMD.

Museum of Art, Rhode Island School of Design, Rhode Island, 1877, costumes+, curator of costume and textiles. Hue, OMD.

Museum of Fine Arts, Boston, Massachusetts, 1870, costumes+. Dru, OMD, CSA.

Museum of Fine Arts, Houston, Texas, 1900, costumes+, curator of textiles and costumes. CSA, OMD.

Museum of History and Industry, Washington, 1914, nineteenth- and twentieth-century costumes (70,000 items including textiles), costumes assistant. CSA, OMD, Hue.

Museum of International Folk Art, New Mexico, 1953, folk costumes+, curator of textiles/costumes. CSA, OMD, Hue.

Museum of the Bedford Historical Society, New York, 1916, costumes+. OMD.

Museum of the City of New York, New York, 1923, costumes+, curator of costumes. Hue, OMD.

Museum of Vintage Fashion, California, 1978, fashion from 1710 to date, clothing from fifty designers, 10,000 items including forty-five accessory types, president and curator. OMD.

National Air and Space Museum, Smithsonian Institution, Washington, D.C., 1946, uniforms+. Hue, OMD.

National Baseball Hall of Fame, New York, 1936, uniforms+. Hue, OMD.

National Historic Oregon Trail Interpretive Center, Oregon, 1992, artifacts, photos+. CSA, OMD.

National Museum of American History, Smithsonian Institution, Washington, D.C., 1846, costumes+. Dru, OMD, Hue.

National Park Service, Harper's Ferry National Historic Park, West Virginia, 1944, artifacts. CSA, OMD.

Natural History Museum of Los Angeles County, California, 1910, artifacts+. CSA, OMD.

Neville Public Museum of Brown County, Wisconsin, 1915, costumes+. Hue, OMD.

New Bern Civil War Museum, North Carolina, Civil War history. CSA.

New Jersey Historical Society, New Jersey, 1845, costumes+. Hue, OMD.

New Milford Historical Society, Connecticut, 1915, costumes+. Hue, OMD.

Nordica Homestead, Maine, 1927, Lillian Nordica collections of opera costumes, jewelry+. Chr, OMD.

North Carolina Museum of History, North Carolina, 1902, costumes, toys+. CSA, OMD.

Northampton County Historical and Genealogical Society, Pennsylvania, 1906, dolls, uniforms+. Hue, OMD.

Oakland Museum, California, 1969, costumes+. Hue, OMD.

Ohio Historical Center, Ohio, 1885, clothing+. Hue, OMD.

Ohio State University, Ohio, costumes. Duf (500 items).

Oklahoma State University, Oklahoma, costumes. Duf (500 items).

Old Fort Meade Museum and Historic Research Association South Dakota, 1964, military memorabilia, 1878–1944. OMD.

Old Sturbridge Village, Massachusetts, 1946, costumes+. CSA, OMD, Hue.

Oregon Historical Society, Oregon, 1873, costumes+. Hue, OMD.

Ossining Historical Society Museum, New York, 1931, costumes, dolls+. Hue, OMD.

Owatonna Arts Center, Minneapolis, 1974, Marianne Young 100-piece costume collection. OMD.

Panhandle-Plains Historical Museum, Texas, 1921, pioneer clothing+. CSA, OMD.

Pascack Historical Society, New Jersey, 1942, local Dutch history, clothing+. OMD.

Peabody Essex Museum, Massachusetts, 1799/1848, early American costumes, portraits+. CSA, OMD, Hue.

Philadelphia Mummers Museum, Pennsylvania, 1976, audiovisuals, Mummers suits, costumes+. OMD.

Philadelphia Museum of Art, Pennsylvania, 1876, American decorative arts+, curator of costume and textiles. Dru, OMD, CSA, Hue.

Phoenix Art Museum, Arizona Costume Institute, Arizona, 1949, eighteenth-through twentieth-century costumes+, curator of costumes. CSA, OMD.

Pilgrim Hall, Massachusetts, 1820, decorative arts+. Hue, OMD.

Plimouth Plantation, Massachusetts, 1947, seventeenth-century English and Native American culture. CSA, OMD.

Plymouth Antiquarian Society, Massachusetts, 1919, costumes+. Hue, OMD.

Porter-Phelps-Huntington Foundation, Massachusetts, 1955, clothing+. Hue, OMD.

Purdue University, Indiana, costumes. Duf (800 items).

Rancho Los Cerritos, California, 1955, costumes+. Hue, OMD.

Riley County Historical Museum, Kansas, 1914, dolls+. Hue, OMD.

Robert Hall Fleming Museum, Vermont, 1931, costumes+. Hue, OMD.

Rochester Historical Society, New York, 1861, costumes+. Hue, OMD.

Rochester Museum and Science Center, New York, 1912, costumes+. Hue, OMD.

Rock and Roll Hall of Fame and Museum, Ohio, 1985, costumes, popular culture+. OMD.

Rockwood Museum, Delaware, 1976, seventeenth- through nineteenth-century American decorative arts+. CSA, OMD.

Rogers Historical Museum, Arkansas, 1975, local history, festivals, quilts+. CSA, OMD.

Rosalie Whyel Museum of Doll Art, Washington, 1989, doll history. CSA, OMD.

Roscoe Village, Ohio, 1968, historic site clothing+. CSA, OMD.

St. Lawrence County Historical Association, Silas Wright House, New York, 1947, costumes+. Hue, OMD.

Sharlot Hall Museum, Arizona, 1929, costumes+. Hue, OMD.

Shelburne Museum, Vermont, 1947, American folk and decorative arts, dolls, circus+. CSA, OMD.

Siloam Springs Museum, Arkansas, 1969, World War II uniforms+. OMD.

Slater Memorial Museum, Connecticut, 1888, costumes+. Hue, OMD.

Smithsonian Institution. *See* Cooper-Hewitt National Museum of Design; National Air and Space Museum; National Museum of American History.

Smithtown Historical Society, New York, 1955, costumes+. OMD.

State Historical Museum of Wisconsin, Wisconsin, 1846, dolls, costumes+. Hue, OMD.

Staten Island Historical Society, New York, 1856, costumes+. Hue, OMD.

Strong Museum, New York, 1968, sociocultural history Northeast United States

1820–date. CSA, OMD.

Textile Museum, Washington, D.C., 1925, 15,000+ historical and handmade textiles+. CSA, OMD, Hue.

Ukranian National Museum, Library and Archive, Illinois, 1952, embroideries, beadwork, folk art+. OMD.

University of Alabama, Alabama, costumes. Duf (741 items).

University of Delaware, Delaware, costumes. Duf (2000 items).

University of Hawaii, Hawaii, costumes. Duf (800 items).

University of Illinois, Illinois, costumes. Duf (1,000 items).

University of Maryland, Maryland, costumes. Duf (2,000 items).

University of Minnesota. *See* Goldstein Gallery.

University of Missouri, Missouri, costumes. Duf (1,200 items).

University of Rhode Island, Rhode Island, costumes. Duf (8,537 items).

Valentine Museum, Virginia, 1892, embroideries, costumes 1600–date+, curator of costumes and textiles. OMD, Hue.

Virginia Polytechnic Institute and State University, Virginia, costumes. Duf (1,325 items).

Walters Art Gallery, Maryland, 1931, decorative arts, jewelry+. Hue, OMD.

Washington State University, Washington, costumes. Duf (516 items).

Waukeshsa County Historical Museum and Library, Wisconsin, 1914, dolls+. CSA, OMD.

Wenham Museum, Massachusetts, 1921, costumes, dolls+. Hue, OMD.

West Point Museum, New York, 1854, uniforms+. Hue, OMD.

Western Reserve Historical Museum, Ohio, 1867, costumes+. Hue, OMD.

Wilmette Historical Museum, Illinois, 1947, costumes+. Hue, OMD.

Winnetka Historical Museum, Illinois, 1988, costumes+. Hue, OMD.

Winterthur. *See* Henry Francis Du Pont Winterthur Museum.

Women's Army Corps Museum, Alabama, 1955, uniforms+. Hue, OMD.

Workman and Temple Family Homestead Museum, California, 1981, costumes+. CSA, OMD.

12

Professional Organizations and Related Conference Proceedings

There are many organizations with interests in costume or fashion. Some restrict membership; some are open to anyone. Traditional domestic associations and organizations can be located by using the standard reference source, *Encyclopedia of Associations*. This directory groups associations by basic type and provides a keyword subject/name index. Information provided includes: association name, address, telephone number, contact person, founding date, purpose and brief description, publications, and conference information. Many museums offer membership in costume-related associations, societies, or friends' groups in order to support those collections in the museum. One example is the Costume and Textile Society founded in January 1984 at the Wadsworth Atheneum, Hartford, Connecticut. These groups hold meetings and programs and, along with various symposia and lectures offered by colleges and universities, add another dimension to the learning process.

Organizations that hold conferences or meetings may not publish the papers presented. Those papers that are published might appear in book form, in the periodical literature, often as a special issue, or as preprints. Some organizations publish abstracts of papers and offer them to conference attendees and/or for sale later. No attempt has been made to identify individual conference proceedings from specific groups; however, in the research for this book generally, several conferences or symposia have been noted from a few groups.

Although the Costume Society of America (CSA) has held an annual meeting or symposium each year since 1975, it was not until 1987 that abstracts of papers presented were published. These publications are noted under the entry for the Costume Society of America. Only a few specific conferences were identified for the Costume Society, although it has held an annual conference since 1967. Published conference proceedings and papers presented can be researched generally by searching various indexes (e.g., *WorldCat, the OCLC Online Union Catalog, Proceedings First,* and *Papers First*). Both *Proceedings* and *Papers First* provide access to conference sources held in the British Library collections since October 1993. Often, though, papers from conferences are noticed only secondarily after a normal literature search has been conducted (in, for example, *ERIC, MLA, Clothing and Textile Arts Index,* or the *Art Index*), and consultation of the source reveals that the paper was presented at a conference.

Encyclopedia of Associations. 28th ed. 1994. Detroit: Gale Research, 1993. 2v. in 4.
————. *International Organizations.* 24th ed. 1990. 2v.
————. *Regional, State, and Local Organizations.* 1994–1995. ed. 1994. 5v.
Encyclopedia of Associations [online]. (current). Available: DIALOG file:114.
Encyclopedia of Associations [CD-ROM]. (current), Available: Silverplatter.
Proceedings First and *Papers First.* October 1993– (for both databases). Updated monthly. Databases are available through the *FirstSearch Catalog service.*
WorldCat, The OCLC Online Union Catalog. Pre 1900-. Updated daily. Available through the *FirstSearch Catalog* or *EPIC services.*

SELECTED ORGANIZATIONS

The following organizations and associations have been verified if possible in the *Encyclopedia of Associations;* conference information is noted. More detailed published conference information is provided for a few of the groups whose publication data appear in *WorldCat, the OCLC Online Union Catalog.* The selected groups reflect business as well as scholarly or professional interests of individuals. Many more domestic organizations can be identified by consulting the *Encyclopedia of Associations* directly.

American Association of Family and Consumer Sciences, 1555 King St., Alexandria VA 22314. Annual conference. Formerly American Home Economics Association founded in 1909.

American Association of Museums, 1225 Eye St. NW, Suite 200, Washington, D.C. 20005. Annual conference.

American Institute for Conservation of Historic and Artistic Works, 1400 16th St. NW, Suite 340, Washington, D.C. 20036. Annual meeting.

Association of Clothing Designers, 475 Park Ave. South, New York, NY 10016. Semi-annual conference.

Association of College Professors of Textiles and Clothing. *ACPTC Combined Pro-*

ceedings/ACPTC Proceedings. 1975 to 1986–. Irregular. *See* International Textile and Apparel Association.

Association of Image Consultants International, 509 Madison Ave., New York, NY 10022. Annual conference.

Clothing Manufacturers Association of the U.S.A., 1290 Avenue of the Americas, Suite 1061, New York, NY 10104. Annual conference.

Costume Society, c/o Pat Poppy, 21 Oak Rd., Woolston, Southampton SO19 9BQ England. Annual conference. Address changes and can be located in *Costume*, the annual publication.

1st, 1967. *La Belle Epoque: Costume 1890–1914.* 65p.

2d, 1968. *High Victorian Costume, 1860–1890.* 53p.

3d, 1969. *Early Victorian Costume, 1830–1860.* 46p.

4th, 1970. *The So-Called Age of Elegance: Costume, 1785–1820.* 50p.

7th, 1973. *Strata of Society.* 56p.

Costume Society of America, 55 Edgewater Dr., P.O. Box 73. Earlville, MD 21919-0073. Annual conference. Early meetings concentrated on several speakers, museum or other institution tours with speakers, and society business. Gradually specific titles were given to the meeting and symposium, and the numbers of papers presented increased.

1st, 1975. Symposium on California Dress and Its History [may not be exact title]. Los Angeles, CA.

2d, 1976–1982. *Annual Meeting and Symposium.* No specific titles given for symposium subjects during this period of time.

9th, 1983. *The Eighteenth-Century.* Los Angeles, CA.

10th, 1984. *Annual Meeting and Symposium.* Minneapolis–St. Paul, MN.

11th, 1985. *The Technology and Industry of Fashion.* New York.

12th, 1986. *20th Century Fashion.* Indianapolis, IN.

Abstracts of papers published for:

13th, 1987. *Costume in the New Republic: The First Five Decades 1780–1830 and the Ways Historic Costume Collections are Used to Educate.* Williamsburg, VA. 19p.

14th, 1988. *Accessories and Professional Practices.* Cincinnati, OH. 32p.

15th, 1989. *Ethnic Dress: Origins and Influences.* Denver, CO. 33p.

16th, 1990. *Appearance and Gender Identity.* Washington, D.C. 43p.

17th, 1991. *American Dress as Social History.* Boston and Plymouth, MA. 33p.

18th, 1992. *Exploring Our Cultural Diversity.* San Antonio, TX. 43p.

19th, 1993. *Costumes and Cultures of the Pacific Rim and Their World Influences.* Seattle, WA, and Victoria, BC. 29p.

20th, 1994. *Dress Addressed: Costume across the Disciplines.* Montreal, Quebec, and Hull and Ottawa, Ontario. 48p.

21st, 1995. *Dressing for an Audience: Creating an Image through Costume.* Dearborn and Detroit, MI.

Costume Society of Ontario, Box 981, Station F, Toronto, ON M4Y 2N9 Canada. 1st workshop, 1971. *Fashions of the Seventies, 1870–1879.* [35]p.

Fashion Group International, 9 Rockefeller Plaza, New York, NY 10020. Annual meeting.

International Association of Clothing Designers, 475 Park Ave. South, New York, NY 10016. Semiannual conference.

International Textile and Apparel Association, P.O. Box 1360, Monument, CO

80132-1360. Annual meeting. *ITAA Proceedings*. 1991– (48th year, 1991). Formerly the Association of College Professors of Textiles and Clothing, founded in 1944.

Jeanswear Communication, 475 Park Ave. South, 17th Floor, New York, NY 10016. Semiannual meeting.

Men's Fashion Association of America, 475 Park Ave. South, 17th Floor, New York, NY 10016. Semiannual meeting.

National Association of Fashion and Accessory Designers, 2180 East 93d St., Cleveland, OH 44106. Annual meeting.

National Association of Milliners, Dressmakers and Tailors, c/o Harlem Institute of Fashion, 157 West 126th St. New York, NY 10027.

U.S. Institute for Theater Technology (USITT), 10 West 19th St., Suite 5A, New York, NY 10011. Annual conference.

13

Periodicals

AMERICAN PERIODICALS' HISTORY

Histories and bibliographies of American periodicals provide background for understanding the development of specialized periodicals devoted to fashion or historical costume. The 1892 study of Philadelphia magazines, 1741 to 1850, by Albert H. Smyth acknowledges the importance of Philadelphia as a cultural center. In his discussions of the magazines and their contributors, he reveals that *Godey's Lady's Book* was the "chief financial success among the Philadelphia magazines" and that its circulation increased to "150,000 a month . . . due to its popular colored fashion plates."[1] In addition Smyth indicates that publisher George R. Graham "first suggested to his friend Charles J. Peterson, then editor of the *Saturday Evening Post*, the publication of a fashion journal, patterned upon the popular French periodicals."[2] The result was *Peterson's Ladies' National Magazine*.

In 1935 Sidney Ditzion compiled an excellent bibliography, *The History of Periodical Literature in the United States*. He identifies Sherer's 1931 article on the French influences in *Godey's* as well as publications on periodical illustrations, women's magazines, and publications on individual periodicals. Frank L. Mott's major five-volume work, *A History of American Maga-*

zines (1938–1968), chronicles the development from 1741 to 1905, with descriptions of twenty-one magazines provided for the period 1905–1930. Women's periodicals' history is included, and it is within these sections that we see the emergence of fashion magazines. In "Women's Dress Again" in volume 3, covering the period 1865–1885, Mott indicates that eighteen fashion magazines were being published in New York in 1880, with *Harper's Bazar* being the "most successful purveyor of styles."[3] During the period 1885–1905 the "fashion plate" periodical ended and the "great journals for women"[4] began, such as *Ladies' Home Journal, Woman's Home Companion, McCall's,* and *Vogue,* the latter two placing more emphasis on fashion in the 1890s.[5] Mott provides histories of individual magazines in each volume plus bibliography.

James P. Wood's *Magazines in the United States,* first published in 1949, indicates six pages containing the subject "fashion" in his index. Wood discusses *Ladies' Home Journal, Good Housekeeping, McCall's, Woman's Home Companion, Harper's Bazaar, Vogue, Glamour, Mademoiselle, Charm,* and *Esquire.* But he emphasizes that it was the fashion magazines *Harper's Bazaar* and *Vogue* whose "influence . . . in the market place is powerful."[6] However, he also states that it was the "fashion departments of the women's general magazines" and the fashion magazines themselves that had a strong impact on the clothing choices and "social activities of American women, . . . for fashion magazines are studied and intensively considered, not merely read."[7] Further recognition is paid by stating, in the 1971 edition, that the fashion magazines have "intensively and extensively influenced, and even directed, American women in one of their deepest interests."

Eugene Exman's *The House of Harper* (1967) provides a more in-depth look at publishing in the nineteenth and twentieth centuries. It has a separate chapter on *Harper's Bazar* from 1867 to 1913, when it was sold to William R. Hearst, who was to reinvigorate it and add an "a" to *Bazar.*[8] Histories of other magazine publishers also provide insights, such as James Wood's *The Curtis Magazines* (1971), which recognized the *Ladies' Home Journal, Saturday Evening Post,* and *Country Gentleman* for their dominance and influence on society for almost a century.[9] *American Mass-Market Magazines* edited by Alan Nourie and Barbara Nourie in 1990 provides a historical overview with information arranged alphabetically by title, with a bibliography of other information sources and publication history for each magazine. Titles of interest include *Cosmopolitan, Colonial Ladies and Gentlemen's Magazine, Esquire, GQ, Graham's Magazine, Texas Magazine, Town and Country,* and *Vogue.* A "Chronology of Mass-Market Titles" appears in the book.

WOMEN'S PERIODICALS

Women's magazines have received considerable bibliographic attention. Bertha M. Stearns wrote five articles in the 1920s and early 1930s. Lawrence Martin wrote in 1928 about the beginnings of *Godey's Lady's Book*. Over twenty years later, Caroline J. Garnsey's article, "Ladies Magazines to 1850," although not documented, contains a check list of titles with dates and place of publication arranged by geographic region. Esther F. Stineman in 1979 analyzed the content of five women's magazines (*Ladies' Home Journal, Redbook, Ms, McCall's, Working Woman*) and stated that "advice on . . . fashion undercuts *Redbook* and other major magazines' more serious messages."[10]

By 1982 a major directory, *Women's Periodicals and Newspapers from the 18th Century to 1981*, was published as a union list of holdings from libraries in Madison, Wisconsin. Compiled by Maureen E. Hady, Barry C. Noonan, and Neil E. Strache it is arranged alphabetically by title, with a variety of indexes: geographic, editors, publishers, subject, foreign-language materials, catchword and subtitle, and chronological. Sixty titles are indexed under the subject of "fashion," eight under "clothes," and four under "fabrics." Nancy K. Humphrey's *American Women's Magazines: An Annotated Historical Guide* (1989) has seventeen citations under "fashion" in the index. She includes a section on women's pages in newspapers. In sections on the nineteenth and twentieth-century magazines, publications on individual periodical titles are located after the general material and are arranged alphabetically by title. Magazines of special interest include *Big Beautiful Woman, Cosmopolitan, Glamour, Elle, Essence, Harper's Bazaar, Good Housekeeping, Ladies' Home Journal, Mademoiselle, McCall's, Seventeen, Vogue,* and *Womensports*. Book and journal article citations in the bibliography have been compiled from twenty-eight various indexing services, most through to the late 1980s. Mary E. Zuckerman's 1991 annotated bibliography is titled *Sources on the History of Women's Magazines, 1792–1960*. Her historiographical review offers an excellent analysis of the sources in the bibliography. The subject index indicates ten citations on fashion generally, sixteen on fashion magazines, and three on fashion plates and illustrations. "Sarah J. Hale and Godey's Lady's Book" contains forty-four references. Periodical articles and monographs make up the bulk of the references, with a separate chapter describing archives and manuscript collections relating to women's magazines. Individual titles with separate bibliographies including secondary and primary source materials include *Butterick Publishing Company* (publications), *Family Circle, Good Housekeeping, Harper's Bazaar, Ladies' Home Journal, McCall's, Pictorial Review, Vogue, Woman's Day,* and *Woman's Home Companion*. Author and subject indexes are provided.

In an earlier article Zuckerman discussed marketing the magazines,

1873–1900, crediting clothing patterns for boosting sales of the *Delineator* and the introduction of advertisements as significant for Curtis Publishing. Judy Massey comments in a 1992 article, "Girl Talk Mags," that "among the most dog-eared periodicals in the middle school and high school libraries are girls' fashion magazines."[11] She discusses articles in *Teen, Seventeen, YM,* and *Sassy.* Ellen McCracken's *Decoding Women's Magazines, from Mademoiselle to Ms* (1993) analyzes advertising and editorial texts. Periodicals featured include *Big Beautiful Woman, Harper's Bazaar, Cosmopolitan, Essence, Family Circle, Glamour, Ladies' Home Journal, McCall's, Mademoiselle, Modern Bride, Redbook, Savy, Self, Seventeen, Teen, Vogue, Woman's Day, Women's Sports,* and *Young Miss.* It contains a chapter entitled "Fashion and Beauty: Transgression, Utopia, and Containment" in which she analyzes the near fusion of advertisements and text or "editorial material" in a number of fashion periodicals. She states that "this cultural continuum is especially well developed in one of the strongest categories of women's publications, the fashion and beauty magazines."[12] Her critique includes *Young Miss, Teen, Seventeen, Mademoiselle, Glamour, Self, Cosmopolitan, Bazaar,* and *Vogue.* She indicates that a direct connection between reading or looking at *Vogue* and actually purchasing clothing or beauty products represents "the epitome of the magazine's success, assuring advertisers that pages purchased in *Vogue* lead directly to sales of products."[13] Although this may be true, no research findings are presented to link purchase of *Vogue* to purchase of goods. In a discussion of *Bazaar,* the point is made that "even if *Bazaar*'s average readers have a household income of $47,739, it is unlikely that they can afford such expensive clothing" as designer dresses, often priced from one thousand to several thousand dollars. McCracken continues that readers can "enjoy the opulent garment . . . even while they know it is out of reach." It may be that the sales of advertised beauty products and less expensive clothing that imitates the original designer fashions are increased more so than expensive designer clothing featured in the magazines. Some graduate research explores these types of consumer issues.

Ditzion, Sidney. "The History of Periodical Literature in the United States, a Bibliography." *Bulletin of Bibliography* 15, no. 6 (January–April 1935): 110; and no. 7 (May–August 1935): 129–130.

Exman, Eugene. *The House of Harper: One Hundred and Fifty Years of Publishing.* New York: Harper & Row, 1967. 326p.

Garnsey, Caroline J. "Ladies' Magazines to 1850." *New York Public Library Bulletin* 58 (February 1954): 74–88.

Hady, Maureen E., Barry C. Noonan, and Neil E. Strache, comps. Edited by James P. Danky. *Women's Periodicals and Newspapers from the 18th Century to 1981. A Union List of Holdings of Madison, Wisconsin Libraries.* Boston: G. K. Hall, 1982. 376p.

Humphreys, Nancy K. *American Women's Magazines: An Annotated Historical Guide.* New York: Garland, 1989. 303p.

McCracken, Ellen. *Decoding Women's Magazines: From "Mademoiselle" to "Ms."* New York: St. Martin's Press, 1993. 341p.

Martin, Lawrence. "The Genesis of 'Godey's Lady's Book.' " *New England Quarterly* 1 (1928): 41–70.

Massey Judy. "Girl Talk Mags." *School Library Journal* 38 (October 1992): 54.

Mott, Frank Luther. *A History of American Magazines.* Cambridge: Harvard University Press, 1936–1968. 5v.

Nourie, Alan, and Barbara Nourie. *American Mass-Market Magazines.* Westport, CT: Greenwood Press, 1990.

Sherer, G. B. "French Culture as Presented to Middle Class America by 'Godey's Lady's Book.' " *American Literature* 3 (November 1931): 277–286.

Smyth, Albert H. *The Philadelphia Magazines and Their Contributors, 1741–1850.* Philadelphia: Robert M. Lindsay, 1892. 264p.

Stearns, Bertha M. "Before Godey's." *American Literature* 2 (1930): 248–255.

———. "Early New England Magazines for Ladies." *New England Quarterly* 2 (1929): 420–457.

———. "Early Western Magazines for Ladies." *Mississippi Valley Historical Review* 18 (1931): 319–330.

———. "New England Magazines for Ladies, 1830–1860." *New England Quarterly* 3 (October 1930): 627–656.

———. "Southern Magazines for Ladies (1819–1860)." *South Atlantic Quarterly* 31 (1932): 70–87.

Stineman, Ester F. "Women's Magazines: Serving up the 'New Woman' in the Same Old Way." *Serials Review* 5 (October 1979): 25–29.

Wood, James Playsted. *The Curtis Magazines.* New York: Ronald Press, 1971. 297p.

———. *Magazines in the United States.* 3d ed. New York: Ronald Press, 1971. 476p. (1st ed. 1949, 2d ed. 1956).

Zuckerman, Mary Ellen (Waller-Zuckerman). "Marketing the Women's Journals, 1873–1900." *Business and Economic History* 18 (1989): 99–108.

———. *Sources on the History of Women's Magazines, 1792–1960.* Westport, CT: Greenwood Press, 1991. 297p.

FASHION PERIODICALS

It is these images—sometimes powerful, provocative, fascinating, and artistic—that have served as the focal point for others also interested in the fashion periodical. Vyvyan B. Holland's *Hand Coloured Fashion Plates, 1770–1899* (1955) and Doris L. Moore's *Fashion through Fashion Plates, 1771–1970* (1971) focus attention on the quality of the plates themselves and fashion information from the plates, respectively. Neither concentrates solely on the periodicals. One booklet produced in 1988 by the National Art Library in London and written by Alice Grant discusses British *Fashion Magazines from the 1890s to the 1980s.* Julian Robinson's *The Fine Art of Fashion: An Illustrated History* (1989) covers the mid-eighteenth century in Europe to today. More specifically it concentrates on the fashion drawings or plates, their creators, and the fashion designers, periodical

editors, and publishers who supported their work. In "Our Fashion In-
heritance," Robinson discusses Western clothing and its importance to
many "ordinary people" as a means of "identification" and "expression,"
allowing for dissension yet also allowing membership in the larger society.
It is because of this significance that clothing has become an interest of
"political scientists, economists, sociologists, psychologists, anthropologists and art historians"[14] as well as the costume specialist. He gives the
artist credit for opening "doors to change" and for representing "people's aesthetic dreams" often even more than the clothing actually worn.
Robinson says that the fashion magazines were introduced in the 1700s
in Europe as a way to reach the expanding middle class and inform them
about clothes.

Other types of publications add to the fashion periodical literature. For
instance Sandra E. Moriarty's "Retrospective Analysis of Nostalgia," a paper presented at a meeting of the Association for Education in Journalism
in 1982, examined "12 magazines representing fashion and design-
oriented publications—both general interest and design trade magazines"
from 1959 through 1979. Articles, advertising artwork, and typography
were studied for nostalgic trends. Kelly Ervin and Linda Jackson's 1990
paper looks at the portrayal of black females in fashion advertisements
from *Cosmopolitan, Glamour,* and *Vogue,* 1986–1988. Findings indicated only
2.4 percent of advertisements included blacks. Both studies are available
as ERIC (Educational Resources Information Center) documents located
in many academic libraries.

Several articles and book chapters discuss fashion periodicals. Donna
Fenn (1981) laments the lack of feminist attitudes in fashion magazines;
Michael H. Randall (1982) reviews two bridal magazines; and Ellen Melinkoff focuses a chapter on "Fashion Magazines in General and *Mademoiselle's* College Issue in Particular" in her *What We Wore* (1984). Two
European journal articles should be mentioned, both published in 1988:
Anna M. Castro's "Pandora between Art and Communication," covering
fashion magazines from the sixteenth century to the present, and Gabriel
Bauret's "Trade Images," which covers fashion magazine history from the
1920s to the present. The latter deals with how the "magazines have affected the relationship between photography and fashion."[15] Barbara Cohen-Stratyner discusses "Fashion Fillers in Silent Film Periodicals." This
1989 chapter shows how interest in fashion was used to attract a wider
audience for both the movie companies and the fashion designers and
retailers. Ten house organs and magazines for the general public are analyzed with the list and three bibliographic guides to film periodicals.
Martha Tarlton and Suzanne LaBrecque (1993) have described twenty-six
fashion merchandising periodicals to assist in collection development activity for fashion merchandising educational programs, which, the authors
state, provide for a "growing number of career options for graduates."[16]

The titles are grouped by focus: "Raw Materials and Manufacturing," "Retailing and General Marketing," "Fashion Merchandising Trade Publications," and "Scholarly Journals." Leslie W. Rabine (1994) analyzes fashion magazines, 1960–1990, for their mix of messages communicated through advertisements, fashion photography, and text. The magazines are shown to exhibit the "two female bodies": one confident, free, and powerful, the other "sociopolitical" where the woman is still subordinate.[17] Her examples include material from *Vogue, Glamour,* and *Essence.* Ingeborg M. O'Sickey exposes the *Barbie Magazine,* 1965–, as the opening act or introduction in the play to influence girls to be consumers of fashion and beauty products and to think in certain ways about their bodies, play that leads to the purchase of fashion magazines such as *Seventeen* and *Mademoiselle* and, later, *Glamour, Elle,* and *Vogue.*[18] Although the trade journal is not concentrated on in this discussion, many do play an important role in promoting fashion business interests and form important cultural links as well. For example an article on Reenie Brown, publisher of *Accessories,* "the fashion industry's largest trade publication," indicates that she also began the Fashion Accessories Expo in 1981 and the Fashion Accessories Benefit Ball in 1990, raising funds for many charities.[19]

Several individual fashion periodicals have been the subject of books. Some of these are commemorative, marking anniversaries with a special edition. Both *WWD* and *DNR,* leading fashion industry journals, have published commemoratives. *Women's Wear Daily* in 1976 published a special supplement to celebrate the United States Bicentennial (see Nyberg), and *DNR (Daily News Record)* issued a centennial issue in 1992 to celebrate its one hundredth year. Others offer a journalistic viewpoint, such as Ruth Finley's *The Lady of Godey's, Sarah Josepha Hale* (1931). Some books are mainly pictorial, offering a look at the past. Stella Blum, then director of the Kent State University Museum, wrote *Fashion and Costumes from Godey's Lady's Book* (1985). *Peterson's Magazine* illustrations are featured in *Civil War Ladies' Fashions and Needle-Arts of the Early 1860's* (1987); hair styles and hair jewelry are included from Campbell's *Self-Instructor in the Art of Hair Work.* The 1990 Dover publication, with introduction by Jean L. Druesedow, curator of the Costume Institute, Metropolitan Museum of Art, is entitled *Men's Fashion Illustrations from the Turn of the Century* and features the *Sartorial Art Journal,* 1900–1910, with illustrations of male upper-class fashions. Some sixty-three fashion illustrations from *Esquire* in the 1930s and 1940s are featured in *Men in Style* (1993) by Woody Hochswender. Senior editor at *Esquire,* Hochswender offers both a men's fashion history and history of the periodical, citing *Gentleman's Quarterly* and *Apparel Arts* as "precursors" but "essentially trade magazines."[20] He indicates that *Apparel Arts* contained wonderful illustrations but was more like a catalog than a periodical.

Both *Harper's Bazaar* and *Vogue* have been the subject of a variety of types of books. Jane Trahey (1967) wrote a history of *Harper's Bazaar*'s first one hundred years, 1867–1967. The work is well illustrated and also contains seventeen literary essays by women writers over the century. Other interesting text is selected for inclusion, such as "Plane Clothes" by Amelia Earhart, and editor Carmel Snow's philosophical thoughts on fashion and *Bazaar*. Trahey has selected, as her title indicates, "sumptuous, precious, moneyed, luxe, tasteful, opulent, and amusing" materials for her work. Carmel Snow herself is the subject of a 1962 volume cowritten with Mary Louise W. Aswell. Stella Blum (1974) edited a pictorial overview of women's and some children's clothing from *Harper's*, 1867–1898, which includes a glossary. Blum also selected work for inclusion in *Designs by Erte* in 1976, which features 310 line drawings and fourteen covers done for *Harper's* between 1915 and 1936. A special feature is the inclusion of letters and comments by Erte.

Vogue has had several commemorative volumes for its thirtieth, sixtieth, seventy-fifth, and hundredth anniversaries. For the thirtieth, a special contest required naming the correct Paris designer for each of twelve illustrated gowns. The prizes were a dress of choice from the twelve shown, an evening gown worth $350, and an afternoon gown worth $275. In addition to reviewing all the features of the magazine, photographs of the Paris and New York editorial staffs and the artists were included. Georgina Howell's sixtieth-anniversary volume celebrates *British Vogue* founded in 1916; her seventy-fifth in 1991 focuses on style. Kennedy Fraser's hundredth, *On the Edge* (1992), looks at fashion photography over a hundred-year period. The journalist viewpoint is represented with *Always in Vogue* (1954) by Edna Woolman Chase, who began work at *Vogue* in 1895 at the age of eighteen and became editor. Bettina Ballard, *Vogue* journalist, recorded her reminiscences in 1960. Neither volume has an index. A biography of Conde Nast, *Vogue* publisher, was written by Caroline Seebohm in 1982.

Textual and visual content has also been the focus of review. *Vogue's First Reader* (1942), with an introduction by Frank Crowinshield, reprints essays written originally for *Vogue* and not published elsewhere. They span a period from about 1935 to 1941, represent the work of some seventy writers, and reveal the literary past of the periodical. The anthology *The World in Vogue* was compiled by the Viking Press and *Vogue* editors in 1963. It covers the period 1893–1962 and reflects periods of prosperity, depression, war, and revolution. I. S. V. Patcevitch, then president of Conde Nast, states in the foreword that although the periodical is "fragile and transitory," certain pieces will maintain "fascination" and "excitement" over time. *The Fifties in Vogue* was written in 1987 by Nicholas Drake, with a foreword by Audrey Hepburn, whose career was chronicled in the magazine. In 1992 *Society in Vogue: The International Set between the Wars* was edited by Josephine Ross.

On the visual side there is *The Art of Vogue Covers* (1984) by William Packer, with over 400 covers in color from 1909 to 1940; Packer lets the illustrations speak for themselves but also offers background information. He also produced *Fashion Drawing in Vogue* (1989). Christina Probert contributed separate volumes on hats, lingerie, shoes, and swimwear appearing in *Vogue* from 1910 to 1980, including many drawings and photographs. The photography itself has been the subject of several volumes, including one by Alexander Liberman, editorial director of all Conde Nast publications, with a focus on color photography (1951); Polly Devlin's fashion photography, 1919–1979 (1979); Valerie Lloyd's photographic covers (1986); and Martin Harrison's "beauty photography" (1987). Liberman's introductory essay in Devlin's volume discusses the evolution from the first photographs, designed to show "women wearing clothes" to the more current (1979) appearance of photographs, which contribute to the "dehumanization" of the model—a person who becomes just a form for the fashion designer, hair designer, cosmetics producer, and other commercial interests, as well as the photographer, to mold and decorate in order to advertise and promote their own interests. Liberman also speaks of the females' "unbreakable spell on the imagination of mankind," which is evidenced by the photographer's work.[21] Harrison's *Beauty Photography in Vogue* concentrates on the photographer's art of capturing the beauty in nudity, cosmetics, close detail, movement, hair, and faces, a further example of the fascination mentioned by Liberman. *Vogue's* representation of society and culture is exemplified by the portfolio of plates published by Random House in 1992, *On the Edge: Images from 100 Years of Vogue*. The text presents a history of the periodical and its cooperative work with editors and photographers.

A third category of books related to fashion periodicals might be those that republish fashion features in periodicals. For example, the "Femme Fashions" column from the *New Yorker* includes commentary by Kennedy Fraser from 1970 to 1981 in his *The Fashionable Mind* (1981). Another example is the "annual worst dressed list" by Mr. Blackwell written for the periodical *American Weekly*, a Sunday newspaper supplement. The 1991 presentation is entitled *Mr. Blackwell's Worst: 30 Years of Fashion Fiascos*. This column features both society and entertainment personalities in their "worst" attire. In 1992, *Glamour Dos and Don'ts Hall of Fame: Fifty Years of Good Fun and Bad Taste* was published, edited by Joanne Mattera. It covered the period from about 1939 to 1989, featuring, for example, large shoulder pads of the 1940s, shirtwaists in the 1960s, miniskirts in the 1970s, and pantsuits of the 1980s.

Ballard, Battina. *In My Fashion.* New York: McKay, 1960. 312p.

Bauret, Gabriel. "Trade Images." *Camera International* (France), no. 17 (Autumn 1988): 80–89.

Blackwell, Mr., with Vernon Patterson. *Mr. Blackwell's Worst: 30 Years of Fashion Fiascos.* New York: Pharos Books, 1991. 140p.

Blum, Stella, ed. *Fashions and Costumes from Godey's Lady's Book.* New York: Dover, 1985. 91p.

———. *Victorian Fashions and Costumes from Harper's Bazar, 1867–1898.* New York: Dover, 1974. 294p.

Castro, Anna M. "Pandora between Art and Communication." *D'Ars* 29, no. 119 (April 1988): 12–19. In Italian.

Chase, Edna Woolman. *Always in Vogue.* Garden City, New York: Doubleday, 1954. 381p.

Civil War Ladies: Fashions and Needle-Arts of the Early 1860's. Primary Source Material from "Peterson's Magazine" 1861 and 1964. Mendocino, CA: R. L. Shep, 1989. 348p.

Cohen-Stratyner, Barbara. "Fashion Fillers in Silent Film Periodicals." In *Performing Arts Resources.* v.14: *Performances in Periodicals,* 127–142. New York: Theatre Library Association, 1989.

Devlin, Polly. *Vogue Book of Fashion Photography, 1919–1979.* New York: Simon and Schuster, 1979. 240p.

DNR, One Hundredth Year. Special Centennial Issue. New York: Fairchild Fashion & Merchandising Group, 1992. 196p.

Drake, Nicholas. *The Fifties in Vogue.* New York: Henry Holt, 1987. 160p.

Erte. *Erte's Fashion Designs: 218 Illustrations from Harper's Bazar, 1918–1932.* New York: Dover, 1981. 71p.

———. *Designs by Erte: Fashion Drawings and Illustrations from "Harper's Bazar."* Selected and with an introduction by Stella Blum. Preface by Eric Estorick. New York: Dover, 1976. 129p.

Ervin, Kelly S., and Linda A. Jackson. *The Frequency and Portrayal of Black Females in Fashion Advertisements.* ED315483. 1990. 17p.

Fenn, Donna. "Fashion Magazines: 99 Ways to Increase Your Insecurity." *Washington Monthly* 13, no. 2 (1981): 28–31.

Finley, Ruth E. *The Lady of Godey's, Sarah Josepha Hale.* Philadelphia: Lippincott, 1931. 318p.

Fraser, Kennedy. *The Fashionable Mind: Reflections on Fashion, 1970–1981.* New York: Alfred A. Knopf, 1981. 270p.

———. *On the Edge: Images from 100 Years of Vogue.* New York: Random House, 1992. 296p.

Grant, Alice. *Fashion Magazines from the 1890s to the 1980s: An Account Based on the Holdings of the National Art Library.* London: National Art Library, 1988. 16p.

Harrison, Martin. *Beauty Photography in Vogue.* New York: Stewart, Tabori & Chang, 1987. 192p.

Hochswender, Woody. *Men in Style: The Golden Age of Fashion from Esquire.* New York: Rizzoli, 1993. 112p.

Holland, Vyvyan. *Hand Coloured Fashion Plates, 1770–1899.* London: B. T. Batsford, 1955. 200p.

Howell, Georgina. *In Vogue: 75 Years of Style.* London: Conde Nast, 1991. 255p.

————. *In Vogue: Sixty Years of International Celebrities and Fashion from British Vogue.* New York: Schocken Books, 1976, 344p.

Liberman, Alexander, ed. *The Art and Technique of Color Photography: A Treasury of Color Photographs by the Staff Photographers of Vogue, House & Garden, Glamour, Balkin [and others].* New York: Simon and Schuster, 1951. 225p.

Lloyd, Valerie. *The Art of Vogue Photographic Covers: Fifty Years of Fashion and Design.* New York: Harmony Books, 1986. 222p.

Mattera, Joanne, ed. *Glamour Dos and Don'ts Hall of Fame: Fifty Years of Good Fun and Bad Taste.* New York: Villard Books, 1992. [n.p.]

Melinkoff, Ellen. "Fashion Magazines in General and *Mademoiselle*'s College Issue in Particular." In *What we Wore: An Offbeat Social History of Women's Clothing, 1950–1980,* 195–203. New York: Wm. Morrow, 1984.

Men's Fashion Illustrations from the Turn of the Century. Jno. J. Mitchell Co. [Illustrations selected by and introduction by] Jean L. Druesedow. New York: Dover, 1990. 103p. Reprint: New York: Jno. J. Mitchell Co., 1910.

Moore, Doris L. *Fashion through Fashion Plates, 1771–1970.* New York: Clarkson N. Potter, 1971. 192p.

Moriarty, Sandra E. "A Retrospective Analysis of Nostalgia." Paper presented at the Annual Meeting of the Association for Education in Journalism, Athens, OH, July 25–28, 1982. ED217454. 30p.

Nyberg, Tobi. *Women's Wear Daily. The Changing American Woman: 200 Years of American Fashion.* New York: WWW, 1976. 147p.

On the Edge: Images from 100 Years of Vogue. Introduction by Kennedy Fraser. New York: Random House, 1992. 296p.

O'Sickey, Ingeborg M. "*Barbie Magazine* and the Aesthetic Commodification of Girls' Bodies." In *On Fashion,* 21–40. Edited by Shari Benstock and Suzanne Ferriss. New Brunswick, NJ: Rutgers University Press, 1994.

Packer, William. *The Art of Vogue Covers.* New York: Bonanza Books, 1984. 256p.

————. *Fashion Drawing in Vogue.* Preface by David Hockney. New York: Thames and Hudson, 1989. 240p.

Probert, Christina, ed. *Hats in Vogue since 1910.* New York: Abbeville Press, 1981. 90p.

————. *Lingerie in Vogue since 1910.* New York: Abbeyville Press, 1981. 95p.

————. *Shoes in Vogue since 1910.* New York: Abbeyville Press, 1981. 96p.

————. *Swimwear in Vogue since 1910.* New York: Abbeyville Press, 1981. 96p.

Rabine, Leslie W. "A Woman's Two Bodies: Fashion Magazines, Consumerism, and Feminism." In *On Fashion,* 59–75. Edited by Shari Benstock and Suzanne Ferriss, New Brunswick, NJ: Rutgers University Press, 1994.

Randall, Michael H. "Bridal Magazines." *Serials Review* 8 (Summer 1982): 29–31.

Robinson, Julian. *The Fine Art of Fashion: An Illustrated History.* New York: Bartley & Jensen, 1989. 208p.

Ross. Josephine, ed. *Society in Vogue: The International Set between the Wars.* New York: Vendome Press, 1992. 192p.

Seebohm, Caroline. *The Man Who Was Vogue: The Life and Times of Conde Nast.* New York: Viking, 1982. 390p.

Snow, Carmel, with Mary Louise Aswell. *The World of Carmel Snow.* New York: McGraw-Hill, 1962. 212p.

Tarlton, Martha K., and Suzanne V. LaBrecque. "Fashion Merchandising Periodicals: A Selected, Annotated Bibliography." *Serials Review* 19, no. 1 (1993): 63–70.

The Thirtieth Birthday of Vogue, 1892–1922. New York: Vogue Company, 1923. 208p.

Trahey, Jane, ed. *Harper's Bazaar, 100 Years of the American Female: The Sumptuous, the Expensive, the Precious, the Moneyed, the Luxe, the Tasteful, the Opulent, and the Amusing Woman from Bazaar.* New York: Random House, 1967. 307p.

Vogue Covers, 1900–1970. Introduction by Grace Mirabella. New York: Harmony Books, 1978. 47p.

Vogue's First Reader. Introduction by Frank Crowninshields. New York: J. Messner, 1942. 557p.

The World in Vogue. Compiled by the Viking Press and Vogue Editors. New York: Viking Press, 1963. 416p.

FASHION-RELATED PERIODICALS

Although not strictly fashion periodicals, there are related types of periodicals that contain fashion and clothing information. First, of course, is the general interest or popular periodical written for the general public. These periodicals contain advertisements as well as illustrations and photographs. Through their vast amounts of advertising, illustrations, and occasional fashion/costume/clothing articles, they offer a visual history of what people from all walks of life wore and are wearing, images and messages created using clothing and accessories (whether being worn by individuals or exhibited alone), and the impact of artistic style changes as well as the technological changes affecting the presentation of these images. Thus, these periodicals serve as an archive of fashion and clothing information. For example *Newsweek*'s February 20, 1995, issue contains an article, "Are We Becoming a Nation of Slobs? From IBM to Church on Sunday, America Is Dressing Down," which is featured on the cover with the statement, "You're Going Out in That?" The issue also contains an advertisement for Marlboro cigarettes picturing the Marlboro man wearing cowboy hat, denim shirt, leather vest, and gloves whose clothes and pose personify the message. A two-page advertisement for milk features color portraits of two famous women. Their clothing, a leopard fur (like?) coat for Joan Rivers and a black turtleneck sweater for Lauren Bacall, is accented by a careful show of jewelry, sophisticated images brought down to earth by a narrow white line of milk above their lips. In the article, clothing is the issue; in the advertisements, the message is not as potent without the careful crafting and presentation of the clothing.

A second group of periodicals focuses on interests or activities where specialized clothing is used. Within their pages, the presence of advertising and/or illustrations and photographs can often provide fashion and clothing information without articles on clothing itself. Depending on the length of time a periodical has been published, it can offer a history of the clothing and related equipment, gear, or accessories. These magazines grow out of people's interest in the subjects and willingness to support the publishers. Ethnic magazines fit into this category. Penelope L. Bullock studied the "Negro Periodical Press in the United States, 1838–1909," for her 1971 Ph.D. dissertation, which was later published as a book, *The Afro-American Periodical Press, 1838–1909* (1981). *Ringwood's Afro-American Journal of Fashion* is described, as well as *Women's World* and *Colored Woman's Magazine*. All three included fashion information, patterns, or illustrations as supplements to articles and other features for the edification of their audiences. Sandra L. J. Ireland's 1990 *Ethnic Periodicals in Contemporary America* provides an annotated directory of the periodicals arranged alphabetically by some eighty-six ethnic group names. Only one entry in the index leads to "fashion"—*EM, Ebony Man Magazine,* focusing on "fashion, grooming, health and fitness." The annotations indicate if photos can be submitted with articles and provide deadline information for submission of advertisements. Maureen Hady, Barry Noonan, and Neil Strache identify several ethnic periodicals as supplying fashion information in their 1982 union list of women's periodicals and newspapers.

The field of fine arts periodicals was analyzed by Stanley T. Lewis in 1962. He indicated that no fashion design periodicals were included in the *Art Index* because apparently "a research need has not been formulated."[22] He also adds that the "visual elements of theatre—scenery design, costuming, lighting and architecture—receive brief attention from today's general theatre periodicals."[23] *World Theatre,* 1950–, does continue to cover this type of subject according to Lewis. The Art Press was the subject of a special issue of *Connoisseur* in 1976. It provided histories of *Burlington Magazine,* 1930–, and *Connoisseur,* 1901–, among other topics. Interests in sewing and other textile arts can involve clothing. For example, quilting periodicals have been reviewed by Gayle Williams (1985) and lacemaking periodicals by Jeanne M. K. Boydston (1989).

Sports periodicals provide a special look at clothing, uniforms, and accessories. In a 1979 article on sports and outdoor recreation periodicals, Marshall Nunn provides a list with dates of publication and where the periodicals are indexed. Jeffrey Levine (1981) reviews four sports magazines: *Sports Illustrated, Sport, Inside Sports,* and *Sporting News.* Color photographs appear in *Sport,* 1946–, and in *Sports Illustrated* from 1954. The annual female swimsuit issue in *Sports Illustrated* and the annual bathing suit issue in *Inside Sports,* mentioned by Levine, attest to the interest in and power of clothing and sex in selling magazines. More scholarly sports periodicals are described by Joan C. Griffith (1986), who indicates that the *Journal of Physical Education, Recreation and Dance,* 1981–, contains many illustrations, which add to its popularity. Michael Miranda and Deborah Mongeau (1991) evaluate physical education, athletic, and sports periodicals for their importance to academic faculty (clothing or uniform issues are not mentioned).

Virginia Seiser (1987) has contributed to the literature on mountaineering periodicals or serials. One of her bibliographic essays describes both commercial and organizational publications and indicates if illustrations or photographs are provided (*Rock and Ice*, 1984–, includes product reviews and color photographs; *Summit*, 1955–, covers cross-country skiing, climbing photographs, and classified ads). Her book, *Mountaineering and Mountain Club Serials* (1990), provides a more comprehensive list of titles and special collections, though no illustration information. It is a look at sport that, despite its dangers, attracts general attention and awe. Other elite sports also have periodicals that might provide illustrations of specialized clothing. For example, Margaret Thwaits's "Survey of Horse Periodicals" (1982) covers some 100 titles and mentions availability of photographs. Sports activities enjoyed by a wider public have their own periodicals (e.g., *Skiing*, 1948–, *Tennis*, 1965–, and *Walking Magazine*, 1986–). All provide excellent materials for fashion and clothing study. These and others can be located by using *Ulrich's International Periodical Directory* and/or the *Standard Periodical Directory*, available at many libraries.

Other "performance" activities—theater, dance, opera, movies, and television—have periodicals that may contain costume articles and/or advertisements for products and performances containing illustrations. Lucy Barton (1961) lists periodicals where materials can be located as sources for historic stage costumes. C. J. Stratman's bibliography, *American Theatrical Periodicals, 1798–1967* (1970), documents the periodicals but does not describe the focus of the contents or indicate if illustrations or advertisements are present; there is no entry for "costume" in the index. Irene Shaland provides annotations for her periodicals list but no subject index. Costume is not mentioned except for *Theatre Crafts*, and availability of illustrations is mentioned for only a few titles, such as *Drama Review* and *Theatre*, New Haven. Dance periodicals have been described by Daniel Uchitelle (1985); of the twelve titles, he notes photographs for two: *Ballet News*, 1979–, and *Dance Magazine*, 1926–. William E. Studwell (1989) reviewed seven opera-specific as well as five general music periodicals. *Lyric Opera of Chicago Annual Report* is mentioned as having "valuable illustrations." Michael H. Randall (1980) notes that movie magazines had an impact from the 1920s to the 1950s, when television took the "dominant" role. The movie magazines usually included photographs; Randall reviews *Photoplay*, 1911–, *Modern Screen*, 1930–, *Movie Life*, 1937–, *Movie Stars*, 1940–, *Movie Mirror*, 1956–, *Photo Screen*, 1965–, *Rona Barrett's Hollywood*, 1969–, and *Rona Barrett's Gossip*, 1972–. Mentioned earlier were the "fashion fillers" added to silent film magazines (Cohen-Stratyner, 1989).

A third, and much smaller, group of periodicals has resulted from interests in studying fashion, clothing, or costume in all their various contexts. Most of these scholarly periodicals are published by professional organizations interested in fostering research and communication in these areas. *Costume*, 1967/68–, is published by the Costume Society in England; its counterpart in the United States, *Dress*, 1975–, is published by the Costume Society of America. Both are annual and contain scholarly articles and book and exhibition reviews, with *Costume* also including a bibliography, "New Books and Articles," from no. 10, 1976–. The *Home Economics Research Journal*, published quarterly from 1972 to 1994 by the American Home Economics Association, has changed its name to the *Family and Consumer Science Journal*, reflecting the continued decline in the use of "home economics" to describe college and university programs of study. The *Clothing and Textiles Research Journal*, 1982–, published by the International Textile and Apparel Association quarterly, is designed to demonstrate the interdisciplinary nature of the field of clothing and textiles, encourage research, and facilitate communication. Newsletters from these organizations also carry information of interest: *CSA News, American Home Economics Association, International Section—International Update,* a newsletter published three times per year, and the *ITAA Newsletter.*

Few exhibition catalogs have been located featuring fashion periodicals. *Fashion Magazines, 1799–1975: An Exhibition* at the Manchester Polytechnic Library was published in 1976.

Barton, Lucy. *Historic Costume for the Stage.* Boston: W. H. Baker, 1961, 1963. 609p.
Boydston, J. M. K. "Hand Lacemaking Periodicals: A Selected Review." *Serials Review* 15, no. 1 (1989): 67–71.
Bullock, Penelope L. *The Afro-American Periodical Press, 1838–1909.* Baton Rouge and London: Louisiana State University Press, 1981. 330p.
Connoisseur 191, no. 769 (March 1976). Special issue with cover title "The 75th Anniversary Issue."
Griffith, Joan C. "Sports Studies." *Serials Review* 15 (Winter 1986): 5–8.
Ireland, Sandra L. J. *Ethnic Periodicals in Contemporary America: An Annotated Guide.* Westport, CT: Greenwood Press, 1990. 222p.
Levine, Jeffrey. "Sports Magazines." *Serials Review* 7 (October 1981): 39–41.
Lewis, Stanley T. "Periodicals in the Visual Arts." *Library Trends* 10 (January 1962): 330–352.
Miranda, Michael A., and Debora H. Mongeau. "An Evaluation of Journals in Physical Education, Athletics, and Sports." *Serials Librarian* 21, no. 1 (1991): 89–113.
Nunn, Marshall E. "Indexing of Sports and Outdoor Recreation Periodicals." *Serials Review* 5 (January 1979): 51–53.
Randall, Michael H. "Movie Magazines." *Serials Review* 6 (April 1980): 19–23.
Seiser, Virginia. *Mountaineering and Mountain Club Serials.* Metuchen, NJ: Scarecrow Press, 1990. 180p.
———. "United States Mountaineering Serials." *Serials Review* 13 (Summer 1987): 15–23.
Shaland, Irene. *American Theater and Drama Research: An Annotated Guide to Information Sources, 1945–1990.* Jefferson, NC: McFarland, 1991. 157p.
Stratman, Carl J. *American Theatrical Periodicals, 1788–1967: A Bibliographical Guide.* Durham, NC: Duke University Press, 1970. 133p.
Studwell, William E. "A Bibliographic Guide to Opera Serials." *Serials Librarian* 16, no. 1–2 (1989): 161–166.

Thwaits, Margaret B. "Survey of Horse Periodicals." *Serials Review* 8 (Summer 1982): 21–26.

Uchitelle, Daniel. "Dance Periodicals." *Serials Librarian* 9 (Summer 1985): 113–117.

Williams, Gayle. "Patchwork in Print: A Survey of Quilting Periodicals." *Serials Review* 11 (Fall 1985): 15–20.

THESES ON FASHION PERIODICALS

Theses have been written on fashion periodicals generally and specifically. Phyllis Tortora wrote "The Evolution of the American Fashion Magazine . . . 1830–1969" in 1972. Esther Stineman and Christina Hoffer look at readership issues in popular women's magazines, 1875–1975, and female adolescent fashion magazine reading, respectively. *Vogue* and *Rags,* 1970/71, are compared for beauty content by Susan Taggart (1977); she concluded that only hair and cosmetics were presented differently. Loretta Taylor (1990) compared fabric information in *Godey's* and *Peterson's,* 1860–1880, to costumes in Canadian museum collections for that period, concluding that few everyday costumes of cotton, linen, and wool are represented in the magazines or collections. Fashion advice for businesswomen, 1920–1940, is analyzed by Teresa Brown (1990), while the perceived value of fashion magazines versus other types of fashion information sources was studied by Melissa Krugs (1991). The feminist perspective is represented by Roberta Linden (1990) in an analysis of *Ladies' Home Journal* and *Chatelaine* and their presentation of women and change from 1955 to 1987.

Individual fashion periodicals have been researched as well. The education and music aspects of *Godey's Lady's Book* were the focus for Nancy Lee (1985) and Julia Kuza (1988), respectively. *Harper's Bazaar* was used by Hae Jeon Kim (1989) to show the influence of Chinese and Japanese design on women's dress during the period 1890–1927. *Seventeen* in 1984 is the major focus of Miriam Heller's (1987) research on advice and/or "answers" given to readers, while Shelley Budgeon (1993) links *Seventeen*'s advertising with femininity. *Vogue*'s graphics from 1929 to 1942 were studied by Marcia Prior-Miller (1981), and *Vogue*'s advertisements for skirts, 1947–1972 were seen as a measure of women's social position by Mary Ellen Brigham (1988). Research on *Women's Sports and Fitness,* 1974–1989, by Barbara Endel (1991) implies that the periodical, reflects fashion, beauty, and feminity interests thus producing "in women an alienation from her bodily being."[24]

As early as 1937 Mauva Reese studied clothing information in several fashion magazines. The day dress from 1890 to 1900 was analyzed by Karen Basralian (1969), while Dana Lacy (1978) analyzed college dress from 1930 to 1950, comparing college photographs and fashion magazine

information. Rhonda Hardy (1981) looked at images of "African-styled dress" in four fashion magazines, 1958–1976. A historical style comparison of fashion magazine content and actual dress of Nebraska women, 1880–1890 was carried out by Lenae Harless (1983). Three other historical analyses focus on sports clothing (*Godey's, Delineator,* and *Ladies' Home Journal*) by Judith Leslie (1985); consumer information on women's fashions (*New York Times*) by Karen Thomas (1986); and "differentiation of women's costume in America," 1770–1910 by Marguerite Connolly in 1987.

Advertising has also been a major interest of students. Trends from 1935 to 1944 were reviewed by Irene Fogel (1946). Newspaper fashion supplements and consumer interest were researched by Christine Love (1986). In 1990 Vickie Graves broke new ground by studying men's interest in fashion, fashion magazines, and actual purchase of clothes. Patricia Kimle (1991) also looks at how consumers evaluate fashion magazine advertising. The relationship of advertising to editorial text is studied by Laura Womack (1991). The images of African Americans or "African-American racial identity" as represented in *Ebony* advertisements, 1950–1991, were researched by Nathaniel Goodlow (1993). Goodlow indicates that these "racial images in the popular culture and the mass media" can contribute to the "transformation" from a racial image that is "disparaged to one that is valued."[25]

Basralian, Karen M. "The American Woman's Day Dress, 1800 [i.e. 1890] through 1900, as Reflected in the American Fashion Magazines." Master's thesis, University of Maryland, 1969.

Brigham, Mary Ellen K. S. "*Vogue* Magazine and Sears, Roebuck & Co., Catalogues: Barometers of Women's Social Position, as Seen through Skirts Advertised 1947–1972." Master's thesis, University of Connecticut, 1988.

Brown, Teresa C. "Advice on Dress and Grooming for Business Women in Selected Periodicals, 1920–1940." Master's thesis, Iowa State University, 1990.

Budgeon, Shelley J. "Fashion Magazine Advertising the Constructions of Femininity in *Seventeen*." Master's thesis, University of British Columbia, 1993.

Connolly, Marguerite A. "Dressing for the Occasion: The Differentiation of Women's Costume in America, 1770–1910." Master's thesis, University of Delaware, 1988.

Endel, Barbara L. "Working Out: The Dialectic of Strength and Sexuality in Women's Sports and Fitness Magazine." Ph.D. diss., University of Iowa, 1991.

Fogel, Irene L. R. "Trends in Advertising in the Fashion Magazine, 1935–1944." Master's thesis, University of Missouri–Columbia, 1946.

Goodlow, Nathaniel Van. "African-American Identity from 1950–1991: A Content Analysis." Ph.D. diss., California School of Professional Psychology, Los Angeles, 1993.

Graves, Vickie L. "A Comparative Study of Men's Fashion Interest in Relationship to Men's Fashion Magazine Use and Influence on Clothing Purchasing Behavior." Master's thesis, Andrews University, 1990.

Hardy, Rhonda I. "The Presence of African-Styled Dress in Selected United States

Magazines Published between 1958 and 1976." Master's thesis, Southern Illinois University–Carbondale, 1981.

Harless, Lenae H. "A Comparison of Style Elements in a National Fashion Magazine with Dress of Nebraska Women from 1880 to 1890." Master's thesis, University of Nebraska–Lincoln, 1983.

Heller, Miriam K. "*Seventeen* Magazine: Answers and Advice in Three Languages (Teenagers)." Ed.D. thesis, Columbia University Teachers College, 1987.

Hoffer, Christina M. "A Cultural Studies Perspective of Female Adolescent Fashion Magazine Reading." Master's thesis, Illinois State University, 1993.

Kim, Hae Jeon. "Far Eastern Influence on Western Women's Dress in *Harper's Bazaar*, 1890–1927." Ph.D. diss., University of Minnesota, 1989.

Kimle, Patricia A. "Consumer Perception and Evaluation of Fashion Magazine Advertisements." Master's thesis, Iowa State University, 1991.

Krugs, Melissa I. "Perceived Value of Fashion Magazines versus Other Types of Fashion Information Sources by Florida State University Women Graduates." Master's thesis, Florida State University, 1991.

Kuza, Julia E. "Music and References to Music in *Godey's Lady's Book*, 1830–1877." Ph.D. diss., University of Minnesota, 1988.

Lacy, Dana. "A Comparison of Fashion Magazines and College Photographs: College Fashions, 1930–1950." Master's thesis, Ohio State University, 1978.

Lee, Nancy L. "*Godey's Lady's Book* and Its Relationship to Adult Education: A Historical Analysis." Ph.D. diss., University of Oklahoma, 1985.

Leslie, Judith E. "Sports Fashions in Society from 1850 to 1920 (Riding Habits, Swim Wear, Bicycle, Golf, Tennis Dresses)." Ph.D. diss., University of North Carolina, 1985.

Linden, Roberta H. "Media Images of Women and Social Change: A Feminist Perspective (Magazines)." Ed.D. thesis, University of Toronto, 1990.

Love, Christine R. "Consumer Interest in a Regularly-Published Newspaper Fashion Supplement." Master's thesis, Louisiana State University, 1986.

Prior-Miller, Marcia R. "*Vogue*, 1929–1942: A Graphic Profile." Master's thesis, University of Missouri, Columbia, 1981.

Reese, Mauva D. "A Study of Clothing Information in Women's Magazines: An Analysis of Contributions Appearing in Four Fashion Magazines for a Period of Three Years." Master's thesis, Texas State College for Women, 1937.

Stineman, Esther F. "What the Ladies Were Reading: Popular Women's Magazines in America, 1875–1975." Master's thesis, University of Chicago, 1976.

Taggart, Susan B. "A Content Analysis of the Fashion Magazines *Rags* and *Vogue*: June 1970–June 1971." Master's thesis, Michigan State University, 1977.

Taylor, Loretta M. "Fabric in Women's Costumes from 1860 to 1880: A Comparison of Fashion Periodicals and Selected Canadian Museum Collections." Master's thesis, University of Alberta, 1990.

Thomas, Karen W. "Consumer Analysis of Adult Female Fashion Information in the *New York Times*, 1891–1940." Master's thesis, Louisiana State University, 1986.

Tortora, Phyllis G. "The Evolution of the American Fashion Magazine as Exemplified in Selected Fashion Journals, 1830–1969." Ph.D. diss., New York University, 1972.

Womack, Laura L. "The Advertising-Editorial Relationship: A Content Analysis of

Three Women's Fashion Magazines.'' Master's thesis, University of Tennessee, 1991.

THE PERIODICALS

This list has evolved from information in several sources that discuss periodicals and specifically indicate titles as fashion periodicals; other titles have been added. Dates and volume information were verified where possible in several standard periodical lists: ULS (*Union List of Serials*, 3d ed., 1965) noted especially for pre-twentieth century titles; NST (*New Serial Titles*, covering the period 1950–1987); Ulrich (*Ulrich's International Periodical Directory*, 1995 ed.); SPD (*Standard Periodical Directory*, 1995 ed.); and Wcat (*WorldCat, the OCLC Online Union Catalog*). A few titles now available full text in the LEXIS/NEXIS (L/N) online service are so noted. Following are the sources that indicate titles as fashion periodicals:

Ba	Barton (*Historic Costume for the Stage*, 1963)
Be	Berger ("Fashion," in *Handbook of American Popular Culture*, 2d ed. 1989)
Bu	Bullock (*Afro-American Periodical Press*, 1981)
Ha	Hady (*Women's Periodicals and Newspapers*, 1982)
Hi	Hiler (*Bibliography of Costume*, 1939) U.S. titles only
Ho	Holland (*Hand Coloured Fashion Plates*, 1955) U.S. titles only
Hn	Hoornstra (*American Periodicals 1741–1900*, 1979)
M	McCracken (*Decoding Women's Magazines*, 1993)
R	Robinson (*The Art of Fashion*, 1988)

American Fabrics and Fashions. 1946–. New York. Be, Ha, ULS.

American Family Journal. 1904–1910(?). New York. Hi, ULS.

American Gentleman and Sartorial Art Journal. 1901–June 1929 as *American Gentleman;* absorbed *Sartorial Art Journal* v.55, no. 1, 1929–. New York. Hi, ULS.

American Girl. 1917–1979. Monthly. New York: Girl Scouts of the U.S.A. Ha, ULS.

American Home. 1928–1978. Monthly. New York. Ha, ULS.

American Home Economics Association. International Section—International Update. Three issues per year. Alexandria, VA.

American Home Magazine. 1897–1898. Monthly. Chicago. Ha, ULS.

American Ladies' Magazine. 1828–1836. Merged into *Godey's Lady's Book.* Hi, ULS.

American Ladies' Tailor and les Parisiennes. 1903–. New York. Hi, ULS.

American Literary Magazine. v.1–5, 1847–1849. Albany, New York; Hartford, CT. Hn, ULS.

American Magazine. v.1–162, 1876–1956. New York. Ba, ULS.

American Woman. 1892(?)–1916(?). Monthly. Augusta, ME. Ha.

American Tailor and Cutter. v.1–37, 1880–1916. ULS.

Animations: A Review of Puppets and Related Theatre. v.1, 1977–Bimonthly. London: Puppet Centre Trust. Wcat.

Apparel Arts. 1931–. See *Gentlemen's Quarterly.*

Art and Archaeology. 1914–1934. Washington, D.C. Ba, ULS.

Art et Decoration. v. 1–67, 1897–1938; n.s. 1939; s3 1946–. Paris. R, ULS.

Art et la Mode. Revue de l'Elegance. 1880–. Paris. Ba, ULS.

L'Art pour Tous. 1861–1906. Paris. Ba, ULS.

Arthur's Home Magazine. v.1–67, 1852–1898. Monthly. Philadelphia. Ha Hn, ULS.

Artist: A Monthly Lady's Book. September 1842–May 1843. New York. Hn, ULS.

Barbie. 1965–. Six issues per year. New York. M, Ulrich, Wcat.

La Belle Assemblee, or Bell's Court and Fashionable Magazine. 1806–1832. Monthly. London. Ba, Ha, R, ULS.

Bicycling. v.1, 1962–. Menlo Park, CA. Be, NST.

Big Beautiful Woman Magazine (BWW). v.1, 1980–. Bimonthly. Century City, CA. NST.

Bobbin. v.1, 1959–. Columbus, SC: South Carolina Needle Trades Manufacturing Association. Be, NST.

Body Fashions/Intimate Apparel. 1974–. New York. Ha, NST.

Le Bon Ton and le Moniteur de la Mode United. 1851–1927(?). New York. Ba, Hi, ULS.

Boston Magazine. v.1–3, 1802–1805; n.s. v.1, 1805–1806. Boston. Hn, ULS.

Boston Miscellany of Literature and Fashion. v.1–3, 1842–1843. Boston, New York. Hn, ULS.

Bride's Magazine. v.1, 1934–. New York. Be, ULS.

Burlington Magazine. v.1, 1903–. London. Ba, ULS.

Burton's Gentleman's Magazine. 1837–1840. Philadelphia. Continued as *Graham's Monthly Magazine.* Be, ULS.

Butterick Pattern Book. 1908–1941. New York. Hi, ULS.

California Apparel News. 1945. Weekly. Los Angeles, CA. Be, HA.

California Stylist. 1937–. Los Angeles. Hi, ULS.

Canadian Conservation Institute. Newsletter (CCI Newsletter). no.1, 1988(?)–. Ottawa. Wcat (no.9, 1992, 2 nos. per year).

Carousel. 1868–1969(?). Irregular. New York. Ha.

Century: A Popular Quarterly. v.1–120, 1870–1930. New York. Ba, ULS.

Children's Vogue. Title varies. 1919–1925. New York. Other titles: *Children's Costume Royal, Children's Royal, Vogue Pattern Book, Vogue Fashion Bi-Monthly.* Wcat.

Claudia. 1965. Monthly. Mexico City, Mexico. Ha.

Clothing and Textiles Research Journal. v.1, 1982–. Monument, CO: Association of College Professors of Textiles and Clothing. NST.

Co-ed. v.1, 1956–. Ten issues per year. Dayton, OH: Scholastic Magazines. Ha, NST.

Colored Woman's Magazine. 1907–1920(?). Topeka, KA. Bu, ULS.

Connoisseur: An Illustrated Magazine for Collectors. v.1, 1901–. London, New York. Ba, Be, ULS.

Conservation Notes. 1982–1987. Materials Conservation Laboratory, Texas Memorial Museum, University of Texas at Austin. Wcat.

Cosmopolitan. v.1, 1886–. Monthly. New York. Be, Ha, Hn, M, ULS. (1989–selected full-text L/N).

Costume: The Journal of the Costume Society. no. 1/2, 1967/68–. Annual. London: The Society. Be, NST.

Costume Journal: A Publication of the Costume Society of Ontario. 1970(?)–. Toronto: The Society. Wcat (v.19, 1989).

Costume Society of Ontario. Newsletter. (CSO News) v.1–14, 1971–1984/85(?). Toronto: The Society. Wcat.

Costume Society of Scotland. Bulletin. 1966–. Edinburgh? The Society. Wcat.

Court Magazine and Monthly Critic. v.1–32, 1832–1848. London. Ba, ULS.

CSA News. v.1, no. 1, September 1974–. (Three per year to Spring 1989; four per year from Summer 1989). Earleville, MD: Costume Society of America. Formerly *Costume Society of America Newsletter* v.1, no. 1, September 1974–v.13, no.3, Winter/Spring 1988. Also newsletters of the regional groups: Region I, New England and the Eastern Provinces (f. 1984); Region II, Eastern (f. 1983); Regions III–IV, Midwest–Northern Mountain/Plains (f. 1982); Region V, Western (f. 1978); Region VI, Southeastern (f. 1985); Region VII, Southwestern (f. 1985); Region VIII, Abroad.

Cutter's Research Journal. v.1, 1989–. Urbana, IL: United States Institute for Theatre Technology. Wcat.

Czechoslovak Woman. 1954–? Quarterly. Prague, Czechoslovakia. Ha, ULS.

Daily News Record. See DNR.

Dance Magazine. 1927–. Monthly. New York. ULS.

Damskii Zhurnal. 1823–1833. Weekly. Moscow. Ha, ULS.

Daughters of America. 1886–1894? Monthly. Augusta, ME. Ha, ULS.

Delineator. v.1–130, 1873–1937. New York. Continued in *Pictorial Review.* Ba, Hi, ULS.

Dell Teen Agers Ingenue (Ingenue). 1959–1973. Dunellen, NJ. Be, NST.

Demorest's Family Magazine (Demorest's Monthly Magazine). v.1–36, 1865–1899(?). New York. ULS.

Designer and Manufacturer: A Magazine Devoted to the Designing and Manufacture of Men's, Boy's and Children's Clothing. 1933–. New York. Hi, ULS.

Designer and the Woman's Magazine. 1894–1926. Monthly. New York. Merged with *Delineator.* Ha, ULS.

DNR: The Magazine. 1892–. New York. Formerly *Daily News Record.* NST, Ulrich.

Dollar Magazine: A Monthly Gazette of Current Literature, Music and Art. v.1–2, 1841–1842. New York. Hn, ULS.

Dress. v.1, 1975–. Annual. Earleville, MD: Costume Society of America. NST.

Ebony. v.1, 1945–. Chicago. Be, ULS.

Ebony Man: EM. v.1, 1985–. New York. NST.

Elegances Parisiennes. 1916–1924. Paris. R, ULS.

Elite: An Illustrated Society Journal Addressed to People of Culture and Fashion. 1881–1908(?) Chicago. Hi, ULS.

Elle. v.1, 1985–. New York. Be, Ha, NST.

Esquire: The Magazine for Men. v.1, 1933–. Monthly. Chicago. Be, ULS.

Esquire Gentleman. v.1, 1993–. New York. Wcat.

Essence. v.1, 1970–. Monthly. New York. Be, Ha, NST (1992– selected full-text L/N).

Evening Fireside. 1804–1806. Philadelphia. ULS.

Excella Fashion Quarterly. 1922–1936. New York. Hi, ULS.

Family and Consumer Science Journal. 1995–. Washington, D.C. Formerly *Home Economics Research Journal,* 1972–1994.

Family Circle. v.1, 1932–. New York. Formerly *Everywoman's Family Circle,* 1932–1958. Be, Ha, ULS.

The Farmer's Wife. v.1–42, 1897–1939. Monthly. St. Paul, MN. Ha, ULS.

Fashion International: News and Views of the International Fashion World. 1972–. Monthly. New York. Wcat.

Fashion for Men. 1980?–. Quarterly. Chicago: Playboy Enterprises. Wcat (v.2, Spring/Summer 1981).

Fashion Service Magazine. 1920–1938. Scranton, PA. Hi, ULS.

Fashions Art. v.1–2, 1934–1935/1936. New York. Hi, ULS.

Femina (Femina Illustration). 1901–1956. Monthly. Paris. Ha, R, ULS.

Femme Chic. 1911–. Paris. R, ULS.

Femme Lines. v.1, 1957–. New York. Be, NST.

Feuillets d'Art. 1919–1920. Paris. R, ULS.

Footwear News. v.1, 1945–. Weekly. New York. Be, ULS.

Frank Leslie's Ladies Journal. 1871–1881. New York. ULS.

Frank Leslie's Lady's Gazette of Fashion and Fancy Needle Work. 1854–1857. New York. Hi, Ho, Hn, ULS.

Frank Leslie's Lady's Magazine. v.1–51, 1857–1882. Monthly. New York. Ha, ULS.

Frank Leslie's Modenwelt. 1870–1871. New York. Hi, ULS.

Gallery of Fashion. 1794–1803. Monthly. London. Ba, Ha, R, ULS.

Gazette des Beaux Arts. 1859–1939. Paris. Ba, ULS.

Gazette des Salons: Journal des Dames et des Modes. 1797–1839. Paris. Ba, ULS.

Gazette du Bon Ton: Arts, Modes. 1912–1925. Monthly. Paris. R, ULS.

Gentlemen's Magazine. 1828–1894. London. Ba, ULS.

Gentlemen's Magazine. 1731–1907. London. R, ULS.

Gentleman's Quarterly. 1931–1956? New York, Chicago. Alternate titles, *Apparel Arts,* 1950–1957; *Esquire's Apparel Arts* 1950–1956. Continued as *GQ.* ULS, Wcat.

Gentlewoman and Modern Life. 1890–1926. Weekly. London. ULS.

Gentry. 1951–1957. New York. ULS.

Glamour. 1939–. Monthly. New York. Be, Ha, M, ULS.

Godey's Ladies' Book. See *Godey's Magazine.*

Godey's Magazine. v.1–137, 1830–1898. Monthly. Philadelphia. Ba, Ha, Hi, Ho, Hn, ULS.

Golf Digest. 1950–. Monthly. New York. Ulrich.

Good Housekeeping. 1885–. Monthly. New York. Ba, Be, Ha, ULS (1989– selected full-text L/N).

GQ, Gentlemen's Quarterly. 1957–. Monthly. New York. London edition 1988–. Be, ULS.

Graham's American Monthly Magazine of Literature, Art and Fashion. v.1–53, 1826–1858. Philadelphia. Ba, Be, Ha, Hi, Ho, Hn, ULS.

Guirlande . . . d'Art et de Littérature. 1919–1920. Paris. R, ULS.

Harper & Queen International. 1981–. London. NST, Wcat.

Harper's & Queen. 1970–1980. London. Continued by *Harper & Queen International.* NST, Wcat.

Harper's Bazaar. v.1, 1867–. Monthly. New York. Ba, Be, Ha, Hi, Hn, M, R, ULS. (1992–selected full-text L/N).

Harper's Bazaar. May 20, 1867–October 1929. New York. Continued as *Harper's Bazaar.*

Harper's Magazine. Title varies. 1850–1879. New York. Ba, ULS.

Hausfrau. 1904–. Monthly. Milwaukee, WI. Ha, ULS.

Hertha. 1914. Bimonthly. Stockholm, Sweden. Ha, ULS.

Home Economics Research Journal. 1972–1994. Washington, D.C. Continued by *Family and Consumer Science Journal.* Be, ULS.

Home-Maker. 1888–1893(?). Monthly. New York. Ha, ULS.

Household Monthly. 1858–1860. Monthly. Lynn, MA; Boston. Ha, ULS.

ITAA Newsletter. v.14, 1991–. Quarterly. Monument, CO: International Textile and Apparel Association. Formerly *ACPTC Newsletter* v.1–13, 1977(?)–1990(?). Wcat.

Illustrated Household Magazine. 1878–1881(?). Monthly. Portland, ME. Ha (also Newburg, NY, from 1867(?)–1875 per ULS).

Illustrated London News. v.1, 1842–. London. Ba, ULS.

Illustration. v.1–102, 1843–1944. Paris. Ba, ULS.

Illustration des Modes. See *Jardin des Modes.*

Impressions: The Magazine for the Imprinted Sportwear Industry. 1977?–. Fifteen issues per year. Dallas. Wcat.

In Fashion. 1985–1989. 1990–. New York. Ulrich, Wcat.

Ingenue. 1959–1973. Dunellen, NJ. Continued by *New Ingenue.* Be, Wcat.

International Designer. Quarterly. New York: International Association of Clothing Designers. NST.

International Monthly Magazine of Literature, Science and Art. v.1–5, 1850–1852. New York. Hn, ULS.

International Saddlery and Apparel Journal. v.12, 1992–. Berea, KY. Formerly *Horse Digest,* 1983–1991. Wcat.

International Studio. 1897–1931. New York. Merged with *Connoisseur.* Ba, ULS.

Jardin des Modes. 1920–. Paris. R, ULS.

Journal des Dames. 1817–1819. London. Ba, ULS.

Journal des Dames et des Modes. v.1–5, 1912–1914. Paris. R, ULS.

Journal des Luxus und der Moden. See *Journal fur Literature.*

Journal für Literatur, Knust, Luxus, und Moden. 1786–1827. Weimar. Ba, R, ULS.

Journal of Physical Education, Recreation and Dance. 1986–. Monthly. Reston, VA. Ulrich.

Journal of Popular Culture. 1967–. Quarterly. Bowling Green, OH. Be, NST.

[Journal of the International Association of Costume] Kokusai Fukushoku Gakkai Shi. no. 1, 1984–. Annual. Tokyo. Wcat.

Judge. 1881–1939. New York. Ba, ULS.

Kids Fashion Magazine. v.1, 1976–. Monthly. Newton, MA. NST.

Lace Collector, a Quarterly Newsletter for the Study of Lace. v.1, 1991–. Plainwell, MI: Lace Merchant. Wcat.

Ladies' Cabinet of Fashion. 1832–1870. Monthly. London. Ha, ULS.

Ladies Companion. v.1–21, 1833–1844. New York. Ba, ULS.

Ladies' Garland. v.1–4, 1824–1828. Harpers Ferry, VA. Hn, ULS.

Ladies' Garland and Family Wreath. v.1–16, 1837–1849; n.s. 1849–1850(?). Philadelphia. Hn, ULS.

Ladies' Home Journal. v.1, 1883–. Monthly. New York. Ha, Hi, ULS (1983– selected full-text L/N).

Ladies' Home Magazine of New York. See *American Family Journal.*

Ladies' Literary Cabinet. 1819–1822. Weekly. New York. Ha, ULS.

Ladies' Monthly Museum. See *Ladies' Museum.*

Ladies' Museum. 1798–1832. Monthly. London. R, ULS.

Lady's Friend. 1864–1873. Monthly. Philadelphia. Ha, ULS.

Lady's Magazine and Museum of the Belles-Lettres. 1770–1837. London. R, ULS.

Lady's Monitor. 1801–1802. New York. Hn, ULS.

Life. v.1, November 23, 1936–. Chicago. ULS.

Lifestyle Apparel News. 1987(?)–1992. Monthly. Scottsdale, AZ. Wcat (v.5, 1991).

MGF (Men's Guide to Fashion). 1985–. Monthly. New York. Ulrich.

M: the Civilized Man. v.1, 1983–. New York. Be, NST.

Madame. v.1–5, 1903–1906. Monthly. Indianapolis. Ha, ULS.

Mademoiselle. 1935–. Monthly. New York. Be, Ha, M, ULS.

McCall Fashion Book. See *McCall's Pattern Fashions.*

McCall's. v.1, 1870–. Monthly. New York. Be, Ha, ULS.

McCall's Pattern Fashions. 1913–1958. New York. Hi, ULS.

Man's Book: A Magazine. 1908–1910. New York. Hi, ULS.

Masculines. 1957–. New York. Be, NST.

Men's Wear. 1896–. New York, Chicago. Hi, ULS.

Metropolitan. 1868–1875. New York. Superseded by *Metropolitan Fashions.* Be, ULS.

Metropolitan Fashions. 1873–1901. New York. Be, ULS.

Mirabella. v.1, 1989–. Monthly. New York. Wcat.

Mirror of Fashion. 1840–1850, n.s. 1853–1855(?) New York. Be, ULS.

Modern Bride. v.1, 1949–. Bimonthly. New York. Be, Ha, ULS.

Modern Screen. 1930–. New York. ULS, Wcat.

Modes. 1901–1925(?) Paris. R, ULS.

Modes et Maniéres d'Aujourdhui. 1912–1920(?). Paris. R, ULS.

Movie Stars. 1940–. New York. Formerly *Movie Stars Parade,* 1940–1958. ULS, Wcat.

National Association of Watch and Clock Collectors Bulletin. 1946–1985. Columbia, PA. Wcat.

Needle and Bobbin Club. New York. Bulletin. 1916–. New York. ULS.

New Calliope. 1984–. Six issues per year. Jackson, TX: Clowns of America International. Wcat, Ulrich.

New Ingenue. 1973–. New York. Be.

New Lady's Magazine. 1786–1795. Monthly. London. Ha, ULS.

New York Times. 1896–. New York. ULS (6/1980–, full-text L/N).

New York Times Magazine. Fashion supplements, titles may vary: "Fashions of the Times for Women," "Fashions of the Times for Men," "Children's Fashions." These can be located through the *New York Times Index* under "Apparel." New York.

Ornament: A Quarterly of Jewelry and Personal Adornment. 1974–. Quarterly. (1974–1979 as *Bead Journal*). San Marcos, CA. Wcat.

Pagentry: The Magazine for the Pageant and Talent Industry. [n.d.] Quarterly. Altamont Springs, FL: World Pageant Association, Pagentry, Talent & Entertainment Services. Ulrich.

Parisiennes. 1899–1929. New York. Hi, ULS.

Peterson Magazine. v.1–113, 1842–1898. Monthly. Philadelphia. Be, Ha, Hn, ULS.

Petit Courrier des Dames. 1821–1868. Paris. Ha, ULS.

Petite: Fashion-Entertainment-Glamour for Women. 1992–. Twelve issues per year. Los Angeles. Ulrich.

Pictorial Review combined with Delineator. v.1–40, 1899–1939. New York. Be, Hi, Hn, ULS.

Playboy. 1953–. Chicago. Be, NST.

Photoplay. v.1–54, 1911–1940. Chicago. ULS, Wcat.

Poughkeepsie Casket. v.1–4, 1836–1841. New York. Hn, ULS.

Printwear Magazine. v.1, 1988–. Monthly. Broomfield, CO: National Business Media. Ulrich, Wcat.

Puritan. v.1–9, 1897–1901. New York. Hi, ULS.

Queen of Fashion. See *McCall's.*

RTW Review: Ready-to-Wear Review. Your Fashion Business News Source. v.1, 1986–. Monthly. Waterford, MI: Danielle Consultants. Wcat.

Redbook Magazine. 1903–. Monthly. New York. Be, Ha, ULS (1989– selected full-text L/N).

Repository of Arts, Literature, Commerce, Fashion and Politics. 1809–1829. London. R, ULS.

Revue de l'Art. 1897–1937. Paris. Ba, ULS.

Ringwood's Afro-American Journal of Fashion. 1891–. Cleveland: Julia Ringwood Coston. Bu.

Royal. v.1–29, 1895–1925. New York. Hi, ULS.

St. Nicholas: A Magazine for Boys and Girls. v.1–67, 1873–1943. New York. Ba, ULS.

Sargant's News Monthly Magazine of Literature, Fashion and the Fine Arts. 1843. New York. Ba, ULS.

Sartain's Union Magazine of Literature and Art. v.1–11, 1847–1852. New York Philadelphia. Ba, ULS.

Sartorial Art Journal and American Tailor and Cutter. v.1–54, 1874–1929. New York. Ba, Hi, ULS.

Sassy. v.1, 1978–. Monthly. Los Angeles. Wcat.

Saturday Evening Post, an Illustrated Weekly Magazine. 1821–1969. Philadelphia. Ba, Hn, ULS, NST.

Scene. Revue des Succès Dramatiques. 1877–1882. Paris. Ba, ULS.

Scribners'. See *Century.*

Self. v.1, 1979–. New York. M, NST.

Seventeen. 1942–. Monthly. New York. Be, Ha, M, ULS (1993– selected full-text L/N).

Sew It Seams. 1986–. Bimonthly. Kirkland, MA. Wcat, Ulrich.

Sew Beautiful. v.1, 1987–. Five issues per year. Huntsville, AL. Wcat, Ulrich.

Sew News: The News of People Who Sew. 1981–. Monthly. Peoria, IL Wcat, Ulrich.

Sibyl, a Review of the Tastes, Errors, and Fashions of Society. 1856–1864. Monthly. Middletown, NY. Ha, ULS.

Sightings. 1965–. Monthly. New York: Institute for Theatre Technology. Formerly *USITT Newsletter.* Ulrich.

Simplicissimus: Illustrierte Wochenschrift. 1896–. Munich. Ba, ULS.

Simplicity Magazine: Simplicity Sewing for Today. Title varies. 1967–. s-a. New York: Simplicity Pattern Co. Ha, SPD.

Skiing. v.11, 1958–. Los Angeles. Continues *National Skiing.* NST.

Social Mirror. 1893–1895(?). Milwaukee. Ha.

Société de l'Histoire du Costume, Bulletin. v.1–2, 1907–1911. Paris. Ba, ULS.

Southern Women's Magazine. v.1–4, 1904–1905. Monthly. Atlanta. Ha, ULS.

Souvenir: A Journal of Literature and Fashion. v.1–4, 1827–1830. Philadelphia. Hn, ULS.

Sports Clothing Diary. 1990(?)–. Annual. Mount Prospect, IL: National Sporting Goods Association. Wcat.

Sports Illustrated. v.1, 1954–. New York. Be, ULS.

Sports Illustrated for Kids. 1989–. Monthly. New York. Ulrich, SPD.

Sportswear Jeans Intern (Jeans Intern). 1982(?)–. New York. Wcat (v.2, 1983).

Stores. (National Retail Dry Goods Association) v.1, 1913–. New York. Be, ULS.

Studio, an Illustrated Magazine of Fine and Applied Art. 1893–. London. Ba, ULS.

Style: A Monthly Magazine of Fashion for Women. v.1–8, 1901–1909. New York. Hi, ULS.

Style-Arts: Feminine Fashions, Accessories, Decoration. v.1, no. 1, 1936. New York. Supersedes *Fashions Art.* Hi, ULS.

Style Sources of American Fashions. v.1–18, 1924–1932. Chicago. Merged with *Women's Wear Daily.* Hi, ULS.

Style Trend: Devoted Exclusively to the Interests of the Washable Garment, Fabric and Related Industries. 1928–1938. Hi, ULS.

Swim Magazine. 1984–. Bimonthly. Pasadena, CA. Ulrich.

Swimsuit International. 1987–. Monthly. New York. Ulrich.

Swimwear USA. v.4, 1987–. New York. Wcat, Ulrich.

TCI (Theatre Crafts International). 1967–. Ten issues per year. New York. Formerly *Theatre Crafts* 1967–1992. SPD, Wcat.

TD&T. v.1, 1965–. q. New York: U.S. Institute of Theatre Technology. Formerly *Theatre Design and Technology* 1965–1989(?). NST, Ulrich, Wcat.

Technology and Conservation. v.1, 1976–. Boston. NST.

Teen. v.1, 1957–. Los Angeles. M, NST.

Tennis. v.1, 1965–. Trumbull, CT. NST, SPD.

Theatre Crafts. See *TCI.*

Today's Secretary. v.1, 1899–. Monthly. New York. Ha, ULS.

Today's Woman and Home. v.1–24, 1905–1928. New York. Hi, ULS.

Town. v.1, no. 1–5, 1807. New York. Hn, ULS.

Town and Country. v.1, 1846–. Monthly. New York. Be, Ha, Hn, ULS.

Twin Cities Woman. 1977–1979. Monthly. Minneapolis. Ha, Wcat.

L'Uomo Vogue. 1968–. Quarterly. Milan. NST.

Vanity Fair. v.1–45, 1913–1936. New York. Merged with *Vogue.* Hi, ULS.

Vie Heureuse. 1902–1909(?). Monthly. Paris. Ha, ULS.

Vie Parisienne. 1863–1970(?). Paris. Hi, ULS.

Visual Merchandising and Store Design. 1922–. Cincinnati, OH. Be, Wcat.

Vogue. v.1, Dec. 17, 1892–. Monthly. New York. Ba, Be, Ha, Mc, Hi, R, ULS. Also Australian, Brazilian, British, French, German, Italian, and Spanish editions.

Vogue Children (Vogue Children's Fashions). v.1, 1963–. s-a. New York. NST, Wcat.

Vogue Hommes. (in English and French) 1976–. Ten issues per year. Paris. Ulrich.

Vogue Pattern Book. 1925–. Greenwich, CT. Hi, ULS.

W (Women's Wear Daily). v.1, 1972–. New York. Be, NST.

Walking. 1986–. Six issues per year. Boston. NST, Ulrich, Wcat (v.9, 1994).

Wearable Crafts. 1991–. Bimonthly. Berne, IN: House of White Birches Publishing. (formerly *Wearable Wonders*). Ulrich.

Western Outfitter. 1969–. Monthly. Houston. Wcat (v.9, 1978).

White Tops: Devoted Exclusively to the Circus. 1927–. Bimonthly. White Stone, VA: Circus Fan Association of America. ULS.

Woman's Day. v.1, 1937–. New York. Be, Ha, ULS.

Woman's Home Companion. v.1–84, 1873–1957. Monthly. Springfield, OH. Ba, Be, Ha, Hi, ULS (1873–1895 as *Ladies' Home Companion*).

Woman's Magazine. v.1–22, 1899–1910. Monthly. St. Louis, MO. Ha, ULS.

Women's Sports and Fitness. v.1, 1979–. Palo Alto, CA. (formerly *Women's Sports* 1974–1978). NST (1983–. L/N full-text).

Woman's Outlook. 1919–1926(?). Biweekly. Glasgow, Scotland. Ha.

Woman's World. 1887–1890. Monthly. London. Ha, ULS.

Woman's World. 1958–1971(?). Quarterly. Karachi, Pakistan. Ha, NST.

Women and Performance: A Journal of Feminist Theory. v.1, 1983–. s-a. New York: New York University Department of Performance Studies. Wcat.

Women's Wear Daily. See *WWD*.

Women's Wear Magazine. Eastern edition. See *Style Sources of American Fashions*.

Working Woman. v.1, 1976–. Monthly. New York. Ha, NST. (1983– selected full-text L/N).

WWD (Women's Wear Daily). 1892–. Daily, New York. Continues *Women's Wear*. Be, Ha, NST (1983–selected full-text L/N).

YM (Young Miss). v.1, 1953–(*Young Miss* 1953–1985; *Young Miss Magazine: YM* 1985–1986; YM 1986–). Bergenfield, NJ. Be, M, NST.

Zeitschrift fur Historische Waffen- und Kostumkunde. Organ des Vereins fur Historische Waffenkunde. v.1, 1892–. Dresden. Ba, ULS.

Zeitung fur die Elegante Welt. v.1–57, 1801–1857(?) Leipzig. Ba, ULS.

Appendix: Clothing and Accessory Terms Used in the *OCLC/WorldCat* Database July 6, 1995 (Sorted For Books, Serials, and Media in English)

Clothing (c) and Accessory (a) Items from *OCLC/WorldCat* Sorted by Number of Hits, Books in English, July 6, 1995.

Clothing Item	c a	OCLC hits	in English	Books in English	Serials in English	Media
clothing and dress	c	07848	07065	05725	00225	00976
men's clothing	c	01162	01065	00793	00143	00112
children's clothing	c	01018	00941	00719	00063	00152
sweaters	c	00357	00302	00284	00007	00011
coats	c	00355	00330	00254	00016	00049
underwear	c	00261	00231	00190	00036	00002
color in clothing	c	00272	00227	00181	00001	00042
fur garments	c	00195	00171	00140	00013	00017
sport clothes	c	00216	00201	00127	00056	00018
trousers	c	00174	00161	00119	00003	00037
skirts	c	00134	00123	00077	00002	00043
work clothes	c	00097	00081	00074	00006	00000
leather garments	c	00098	00081	00071	00004	00006
t-shirt+	c	00117	00108	00059	00006	00040
kimonos	c	00230	00055	00052	00001	00002
jeans / clothing	c	00084	00072	00051	00004	00013
maternity clothes	c	00037	00034	00033	00000	00001
blouses	c	00076	00065	00032	00003	00030
sleepwear	c	00046	00043	00031	00003	00009

overalls	c	00026	00026	00025	00000	00000
cloaks	c	00041	00031	00023	00002	00005
vintage clothing	c	00021	00020	00016	00002	00002
uniforms sports	c	00021	00019	00014	00001	00004
riding habit	c	00023	00021	00011	00002	00008
smocks	c	00014	00013	00011	00000	00002
teenage boys clothing	c	00015	00015	00010	00002	00003
raincoats	c	00011	00011	00010	00001	00000
kilts	c	00010	00010	00008	00000	00001
waists	c	00010	00009	00007	00000	00001
bodices	c	00023	00021	00005	00000	00016
bloomer costume	c	00013	00006	00005	00000	00000
evening gowns	c	00008	00006	00003	00000	00003
leather jackets	c	00005	00004	00003	00000	00001
aloha shirts	c	00003	00002	00002	00000	00000
jewelry	a	04946	03644	03162	00204	00240
shoes	a	01853	01576	01305	00097	00090
boots	a	01213	01060	00911	00081	00034
hats	a	00983	00837	00681	00015	00103
eyeglasses	a	00892	00654	00545	00015	00066

footwear	a	00785	00631	00524	00091	00009
hosiery	a	00549	00486	00384	00074	00009
buttons	a	00309	00274	00239	00017	00016
millinery	a	00325	00304	00232	00041	00007
gloves	a	00341	00299	00217	00015	00063
dress accessories	a	00221	00180	00144	00021	00014
handbags	a	00220	00101	00088	00004	00009
shawls	a	00102	00066	00063	00000	00000
scarves	a	00082	00065	00052	00000	00012
collars	a	00080	00070	00043	00000	00027
belts / clothing	a	00075	00047	00041	00000	00006
vests	a	00047	00042	00038	00000	00004
handkerchiefs	a	00040	00031	00029	00002	00000
headgear	a	00019	00019	00019	00000	00000
neckwear	a	00017	00014	00013	00000	00001
buttonholes	a	00027	00027	00012	00000	00015
cowboy boots	a	00016	00014	00011	00000	00002
cuffs / clothing	a	00018	00018	00008	00000	00010
stoles / clothing	a	00007	00007	00005	00001	00001

Clothing Items from *OCLC/WorldCat* Sorted by Number of Hits, Serials in English, July 6, 1995 (Clothing [c]/Accessory [a])

Clothing Item	c a	Serials in English	OCLC hits	in English	Books in English	Media
clothing and dress	c	00225	07848	07065	05725	00976
jewelry	a	00204	04946	03644	03162	00240
men's clothing	c	00143	01162	01065	00793	00112
shoes	a	00097	01853	01576	01305	00090
footwear	a	00091	00785	00631	00524	00009
boots	a	00081	01213	01060	00911	00034
hosiery	a	00074	00549	00486	00384	00009
children's clothing	c	00063	01018	00941	00719	00152
sport clothes	c	00056	00216	00201	00127	00018
millinery	a	00041	00325	00304	00232	00007
underwear	c	00036	00261	00231	00190	00002
dress accessories	a	00021	00221	00180	00144	00014
buttons	a	00017	00309	00274	00239	00016
coats	c	00016	00355	00330	00254	00049
hats	a	00015	00983	00837	00681	00103
eyeglasses	a	00015	00892	00654	00545	00066
gloves	a	00015	00341	00299	00217	00063
fur garments	c	00013	00195	00171	00140	00017
sweaters	c	00007	00357	00302	00284	00011

Category						
work clothes	c	00006	00097	00081	00074	00000
t-shirt+	c	00006	00117	00108	00059	00040
leather garments	c	00004	00098	00081	00071	00006
jeans / clothing	c	00004	00084	00072	00051	00013
handbags	a	00004	00220	00101	00088	00009
trousers	c	00003	00174	00161	00119	00037
blouses	c	00003	00076	00065	00032	00030
sleepwear	c	00003	00046	00043	00031	00009
skirts	c	00002	00134	00123	00077	00043
cloaks	c	00002	00041	00031	00023	00005
vintage clothing	c	00002	00021	00020	00016	00002
riding habit	c	00002	00023	00021	00011	00008
teenage boys clothing	c	00002	00015	00015	00010	00003
handkerchiefs	a	00002	00040	00031	00029	00000
color in clothing	c	00001	00272	00227	00181	00042
kimonos	c	00001	00230	00055	00052	00002
uniforms sports	c	00001	00021	00019	00014	00004
raincoats	c	00001	00011	00011	00010	00000
stoles / clothing	a	00001	00007	00007	00005	00001
maternity clothes	c	00000	00037	00034	00033	00001

		00000	00026	00026	00025	00000
overalls	c	00000	00026	00026	00025	00000
smocks	c	00000	00014	00013	00011	00002
kilts	c	00000	00010	00010	00008	00001
waists	c	00000	00010	00009	00007	00001
bodices	c	00000	00023	00021	00005	00016
bloomer costume	c	00000	00013	00006	00005	00000
evening gowns	c	00000	00008	00006	00003	00003
leather jackets	c	00000	00005	00004	00003	00001
aloha shirts	c	00000	00003	00002	00002	00000
shawls	a	00000	00102	00066	00063	00000
scarves	a	00000	00082	00065	00052	00012
collars	a	00000	00080	00070	00043	00027
belts / clothing	a	00000	00075	00047	00041	00006
vests	a	00000	00047	00042	00038	00004
headgear	a	00000	00019	00019	00019	00000
neckwear	a	00000	00017	00014	00013	00001
buttonholes	a	00000	00027	00027	00012	00015
cowboy boots	a	00000	00016	00014	00011	00002
cuffs / clothing	a	00000	00018	00018	00008	00010

Clothing Items from *OCLC/WorldCat* Sorted by Number of Hits, Media, July 6, 1995 (Clothing [c]/ Accessory [a])

Clothing Item	c a	Media	Books in English	Serials in English	OCLC hits	in English
clothing and dress	c	00976	05725	00225	07848	07065
jewelry	a	00240	03162	00204	04946	03644
children's clothing	c	00152	00719	00063	01018	00941
men's clothing	c	00112	00793	00143	01162	01065
hats	a	00103	00681	00015	00983	00837
shoes	a	00090	01305	00097	01853	01576
eyeglasses	a	00066	00545	00015	00892	00654
gloves	a	00063	00217	00015	00341	00299
coats	c	00049	00254	00016	00355	00330
skirts	c	00043	00077	00002	00134	00123
color in clothing	c	00042	00181	00001	00272	00227
t-shirt+	c	00040	00059	00006	00117	00108
trousers	c	00037	00119	00003	00174	00161
boots	a	00034	00911	00081	01213	01060
blouses	c	00030	00032	00003	00076	00065
collars	a	00027	00043	00000	00080	00070
sport clothes	c	00018	00127	00056	00216	00201
fur garments	c	00017	00140	00013	00195	00171
buttons	a	00016	00239	00017	00309	00274

bodices	c	00016	00005	00000	00023	00021
buttonholes	a	00015	00012	00000	00027	00027
dress accessories	a	00014	00144	00021	00221	00180
jeans / clothing	c	00013	00051	00004	00084	00072
scarves	a	00012	00052	00000	00082	00065
sweaters	c	00011	00284	00007	00357	00302
cuffs / clothing	a	00010	00008	00000	00018	00018
footwear	a	00009	00524	00091	00785	00631
hosiery	a	00009	00384	00074	00549	00486
handbags	a	00009	00088	00004	00220	00101
sleepwear	c	00009	00031	00003	00046	00043
riding habit	c	00008	00011	00002	00023	00021
millinery	a	00007	00232	00041	00325	00304
leather garments	c	00006	00071	00004	00098	00081
belts / clothing	a	00006	00041	00000	00075	00047
cloaks	c	00005	00023	00002	00041	00031
uniforms sports	c	00004	00014	00001	00021	00019
vests	a	00004	00038	00000	00047	00042
teenage boys clothing	c	00003	00010	00002	00015	00015
evening gowns	c	00003	00003	00000	00008	00006

underwear	c	00002	00190	00036	00261	00231
vintage clothing	c	00002	00016	00002	00021	00020
kimonos	c	00002	00052	00001	00230	00055
smocks	c	00002	00011	00000	00014	00013
cowboy boots	a	00002	00011	00000	00016	00014
stoles / clothing	a	00001	00005	00001	00007	00007
maternity clothes	c	00001	00033	00000	00037	00034
kilts	c	00001	00008	00000	00010	00010
waists	c	00001	00007	00000	00010	00009
leather jackets	c	00001	00003	00000	00005	00004
neckwear	a	00001	00013	00000	00017	00014
work clothes	c	00000	00074	00006	00097	00081
handkerchiefs	a	00000	00029	00002	00040	00031
raincoats	c	00000	00010	00001	00011	00011
overalls	c	00000	00025	00000	00026	00026
bloomer costume	c	00000	00005	00000	00013	00006
aloha shirts	c	00000	00002	00000	00003	00002
shawls	a	00000	00063	00000	00102	00066
headgear	a	00000	00019	00000	00019	00019

Notes

CHAPTER 1

1. Jackson Kesler, *Theatrical Costume, a Guide to Information Sources* (Detroit: Gale, 1979), x. The three Ph.D. dissertations mentioned are G. Richardson, "The Costuming on the American Stage, 1751–1901: A Study of Major Developments in Wardrobe Practice and Costume Style" (University of Illinois, 1953), J. Loring, "Costuming on the New York Stage from 1895 to 1915 with Particular Emphasis on Charles Frohman's Companies" (State University of Iowa, 1960), and J. Paterek, "A Survey of Costuming of the New York Commercial Stage: 1914–1934," 3 v. (University of Minnesota, 1961).

2. H. M. Larson, *Guide to Business History* (Cambridge, MA: Harvard University Press, 1948), 1082, and item 2436. Notes A. B. Young's *Recurring Cycles of Fashion, 1760–1937* (New York: Harper, 1937).

3. R. W. Lovett, *American Economic and Business History Information Sources* (Detroit: Gale, 1971), 11.

4. L. M. Daniells, *Business Information Sources* (Berkeley: University of California Press, 1993), xvi.

5. J. T. Vogel and B. W. Lowry, *The Textile Industry: an Information Sourcebook* (Phoenix, AZ: Oryx Press, 1989), vii.

6. T. J. Schlereth, "Material Culture Studies in America, 1876–1976," in *Material Culture Studies in America* (Nashville, TN: American Association for State and Local History, 1982), 6–8.

7. *New York Times Book Review*, December 14, 1941, 4.

CHAPTER 3

1. D. M. Gorsline, *A History of Fashion* (London: Fitzhouse Books, 1953), xii.

2. M. P. Murray, *Changing Styles in Fashion* (New York: Fairchild, 1989), 242.

3. See *National Union Catalog Pre-1956 Imprints* 154 (1971): 106–109.

4. E. McClellan, *Historic Dress in America, 1607–1870* (New York: Tudor Pub. Co., 1937), 26.

5. To locate U.S. documents on military uniforms, consult indexes outlined in chapter 7 in the last section, "Types of Publications."

6. *Library Journal,* November 15, 1965, 4955.

7. E. Warwick and H. C. Pitz, *Early American Costume* (New York: Century Co., 1929), v.

8. A. Train, Jr., *The Story of Everyday Things* (New York: Harper & Brothers, 1941), 4.

9. Ibid., 356.

10. I. Brooke, *English Children's Costume since 1775* (London: A. & C. Black, 1930), 4.

11. J. Dorner, *Fashion: The Changing Shape of Fashion through the Years* (London: Octopus Books, 1974), 9.

12. P. F. Copeland, *Working Dress in Colonial and Revolutionary America* (Westport, CT: Greenwood, 1977), xv.

13. L. Baumgarten, *Eighteenth-Century Clothing at Williamsburg* (Williamsburg, VA: Colonial Williamsburg Foundation, 1986), 5.

14. F. Chenoune, *A History of Men's Fashion* (Paris: Flammarion, 1993), 2.

15. M. E. Tillotson, *History of the First Thirty-Five Years of the Science Costume Movement* (Vineland, NJ: Weekly-in-Dependent, 1885), title page.

16. B. J. Mills, *Calico Chronicle* (Lubbock, TX: Texas Tech Press, 1985), 7–8.

17. C. B. Kidwell and M. C. Christman, *Suiting Everyone* (Washington, D.C.: Smithsonian Institution Press, 1974), 13.

18. O. Thieme et al., *With Grace and Favor* (Cincinnati, OH: Cincinnati Art Museum, 1993), v.

19. D. L. Cohn, *The Good Old Days* (New York: Simon and Schuster, 1940), 469.

20. E. Melinkoff, *What We Wore, an Off Beat Social History of Women's Clothing, 1850–1980* (New York: W. Morrow, 1984), 185.

21. R. Martin and H. Koda, *Jocks and Nerds* (New York: Rizzoli International, 1989), 1.

22. J. Gaines and C. Herzog, eds., *Fabrications: Costume and the Female Body* (New York: Routledge, 1990), 19.

23. B. A. Schreier, *Mystique and Identity* (Norfolk, VA: Chrysler Museum, 1984), 16.

CHAPTER 4

1. I. Brooke, *Dress and Undress: The Restoration and Eighteenth Century* (Westport, CT: Greenwood, 1958).

2. D. D'Arcy, "Lingerie Is Front and Center at the MET," *Los Angeles Times,* May 7, 1993, E:4, *Lexis/Nexis:* NEWS library/CURNWS file.

3. *Dissertation Abstracts International* 48B (1987): 110.

4. Ibid. 51A (1991): 3001.

5. F. Deford, "How It All Began," *Sports Illustrated* 70, no. 6 (February 1989): 38–41, 52, 54, 56.

6. *Sports Illustrated* 70, no. 6 (February 1989): 64.

7. *Home Economics Research Abstracts—1969: Textiles and Clothing* (1970): 74.

8. *American Denim: A New Folk Art* (New York: H. N. Abrams, 1975), 135.

9. *Dissertation Abstracts International* 55A (1995): 2150.

10. Promotional sheet describing *The Wedding Dress* by Maria McBride Mellinger published by Random House with price and order information, n.d. [1993?].

11. M. Baerwald and T. Mahoney, *The Story of Jewelry* (London: Abelard-Schuman, 1960), 185.

12. "Paying Tribute to Wearable Art," *New York Times*, Section 1, Part 2, April 26, 1992, 48. *Lexis/Nexis:* NEWS library/CURNWS file.

13. *Dance: A Very Social History* (New York: Metropolitan Museum of Art: Rizzoli, 1989), 90.

14. *Dissertation Abstracts International* 49A (1989): 2025–2026.

15. M. Jacobs, "Antiques: Cape May to Recall Victorian Era," *New York Times*, Section 11NJ, October 6, 1985, 23. *Lexis/Nexis:* NEWS library/ALLNWS file.

16. A. Gilbert, "Vintage Clothing: It Just Gets Better with Time," Gannett News Service, October 6, 1993. *Lexis/Nexis:* NEWS library/ALLNWS file.

CHAPTER 5

1. F. R. Parsons, *Psychology of Dress* (Garden City, NY: Doubleday, 1923), vii.

2. M. J. Horn, *Second Skin* (Boston: Houghton Mifflin, 1968), viii.

3. A. Hollander, *Seeing through Clothes* (New York: Viking, 1978), 311.

4. Ibid., xvi.

5. ED138994, ERIC Document Abstract.

6. P. Glynn, *In Fashion* (New York: Oxford University Press, 1978), 13.

7. S. and E. Ewan, *Channels of Desire* (New York: McGraw-Hill, 1982), 187.

8. V. Steele, *Fashion and Eroticism* (New York: Oxford University Press, 1985), 4.

9. Ibid., 8.

10. A. Ribeiro, *Dress and Morality* (New York: Holmes & Meier, 1986), 15.

11. Ibid., 17.

12. Ibid., 18.

13. Ibid., 17.

14. S. B. Kaiser, *Social Psychology of Clothing and Personal Behavior*, 2d ed. (New York: Macmillan, 1990), 25–27.

15. N. Joseph, *Uniforms and Nonuniforms* (Westport, CT: Greenwood, 1986), 195.

16. J. Gaines and C. Herzog, eds., *Fabrications: Costume and the Female Body* (New York: Routledge, 1990), 19.

17. Ibid., 296.

18. P. A. Cunningham and S. V. Lab, eds., *Dress in American Culture* (Bowling Green, OH: Bowling Green State University Popular Press, 1993), 215.

19. S. Benstock and S. Ferriss, eds., *On Fashion* (New Brunswick, NJ: Rutgers University Press, 1994), back cover.

20. G. Lipovetsky, *Empire of Fashion* (Princeton, NJ: Princeton University Press, 1995), ix.

21. Ibid., x.

22. Ibid., 5.

23. *Home Economics Research Abstracts, Textiles and Clothing* 3 (1974): 51.

24. *Dissertation Abstracts International* 53A (1993) 3347.

25. *Masters Abstracts International* 30 (Winter 1992) 1136.

CHAPTER 8

1. "The Lighthouse, Looking Backward," *Wilson Bulletin for Librarians* 12 (February 1938): 410.

2. *National Union Catalog Pre 1956 Imprints* 1 (1968): viii.

3. *Poole's Index to Periodical Literature* 1, part 1 (1891; reprinted 1963): iii.

4. "The Lighthouse," *Wilson Bulletin for Librarians* 12 (September 1937): 45.

5. *Index to Periodical Articles by and about Negroes (Formerly Index to Selected Periodicals) 1960–1970* (Boston: G. K. Hall, 1971), iii.

6. *Cumulated Magazine Subject Index, 1907–1949* 1 (1964): iii.

7. *Information Industry Directory* (Detroit: Gale Research, annual).

8. A. M. Boyd and M. V. Miller, "A Reading List on Historic and Fancy Costume for Domestic Art, Amateur Theatricals, Historical Pageants and Festivals," *Historical Outlook,* 12 (February 1921): 59–61.

9. I. Monro and D. E. Cook, eds., *Costume Index* (New York: H. W. Wilson Company, 1937), iii.

10. I. Monro and K. M. Monro, eds., *Costume Index. Supplement* (New York: H. W. Wilson Company, 1957), v.

11. R. Colas, *Bibliographie Générale du Costume et de la Mode,* 2 vols. (Paris: Librarie René Colas, 1933).

12. H. and M. Hiler, *Bibliography of Costume* (New York: H. W. Wilson Company, 1939), iii.

13. *National Union Catalog Pre 1956 Imprints* 245 (1973): 568.

14. H. Hiler, *From Nudity to Raiment: An Introduction to the Study of Costume* (New York: E. Wehye, 1929), 2.

15. "The Lighthouse," *Wilson Bulletin for Librarians* 13, no. 6 (February 1939): 434.

CHAPTER 9

1. *Awards, Honors and Prizes,* 8th ed. (Detroit: Gale Research, 1989) 1:10.

2. Ibid., 1:928.

CHAPTER 11

1. A. L. Lafferty, "Contents and Services of Museum Costume Collections in the United States, 1963–1964" (master's thesis, Texas Women's University, 1968), 13.

2. Ibid., 70.

3. Ibid., 68.

4. Ibid., 17.

5. Ibid., 33.

6. C. Lubell, *Textile Collections of the World* (New York: Van Nostrand Reinhold, 1976), 1:6.

7. F. J. Duffield, *Resources in the Form of Collections of Historic Costumes . . .* (1979), 1.

8. F. J. Duffield, "University and College Historic Costume Collections," *Theatre Design and Technology* 16 (Winter 1980): 20.

9. M. Perkko, "Costumes as Indicators of Community," *Museum International* 45, no. 3 (1993): 25.

10. Lafferty, "Contents," 71.

11. T. R. Adam, *The Museum and Popular Culture* (New York: American Association for Adult Education, 1939), 170.

12. H. and M. Katz, *Museums, U.S.A.: A History and Guide* (Garden City, NY: Doubleday, 1965), 254.

13. K. Hudson, *Museums of Influence* (Cambridge: Cambridge University Press, 1987), 151.

14. *CSA News,* 20, no. 4 (Spring 1955): 10–11.

15. Metropolitan Museum of Art, New York, *Women in White: Addresses* (Boston: Bullfinch Press, 1989).

CHAPTER 13

1. A. H. Smyth, *The Philadelphia Magazines and Their Contributors, 1741–1850* (Philadelphia: R. M. Lindsay, 1892), 207.

2. Ibid., 225.

3. F. L. Mott, *A History of American Magazines* (Cambridge, MA: Harvard University Press, 1938–1968), 3:97.

4. Ibid., 4:359.

5. Ibid., 3:360.

6. J. P. Wood, *Magazines in the United States* (New York: Ronald, 1949), 126; (1971 ed.), 128.

7. Ibid.

8. E. Exman, *The House of Harper* (New York: Harper & Row, 1967), 126.

9. J. P. Wood, *The Curtis Magazines* (New York: Ronald, 1971), viii.

10. E. F. Stineman, "Women's Magazines," *Serials Review* 5 (October 1979): 26.

11. J. Massey, "Girl Talk Mags," *School Library Journal* 38, no. 10 (October 1992): 54.

12. E. McCracken, *Decoding Women's Magazines from Mademoiselle to Ms* (New York: St. Martin's Press, 1993), 135.

13. Ibid., 169.

14. J. Robinson, *The Fine Art of Fashion* (New York: Bartley & Jensen, 1989), 30–31.

15. *ARTbibliographiew Modern,* DIALOG online database, file 56. AN 277701 2104421.

16. M. K. Tarlton and S. V. LaBrecque, "Fashion Merchandising Periodicals," *Serials Review* 19, no. 1(1993):63.

17. S. Benstock, and S. Ferriss, *On Fashion* (New Brunswick, NJ: Rutgers University Press, 1994):66.

18. Ibid., 24.

19. "Kappa Publishes Fashion Trade Magazine," *Key of Kappa Kappa Gamma* 112, no. 3 (Fall 1995): 47.

20. W. Hochswender, *Men in Style* (New York: Rizzoli, 1993) 7.

21. A. Lieberman, Introduction to P. Devlin, *Vogue Book of Fashion Photography, 1919–1972* (New York: Simon and Schuster, 1979), 23.

22. S. T. Lewis, "Periodicals in the Visual Arts," *Library Trends* 10 (January 1962): 342.

23. Ibid., 346.

24. *Dissertation Abstracts International* 52A (January 1992): 2459.

25. Ibid., 54A (July 1993): 329.

Author Index

Abbott, Carmen M., 31
Abe, Kazuo, 167
Abramson, Glenda, 16
Ackerman, Evelyn, 29
Adam, Thomas R., 187
Adams, Amelia E., 109
Adams, Eeba, 84
Adams, George E., 84
Adams, Jane F., 133
Adams, Shirley, 66
Akers, Edna, 113
Alabama Educational Television Network, 92
Albert Lea Hide & Fur Co., 66
Albrecht, Juliana, 57, 133
Alexander, Lois K., 101
Alexander, Nancy, 53
Allen, Barbara, 35
Allen, Helen H., 112
Allen, Rebecca, 7
Alto, Vonnie R., 80

American Apparel Manufacturers Association, 62
American Craft Museum, 76
American Entrepreneurs Association, 68
American Home Economics Association, 130
American Optometric Association, 82
Anderson, Carma, 31
Anderson, Clarita, 134
Anderson, Virginia L., 36
Anspach, Karlyne A., 99
Anthony, Pegaret, 130
Apparel Institute, 51, 62
Argent, Jeanne, 66
Armour, Robert A., 5
Armstrong, Alan, 23
Arnim, Faye, 55
Arnold, Janet, 1, 130
Ash, Lee, 172
Aswell, Mary L., 210

B. B. Menzel & Co., 55
Bach, Pieter, 46, 186
Baclawski, Karen, 124
Bacon, Elizabeth E., 12
Bader, Iva M., 132
Baerd, Tyler, 80
Baerwald, Marcus, 74
Bailey, Albina, 45
Bailey, Florence H., 36
Bailey, Margaret J., 87
Bailey, R., 104
Bailey, William G., 105
Baker, Blanch M., 5
Baker, Lillian, 75
Baker, Roberta H., 30
Balay, Robert, 123–124
Balch Institute for Ethnic Studies, 72
Baldwin, Lois M., 110
Ball, Joanne D., 75
Ball, Verna D. B., 167
Ballard, Battina, 210
Barker, S. Omar, 64
Barnes, Ruth, 104
Bartis, Peter T., 7
Barton, Lucy, 90, 216
Bartsch, Donna, 23, 133
Basralian, Karen M., 71, 218
Batterberry, Ariane, 19
Batterberry, Michael, 19
Baum, Gretchen, 50
Baum, Shelly J., 118
Baumgarten, Linda, 24
Bauret, Gabriel, 208
Baylor, Don, 160
Beagle, Peter, 64–65
Beard, Charles, 124
Beaton, Cecil, 87
Beaudoin-Ross, Jacqueline, 130
Beck, S. William, 83
Beeson, Marianne S., 100
Bell, Quentin, 98
Ben-Yusuf, Anna, 80
Bennett, Debra S., 31
Benstock, Sheri, 104
Berg, Donna L., 124
Berger, Vicki L., 2, 103
Bergler, Edmund, 98
Berlin Glove Company, 66

Bernard, Barbara, 32
Bernard, Christopher, 105
Bernfeld, Dan, 186
Billings, Victoria C., 119
Binder, Anna L., 80
Bishop, Edna B., 163
Bivin, Rolalie J., 115
Bjerke, Gene, 166
Blackstock, Pamela, 130
Blackwell, Mr., 211
Blau, Clare, 81
Blauer, Ettagale, 77
Bloom, Elliot P., 92
Blum, Dilys E., 81
Blum, Stella, 33–34, 209–210
Blumberg, Rhoda, 57
Bodine, Sarah, 77
Boloz, Sigmund A., 70
Bolton, Mary J., 110
Bonapfel, Robert H., 62
Bond, Larry, 93
Borland, Glenn F., 70
Boswell, Thom, 91
Boucher, Francois, 13
Bowler, Bobbi R., 162
Bowser, Debra J., 116
Boxer, Joe, 53
Boydston, J.M.K., 215
Boynton, Bonnie, 35
Brackman, Barbara, 80
Branch, Roxanne M., 64
Brandt, Brenda, 31, 133
Brigham, Mary E., 60, 112, 218
Briscoe, Emma H., 23
Britton, Sherry, 62
Bronson, L. D., 82
Brooke, Iris, 23, 79
Brown, Dorothy F., 83
Brown, Elizabeth S., 30
Brown, Mary L., 113
Brown, Reenie, 209
Brown, Teresa C., 218
Brunson, Deborah L., 53
Brusstar, Lorna T., 85
Buck, Anne, 124
Budgeon, Shelley, 105, 218
Bullen, Nicholas, 72
Bullock, Penelope L., 215

Bundy, Elizabeth, 60
Burberry's of London, 51
Burch, Janis G., 31
Burns, Marilyn M., 36
Burton, Mary E., 110
Butterick Fashion Marketing Co., 55, 66
Buys, Bonnie, 163
Buzzaccarini, Vittoria de, 83

C. J. Bailey & Co., 51
C. W. Hyer & Sons, 79
Calandro, Donna F., 117
Calasibetta, Charlotte M., 124, 126
Caldwell, Lark F., 118
Calveri, Karin L. F., 23
Cantua, Willette D., 36
Carnes, Valerie, 100
Carrillo, Loretta, 101
Carter, Alison, 53
Carter, Ernestine, 32
Carter, Robert A., 133
Carver, Marie N., 132
Cassidy, Louise, 110
Castro, Anna M., 208
Catlin, Amy, 35
Caulfeild, Sophia F. A., 126
Cederwall, Sandraline, 76
Cerny, Catherine A., 36, 104,
Chambers, Bernice G., 12
Chang, Younhwa, 117
Chas. Goldstein & Company, 55
Chase, Edna W., 210
Cheney Brothers, 58
Chenoune, Farid, 25
Chierichetti, David, 87
Christensen, Erwin O., 183
Christman, Margaret C., 28
Church, Helen L., 64
Cianni, Vincent, 72
Clabburn, Pamela, 126
Clapp, Jane, 137
Clark, Fiona, 80
Clark, Lori J., 120, 167
Clarke, Mary, 85
Clayton, Mary K., 16
Clements, Patricia S., 58
Clifford, Marilyn W., 30

Clift, Virgil A., 16
Cochran, Mary F., 114
Cockrell, Rachel H., 53
Cohn, David L., 32
Cohn-Stratyner, Barbara, 208
Colburn, Carol A., 31, 149
Colchester, Chloe, 6, 126
Coleman, Dorothy S., 47
Coleman, Elizabeth A., 25, 28, 30, 47, 186
Coleman, Evely J., 47
Collard, Eileen, 52
Collazzo, Charles J., 133
Collins, C. Cody, 84
Colmer, Michael, 52–53
Compton, Norma H., 58, 114
Compton, Rae, 50
Connolly, Lois, 136
Connolly, Marguerite A., 119, 219
Cook, Dorothy E., 131
Copeland, Peter F., 24, 46, 61
Copley, Ellie, 163
Corbin, Krestine, 66
Cornwel, Rebecca A., 31
Cornwell, Felicia M., 115
Corrigan, Barbara, 63
Corson, Richard, 82
Costume Society of America, 130, 184
Coulter, Linda S., 120
Crawford, Elizabeth G., 54
Crawford, Morris de Camp, 52, 127
Crisp, Clement, 86
Crocker Art Museum, 29
Crowninshields, Frank, 210
Cubbs, Joanne, 35
Cumming, Valerie, 34, 84
Cunningham, Patricia A., 30, 104, 133
Cunnington, C. Willett, 52, 124
Cunnington, Phyllis, 54, 124
Curran, Mary J., 89
Curtis, John H., 82
Cushing, Helen G., 131

Dalzell, Frederick A. B., 89
Damhorst, Mary L., 136
Damme, Regine van, 63
Daniells, Lorna M., 4
Danto, Arthur C., 77

Darlington, Anne, 163
Dartmouth College, Museum Galleries, 29
Dauterman, C. C., 133
Davenport, Millia, 12–13
Davidson, Derek C., 82
Davies, Stephanie C., 124
Davis, Fred, 104
Dayton Co., 55
De Marly, Diana, 11, 20
Dean, Tammera S. H., 89
DeLano, Sharon, 80
DelGaudio, Sybil, 88
DeLong, Marilyn R., 103
Delpierre, Madeleine, 124
Denver Dry Goods Co., 79
DePaul, Frances T., 35
Devitt, Annette, 117
Devlin, Polly, 211
Dickey, Susan J., 46
Dickinson, Joan Y., 74
Dispenza, Joseph E., 100
Ditzion, Sidney, 203
Doelken, Theodor, 128
Doering, Mary D., 134
Dolan, Maryanne, 93
Dominique, Michael J., 31
Donaldson, Edith C., 36
Dong, John G., 130
Donovan, Carrie, 14
Dorner, Jane, 23, 32
Dotson, Jim, 163
Dowlen, Rowena P., 133
Drake, Nichols, 210
Drayton, Grace G., 45
Dreher, Denise, 80
Driscoll, Bernadette, 66
Druesedow, Jean L., 85, 186, 209
Drutt, Matthew, 77
Duce, Leora L. G., 112
Duffield, Frances J., 185
Dunnigan, Timothy, 35
Duntley, Linda K., 116
Durfee, Paulette, 163
Durst, Elaine A., 56
Duvalos, Shirley, 165

E. E. Atkinson & Co., 55
Eagon, Mary A., 72

Earhart, Amelia, 210
Earle, Alice M., 20, 124
Edelman, Phyllis C., 134
Edelstein, Sally, 45
Edes Robe Tanning Co., 66
Edlefsen, David, 76
Edmonds, Linda L., 115
Edmunds, Alice, 63
Edwin Clapp & Son, 78
Eicher, Joanne B., 99, 104, 130, 137
Eiger, Janet N., 35
Ekeland, Barbara K., 30
Eldridge, Charlotte B., 46
Eliade, Mircea, 17
Elliott, Shirley D., 116
Ellsworth & Thayer Mfg. Co., 55
Endel, Barbara L., 218
Enis, Ben A., 165
Erte, 210
Ervin, Kelly S., 208
Esmerian, Ralph, 75
Estorick, Eric, 212
Ettinger, Roseann, 34, 75, 93
Evans, Mary, 90
Everett, Karen, 166
Ewan, Elizabeth, 100
Ewen, Stuart, 100
Ewing, Elizabeth, 32, 52
Exman, Eugene, 204

Fahy, Neal, 168
Fargo, Barbara M., 30
Farnfield, Carolyn A., 6
Farrell, Jeremy, 83
Farrell-Beck, Jane, 133, 136
Farren, Mick, 67
Fasel, Marion, 75
Fashion Institute of Technology, 53, 57, 130, 133
Fehr, Barbara, 63
Feinman, Jeffery, 68
Feldkamp, Phyllis, 29, 100
Feldman, Elane, 34
Felger, Donna H., 46, 72
Fenn, Donna, 208
Fennelly, Catherine, 23
Ferrell, J., 70
Ferriss, Suzanne, 104
Figg, Laurann, 31

Figliulo, Susan, 68
Filene, Adele, 130, 150
Finlayson, Bliss B., 113
Finlayson, Iain, 64
Finley, Ruth E., 209
Fischer, Gayle V., 135
Fleetwood, Shianne, 166
Flint, M. Elaine S., 115
Flood, Jessie B., 86
Flores, Bob, 70
Flugel, John C., 98
Focht, Brenda B., 29
Fogel, Irene L. R., 219
Folkers, Treva A., 85
Foote, Shelly J., 76
Forbes, Bessie B., 110
Ford Motorsport/PMI, Ltd., 58
Foreman, Lois J., 30
Formanek, Janet L., 118
Formanek-Bronell, Miriam, 46
Foster, Virginia B., 113
Fox, Patty, 105
Francis, Lucinda F., 168
Fraser, Kennedy, 210–11
Freeman, Jack, 12
Fresener, Pat, 69
Fresener, Scott, 68
Friedman, Jay, 161
Frommer, D. W., 79
Fullam, Melissa L., 35
Fuller, Jane M., 168
Funderburk, Jane A. U., 120, 167

Gaines, Jane, 34,103
Gale, William, 14
Gallup Organization, 58
Gamber, Wendy, 80
Gardner, Linda V., 120
Garnsey, Caroline J., 205
Gehret, Ellen J., 23
Geist, Christopher D., 172
Gere, Charlotte, 74
Gerson, Roselyn, 93
Gibson, Ray, 68
Gibson-Quick, Robyn, 36
Gifford, Beverly, 70
Giles, Cynthia, 93
Gilgun, Beth, 25
Gillespie, Karen R., 133

Giorgi, Sue T., 109
Gipson, Kay G., 113
Glatt, Hillary, 7
Glickman, Albert S., 110
Glosson, Eunice A., 26, 90
Glynn, Prudence, 32, 100
Goings, Barbara D., 112
Goldin, Leslie, 55
Goldman, Larry, 72
Goldstein Gallery, Univ. of Minnesota, 72
Goodlow, Nathaniel Van, 219
Goodwear Knitting Mills, 50
Gordon, Beverly, 64, 136
Gorn, Elliot, J., 16
Gorseline, Douglas, 19
Gradwohl, Eleanor, 112
Grant, Alice, 207
Grass, Milton E., 83
Grattaroti, Rosalie, 68
Grauch, Arlene E., 88
Graves, Vickie L., 219
Greeman, John, 63
Green, Larry, 160
Greer, Rebecca W., 114
Gregorietti, Guido, 110
Greyser, Stephen A., 165
Griffin, Gary M., 53
Griffith, Joan C., 215, 217
Grimble, Frances, 94
Grimkee, Sarah M., et al, 99
Grossbard, Judy, 57
Grounds, Cynthia T., 31
Guerin, Polly, 168
Guernsey, E., 52
Gummage, M. E. "Manny," 81
Gurel, Lois M., 100

H. B. Mackie Fur Coat & Robe Co., 55, 66
H. J. Justin & Sons, 79
Haan, Johannis Dirk de, 83
Hackler, Nadine, 60
Hady, Maureen E., 205
Haines, Elizabeth, 46
Haines, Frank, 46
Hall, Helen F., 55
Hall, John P., 78
Hall, Lee, 20

Hall, Nancy, 69
Hall, Tami W., 112
Halleran, Kristine, 31
Hallmark Gallery, 72
Halversen, Jackie F., 62
Hamblin, Dora J., 82
Hamilton, Coradel, 112
Hanson, Robin, 84
Hardy, Mamie L., 110
Hardy, Rhonda I., 219
Harless, Lenae H., 219
Harlow, Eve, 63
Harmel, Melissa, 72
Harmuth, Louis, 125
Harp, Shelley S., 167
Harp, Sue, 120
Harper, Jereleen H., 168
Harper, William, 76
Harris, Julie, 87
Harris Furs, 55
Harrison, Martin, 211
Hartley, Elizabeth F., 23
Hartung, Sara J., 113
Hartzog, Martha, 81
Havasy, Jamie, 109
Haven, Dorothy C., 90
Hawes, Elizabeth, 98
Hawthorne, Rosemary, 83
Hay, Susan A., 29
Haynie & Co., 55
Head, Edith, 87
Healy, Debra, 75
Heller, Miriam K., 218,
Helvenston, Sally, 30–31, 136
Henessee, Judith, 100
Hennessy, Karen E., 117
Hennings, Kyle L., 187
Henry, Sondra, 63
Henshaw, Betty L., 30
Hepburn, Audrey, 210
Herman, Lloyd E., 77
Herring, Margaret T., 53
Hersh, Tandy, 52
Herzog, Charlotte, 34, 103
Hickman, Joan T., 118
Hieronymus, Anne K., 114
Higbee, Arthur L., 163
Higbee Co., 55

Hiler, Hilaire, 3, 130, 149
Hiler, Meyer, 130, 149
Hill, Joe M., 168
Hirsch, John E., 90–91
Hochswender, Woody, 209
Hodges, Lloyd C., 115
Hodgkins, Betty J., 110
Hoffer, Christina M., 218
Hoffman, Adeline M., 132
Hoffmann, Frank W., 105, 135
Hofsess, L. F., 85
Holding, Ralph O., 84
Holland, Vyvyan B., 207
Hollander, Anne, 100
Holloman, Lillian O., 24
Holman, David, 66
Holt, Karen R., 53
Hoolt, Thomas, 109
Horn, Marilyn J., 99
Hornback, Betty C., 35
Horne, Lena, 119
Horning, Priscilla, 114
Hosking, Susan L., 76
Houck, Catherine, 14
Houdek, Mary F., 35
Howell, Gorgina, 210
Huddleson, Julia E., 78
Hudson, Kenneth, 188
Hudson, Peyton B., 163
Huenefeld, Irene P., 185
Huepenbecker, Agatha L., 110
Hummel, Edith M., 84
Humphreys, Nancy K., 205
Hunt, Lucille A., 110
Hunt, Patricia K., 31
Hunter, Margaret, 36
Hurlock, Elizabeth B., 98
Hurst, Marie J., 112
Hutinger, Patricia, 70
Hutton, Sandra S., 138, 150–51

Inge, M. Thomas, 101, 1031
International Latex Corp., 162
International Tennis Hall of Fame, 58
Iowa State University, 165
Ireland, Sandra L. J., 215
Irick-Nauer, Tina, 93
Ironside, Janey, 125

Jachimowicz, Elizabeth, 29
Jackson, Linda A., 208
Jacob, John B., 109
Jacobs, Laura, 46
Jacobsen, Mary A., 36
Janes, Karen, 36
Jeanswear Communications, 164
Jelen, Janet L., 30
Jennings, Harriet T., 6
Jennings, Julie S., 65
Jerde, Judith, 15, 125
Johnson, Dorma L., 113.
Johnson, Joyce S., 115, 136
Johnston, Moira, 100
Joinder, Betty, 85
Jones, Carolyn A. C., 110
Jordan, Oscar, 69
Joseph, Nathan, 102
Justin, H. J., 80

Kaiser, Susan B., 102, 136
Kalamazoo Corset Co., 52
Katz, Herbert, 187
Katz, Marjorie, 187
Kazanjian, Dodie, 105
Keenen, Beverly D., 110
Keeney, Margaret A., 114
Kellogg, Bill, 70
Kelly, Alberta, 82
Kemper, Rachel, 12
Kennett, Frances, 93
Kerr, Norman, 33
Kerr, Robert R., 28
Kerr, Rose H., 90
Kesler, Jackson, 2, 135
Khachaturian, Janet L., 117
Kidwell, Claudia B., 28, 57, 134
Kim, Hae J., 31, 218
Kim, Hye K., 36
Kim, Youn-Kyung, 120
Kimle, Patricia A., 219
King, Dorothy W., 110
Klapper, Marvin, 126
Kleeberg, Irene C., 62
Kleibacker, Charles, 164
Klein, Christine, 133
Klickmann, Flora, 51, 52
Klopp, Bernie, 69

Klopp, Linda, 68
Kneitel, Ken, 68
Koda, Harold, 30, 33, 35, 53
Koester, Ardis W., 12, 69
Kogos International Corp., 62
Kohler Arts Center, 35
Konetschni, Walter, 136
Kontos, Paulette G., 35
Korslund, Lois N., 113
Kotlarczyk, Lynne M., 56
Kotler, Philip, 165
Kowal, Cal, 68
Kozloski, Lillian D, 61
Kraditor, Aileen S., 99
Krashes, Laurence S., 74
Kraus, Richard G., 86
Krugs, Melissa I., 120, 218
Kuennen, Catherine M., 89
Kunzle, David, 53
Kuza, Julia E., 218

L. S. Donaldson Co., 55
La Barre, Kathleen M., 93
La Cross, Richard B., 61
Lab, Susan V., 104
LaBrecque, Suzanne, 208
LaClaire, Joyce, 62
Lacy, Dana, 218
Ladbury, Ann, 72
Editors of Ladies' Home Journal Needle & Craft, 50
Lafferty, Ann A., 184–5, 187
Lamancusa, Kathy, 160
Lambert, Eleanor, 1
Lancour, J., 133
Land's End, Inc., 58
Landrum, Larry N., 7
Langner, Lawrence, 99
Lansdell, Avril, 61
Larson, Henrietta M., 4
Larson, Joyce M., 31
Lauer, Jeanette C., 15, 102
Lauer, Robert H., 15, 102
Laver, James, 32, 90
LaVine, Robert, 87
LaVita, James, 86
Lawrence, Hazel M., 110
Lawson, Donna, 63

Layton, Peggy D., 63
Lebensburger, Myron M., 168
Lee, Jin-Kook, 113
Lee, Nancy L., 218
Lee-Potter, Charlie, 57
LeeWards Creative Crafts Center, 71
Leggett, Liza, 92, 120
Lennon, Sharron J., 136
Leslie, Judith E., 57, 114, 219
Leslie, Serge, 135
Lesse, Elizabeth, 87
Leu, Brian Y. N., 133
Levenstein, Bruce, 68
Levi Strauss and Company, 63
Levine, Jeffrey, 215
Lewis, Martha A., 121
Lewis, Stanley T., 215
Liban, Felicia, 160
Liberman, Alexander, 211
Library Association, 130
Lincoln, Dorothea C., 70
Linden, Roberta H., 218
Lindsay, Irina, 57
Linton, George E., 126
Lipovetsky, Gilles, 104
Little, David, 93
Lloyd, Valerie, 211
Loba, Frances B., 187
Lockard, Dora M., 60
Lokken, Doris E., 109
Lopez, Nylda N., 116
Lord, M. G., 46
Lord, Marcia, 186
Los Angeles County Museum of Art, 29
Lose, Patrick, 51
Love, Christine R., 219
Love, Harriet, 93
Lovett, Robert W., 4
Low, W. Agustus, 16
Lowe, Claudia J., 5
Lowry, Barbara W., 6
Lubell, Cecil, 185
Lundeen, Shirley M., 109
Lurie, Alison, 102
Lyle, Mary F., 112
Lynnlee, J. L., 75

MacIntosh, Eileen, 94
Mack-Keeles, Vermell, 120
Mackey, Margaret G., 90
Madeira, Elizabeth A., 122
Maeder, Edward, 29, 88
Magriel, Paul D., 135
Mahoney, Tom, 76
Maiwiejczyk-Munigumery, Marion A., 91
Maloney, Bill, 68, 69
Mandeville, A. Glenn, 46
Manento, Theresa M., 92
Manhart, Tom, 74
Manley, Jamine W., 114
Margaret Woodbury Strong Museum, 29
Martin, Diana, 68
Martin, Lawrence, 205,
Martin, Lee, 160
Martin, Richard, 12, 25, 30, 33, 35, 53, 127
Mason, Anita, 124
Massey, Judy, 206
Massey, Pat, 66
Mattera, Joanne, 211
Matthews, Linda M., 168
May, Anita, 110
Mayer, Sister M. L., 36
McBride, Jean E., 63
McBride-Mellinger, Maria, 72
McCarney, Kathleen, 187
McCarthy, Bill, 15
McClellan, Elisabeth, 20
McCool, Mary, 70
McCormick, Kari L., 117
McCormick, Terry, 93
McCoy, Sharon, 63
McCracken, Ellen, 206
McDowell, Colin, 125
McGee, Diane, 93
McGruder, Diana L., 116
McKune, Ann, 73
McPharlin, Paul, 22
McRobbie, Angela, 101
Melinkoff, Ellen, 33, 208
Men's Fashion Association of America, 33, 164
Merrifield, Heyoehkah, 75

Metropolitan Museum of Art, 138
Metzger, Paul, 135
Meyers, Carol A., 112
Milbank, Caroline R., 28, 103, 127
Miller, Elizabeth S., 57
Miller, Kimberly A., 115
Miller, Martha S., 113
Miller, Mary G., 59
Miller, Maryann T., 59
Miller, William G., 172
Mills, Betty J., 27–28, 45, 71
Mills-Godfrey, Marian, 93
Mint Museum of Art, 30
Mirabella, Grace, 214
Miranda, Michael A., 215
Mitchell, Roberta, 110
Molloy, John T., 100
Mongeau, Deborah H., 215
Monro, Isabel, 130, 148
Monro, Kate M., 131, 153
Monsarrat, Ann, 72
Montgomery, Florence M., 126
Montroll, Heidi S., 71
Moore, Doris L., 207
Moore, Kathleen A., 112
Morales, Barbara A., 118
Moriarty, Sandra E., 208
Morra, Marisa, 134
Morris, Adah V., 131
Morris, Judson H. Jr., 70
Morris, Katherine, 110
Morris, Robert L., 76
Morrow, Phoebe M., 118
Moses, H. Vincent, 29
Moss, Miriam, 61
Moss, Roberta, 66
Mott, Frank L., 203–4
Murrah, Judy, 51
Murry, Maggie P., 20
Museums at Stony Brook, 72
Musser, Cynthia, 48

Nasr, Insaf H., 36
Nassau, Ruth S., 167
National Book League (Great Britain), 130
Neff, John H., 68
Newman, Harold, 124

Newton, Audrey, 132
Newton, Stella M., 26
Nicholas, Kristin, 50
Nicholson, Joan, 100
Noel, Juanita M., 120, 167
Noonan, Barry C., 205
Nordquist, Barbara K., 24
Norfleet, Barbara P., 72
Norton, Deborah L., 76
Noss, Aagot, 186
Nourie, Alan, 204
Nourie, Barbara, 204
Nunn, Marshall E., 215
Nyangoni, Betty, 70
Nyberg, Tobi, 24, 209
Nystrom, Esther, 71
Nystrom, Paul H., 129

O'Donnell, Victoria, 68
O'Donnol, Shirley M., 90
O'Hara, Georgina, 14
O'Sickey, Ingeborg M., 209
Oberly, Michelle, 30
Oberseider, Nancy L., 26
Oden, Walter E., 70
Ohio Agricultural Experiment Station, 63
Okkonen, Marc, 89
Olian, Jo Anne C., 15, 34
Oliver, Nancy A., 109
Oliver, Valerie B., 2, 130
Olsheim, Linda, 1
Ordonez, Margaret T., 31
Organ, Helen D., 66
Orkus, Judith O., 119
Orme, Kathryn, 119
Ott, Peggy S., 52
Otten, Patricia, 132
Owen, Bobbi, 90, 127

Pace, Angella M., 64
Packer, William, 211
Packhman, Jo, 72
Pahopin, Jo S., 110
Palmer, Alexandra, 134
Palmer, Pati, 66
Paoletti, Jo B., 31, 36, 120, 134, 136
Pape, Sara M., 36

Parezo, Nancy J., 7
Parke-Bernet Galleries, 55
Parker, Donna, 134
Parker, Georgia H., 30
Parsons School of Design, 68
Parsons, Frank A., 97
Parvis, Paul, 130
Pasnak, Mary F. D., 112
Patcevitch, I.S.V., 210
Patterson, Janice L., 119
Patterson, Vernon, 212
Patton, Eleanor N., 90
PB Eighty Four, 55
Pecotte, Linda S., 92
Peeples, H. I., 68
Peiss, Kathy, 26
Penalis, Frances M., 117
Pender, Minnie L., 113
Perkins, Olive, 118
Perkko, Mariliina, 186
Perry, Ruth M., 7
Person, Brenda E., 127
Persons, Billie, 66
Peterson, Fran, 161
Pfeiffer, Nancy, 60
Pforringer, W., ed., 78
Phillips, Angelene C., 113
Phillips, Joana W., 23
Picken, Mary B., 124
Pietsch, Jeanine M., 120
Pipkin, Alison L., 114
Pitz, Henry C., 21
Pletsch, Susan, 66
Plunkett, E. M., 13
Plymouth Fur Company, 55
Polhemus, Ted, 101
Pond, Mimi, 78
Prelle-Tworek, Martin E., 85
PRIDE Foundation, 132
Prior-Miller, Marcia R., 218
Pritchard, Susan P., 36, 135
Probert, Christina, 53, 72, 78, 80, 211
Procter, Lynn, 101
Proddow, Penny, 75
Prucha, Francis P., 5
Pullen, Martha C., 94
Purdy, Jane B., 30
Putney, Cornelia F., 86

Quimby, Harold R., 78
Quinn, Andrea, 68, 69

R. J. Reynolds Tobacco Co., 58
Rabalais, Pamela P., 31
Rabine, Leslie W., 209
Radcliffe, Pamela M., 31
Rainwater, Dorothy T., 75
Raison, Vicki L., 187
Ralston, Valerie H., 9
Ramsdell, Carol E., 53
Randall, Michael H., 208, 216
Randers-Pehrson, Justine D., 82
Ranson & Horton, 55
Rasch, Robert, 160
Ratner, Harry, 164
Redwine, Ann E., 113
Reed, Margaret D., 112
Reedstrom, Ernest L., 27
Reese, Mauva D., 218
Regan, Michael, 88
Rego, Antoinette D., 167
Reich, Naomi, 132
Reis, Mitch, 89
Reitz, Jan. J., 35
Renner, Julie A., 31
Revere, Helen J., 35
Rexford, Nancy, 15, 25
Rey, Ernabeth E., 31
Reynolds, Jeannette, 11, 62
Rhode Island School of Design, Museum of Art, 29
Rhodes, Vicki, 68
Ribeiro, Aileen, 101
Ricca, Barbara L., 57
Richardson, Genevieve, 90
Richardson, Susan O., 118
Rieff, David, 80
Riggs, Terri A., 26
Riley, Patricia, 60
Riney, Hal, 76
Riquier, Aline, 70
Roach, Mary E., 99, 110
Roberts, Thelma A., 125
Robins, Bill, 124
Robinson, Fred M., 81
Robinson, Julian, 207–8
Roche, Daniel, 105

Rockford Overalls Mfg. Co., 61
Rosamond, Peggy J., 45
Rosen, Edward, 82
Rosenbloom, Jonathan, 63
Rosencranz, Mary L., 99
Rosenthal, J. William, 82
Ross, Josephine, 211
Rowland, Andra, 63
Rowland, Rachel, 113
Roy, Billie, 46
Rubenstein, Ruth P., 105
Rubin, Galye S., 67
Rudofsky, Bernard, 98
Rufy, Celia, 15
Ruiz, Joyce, 120
Runbeck, Dorothy C., 113
Russell, Douglas A., 13
Rust, Terrie E., 57
Ryan, Mary S., 99
Ryan, Mildred G., 98

Saccone, Peter R., 70
Saks & Company, 55
Sallee, Lynn, 75
Sandage, Pamela J., 36
Saward, Blanche C., 126
Sawin, Sylvia D., 46
Schlegel, Lee-Lee, 50
Schlereth, Thomas J., 6
Schneirla, Peter, 75
Schoeffler, Oscar E., 12, 14
Schoelwer, S. P., 35
Schoen, Wendy P., 94
Schoeser, Mary, 15, 68
Schon, C., 70
Schoolman, Maria J., 100
Schreier, Barbara A., 30, 35
Schwab, R. G. Jerry, 70
Schwartz, Gary H., 58
Schwebke, Phyllis W., 55
Schwerin, Jules V., 72
Scott, Clarice L., 61
Seebohm, Caroline, 210
Segesser, B. ed., 78
Seiser, Virginia, 215–16
Seitz, Kristina N., 92
Sennett, Richard, 104
Serra, Christina M., 31

Serter, Sam, 55
Severn, William, 81
Shaland, Irene, 217
Shaw, Lloyd, 86
Shaw, William H., 27
Shawer, Katherine, 80
Sheehy, Eugene P., 123, 127
Shenoi, Suman A., 30
Sherer, G. B., 207
Sherlock, Ruth, 118
Sherman, Kathy L., 36
Shirley, Jeanne C., 118
Shively, Eva, 133
Shore, Joyce E., 31
Showalter, Martha, 112
Sibbett, Ed, 68
Sibley, Lucy A. R., 30
Sibson, Sandra J., 36,
Siegman, Gita, 167
Silverman, Debora, 103
Simabur, Djas W., 120
Simmons, Melissa A., 55
Simpson, J. A., 124
Simpson, Linda D., 110
Simpson, Lorraine H., 30
Simpson, Mary M., 109
Singletary, Betty L., 89
Sinsheimer, Allen, 168
Sloan, Alfred V., Jr., 12
Small, Ken, 23
Smith, Arthur L., 166
Smith, Barbara C., 26
Smith, Dorothy J., 30,
Smith, Greta, 161
Smith, Loretta J. H., 117
Smith, Sweetman R., 12
Smyth, Albert H., 203
Snow, Carmel, 210
Snyder, Linda A., 59
Sohn, Marjorie A., 109
Sommar, Helen G., 6
Sooy, Louise P., 90
Southeby's, 46
Spicer, Christopher H., 70
Spicer, Margaret E., 29
Starke, Barbara M., 24
Starnes, Jane E., 40
Steadman, Saundra N., 119

Stearns, Bertha M., 205
Steele, H. Thomas, 68
Steele, Valerie, 12, 101
Stegemeyer, Anne, 126
Stell, Roxanne, 113
Stephen Ballard & Co., 52
Stephens, Anne C., 110
Stephenson, Lois, 57, 135
Stephenson, Richard, 57, 135
Stern, Bert, 64
Stevenson, Pauline, 72
Stieglitz, Cliff, 68, 163
Stineman, Esther F., 205, 218
Stolz, Lyla J. M., 109
Storm, Penny, 103
Stoten, Mary R., 113
Stout, Shari A., 113
Stowell, Donald C. Jr., 90
Strache, Neil E., 205
Stratman, Carl J., 216
Stroup, Ann H., 361
Strute, Karl, 128
Studwell, William E., 216
Sturtevant, William C., 17
Stewart, Marian G., 118
Surerus, Jo A. M., 113, 117
Swan, Susan B., 126
Swann, June, 78
Swanson, Charlotte L., 113
Sweet-Orr, Inc., 62
Swift, Gay, 126
Sylbert, Viola, 55
Szybillo, George J., 115

TAG Heuer, 75
Taggart, Susan B., 218
Takamura, Zeshu, 125
Tammen, Jo A., 78
Tarlton, Martha, 208
Tarrant, Naomi E. A., 93, 150
Tatarka, Bernadette, 168
Tate, Sharon L., 46
Taylor, Loretta M., 218
Taylor, Nancy J., 31
Terasawa, Haruko, 110
Thackeray, Renee, 116
Thieme, Otto C., 29, 30
Thom McAn Shoe Co., 161

Thomas, Karen W., 219
Thomas, Mary, 126
Thompson, Elizabeth J., 136
Thorne, Tony, 105
Thwaits, Margaret B., 216
Tierney, Tom, 45
Tillotson, Mary E., 26
Tindel, Cynthia J., 35
Tingle, Jennifer, 35
Todd, Eric C., producer, 164
Tolman, Ruth, 162
Tony Lama (firm), 79
Topple, Raymond S., 163
Torbet, Laura, 68
Tortora, Phyllis G., 218
Tosa, Marco, 71
Trahey, Jane, 210
Train, Arthur, Jr., 21
Trautman, Patricia, 133
Trayte, David J., 31, 119
Truesdell, Bill, 184
Turner, Helen, 55

Uchitelle, Daniel, 216
Ulseth, Hazel, 45
Union Special Corporation, 63, 70
University of Texas at Austin, General
    Libraries, 130
University of Wisconsin, Agricultural
    Experiment Station, 63

Vachon, Diane L., 71
Valency, Maurice, 12
Van Brunt, Nancy K., 53
Vogel, J. Thomas, 6
Von Rosenstiel, Helene, 126
Vreeland, Diana, 32, 34, 88

W. S. Nott Company, 52
Walker, Norma P., 115
Ware, Jane, 48
Wares, Lydia J., 20
Warner, Patricia C., 57, 134
Warning, Margaret C., 110
Warwick, Edward, 21
Wass, Ann B., 134
Watanabe, Mitsuru S., 78
Watkins, Josephine E., 128

Watson, Phyllis, 85
Watts, Margaret W., 61
Waugh, Norah, 52
Webster, Sandra B., 163
Wehrle, Louise, 136
Weibel, Kathryn, 26
Weidt, Maryann N., 63
Wein, Len, 163
Weiner, E.S.C., 124
Weisfeld, Zelma H., 130
Weitz, John, 60
Wertheim, Arthur F., 134
Wheeler, Mary B., 172
White & Davis, 79
White, D. Douglass, 115
White, Ed, 69
White, Gerry S., 117
Wienslaw, Arthur E., 133
Wilckens, Leonia von, 124
Wilcox, Ruth T., 19, 56, 78, 80, 124, 130
Wilgus, Virginia R., 118
Willett, Ann M., 110
Williams, Elsie K., 92
Williams, Gayle, 215
Williams, Iona S., 110
Williams, Joan, 118
Williams, Peter W., 16
Williams, Susan R., 119
Williams-Mitchell, Christobel, 61
Willman, Polly, 130, 132, 150
Wilmeth, Don B., 5
Wilson, Anna C., 30

Wilson, Charles R., 16
Wilson, Elizabeth, 92
Wilson, Eunice, 78
Wilson, Janelle L., 120
Winakor, Geitel, 133
Windsor, Jane W., 55.
Wingate, Isabel B., 125
Winick, Charles, 99
Winters, Arthur A., 167
Winters, Carol, 163
Wohl Shoe Company, 78
Womack, Laura L., 219
Wood, Jame P., 204
Woram, Catherine, 72
Worrell, Estelle A., 22–23, 26, 90
Wright, Meredith, 24, 186
Wycoff, Alexander, 21

Yang, Cheng-Yuan Y., 120
Yarwood, Doreen, 3, 14, 130
Yener, Barbara A. V., 117
Yeshiva University Museum, 72
York, Marjorie O., 118
Young, Agnes, 23, 98
Young, Catherine A., 36
Young, Mary J., 110

Zalaznick, Sheldon, 100
Zapata, Janet, 74
Ziegert, Beate, 29
Zieman, Nancy L., 60, 163
Zimmerman, Catherine S., 72
Zuckerman, Mary E., 205–6

Subject and Selected Title Index

Academic American Encyclopedia, 13

Access, The Supplementary Index to Periodicals, 151

accessories, 74–85; bibliographies, 132–24; collecting, 93–95; design, 144; for men (1900–1970s), 14; in performance, 85–93; trade publication, 209

address books, 189

Adolescent Girls Skirts, 60

adult education, 187

Adventure Comics, 163

advertisements: black women in, 208; bra, 99; company logos on buttons, 84; corsets, 84; dolls, paper dolls, 45–46; eyeglasses, 82; fashion video, 117; hosiery, 83; housewife, 35; jeans, 64; leather jackets, 66–67; men's wear, 33, 34; museums and museum exhibitions, 188–89; *New York Times* (1865–1914), 120, 167;

Sears fashions (1919–1930/31), 33; skirts (1947–1972), 60; tennis (1874–1940), 58; U.S. Bicentennial, 24; use in marketing magazines, 206; *Vogue* (1947–1972), 218

advertising: aesthetics and gender in, 168; artwork representing nostalgia (1959–1979), 208; campaigns, 120; clothing and, 166–69; editorial texts and, 206; ephemera, 58; evaluation by consumers, 219; fashion and adolescents, 121; fashion and indifference in society, 105; femininity and, 218; feminist thought on, 103; history (1950–1969), 167; industry history, 4; influences, 120–21; jeans and denim garments, 64; methods (1929), 98; pamphlets, bibliography, 101; photography award, 167; popular press and, 100; promotions for men's fashions, 33; sports clothes,

58; television commercial award, 167; trends, 120, 167, 219

advice: books, 100; buying jeans, 164; clothing selection, 98; color in clothing, 163–64; teenagers in *Seventeen*, 218; wearing gloves, 162; wearing jewelry, 160; wedding and etiquette (1880–1919), 136

Aesthetics and Clothing, 130

affordability of clothing, 102

African-styled dress (1958–1976), 219

Afro-Americans: dress (1700s–1980s), 24; encyclopedia, 15; images in *Ebony* advertisements (1950–1991), 219; women's dress (1870–1915), 20, 31. *See also* Blacks

Alaska Cooperative Extension, 55

Alaska Furs and Fur Garments, 55

alternative fashion force, 101

Amanda paper dolls, 27

American History and Life, 151

American Association of Family and Consumer Sciences, 200

American Association of Museums, 183, 200; and the *Art Index*, 142

American Denim Council, 63

American Home Economics Association, International Section-International Update, 217

American Institute for Conservation of Historic and Artistic Works, 200

American Library Association, 143, 147

American Red Cross, 134

American Sociological Association, 143

American Theatrical Periodicals (1798–1967), 216

anthropological perspectives, 100

antifashion, 25, 104

antiques as an investment, 5

Apparel Arts, 209

apparel manufacturer and fabric producer, 6

appearance: enchantment of, 105; social meaning of, 102

appliqué, 51

aprons (1942), 61

archives and manuscripts collections, 1, 27, 172

Arizona clothing (1880–1930), 31

art: art deco influence (1915–1925), 36; *Art Index*, 151; art periodicals, 144; Art Reference Round Table of ALA, 147–48; *ARTbibliographies Modern*, 151; *Arts and Humanities Citation Index*, 152; clothes and, 100; fine art periodicals, 215; graphics in *Vogue* (1929–1942), 218; society and, 100

Artwear Gallery, 76

Association of Art Museum Directors and the *Art Index*, 142

Association of Clothing Designers, 200

Association of College and Research Libraries, 148

Association of College Professors of Textiles and Clothing, 200

Association of Fashion, Advertising and Editorial Photographers, award, 167

Association of Image Consultants International, 201

"Attractions of Underclothes," 101

auction catalogs, 55

automobile coats, 51; motorcoat, 134; stormy weather outerwear, 52

automobile fur garments, 55

Awards: *Awards, Honors and Prizes*, 167; Academy Awards (1948–1979), 87; *Advertising Age*, 167; Communications Excellence to Black Audiences (CEBA) awards, 167; costume design, 91; Coty, 2; Cutty Sark Men's Fashion Design Awards, 33; Donaldson Awards, 91; film costume designers to 1975, 87; Hall of Fame, 2; Lulu awards, 33; Marharam, 91; Oscar nominees and winners, 87; Society of Film & Television (England), 87

Badger Knitted Sports Wear, 50

Ballard, Bettina, 210

ballet, 85

Ballet News, 216

barbie doll, 46, 104

Barbie Magazine, 104, 209

baseball: caps, 103; catchers, 84; gloves, 162; suits, 22; uniforms, 89

Bata Ltd: Bata Shoe Museum Foundation, 79; Bata, Thomas, 161; footwear history, 79

bathing and its "Cultural Environment," 57

bathing suits: in Sears catalogs, 32; for women, 57. *See also* swimsuits; swimwear

Bazaar. See Harper's Bazaar

beauty, 105; captured in photography, 211; content in *Vogue* and *Rags*, 218; and femininity, 218

Bel Geddes, Norman (1915–1935), 92

Bernstein, Aline (1915–1935), 92

BHA: Bibliography on the History of Art, 152

Bi-Folkal Productions, 166

bibliographies: Afro-American dress, 24; American costume (1840–1925), 19; *American Denim,* 64; American fashion designers, 103; American periodicals' history, 206–7; American style history, 28; American women's periodicals, 206–7; barbie doll clothes, 46; *Bibliographic Index,* 129; *Bibliography of Costume,* 130, 149, 152; *A Bibliography of Dancing,* 135; *Bibliography of Recent Books Relating to Costume,* 152; blazers, 132; bridal costume history, 72; buttons, 83; *Changing World of Fashion* (1900–1979), 32; clothing manufacturing history, 29; Colas, 149; colonial work clothes, 24; corset, 53; costume history (1607–1790), 21; *Couture: The Great Designers,* 127; cowboy hat, 81; cross culture focus, 99; *CSA News,* 130; *Dictionary of Costume,* (1969), 130; eyeglasses, 82; *Fashion and Eroticism,* 101; fashion encyclopedia, 14; fashion periodicals, 217–18; "Fashion/Textiles/Beauty/Culture," 135; feminism and consumerism, 103; feminist perspective, 104; footwear, 78; frontier clothing, 61; fur

craftsmanship and furs, 55–56; gloves, 84; hatmaking, 80; historic western dress, 27–28; *Hollywood Costumes,* 103; Hollywood film costume, 87; Hollywood jewels, 75; hosiery industry, 83; jeans, 63–64; jewelry, 74; men's clothing, 34; native Americans, 7; psychological, sociological and cultural aspects of clothing, 105–8; radio and television programs, 101; ready-to-wear women's clothing (1865–1914), 167; skating costume history, 57; sociocultural significance of dress, 130; space suit and gear, 61; specialized, 129–38; *Sternberg, Dietrich and Costume,* 88; swimwear, 57; 20th century fashion, 93, 100; underwear, 53; vintage fashion sewing, 94; white wedding, 72; women's periodicals (1792–1960), 205

bicycle wear, 57, 114

Big Beautiful Woman, 205

biographical dictionaries and related sources, 126–28

Biography Index, 127

birthstones, 74

Black Fashion Museum, 101

black gown and dance, 85

black is beautiful, 26

black leather jacket, 67

Blacks, 101

Blackwell, Mr., 211

blazers, 132; tailoring of, 163

bloomer costume, 57

body garments: 1970s, 53; packaging, 53; sculpture, 53

bonnets, 21

book chapters, 141

Book of Costume, 13

Books in Print, 152

books, 139–40

boots, 79–80

boxer shorts, 53

Boy Scout uniforms, 89

boys: clothing (1860–1919), 134; as focus for research, 110–112

brand name. *See* label issues

brassiere, 53, 99
breeches, 90
Breen, Dorothy, 148
Brides in Vogue since 1910, 72
British Vogue, 210
broadcasting fashion news (1929), 98
Broadway: costume design and designers, 90–91, 127; fashion news, 98
Brooklyn Museum, 166, 188
Brown, Reenie, 209
buckskin and frontier clothing (1820–1879), 66
Buffalo Bill Museum, 188
Burlington Magazine, 215
Busch Entertainment Group, 184
business literature guides, 4–5
"Businessman," 34
Business Periodicals Index, 152
business suit (1901–1950), 168
bustle fashion, 30, 101
Butterick Fashion Marketing, 51
Butterick Publications, 165, 205
buttons, 83–84, 133

C. J. Bailey & Co., 51
calico, 27
California history (1769–1847), 90
Calvin Klein advertising, 120
Canada, 130
"Cape of Puritan Woman," 90
caps, 103
cards, 189
career hat set, 161
cartoons: clothing, 99; Disney characters, 102; gender and appearances, 136; housewife, 35; male image (1880–1910), 120; museum collections of, 184; t-shirts, 163
casual fashion, 99
catalogs, 101
CD-ROM databases, 146
CEBA. *See* Communications Excellence to Black Audiences
Centennial Exhibition in Philadelphia (1876), 188
ceremonial and religious items, 5
ceremonies and clothing, 151
Channel, Gabrielle, 36

Channels of Desire, 100
charm bracelet, 75
Charm, 204
Chatelaine, 218
Chesterfield coat, 34
children: as focus for research, 110–12; as symbol bearers, 102
"Children in North America" (1585–1790), 21
children's apparel industry, 5
children's clothing, 100, 136; athletic shoes, 78; British focus, 23; children's plays, 90; coats, 51; cowboy clothing for, 34; dolls and, 22; fur automobile garments, 56; health advice and, 31; history, 19; (1607–1910), 22; (1890–1930), 30; (1930–1941), 36; (1950s), 93; literature guides, 1, 5; overalls, 22; play clothing, 31, 111; and society (1841–1885), 30; underwear history, 53; used to study childhood, 23
choices, 100
chronology of major clothing events, 20
Chrysler Museum, 35
Cincinnati Art Museum, 29
circus and variety shows, 5
circus costume (1866–1980s), 91
Circus World Museum, 188
citation indexes: *Arts and Humanities Citation Index*, 144; *Social Sciences Citation Index*, 156
Civil War clothing for women, 31
"Clothing," 12, 15
clothing: and accessories, 85–93, 132–34; affordability, 102; and behavior as focus for student research, 112–15; consciousness, 100; criticism, 101–2; design influences on, 35–36; education history, 142; fetishism in MTV, 120; protective and safety issues, 144; purchase, 92
"Clothing and Personal Adornment," 15
Clothing and Textile Arts Index, 150–52
Clothing and Textiles Research Journal, 217

Clothing Behavior Index, 152
Clothing Index, 153
"Clothing Industry," 13
Clothing Manufacturers Association, 201
coats, 51–52: Chesterfield, 34; men's 19th century, 134; media publications on, 162–63; motorcoat, 134; tailoring, 163. *See also* automobile coats
Colas, René, 149
collecting and collectibles: buttons, 83–84; clothing and accessories, 93–95; eyeglasses, 82; jewelry, 160; museums and popular pastime, 187–88
Collecting Costume, 93
College and Research Library News, 172
Colliers Encyclopedia, 12
Colonial Clothing (1760–1880), 165
Colonial Ladies and Gentlemen's Magazine, 188
Colonial Williamsburg, 165, 188
color: behavioral studies, 116–17; dance clothing fabrics, 85; impact in men's fashion history, 14; media publications on, 163–64; quotes from literature on, 98
coloring books, 46
comic strips, 136
Common Threads, 20
Communications Excellence to Black Audiences awards, 167
comparative study of clothing (1900–1909), 36
competition, 98
Comprehensive Dissertation Index, 153
Computer T-Shirts, 68
computer used to create t-shirts, 70
conference proceedings, 199–202
conferences, 188
conformity: in children's clothing, 111; in adolescent girls, 117
Connoisseur, 215
conservation, 1
conservatism and fashion, 99
consumer issues, 115–16
consumer surveys, 5

consumerism: and democracies, 105; and photography, 104
consumers, 100
"Consummate Fashion," 105
contests: jeans decoration, 63; t-shirt, 68; for *Vogue*'s thirtieth year celebration, 210
cords, 104
Cornell University, 30
corsets, 52–53, 101–2
Corsets and Crinolines, 52
cosmetics, 12; advertising promotions, 35; Afro-American, 24
Cosmopolitan, 204–5; advertising and text study, 206; black females in (1986–1988), 208
costume: as art, 15; in art history literature, 144; collections, 1, 46, 125–87; colonial period to the 1970s, 15; history, 165–66; ideologies and, 3, 149; in film and television periodicals, 144 (*see also* film and films); illustrations and plates in books, 147–49; jewelry, 75; museums and collections, 183–97; stage and, 2, 5; stage design and, 166; symbolism, 102; tourism and, 93; uniforms and nonuniforms, 102; western square dancing, 86; Williamsburg, VA, 24
"Costume," 13
Costume (Costume Society), 130, 150, 216–17
"Costume and Customs: The Vanishing Difference," 99
Costume and Textile Society, 199
Costume Index, 130, 147–49, 153
Costume Institute. *See* Metropolitan Museum of Art
Costume Society, 150, 201
Costume Society of America (CSA), 150, 200–201; membership directory, 127; museum category members list, 184
Costume Society of Ontario, 201
costumed dressing in the 19th century, 104
costumed interpreters, 188
Coty Award winners (1943–1975), 2

Country Gentleman, 204
couture, 127
cowboy, 102, 104; boots, 79–80; clothing for children, 34; dances, 86; hat,
81; museums, 184; type of man and
style, 34; urban, 103
crinoline (1850–1870), 31
Crocker Art Museum, 29
cross cultural communication and
clothing, 99, 118
CSA News, 130, 217
cultural studies and feminism, 104
cultural studies movement, 102
culture as focus of research, 118–19;
mass culture and fashion, 105; and
men's fashion advertising, 168
Culture of Clothing, 105
Culture of Fashion, 105
*Cumulated Magazine Subject Index 1907–
1949,* 153
Cumulative Book Index, 153
Current Biography, 204
Curtis Magazines, 204, 206
Customs Service, 89
Cutty Sark Men's Fashion Design
Awards, 33

DailyNews Record (DNR) commemorative publication, 209; men's fashion-
promotions, 168
Dakotas (1861–1889), 31
dance costume, 2, 5, 135
dance clothing and accessories, 85–87
Dance Magazine, 216
"Dandy," 34
Danner, Caroline Burford, 35
database creation, 49–50
dating clothing, 1, 31; women's underwear, 54
DC Comics, 163
De Weese swimwear (1930s–1970s), 24
Debonair sports fabric, 58
decoration vs. modesty, 98
dehumanization, 211
Delineator (1850–1920), 219
democracies, 100, 105
denim: jeans and folk art, 63; play
clothes, 34; sex and homosexuals,

64; sports clothing, 58; symbolism,
64; vintage, 93
Denim: An American Legend, 64
Denim Council, American, 63
Denim Overalls Clubs, 104
department and specialty stores, 4; relations with, 103
desexualization, 99
Design and Applied Arts Index, 153
designers: Afro-American, 24, 101, 127;
biographies of U.S., 28–29; Broadway costume designers (1915–1985),
90–91; fashion designers, 1, 103,
127; film costume, 87–88; hats, 161;
musician designers, 101; street designers, 101; theatrical, 2
diamonds, 74
Diana Vreeland: Immoderate Style, 35
dictionaries, 123–28; of buttons, 83; of
costume, fashion, clothing and
dress, 124–25
directories: associations, 199; libraries,
172; museums, 189–90; research
centers, 171–72; women's periodicals, 205
disabled and clothing, 132
display of merchandise, 5
disposable clothing, 151
Dissertation Abstracts Online, 153
doll clothes, 46, 71; shoes, 161; underwear, 46; wedding dress, 46, 72
doll collections, 184; auction catalogs,
46; directories, 46, 186
doll industry, gender issues (1830–
1930), 46
dolls: and children's clothing, 22; Barbie, 46, 104; character dolls, 148;
and doll houses, 184; fashion dolls,
151; Gody Lady Doll, 46; hat making
for (1855–1916), 81; "Harvest
Spirit," 46; paper dolls, 27, 45, 101;
representing U.S. history, 45–48; Rodeo Rosie, 46; Savvy Shopper Barbie, 46; Shelburne Museum, 188
Dollywood, 184
Donaldson Awards (1943–1954/55), 91
Dover paper doll series, 45

Drama Review, 216

drawings: Gorsline, D. W., 19; Mc-
    Pharlin, P., 22; Pitz, H. C., 21; Price,
    R., 34; Reedstrom, E. L., 27; Steel,
    S. B., 20; Trout, C. W., 20; Wilcox,
    R. T., 19, 56; Worrell, E. A., 26–27

"Dress", 11

Dress, 216–17

dress: and college (1930–1950), 218;
    eastern influences on western dress,
    30; and Indian white relations
    (1834–1862), 31; and society, 105

Dress, Adornment, and the Social Order,
    99

Dress and Morality, 101

Dress and Popular Culture, 104

Dress Codes, 105

dress reform, 26, 30, 104

dresses, 101; day, 71, 112, 113, 218;
    evening, 71, 85; Miss America Pag-
    eant (1921–1987), 91; party, 112;
    school, 112; tennis, 114

Dress in American Culture, 104

dressing for the occasion, 119

dressmaking trades (1860–1930), 81

Earle, AliceMorse, 119

Ebony (1950–1991), 219

eclecticism, 102

economics and apparel, 100

ecowear in the 1990s, 34

Education Index, 142, 153

education: continuing, in museums,
    187; indexes, 142–44

Educational Resources Information
    Center (ERIC), 143–44, 153

Egyptian influences: on 20th century
    fashion, 36; on American jewelry, 76

elderly and clothing, 132

electronic indexes and abstracts, 146–
    47

electronic literature searching tech-
    niques, 2

Elle, 144, 205

EM, Ebony Man, 215

embroidery: design, 144; dictionaries,
    125–26; in *Encyclopedia of World Art*,
    15; in vintage fashions, 94

*Empire of Fashion: Dressing Modern De-
    mocracy*, 104–5

"Enchantment of Appearances," 105

Encyclopedia of Associations, 127, 199

Encyclopedia of World Art, 15

encyclopedias, 11–17

entertainment and performance activi-
    ties, 5

Entertainment Memorabilia, 92

EPIC, 140

ERIC. *See* Educational Resources Infor-
    mation Center

eroticism and fashion (1820–1928),
    101

Erte, 210

Esquire, 204, 209

*Esquire's Encyclopedia of 20th Century
    Men's Fashion*, 14

Essay and General Literature Index, 153

Essense, 205, 209

Essex Institute, 79; John Ward House,
    188

ethics in clothing, 98

ethnic: clothing, 36, 104; periodicals,
    215

etiquette and advice, 136

European fashion, 32

evening clothes, 85

evening gowns, 91

"evening glamour" in Hollywood cos-
    tumes (1930s), 88

"Evolution of Garments," 98

exhibitions: catalogs, 101; for fashion
    and costume history, 39–40; Holly-
    wood costume, 88; indexes, 137,
    140–41; jewelry, 76; material culture,
    7; 19th–20th century costume, 28–
    30; 20th century clothing, 34–35

exhibits: Black Fashion Museum, 101;
    design of, 144; international design,
    74–75; vintage items, 94

"Exoticism in Art," 30

eyeglasses, 82–83, 151, 162

"Fabric of Dance,"85

fabric producer and apparel manufac-
    turer, 6

fabrics, 127

fads, 105, 112, 118, 119, 151
Fairchild Visuals, 167
Fairchild's: Dictionary of Fashion, 124;
    Dictionary of Textiles, 125; *Who's Who
    in Fashion*, 126
Family and Consumer Science Journal, 217
Family Circle, 205
fans, 184
"fantastic fashion hoax," 98
Farmers' Village of Cooperstown, 188
"Fashion," 12, 15
Fashion Accessories Benefit Ball, 209
Fashion Accessories Expo, 209
fashion advertising, 167, 168
fashion and clothing, 12, 14
fashion and costume indexing and ab-
    stracting services, 1–4, 147–51
fashion and costume museums, 186
Fashion and Eroticism (1820–1928), 101
fashion and influences of music video,
    92
fashion and social and art trends
    (1870–1900), 30; and social life, 102
fashion art and artists, 207
fashion as an art, 100
"Fashion/Body/Consumer Culture,"
    104
fashion codes, 104–5
fashion cycles, 20, 23; bridal gowns
    (1969–1988), 72; women's daywear
    (1952–1992), 92; work clothes
    (1947–1962), 62
fashion design, 144
fashion designers. *See* designers
fashion dolls, 20, 98
fashion editorials. *See* advertisements,
    advertising
fashion elite, 119
Fashion Encyclopedia, 14
fashion features in periodicals, 211
"Fashion Fillers in Silent Film Periodi-
    cals," 208
Fashion Group International, 201
fashion groupies, 100
*Fashion Guide: An International Designers
    Directory*, 126
fashion history, 165–66
fashion houses after WWII, 127

fashion illustrations, 144
fashion industry (1970s), 1–2
Fashion Institute of Technology, 53,
    57
fashion leaders, 112
fashion magazines and periodicals, 33,
    104, 120, 207–14, 221–229; analysis
    of messages (1860–1990), 209; Brit-
    ish (1890s–1980s), 207; exhibit, 217;
    fashion plates in, 20, 207
feminist thought, 103; history (1830–
    1969), 218; list by country (1939), 3;
    theses on, 218–21. *See also* periodi-
    cals
fashion meanings, 102
fashion models, 100, 211
fashion perception, 92
fashion plates, 20, 207
fashion publications, 14
fashion retailing effects, 102
Fashion Sales Promotion, 167
fashion shows, 98, 104; in films, 34; in-
    dex to articles on, 151; as promo-
    tional devices, 93; video, 167
fashion supplements in newspapers,
    219
fashion system model, 104
fashionable women (1810–1970s), 26
Fashion of a Decade series, 34
fashions (1950s), 34
"feminine mystique," 35
femininity: and advertising, 218; and
    beauty, 218
feminism, 104
feminist: literature, 144; perspectives
    on fashion magazine images, 218;
    perspectives on film costume, 103;
    writings of the 19th century, 99
Fiesta de San Jacinto, 28
Fiesta Texas, 184
film and films: clothing and accesso-
    ries, 87–88; costume, 103; costume
    influence on fashion (1930s), 36;
    impact of fashion in, 104; and jew-
    elry, 75; research collections, 5; si-
    lent film fashions, 104; silent film
    periodicals, 208; and society, 5; stu-
    dios (1915–1960s), 87; and swim-

wear, 57; and television periodicals, 144; titles, 87; t-shirt spin-off products, 68; uses in museums, 188; women and fashion in, 34

Film Costume, 135

Film Literature Index, 153

film studios (1915–1960s), 87

filmographies (1915–1960s), 87

First Ladies' Gowns, 166

FirstSearch, 140

fitness industry, 5

Five Centuries of American Costume, 19

flapper fashion, 35, 101

Florida frontier costume (1824–1861), 31

folk art clothing, 68, 103

folk costume, 102

folklife, 7

folklore, 104

Footloose in History, 161

footwear, 172. *See also* boots; shoes

Ford, Henry (1926), 188

foreign influences, 119

4–H uniforms, 89

Fraser, Kennedy (1970–1981), 211

freedom of choice, 98

French influences (1917–1927), 36

frontier clothing: Arizona, 133; Florida, 31; Texas, 66

Frostline Kits, 163

"Fundraising Fair," 136

"Fur Coat, Great Western," 55

fur garments, 55–56; Alaska furs, 55; care for natural and man-made, 66; coats, 55; fake fur and fur-like fabrics, 66, 100; fur decoration on clothing, 55; history, 3–4; muffs, 136; Ohio fur industry and fashions (1900–1980), 56; purchase and care for, 55–56

fur trade history, 4

furriers, 55

furs, 3, 55

"Furs for Christmas," 55

gay men's clothing influences, 25

gender: and aesthetics in men's fashion advertising, 168; differences, 102; and dress, essays, 104; identity and quilted garments, 104; issues (1780–1980s), 25–26; issues in doll industry (1830–1930), 46; and seduction, 105

Gentleman's Quarterly, 209

Georgia women's dress (1870–1915), 31

Gibson Girl, 28, 103

gift giving, 104, 119

girdle belt, 53

glamorize with fur, 55

Glamour Do's and Don'ts (1939–1989), 211

glamour in Hollywood costumes (1930s), 87–88

Glamour, 204–5; analysis of, 206; black females in (1986–1988), 208; messages (1960–1990), 209

"Glamorous Fashion," 87

glossaries: in *Book of Pearls*, 74; buttons, 83; costume history, U.S., 21; in *Encyclopedia Americana*, 12; fur fashions, 56; gloves, 84; hatmaking, 80; hats (1750–1800), 81; hosiery (1600–1990), 83; jewelry (1840–1980s), 75; men's fashion terms, 14; millinery and dry good terms, 80; in *Plain and Fancy* (1700–1850), 126; in review of *Harper's Bazaar* (1876–1896), 210; shoe leathers, 78; textile terms, 6, 20; in *20,000 Years of Fashion*, 14; Victorian and Edwardian fashion, 30; western clothing history, 27; work clothes, 61

glove industry, 5

gloves, and glovemaking, 84–85; baseball gloves, 162; catchers, 84

Godey Lady Doll, 46

Godey's and Peterson's (1860–1880), 218

Godey's Lady's Book, 150, 203, 209; bibliography, 205; education aspects, 218; music aspects, 218; sports clothing in (1850–1920), 219

golf: and sweaters (1919), 57; wear for women, 114

Good Housekeeping, 204–5

Goodwear Knitting Mills, 51

Gorsline, Douglas W., 12, 19
gowns, 166
GQ, 204
Graham's Magazine, 204
Green, Margaret, 148
Gummage, M. E. "Manny," 81
gymsuit, 104

H. W. Wilson Company, 139, 141–43, 147
hair styles and hair jewelry, 209
Hale, Sarah J., 205, 209
Hall of Fame awards, 2
hand-me-downs, 118
handbags, 93
Harlem Institute of Fashion, 101
Harper's Bazaar, 204–5, 209–10; Asian design influences in (1890–1927), 218; bibliography, 205; eastern influences on dress, 31, 128; pictorial review of (1876–1896), 210
Harper, William, 76
hats and millinery, 80–82; bowler hat, 81; couture, millinery, 127; 18th century fashions, 80; hard hats, 161; hats puzzle, 161; history, 21; making for dolls (1855–1916), 81; media publications, 160–61; milliners, 80; millinery trades (1860–1930), 81; in Sears catalogs, 32; straw hats, 130; in Vogue (1910–1980), 80; wearable art, 161; women's (1750–1800), 80
Hawaiian shirt, 68
HEADstrong Coalition, 161
health and clothing, 31
Hearst, William R., 204
Hennessy, G. Michael, 55
Hepburn, Audrey, 210
heroine on screen, 100
high heels, 101
Hiler, Hilaire: costume collection, 148; costume library, 149
historical societies and organizations: directory, 172; state historical societies, 143
histories: American, 5–6, 143; clothing industry, 4; costume and fashion, 3, 19–48; fashion, 101; films and film

industry, 87–88; footwear, 78–79; gloves, 84; hats, 80–82; hosiery, 83; magazines, American (1741–1930), 203–4; sports clothes, 56–57; t-shirts, 68; wedding dress, 71–72; work clothes, 61–62
Hollywood: bibliography, 104; fashion and costume design, 87–88; film costume influence on fashion (1930s), 36; icon maker, 100; jewels and jewelry, 75; slides and microfiche, 166; star style, 105
Home Economics Education Board, 99
Home Economics Research Abstracts, 153
Home Economics Research Journal, 217
home sewing and sewers, 118
horse/equestrian periodicals, 216
hosiery, 5, 83
housewife, 26, 35
"Human Packaging, Preserving," 186
Humanities Index, 153
humor and male image (1880–1910), 31
"Hunter," 34
hunting shirt, 103
Hutton, Sandra S., 150

ice shows (1866–1980s), 91
"Icons of Popular Fashion," 100
identity through clothing, 36
illustrations (see also art; drawings; photographs): American (1440–1790/1800), 21; criticism for costume study, 21; 16th century European, 14; theatrical portrait engravings (1760–1860), 91
images: feminist thought on, 103; private and public, 105; in sale catalogs, 121
immigrants, Laotian, 35
Index of American Design, Textiles, Costume and Jewelry, 165
Index to American Periodicals of the 1700s, 153
Index to Black Periodicals, 153
indexing and abstracting services, 139–57

Indian influences (1960–1975), 36
Indianapolis Museum of Art, 34–35
indifference and fashion, 105
individual differences, sex differences, 98. *See also under* gender
individualism and fashion, 105
industrial revolution, 30
Information Industry Directory, 147
information sharing, 188
InfoTrac, 154
Infra-Apparel, 53
Inside Sports, 215
International Association of Clothing Designers, 201
International Textile and Apparel Association, 201–2
Internet, 140
ITAA Newsletter, 217

jackets, 51, 66–67
jazz dance, 85
jeans, 63–64, 101, 103–4; as object of American history study, 63; and denim printed ephemera, 64; buttons, 84; contests, 63; film, 165; index to articles on, 151; making and decorating, 63; manufacturing, 63; media publications, 164–65; purchasing of, 63; recycling, 63; serviceability of (1950s), 63; sexual aspects and homosexuals, 64; symbolism, 64; video, 164
"Jean"ealogy, 165
Jeans Battles, 164
Jeanswear Communication, 164, 202
jewelry, 74–78; Afro-American, 24; American art jewelry, 76; bibliographies, 133; collections, 184; collector guides, 75; design, 144; dictionaries, 124; Egyptian influence on (1869–1925), 76; in *Encyclopedia Americana*, 12; in *Encyclopedia Britannica*, 11; for hair, 76; history (1830–1914), 74; identification (1840–1980s), 75; *Index to American Design*, 165; manufacturers (1840–1980s), 75; media publications, 159–60; men's, 74; mourning and memorial, 134; na-

ture themes, 75; patriotic, 75; seasonal collections, 75; sport themes, 74–75, 89
Jewish: culture, 15; immigrants and clothing, 30
"Jock," 34
Jocks and Nerds, 33–34
"Joe College," 34
Jones, Robert Edmond, 92
Journal of Physical Education, Recreation and Dance, 215
"Justin's Celebrated Cowboy Boots," 80

Kalamazoo Corset Co., 52
Kansas women's clothing, 30, 31
knit fabrics, 62
Kohler Arts Center, 35

label issues, 5, 113, 117; brand name, 117; "Crafted with pride in the USA," 113, 115, 117; country-of-origin, 113, 117, 121; "Made in the USA," 115; tradenames, 14; tradenames of jewelry, 75; video advertisements and music influence, 117
Labels and Tags: An International Collection of Great Label and Tag Designs, 167
lace, 15; lacemaking periodicals, 215
lace wedding dress (1910), 72
Ladies' Home Journal, 204–5; bibliography, 205; Needle&Craft, knitting patterns, 50; sports clothing in (1850–1920), 219; women and change, 218
leather and suede wear, 66–67
leathermen (1960–199), 67
leatherwork, 66
leisure, 57, 105
leisure time clothing, 102
lesbian fashion, 166
Levi Strauss & Co., 63, 164, 171
LEXIS/NEXIS, 145, 154
libraries and research centers, 173–81
library collections, 171–72
Library of Congress, 139–40
lingerie, 52–53, 101

literature guides, 1–9
looks in clothing, 99
Looney Tunes, 163
Los Angeles Times Index, 154
Los Angeles County Museum of Art, 29, 88
luggage and leather goods (1900–1970s), 14
Lulu awards for fashion journalism, 33
Lycoming Rubber Co., 52

Mackintoshes, 51–52
Mademoiselle, 33, 204–6
Madonna's use of fashion, 104
mail order catalogs. *See* sale catalogs
Maine mittens, 84–85
make-up, 5, 13
making jewelry, 160
making objects, 188
making shoes, 161–62
"Man about town," 34
mannequins, 98
manual vs. electronic literature searching, 2
manufacturing history, 4; U.S., 29
manuscripts and archives collections, 172
Marharam Awards (1964/65–1985/86), 91
marionetts/puppets, 5, 13
marketing jeans, 164
marketing women's magazines, 205–6
marriage and family, 154; notices, 144
mass communication and democracies, 105
mass images in American society, 100
master's theses, 137
Masters Abstracts and Masters Abstracts International, 154
material culture, 6, 7, 21
material culture and costume, 144
"Material Culture Studies in America" (1876–1976), 6–7
maternity, and nursing wear, history and bibliography, 3; maternity clothes (1850–1990), 104; behavioral studies, 114
McCall's, 204–5

McKissik Museum, 54
McPharlin, Paul, 22
meanings of fashion, 102
media, 166–69
media: and democracies, 105; relations with, 103; slides and videotapes, 33
media (print and electronic) and clothing, 120–21
media publications: featuring clothing and accessories, 159–69; featuring fashion and costume history, 165–66
membership directories. *See* organizations
men as focus for research, 109–10
men's clothing, 102. *See also Esquire*. adoption by women, 25; furs, 55; history (1760–1990), 25; history (1861–1982), 27; history (1900–1910), 209; history (1930s–1940s), 209; history (1965–1980), 33; jewelry, 74; night shirts in Sears catalogs, 32; North Carolina (1860–1870), 31; urban (1810–1980), 30; underwear, 53
men's fashion: advertising, 168; awareness, 119; filmstrips and poster, 166; promotions, 33
Men's Fashion Association of America, 33, 164, 202
men's interest in fashion, 219
Merrifield, Heyoehkah, 75
Metropolitan Museum of Art: annual report, 137; Costume Institute, 188; exhibits, 34, 35, 53, 83; library catalog, 137; Neighborhood Exhibits, 187; Textile Gallery opening, 22
middy for girls, 22
"Military man," 34
Miller, Nicole, 46
millinery/milliners. *See* hats
mind and expression in material subjects, 98
miniatures (toys), 151
miniskirts on the 1970s, 211
Minnesota: James J. Hill family (1863–1916), 31; women's clothing history, 30

Mirror, Mirror: A Social History of Fashion, 19
mirrors, 100
Miss America Pageant (1921–1987), 91
mittens and gloves, 84–85
MLA (Modern Language Association) International Bibliography, 154–55
modern dance, 85
Modern Screen, 216
modesty vs. decoration, 98
mourning dress, 20
Molly's Manhattan Show and Sale of Vintage Fashion and Antique Textiles, 94
morality and dress, 101
Mormon clothing (1840–1860), 31
Morris, Robert L., 76
motorcycle helmet, 133, 161
mountaineering periodicals, 215–16
movie(s). *See* film and films
movie magazines, 216
movie stars, 53, 75
movies and feminist thought, 103. *See also* feminism; feminist
Ms, 205
MTV and clothing, 120
Murphy, Jean, 148
Museum and Popular Culture, 187
Museum of Costume, 32
Museum of London, 34
museums: bulletins and annuals, 142; collections, 3; costume and textile associations sponsored by, 199; and fashion designers, 127; history of, 187–89; members of the Costume Society of America, 184; *Museum Publications*, 137; New England costume, 25; relations with, 103
Museums, American Association of, 200
Museums of Influence, 188
music: fashion and, 101; fashion video, 117; Madonna and fashion, 104; musical revue costume, 90; musical theater, 136; musicals, 5; musician fashion designers, 101; popular, 104; videos, 102; videos' influence, 92
Music Index, 155

Muzzleloader, 25
Mystic Seaport, 188

Nast, Conde, 210
National Association of Fashion and Accessory Designers, 202
National Association of Milliners, Dressmakers and Tailors, 202
National Cowboy Hall of Fame, 188
National Gallery of Art, 165
National Geographic, 149
National Museum of History and Technology, 165
National Newspaper Index, 155
National Union Catalog Pre 1956 Imprints, 140, 155
native Americans, 7, 15, 36
Navaho costume, 36
Nebraska women's dress (1880–1890), 219
Neighborhood Exhibits, 187
"Nerd," 34
New Catholic Encyclopedia, 15
New England: clothing (1760–1937) collections, 186; costume history, 23; rural clothing (1795–1930), 24
New York Fashion, 28
New York and Hollywood Fashion and Costume Design, 166
New York Public Library, 143
New York Times: consumer information on women's fashion (1891–1940), 219; "Femme Fashions" column (1970–1981), 211; *New York Times Index*, 155; ready-to-wear advertisements (1865–1914), 167
Newsbank, 155
newspapers, 6, 145
night shirts, 32
Nineteenth Century Readers' Guide to Periodical Literature, 155
North Carolina men's clothing (1860–1870), 31
nostalgia (1959–1979), 208
note cards, 189
novels, 102
novelty, 105, 109
nudity in art, 100

nurses' riding uniforms, 134
nylon in underwear history, 52
"nylons in America," 83

Oakley eyeglasses, 82
occupational clothing, 102
Occupational Safety and Health, 155
OCLO Online Union Catalog 140, 155
Official Museum Directory, 183
Ohio fur industry and fashions (1900–1980), 56
oiled clothing, 52
Olathe Cowboy Boots & Shoes, 80
Old Sturbridge Village, 188
Old Tuscon Studios, 184
olympics clothing and accessories, 89
On Fashion, 104
online databases, 146
opera periodicals, 216
opinions on fashion, 102
opthalmic lenses, 162
organizations, 127, 199–202
Oscar nominations and winners (1948–1975), 87
outerwear: as focus of research, 113–15; selection, 110; stormy weather, 52; underwear as, 53
overall dress, 162
overalls, 22, 61–62, 101
Overalls Clubs, 104
Oxford English Dictionary, 123

paintings forcostume study, 13
pajamas, 136
Paley, Albert, 76
Panhandle-Plains Historical Museum, 188
pantines, 98
pants, 63
pantsuits of the 1980s, 211
paper clothes, 104
Papers, 155
papyrotamia, 98
parkas, 55, 66
"participative museum," 186
patchwork, 60, 151

pattern information, 5
patterns: basic clothing (1840–1920), 27; designs and sources, 25; New England clothing (1795–1930), 25
pearls, 74
Pennsylvania costume history, 23
performance: activities, 135–136; costume and fashion, 85–93; periodicals, 216
periodicals, 203–29; advertising, 167; American history of, 203–7; buttons, 83; dance, 135; eighteenth century (1741–1799), 61, 144; fashion-related periodicals, 214–18; film magazines, 5, 87; folklife, 7; for stage costumer, 90; illustrations and covers, 58; indexes to articles in, 141–45; list, 221–29; mass market, 204; material culture, 7; merchandising, 208; native Americans, 7; textiles, 6; wedding customs, 72; women's, 205–6
Peterson's Ladies' National Magazine, 203, 209
petticoats (1820–1928), 52, 101
Philadelphia Mummers, 103
Photo Screen, 216
photographs: black personalities, 101; buttons, 84; couture fashion, 127; Hollywood, 75, 87–88; men's clothing, 27, 33–34
photography: advertising award, 167; fashion photography, 208; impact of fashion in, 104; t-shirt and artistic photography, 68
Photoplay, 216
Pictorial Review, 205
pinup girl, 100
pioneer clothing, 31, 104
Pitz, Henry C., 21
Plain and Fancy: American Women and their Needlework, 126
plain style clothing, 101
"Plane Clothes," 210
plantation clothing practices, 30
play and costume (1890–1930), 31

play clothing for children, 111
Playboy foldout, 100
plays, 91
Playtex gloves, 162
pleated skirts, 60
Plimouth Plantation, 188
poems, 144
Poiret, Paul (1905–1915), 36
Poole's Index to Periodical Literature, 155
popular culture, 102; American, 7; bibliographies, 134–36; and clothing, 30; and fashion awareness, 119; and fashion awareness in men, 119; images of women (1827–1977), 26; jewelry, 74–76; native American Indians, 15; periodicals, 144
popular literature, 102
popular personalities and their eyeglasses, 82
populist model, 104
postcards, 58
postmodernism and photography, 104
power, 105
"Presidency and Contemporary Fashion," 105
price guides, 93–95
Price, Robert, 34
primary sources: of British materials, 1; discussion and sources, 3; eighteenth century, 124; from European journals, 52; letters (1950–1980), 33; quotations, 20; *Textiles in America* (1650–1870), 126; U.S. clothing manufacturing, 29; on wedding customs, 72
product research, 171
promotional activities using the t-shirt, 70–71
protective garments, 84–85
psycholoanalytic cases, 98
Psychological Abstracts, 156
psychology of clothes, 97–98
PsycINFO and *PsycLIT*, 156
Public Health Service, 89
"Public Opinion and Influence," 104
publications, 187–88

punks, 104
puppets and marionettes, 5, 13
"Puritan Maiden," 90

Quaker dress, 20
Queens Borough Public Library, 148–49
quilted apparel and gender, 104
quilted patchwork, 51
quilting periodicals, 215
quilted petticoats, 52

radio programs in blackfashion history, 101
Rags vs. Vogue, 218
rain coats, 51
Ranching Heritage Center, Texas Tech University, 27
Readers' Guide to Periodical Literature, 156
ready-to-wear: essays on, 100; history (1890–1900), 30; industry and the fashion show, 104; women's clothing advertisements (1865–1914), 167
Reagan's America, 103
"Rebel," 34
recycling: of clothing, 151; feed sacks and flour bags, 136; shoes, 161
Redbook, 205
redcaps, 103
Reedstrom E. L., 27
reenacters, 25
regional: resources for folklife study, 7; studies of historic clothing, 31
Religion Index, 156
religious and ceremonial costume, 5
religious clothing, 15
remodeling and renovating clothes, 136
research centers, 171–81
Research Libraries Information Network (RLIN), 140, 156
resorts, 189
riding costume, 113
riding habit, 20

riding habit and clothing for women,
57, 114, 134
Ringling Circus Museum, 188
rings, 74
Rock and Ice, 216
rock: music and music videos, 102;
stars, 100
Rona Barrett's: *Gossip*, 216; *Hollywood*,
216
rubber clothing, 52
running clothing for women, 134

safety issues, 160–61, 162
sailor suits, 22
sale catalogs: discussion, 4; images,
121; jean and denim clothing, 64;
men's underwear, 53; shopping,
120; tall and large women, 120
San Francisco Chronicle (1910–1915), 36
Sartorial Art Journal (1900–1910), 209
satisfaction and clothing, 151
Saturday Evening Post, 204
Schomburg Collection of Negro Literature and History, 143
school uniforms, 89
science costume movement, 26
SCIPIO Art Sales Catalog, 140
Sears catalogs, 32, 34; advertisements,
60, 112, 168; fashions, 33; and style
and custom, 30
second hand clothing, 138
Second Skin, 99
seduction and fashion, 105
Self, 206
Selling Culture, 103
servant: costume, 23; dress, 26
Sevareid, Eric, 164
Seventeen, 205; advertising and text,
206; advice analyzed, 218
Seventh Avenue, 13
sewing, 92
"Sewing with Nancy," 60
Sharaff, Irene, 88
shirt, 100
shirtdress, 24
shirtwaist, 28, 211
shoes, boots, and footwear, 78–80, 102;
bibliographies, 133; media

publications, 161–62; women, 25, 78;
Yankee craftsmanship, 78
shoes in sport, 78
Shoes in Vogue (1910–1980), 78
Shoes Never Lie, 78
shopping and risk measurement, 121
short gowns, 134
shorts, 53
shoulder pads of the 1940s, 211
showgirl costume (1866–1980s), 91
Simonson, Lee (1915–1935), 92
simplicity: in American fashion style,
28; in dress, 104
"Sirens of Style," 100
skating costume, 57, 91, 135
ski sweaters, 50
Skiing, 216
skirts, 60–61; equestrienne, 133; hobble, 101; media publications, 162–
63; patchwork, 60; winter, 112
slacks, 61, 62
slave clothing, 20, 24
sleeves, 21
slipdress, 53
slips, 114
Smithsonian Institution, 165
Snow, Carmel, 210
social history, 35
social life and fashion, 102
Social Sciences and Humanities Index, 156
Social Sciences Citation Index, 156
Social Sciences Index, 156
*Society in Vogue: The International Set be-
tween the Wars*, 211
Society of Film & Television (England)
awards, 87
sociocultural aspects/significance of
dress, 99, 130
Sociofile, 156
Sociological Abstracts, 156
Somper, Frank, 55
sophistication of black gown, 85
southern culture, 15
southwest, 7
Space Gear: Outfitting the Astronaut, 61
Sport: online database, 156; periodical,
215
Sport Discuss, 156

sport themes in jewelry, 74–75
"Sporting Dress," 100
Sporting News, 215
"Sports and the Common Man," 56
sports and non-military uniforms, 88–90
sports clothes, 56–60, 103; behavioral studies, 114; coats, 51; exhibit, 57; gloves for baseball catchers, 84; men's influence on women's, 134; in periodicals (1850–1920), 219; purchasing of, 58; sale catalogs and other advertising ephemera, 58; shoes, 78; sports fashions as reflection of society (1850–1920), 57; in *Vogue* (1910–1980s), 57; women's sports and physical education (1860–1940), 57
Sports Illustrated, 58, 89, 215
sports museums, 184
sports periodicals, 215
sports uniforms, 89
"Sportsman," 34
sportswear, 34, 57
Spratling, William, 76
square dancing, 86
stage clothing, costume, and accessories, 90–92
state historical societies, 143
statistics on textile and apparel, 4
Staunton Suit, 32
Steel, Sophie B., 20
Sternberg, Dietrich and Costume, 88
stockings, 32, 83
Story of Everyday Things, 7
Strauss, Levi, 63, 164
street fashion, 100, 104
street fashion designers, 101
"street wear," 53
striptease, 99
study and teaching, 99–100; fashion system model and populist model, 104
suedes, 66
Suiting Everyone: The Democratization of Clothing in America, 28, 166
suits: advertisements (1901–1950), 168; business, 101; business for men

(1950–1988), 109; grey flannel, 100; miniskirted (1990s), 34; Staunton suit, 32; suiting fabrics, 113; women's, 113
Summitt, 216
sumptuary laws, 23
sunglasses, 82
Sunglass Story, 162
suspenders, 83
sweaters, 50–51; behavioral studies, 114; cardigan, 34; and golf, 57
swim wear, 24, 57, 114, 133
swimsuit issue, 58
swimsuits, 91
symbolism: in costume, 102; of clothing, 104, 119
symbols, 105
Symposia, Costume Society of America, 201

t-shirts, 68–71, 100, 102; cartoon decoration, 22; *Computer T-Shirts*, 68%ntests, 68; created on a computer, 70; decorating of, 68; educational uses of, 70–71; index to articles on, 151; mediapublications, 162–63; messages, 70; tennis theme, 58
taste, 105
tea gown (1820–1928), 101
teaching. *See* study and teaching
Teen, 206
teenage girls' clothing (1950s), 36
television, 92–93; commercials, 120, 167; costume and other collectibles, 92; fashions influence, 92; and film periodicals, 144; influence on girls' clothing practices, 120; MTV and clothing, 120; programs, 101, 102; "Sewing with Nancy," 60; shopping channels, 120; sitcoms, 136; *Through the Looking Glass*, 93
Tennessee women's dress (1895–1910), 31
tennis, 58, 114
Tennis, 216
tests and measures, 99
Texas Magazine, 201

Texas women's clothing (1830–1910), 27

Textile Collections of the World, 185

textiles: artists and designers, 6; content (1860–1880), 218; design, 144; dictionaries, 15, 125–26; early American, 166; electronic information sources, 6; in *Encyclopedia of World Art*, 15; galleries and museums, 6, 46, 184–86; glossary, 6, 20; literature guides, 6; new textiles, 6; periodicals, 6; photographs, 6; *Textiles, Costume and Jewelry, Index of American Design*, 165; *Textiles in America* (1650–1870), 126; "Textiles in Fashion," 6; by Wamsutta (1946–1976), 24

theater and costume design, 166

theater costume, 2, 13, 135

Theatre, 216

Theatre Craft, 216

theme park members, 184

theories, 3, 101, 105

theses and dissertations, 145–46; on clothing history, 35–36; on costume museums, 190; on material culture, 7; on aspects of clothing, 108–121

tie-signs, 105

Tiffany & Co., 75

Tiffany, Louis Comfort, 74

toiletries for men, 14

Tony Award winners (1947–1986), 91

Tony Lama (firm), 80

tourism, 93, 189

Town and Country, 204

trade literature, 4

tradenames. *See* label issues

tradition and fashion, 105

trenchcoat, 51

trends in advertising, 167

trousers, 61–63, 104

Trout, Cecil W., 20

20,000 Years of Fashion (1967), 13

Two Centuries of Costume in America, 20

ultrasuede, 66

UnCover, 147, 157

Undercover Story, 53

underwear, 52–53, 102; cutting and making, 52; female, 52, 101; history, 53; industry, 5; "invisible" and "everywhere," 52; knitted, 52; men's boxer shorts, 168; Merry Widow Bras, 35; in Sears catalogs, 32; wedding fashions, 72

uniforms: American Red Cross, 134; baseball, 89; Boy Scouts, 89; 4–H, 89; history of U.S., 20–21; industry, 5; military of the world, 12; nurses (1860–1915), 89; prisoners, 102; school, 89; sports, 89; theater, 5; *Uniforms and Nonuniforms*, 102; U.S. Customs Service, 89; U.S. Public Health Service, 89

unisex styles, 104

United States Bicentennial, 23

United States federal documents, 137

United States Institute for Theater Technology, 202

universities and other nonprofit institutions, 171–81

Up from the Pedestal, 99

urban cowboy, 103

vanity cases in film, 75

variety entertainments, 5

vests, 51, 63

Victoria's Secret catalog, 52–53

Vidal, Gore, 100

video, 104, 117

Village Voice, 144

Vintage Denim, 93

vintage fashions, 93, 94

vintage items, 93–95

Virginia costume, 24, 26

Visible Self: Perspectives of Dress, 99

visual print sources, 3

Vogue, 204–5, 209–11; advertisements and text, 206; beauty, 218; bibliography, 205; black females in (1986–1988), 208; bridal fashions (1910–1980s), 72; color photography, 211; covers, 211; drawings and photographs (1919–1980), 211; *Everything about Sewing* series, 51; fashion photography (1919–1979), 211; furs and

fur-like fabrics, 55; graphics (1929–1942), 218; hats (1910–1980), 80; history of (1893–1962), 210; lingerie in (1910–1980), 53; literary essays (1935–1941), 210; messages in (1960–1990), 209; photographers and editors, 211; photography, 211; shoes in (1910–1980), 78; skirts (1947–1972), 60, 218
Vreeland, Diana, 85, 103

Wadsworth Atheneum, Costumeand Textile Society, 199
Walking Magazine, 216
Wall Street Journal Index, 157
Wamsutta's fabrics (1846–1976), 24
war: impact on advertising, 167; impact on clothing, 35
watches, 32, 74, 75–76
Wayside Inn, 188
wearable art, 35, 76, 161
wedding dress, 71–74; advice and etiquette (1880–1910), 136; art, design, construction, workmanship, 72; costumes as museum assets, 186; cowboy style hat, 81; exhibits, 29, 72; headwear, 161; history, 20; in paintings and illustrations, 72; index covering, 144; military bride, 72; paper dolls, 45; Victorian dress, 72; white Wedding, 72
"wedding glamour," 88
Weisskopf, Walter, 100
Western Heritage Center, 188
western historic dress, 27. *See also* frontier clothing
western supplies, 80
white collar, 102
white wedding, 72
Whitworth Art Gallery, 88
Who's Who in Designing: America's Foremost Clothing Designers, 126
Who's Who in Fashion, 126
Wilcox, Ruth, 148
Wilcox, Ruth T., 19, 56

Will Rogers Memorial, 188
Wilson, H. W., 150. *See also* H. W. Wilson Company
Wilston, Harry, 74
wish fulfillment, 103
witch, 104
Wolfe, Thomas, 100
Woman's Day, 144, 205
Women Studies Abstracts, 157
Woman's Home Companion, 204, 205
women's clothes (1990s), 34
women's costume (1770–1910), 219
women's fashion, 30, 166
women's pages in newspapers, 205
women's periodicals, 205–207, 218
Women's Sports and Fitness, 218
women's status and fashion, 99
Women's Wear Daily (WWD), 24, 209
Womensports, 205
work clothes, 61–63; history (1710–1810), 24; index to literature on, 144; nurses uniforms (1860–1915), 89; relaxed office wear (1990s), 34; western, 27; for women (early 1940s), 61
"Worker," 34
Working Woman, 205
Works Progress Administration, 165
World Book Encyclopedia, 13
world fairs. *See* Exhibitions
World Institution of Black Communications, 167
World War I, 104
World War II, 127
WorldCat, See OCLC Online Union Catalog
Worldwide Art Catalogue Bulletin, 157
Worrell, E. A., 26–27
"worst dressed list," 211

Yankee Denim Dandies, 63
Young Miss, 206
youth, 99, 105
youth market, 5

Zoot Suits and Second-Hand Dress, 101

About the Author

VALERIE BURNHAM OLIVER is a reference librarian and liaison to the School of Engineering and Mathematics Department at the Homer Babbidge Library, University of Connecticut. She has developed a special interest in both costume and textile literature and is a longtime member of the Costume Society of America. Her background in mathematics influenced the analytical approach she brings to the compilation of this work.

ISBN 0-313-29412-7

90000>

EAN

9 780313 294129

HARDCOVER BAR CODE